RE

Intelligence:
Heredity and Environment

A Series of Books in Psychology

Editors:

Jonathan Freedman
Gardner Lindzey
Richard F. Thompson

Intelligence: Heredity and Environment

Philip E. Vernon
The University of Calgary, Alberta

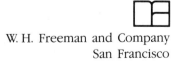

W. H. Freeman and Company
San Francisco

Library of Congress Cataloging in Publication Data

Vernon, Philip Ewart.
　Intelligence, heredity and environment.

　(A Series of books in psychology)
　Bibliography:　p.
　Includes indexes.
　1.　Intellect.　2.　Nature and nurture.　I.　Title.
BF431.V397　　　　153.9′2　　　　78-11975
ISBN 0-7167-0738-1
ISBN 0-7167-0737-3 pbk.

Printed in the United States of America

1　2　3　4　5　6　7　8　9

Contents

Preface

So much has been written about the relative influences of
heredity and environment on the growth of intelligence, particularly since Arthur Jensen's article on boosting IQ appeared in
1969, that many psychologists may query the need for yet
another book. The same controversy has been going on for over
50 years, and it is doubtful that any of the protagonists have ever
been persuaded to change their views. My excuse for adding to
the literature is that there is important evidence on both sides
and therefore the only logical verdict is that both are partially
right. It should be possible to reconcile the conflicting claims
and to adopt an eclectic position that gives due weight to all the
relevant evidence. In this volume, then, I have tried to summarize
all the major investigations that indicate environmental and
genetic effects and to show that the gap between them is much
smaller than is generally believed. Earlier writers have probably
exaggerated the degree of heritability of intelligence, and more
recent workers have scaled down their estimates. Contrariwise,
the advocates of environmentalism have often failed to provide
adequate scientific proof for the malleability of children's traits
and abilities by the environment in which they are reared, or to
recognize that rather limited effects can be brought about by
environmental changes.

Another reason for my survey is that since 1969 a considerable amount of research and critical writing has been published that does not consist merely of ideologically biased arguments. By taking into account both the work of Jensen himself and that of, say, Heber, it should be possible to arrive at a clearer picture. No one, of course, can be wholly impartial in this area, but I have tried to give a fair presentation and evaluation of the different views and of research results. I have also been disturbed by the current unpopularity of intelligence tests in the United States (and elsewhere) and have therefore tried to analyze the reasons for this situation and how far it is justified.

This book is inevitably technical in places, though it has been simplified considerably for the nonpsychologist. A glossary provides definitions of most technical terms, especially those from statistics or genetics.

This is probably the last new book that I will write (though I hope still to be able to revise old ones). If it does anything to persuade psychologists and students that both genetic and environmental factors are important and that intelligence testing, if looked at in this light, still has a major role to play in psychological theory and educational practice, I will regard it as the culmination of over 50 years that I have spent in the field of mental measurement.

I would like to record my thanks, first to my wife Dorothy, who has assisted me in my cross-cultural studies and in many other ways. Second, my sister, Professor M. D. Vernon, and my colleagues, Dr. Hugh Lytton and Dr. Ian Brooks, have helped greatly in reading and criticizing parts or all of the book, though this does not mean that they subscribe to all my conclusions. Dr. Arthur Jensen also gave generous assistance, particularly in explaining statistical methods or findings, without any attempt to influence my interpretations or to convert me when our views differed. Owing to the hospitality of the Center for Advanced Study in the Behavioral Sciences, and the financial support of the Canada Council, I was able to make a good start, during the summer of 1975, on what I knew to be the most difficult assignment of my career.

September 1978   Philip E. Vernon

IMPORTANT NOTE TO THE READER

On several occasions during the writing of this book, new information has been published that required rewriting certain sections. It was not until printing was complete that new evidence appeared on the trustworthiness of Burt's data, which is discussed on pages 170–173. In this section I raise several criticisms of Burt's methods and conclusions but deny that he perpetrated systematic fraud. This view was entirely justified by the evidence in 1978. Now, however, a biography of Burt is to be published by an author with impeccable credentials who had access to Burt's own diaries (Leslie S. Hearnshaw, *Cyril Burt, Psychologist,* Ithaca: Cornell University Press, 1979, in preparation). He finds that Burt did perpetrate systematic fraud from about 1950 onwards, so that the articles by Burt and Howard (1956) and Burt (1966) are worthless apart from their contributions to genetical-statistical methodology. I have to admit, then, that this section of Chapter 11 needs drastic revision.

December 22, 1978   Philip E. Vernon

I

The
Nature of
Intelligence

1

Introduction: Intelligence Testing Past and Present

There are so many excellent books describing the origins and development of intelligence tests and their underlying principles that only a brief historical sketch of some of the highlights is needed here. Indeed, I am less concerned to describe the rise of intelligence testing than to explore its decline and its current status in the mid-1970s.

EARLY TESTS

In the nineteenth century, Itard had devised certain performance tests, not so much for assessments of intelligence as for training devices in his work with an imbecile boy. L. A. J. Quetelet and Francis Galton had noted that many human attributes tend to be distributed in accordance with the normal, or Gaussian, curve, and Galton had first proposed scaling human mental capacity along such a curve. He distinguished 14 steps, or grades, from what he termed the most illustrious and eminent at the top, to the imbeciles and idiots at the bottom, but he lacked any objective means of assessing an individual's grade. He was particularly interested in parent–child resemblance, hoping to show that ability was, in the main, hereditarily determined, though he was aware that most eminent individuals were reared in intellectually stimulating environments and admitted that genius depended considerably on strength of character as well as on intellect. Galton's discovery of filial regression to the mean led to a technique of statistical analysis: the product–moment correlation for measuring the degree of resemblance between two or more sets of measurements of abilities. This technique, when applied in the 1880s to school and university examination marks, showed the remarkable lack of correlation, or unreliability, between marks given to the same examination scripts by independent markers.

Experimental psychologists had begun to explore mental capacities using quantitative techniques such as Ernst Weber's and Gustav Fechner's psycho-physical methods for measuring the acuity of vision, hearing, and touch; Hermann von Helmholtz's work on the speed of reaction to stimuli; and Hermann Ebbinghaus's pioneer studies of memorizing and retention. However, these early psychologists were more concerned with perceptual and intellectual functions in the average or typical human being than, like Galton, with individual differences.

At about the same time, under the influence of Darwin and Spencer, many naturalists were concerned with the evolution of abilities in animal species, from the tropisms, reflexes, and rigid instincts of lower species up to the adaptability and intelligence of humankind. And this interest was complemented by anatomical and physiological studies of the central nervous system, which showed that as neural interconnections, particularly those in the cortical brain centers, become more complex, so does behavior. Intelligence was thus conceived as an innate property or attribute that chiefly differentiated humans from subhuman species, though its rudiments could also be seen in some behavior of mammals and birds, especially of monkeys and the great apes—the nearest relatives to humans in the evolutionary tree.

In 1884, Galton arranged to test visitors to the International Exhibition in London; Joseph Jastrow similarly tested many visitors of different races or nationalities at the Chicago Exposition in 1893. Both used a variety of simple sensory or motor tests. However, as we all know, the first intelligence test for practical use was produced by Alfred Binet and Theodore Simon between 1905 and 1911. Binet, who had made many observations of the growth of his own daughters' mental functions, was asked by the Parisian education authorities to devise a method for identifying those children who were too dull to be educated in ordinary schools. He conceived of a series of mental tasks that would be characteristic of the development of normal children of a given age. The experimental psychologist's tests of sensory acuity and reaction time, often involving elaborate equipment, seemed to him less promising than simple verbal and practical problems that sampled the higher mental functions of comprehension, reasoning, judgment, and adaptation. He chose tasks that were much more readily accomplished by older than by younger children, and also by children identified by their teachers as bright rather than by those regarded as dull. Binet realized that such tasks must be applied and scored in a standard manner if results were to be reliable. The Binet-Simon scale was also the first attempt to provide a numerical scale of levels of intelligence, later referred to as Mental Ages.

FURTHER WORK IN THE EARLY TWENTIETH CENTURY

While Binet was working in Paris, Charles Spearman in London was approaching mental testing from a very different, statistical, angle. He pointed out that there was no agreement among psychologists as to the definition of intelligence. Some writers, as he put it, conceived of intelligence monarchically, as a kind of superpower of the mind that determined all human abilities. Others adhered to nineteenth-century faculty theory, regarding the mind as made up of a series of separate powers such as reasoning, memory, imagination, and so on, and this he called the oligarchic view. Still others, particularly in the United States, held to the anarchic view that humans possessed a host of specific abilities, largely unrelated, for different tasks. Spearman realized that the problems of definition could not be solved by speculative or theoretical argument; it was necessary instead to find out how actual measurements of different abilities correlated with one another. His own investigations led him, in 1904, to the so-called Two Factor Theory. This theory stated that there was something common to all abilities, which Spearman called g or general factor, and that, in addition, every ability involved a specific or s component peculiar to itself. We will further explore the development and implications of factor analysis in Chapter 4. Meanwhile, it is sufficient to point out that Spearman's approach complemented Binet's. The Binet-Simon scale consisted of a largely haphazard collection of mental tasks; Spearman's type of analysis provided some justification for the scale, because each of the tasks or items would be a partial measure of g. Thus, overall performance, or Mental Age, would tend to give a good measure of the general factor, because the specific elements in the various items are uncorrelated; that is, they would tend to cancel one another out and not bias the total score in any particular direction. Spearman avoided the controversial and vague term *intelligence*. His g was a mathematically defined highest common component, which, presumably, represented the core of what was involved in intelligence.

Also at about the same time, E. L. Thorndike, in the United States, became interested in assessimg educational achievements of school children by methods more objective than the traditional teacher exercises and the essay-type examination. His solution was a new type of test, consisting of many short questions, each with only one right answer. He and his colleagues produced a number of such tests in different school subjects, with norms based on the typical scores of children of different ages or in different school grades.

The Binet-Simon test was quickly taken up by psychologists in other countries, including Henry H. Goddard in the United States and Cyril Burt in England, who translated and restandardized it. In 1916, L. M. Terman, of Stanford University, published a more extensive revision, which covered almost the whole range of intelligence, from 3 years to adult levels. Louis Stern had noted that as children grew older, the spread of Mental Ages between the bright and the dull increased; he suggested that taking the ratio of Mental Age to true, or chronological, age would yield a figure that remains relatively constant at all ages. Terman multiplied this ratio by 100 to yield the Intelligence Quotient, or IQ. Thus, children are normal for their age would score close to 100; the very bright might go up to 150, or even 200; the borderline feeble-minded would usually score about 70; and imbecile or idiot IQs might drop to 20 or below. However, it was also found that M.A. scores increased little, if at all, beyond the age of about 14 to 15. (Indeed, the average performance for recruits in the United States army in 1917–1918 corresponded to a M.A. of only 13 years.) Hence, it became customary to divide an adult's Mental Age by 14 or 15 instead of by chronological age in order to obtain his or her IQ. The Stanford-Binet was the most widely used individual intelligence test until it was replaced, in 1937, by the Terman-Merrill tests, Forms L and M.[1]

[1] Though often referred to as Stanford-Binet or Revised Stanford-Binet scales, the 1937 and 1960 revisions will be called the Terman-Merrill tests throughout to avoid confusion. Occasionally, however, Binet is used to refer to all tests of this type.

This makeshift device for coping with the gradual slowing of mental growth in adolescence was rather unsatisfactory, and when later it was realized that the spread, or Standard Deviation, of IQs differed considerably from one test to another or from one age group to another, the Moray House testing unit at Edinburgh, under Godfrey Thomson, substituted what are called Deviation Quotients for all their tests. Deviation Quotients are standard scores that convert the raw scores onto a scale with a mean of 100 and Standard Deviation 15 (or other arbitrary figure) for each age group separately. Thus, they no longer involve M.A.'s and chronological ages but are comparable from one test or age group to another. David Wechsler later adopted the same device for his well-known series of intelligence scales (1958), as did Q. McNemar in the 1960 revision of the Terman-Merrill scale Form LM (a combination of Forms L and M).

GROUP TESTS OF INTELLIGENCE

Around 1915, A. S. Otis in the United States and Burt in England were experimenting with group tests of intelligence. Not only could these be given to large numbers of children (or adults) simultaneously, with great savings in time, but they could be administered by teachers or others who had not been trained in the rather elaborate techniques required for Binet testing. Group intelligence tests, patterned on group achievement tests, usually contained large numbers of short items with multiple-choice answers, the testee having to underline or otherwise indicate the correct choice. Though less varied in content than Binet's or Terman's tests, they covered much the same intellectual processes—such as grasping relations (e.g., analogies) and reasoning—problems, classification, everyday information, vocabulary, and so on. Although such tests were almost wholly verbal, they could also be based on pictorial materials or figures and shapes, which would be more suitable for people with language difficulties. At about this period, a number of individual practical or performance tests were constructed by Rudolph Pintner and Donald G. Paterson and others, using pictures, blocks, and shapes to supplement the Binet-type of test.

When the United States entered World War I in 1917, psychologists were rapidly able to produce the Army Alpha test (verbal) and the Army Beta test (nonverbal), which were applied to nearly 2 million men in the next two years, and proved to be of considerable value in allocating recruits to jobs requiring higher or lower intelligence and weeding out those who were too dull to be trainable. Naturally, this gave a boost to group testing, and in the 1920s many other similar tests were constructed for use with children as young as those in first grade and up to college level. Intelligence testing had come of age. Instead of being used, as Binet, Goddard, and Burt first envisaged, mainly for clinical examination of intellectually handicapped children and adults, it provided a means for categorizing the abilities of people of all ages. Testing was extended to job selection (especially in the civil and armed services) and to college entrance and scholarship awards. By the 1960s, according to a rough estimate by Goslin (1963), over 200 million tests of intelligence or achievement were being given annually in the United States.

The United Kingdom was not far behind in per capita test consumption, because from the 1940s to the 1960s almost all children 10½ to 11½ years of age took group tests for allocation to schools, the famous eleven-plus examinations.[2] New versions of intelligence tests were constructed annually. All recruits to the British armed forces in World War II were tested, and the civil service and many commercial or industrial firms likewise tested prospective employees. Even if not on such an elaborate scale, testing was widely adopted in most European and other technologically advanced countries (except those behind the Iron Curtain), mainly for educational or for vocational classification, and for diagnosis, counseling, and selection.

ASSUMPTIONS UNDERLYING INTELLIGENCE TESTS

Testers made assumptions

What were the basic assumptions underlying the theory and practice of intelligence testing in the 1920s and 1930s? First, it was assumed that intelligence is a recognizable attribute that is responsible for differences among children and adults in their learning, reasoning, and other cognitive capacities. It is a homogeneous entity or mental power that, like height or weight,

---

[2] The eleven-plus examination was used in England to pick the top 20 percent or so of those leaving elementary school for admission to academic high schools (known as grammar schools), almost all the remainder going to the less exacting modern schools. It took various forms in different education districts, but most commonly consisted of three standardized objective tests—verbal reasoning (or intelligence), English, and arithmetic.

can vary in amount or in rate of growth or decline but is essentially stable in its nature throughout life. Second, although obviously intelligence is not measurable in the same sense as physical attributes like height, the sampling of appropriate mental tasks and standardizing or norming the scores against the distribution in the general population yield IQs, which can be accepted as quantitative measures of intelligence. Third, intelligence is essentially innate, being determined by the genes that the child inherits from his or her parents; hence, it develops or matures with age, irrespective of the environment in which the child is reared. It reaches its maximum by around 15 years and then stays constant until senility sets in. Thus, the IQ obtained from a reliable intelligence test in childhood indicates the educational and vocational level that the person can be expected to attain in his later school career and in adult life. Writing on general intelligence in 1933, Burt said: "Fortunately it can be measured with accuracy and ease."

Though all these basic assumptions contain some grain of truth, as I shall argue below, they have been hotly contested and would certainly not be accepted by the great majority of psychologists in the 1970s, at least in the extreme form given above. How is it that the testing movement, long regarded as a major achievement of applied psychology and accepted by most laypeople as veridical, is now so widely distrusted and criticized and is even in some danger of abolition in the United States, where it once flourished most luxuriantly?

Already in the early 1920s, there were objections when the results of Army Alpha testing were published (Yoakum and Yerkes, 1920; Bagley, 1924) and scores were classified according to recruits' national or racial origin. Considerable differences occurred between the mean or average scores of recruits of Anglo-American or northwest European descent and those descended from southern and eastern Europeans; the lowest mean scores were obtained by American blacks. But doubts were cast on the interpretation of these as differences in innate intelligence when it was noted that the lower scoring groups were also poorest in socioeconomic advancement and in educational facilities. It appeared at least as plausible that the differences arose from the more privileged or more deprived environments in which these groups grew up. For example, Gordon (1923) carried out a study of canal boat and gypsy children in England who received little if any schooling; on the Binet test, they were of nearly average intelligence up to the age of 6, but thereafter their M.A.'s failed to progress as lack of schooling made itself felt, and their IQs consequently declined. However, on performance tests there was no such marked difference from the norm. Similar results were obtained in the United States with children living in isolated rural communities or mountainous parts of Kentucky (Hirsch, 1928), and in some of the early studies of American Indians (e.g., Klineberg, 1928).

Proponents of testing were unwilling to admit that such findings implied that intelligence was not inherited but dependent on environmental conditions in the home and on schooling. They did, however, concede that tests should make use of words, concepts, or practical skills that all testees would have had the opportunity to acquire. Essentially, tests should measure the capacity to think or reason with familiar words rather than with acquired knowledge. This implied that verbal tests, even if translated, might be inappropriate for natives of some underdeveloped countries or American immigrants, though it was still believed that most nonverbal or performance tests could yield valid comparisons of intelligence, because pictures, shapes, figures, and the like would be understood in all cultural groups.

However, in 1928, several studies of adopted or foster children reported substantial rises in IQ among children removed from orphanages or poor homes and brought up in better, more intellectually stimulating homes. The estimated effects of improved environment were about 10 to 20 IQ points. Other psychologists had studied the constancy of IQs on retesting and found much more variability with growth than had been suspected. In 1937, Newman, Freeman, and Holzinger published their classic study of identical, or monozygotic, twins, including 19 pairs who were separated at or soon after birth and brought up in different environments. Though the IQs of separated pairs showed a high correlation, attributed to their having identical genes, there were also marked discrepancies, ranging up to 24 points, between a few pairs whose homes and schooling had been very different, thus again demonstrating the effects of environment. (All these points will be expanded in later chapters.)

Particularly shocking were the results of a series of studies of environmental influences issued by Beth L. Wellman, H. M. Skeels, and M. Skodak at the University of Iowa, in the late 1930s. These were challenged by followers of Terman (see McNemar, 1940), who noted numerous technical defects in the tests used, in control of conditions, and in statistical analyses of results. Nevertheless, there remained wide differences of views, and a scholarly survey of the whole area by R. S. Woodworth in 1941 concluded that both heredity and environment are important in intellectual development, even though some of the claims for large environmental effects were exaggerated.

INTERACTIONIST THEORY
OF HEREDITY AND ENVIRONMENT

The next highlight was the publication of D. O. Hebb's *The Organization of Behavior* (1949), in which he pointed out that much of the disagreement over the nature–nurture problem was merely semantic, because people were in fact using the term *intelligence* in two very different senses. He proposed to alleviate the confusion by separating these two meanings, calling them Intelligence A and Intelligence B, respectively.

Intelligence A is the basic potentiality of the organism, whether animal or human, to learn and to adapt to its environment. Thus, humans differ from apes, and apes from less evolved species, in intelligence. Intelligence A is determined by the genes but is mediated mainly by the complexity and plasticity of the central nervous system. Some humans are endowed with more of those genes that make for high intelligence than others, and therefore they have a greater potentiality for any kind of mental development. Intelligence does not, however, develop in a vacuum; the degree to which the potentiality is realized depends on suitable stimulation from the physical and social environment in which the child is reared. Intelligence A can be compared to the seed of a plant; to obtain a flourishing plant, one needs not only good seed but also certain environmental conditions, such as moisture, light, warmth, and nutriment.

Intelligence B is the level of ability that a person actually shows in behavior — cleverness, the efficiency and complexity of perceptions, learning, thinking, and problem solving. This is *not* genetic, nor is it merely learned or acquired. Rather, it is the product of the interplay between genetic potentiality and environmental stimulation, whether favorable or unfavorable to growth. Note that we cannot observe, let alone measure, Intelligence A, at least by currently available techniques. Even in the early months of life, the degree of mental development that we infer from an infant's alert and apparently advanced behavior has been affected by suitable nutrition during and since pregnancy, by birth conditions, by the parents' handling of the infant, and by other environmental circumstances. Insofar as the stimulation is provided by members of a particular cultural group, the "content" of a person's Intelligence B is bound to differ from one culture to another. For example, middle-class whites, lower-class whites, and, say, Chinese each tend to implant different concepts and skills that are habitual and valued in their cultures. Hence, children reared in such different groups will build up Intelligence Bs that differ in quality not merely in quantity.

Hebb's distinction resembles the biologist's distinction between genotype and phenotype. Geneticists never claim that particular genes always determine particular attributes, but they admit that the way the genes express themselves depends on the particular environmental conditions.

Hebb's formulation would appear to have settled the nature–nurture controversy. But there were still wide differences between those who regarded observed intelligence as mainly innate (thus confusing B with A) and others who virtually ignored A and attributed individual differences almost wholly to differences in environmental stimulation and learning. An influential book by J. McV. Hunt, *Intelligence and Experience* (1961) set forth Hebb's interactionist theory particularly clearly and showed that much the same view was implied by Jean Piaget's writings on child development. But he strongly criticized the earlier assumption (for example, that of Arnold Gesell and Terman) that intellectual growth arises purely from the maturation of genetic capacities — in other words, that, in a sense, it is predetermined. Hunt went to far as to claim that by applying what we have learned from Piaget, we could raise the effective Intelligence B of the population by 30 IQ points. Thus, he was a leading advocate of the American Head Start programs in the 1960s, which were designed to increase the intelligence of deprived children by providing kindergarten or preschool training before they entered first grade, or, if they had entered school, by giving them compensatory education to boost their Intelligence B and learning capacities. It was hoped in this way to break the vicious circle whereby children from poor backgrounds come to school with low Intelligence B, fail to make progress, suffer increasing frustration and resentment, and thus fall more and more below the average in achievement.

Head Start programs varied widely in their objectives in different parts of the United States, and many of them failed to provide any satisfactory evidence of how effectively they had worked. But thorough surveys by the Westinghouse Learning Corporation in 1969 and the American Institutes for Research in 1971 covered all those programs in which the children's progress had been reliably measured (usually by some form of intelligence or group achievement test) and compared them with the progress of a control group of similar children who had not received any special provision. In the great majority of Head Start and other compensatory programs, there was either no difference at all or else a temporary gain (possibly a kind of Hawthorne effect), which faded within a year after its completion. However, the few programs that focused on linguistic drills or other clearly defined study skills (e.g., Bereiter and Engelmann, 1966) did seem to offer more positive evidence of effectiveness.[3] Other writers have stated that the programs were more effective in improving social adjustment, confidence, and attitudes to schooling among children who had attended, though the personality tests that were given in some schools failed to reveal significant differences.

A common response to these disappointing findings was that the programs were "too little and too late": A few hours of schooling a day for 5-year-olds could hardly be expected to overcome the effects of 5 years of upbringing in unstimulating homes and a deprived environment. Nevertheless, many psychologists who favored environmentalist theories clearly had expected Head Start programs to be worthwhile (e.g., Freeburg and Payne, 1967).

THE WORK OF A. R. JENSEN AND ITS CONSEQUENCES

In 1967, A. R. Jensen, a psychologist at the University of California, Berkeley, who was particularly interested in mental testing and intellectual development, published an article that attached prime importance to environmental disadvantages in producing low IQs among ethnic minority children, such as United States blacks, and white slum dwellers. He stressed that standard tests underestimate the abilities of children who have had less exposure to mental stimulation than those reared in more favorable circumstances. Thus, it seemed a remarkable *volte-face* when his now-famous article "How much can we boost IQ and scholastic achievement?" appeared in the *Harvard Educational Review* in 1969. Presumably, the virtual failure of Head Start had prompted him to accord more weight to genetic factors

[3] A useful summary of findings is given by Jensen in *Genetics and Education* (1972), pp. 60–63. Later research by Miller and Dyer (1975) has cast doubt on the permanency of the effects of the Bereiter-Engelmann program (see p. 147).

Recently (see Lewin, 1977) claims have been made that long-term effects of Head Start were found, even ten years later. For instance, smaller proportions of attenders than nonattenders had to be placed in special schools or classes. While such improvement is not, of course, impossible, it is so improbable that I have not altered what I originally wrote about Head Start in this chapter and in Chapters 9 and 10.

as the cause of school failure; and he reacted against the exaggerated environmentalism of so many psychologists and sociologists in the late 1960s who appeared to believe that children are infinitely malleable and that any intellectual deficiencies can be made up by improving social conditions and education. Jensen also regarded it as sound scientific strategy to put forward two contradictory hypotheses to explain the same phenomenon, and to survey all available and scientifically acceptable evidence and design further researches that would help to decide between these hypotheses.

His arguments for genetic factors in individual differences won wide respect for his scholarship and expertise in genetics and statistics, though also, of course, considerable opposition. But the section of the article that chiefly led to the violent explosion of public and academic opinion was that which extended his conclusions to social class and race differences. He wrote:

> We are left with various lines of evidence, no one of which is definitive alone, but which, viewed all together, make it a not unreasonable hypothesis that genetic factors are strongly implicated in the average Negro–white intelligence difference. The preponderance of the evidence is, in my opinion, less consistent with a strictly environmental hypothesis than with a genetic hypothesis, which, of course, does not exclude the influence of environment or its interaction with genetic factors.

[margin note: negroes— less intelligence]

Note that he was not claiming the genetic inferiority of blacks as a proven fact, only as a hypothesis meriting investigation; but his cautious qualifications were ignored by his critics.

There is no need to detail the extraordinary persecutions and misrepresentations to which Jensen was subjected by the press, student political groups, and even reputable social scientists; the denial to him of free speech at conventions or lectures; the witch hunt reminiscent of the McCarthy era directed against him and any psychologist who dared to support any of his views or his right to publish and carry on further research (see Jensen, 1972). Richard Herrnstein at Harvard, W. Shockley at Stanford, and Hans Eysenck in London were particularly attacked; but others who, like myself, expressed their disagreement with some of Jensen's conclusions yet supported him in other respects were likewise traduced.

[margin note: attacked]

It was natural that black students and black psychologists were in the forefront of the battle, because Jensen appeared to be saying that blacks are innately less intelligent than whites and always will be, whatever we do to try to overcome discrimination in employment, housing, education, and so on. Although he reiterated that environmental differences are also important and there is an enormous amount of overlapping in IQ distributions (i.e., there are a great many high-intelligence blacks and low-intelligence whites), and that people should be assessed for their individual abilities and traits, not by their membership in one racial group or another, he was dubbed and treated as a racist. It was indeed unfortunate that publication of the 1969 article coincided with the peak of college student activism against "the Establishment" and the pressures for black power. Thus, A. M. Shuey's books on black intelligence, published in 1958 and considerably expanded in 1966, caused far less stir, although they argued much more dogmatically than Jensen did that there are genetic differences between whites and blacks. Reviews of Shuey's books in professional journals (e.g., Dreger and Miller, 1960; 1968) were generally critical, but they consisted of rational discussion rather than emotive attacks. However, a majority of social scientists in the United States had veered strongly to environmentalism in the 1960s and believed that all social problems of race relations, economic inequities, school failure, and so on could be ameliorated by improving the environment. Thus, Jensen's attack on their suppositions came as a shock and could not be evaluated rationally.

The furor has by now considerably abated, though the term *Jensenism* is still frequently used to describe the heresy of imputing an important genetic component in intelligence, and particularly in explaining differences between racial or ethnic groups or social classes. Innumerable articles and books have been published attacking it, mostly in highly emotional and abusive fashion, though more recently there have been several more serious and logical discussions of the issue, on which I will draw in succeeding chapters. Moreover, many research investigations into both genetic and environmental factors (e.g., early intervention experiments) have been planned and carried out all the more carefully because the controversies over Jensen's writings exposed the weaknesses of earlier work.

The whole deplorable incident, then, has had some benefits; it has advanced our knowledge and understanding, even if it has not led to many clear-cut answers or to a greater consensus of views. On the other hand, it has increased critical attitudes toward tests among the general public, educational administrators, and teachers alike.

GROWING OPPOSITION
TO INTELLIGENCE TESTING

Though Jensen's publications and the ensuing controversies were certainly not mainly responsible for the growing opposition to testing, his work probably did further polarize supporters and critics. Several books (such as Gross, 1962; Hoffman, 1962; and Goslin, 1963) had pointed out weaknesses, misinterpretations, and overuse of tests in the early sixties. Civil rights legislation had been enacted, and many parents had successfully contested in the courts the assignment of their children to special schools or classes on the basis of low IQ. Likewise, it had been ruled in a number of suits that employers could not refuse to employ blacks or others who obtained low test scores, unless clear evidence was available that suitability for the job depended on intelligence — a reasonable claim, but one that is very difficult to prove in practice.

Since 1970, several states have enacted, or at least considered, legislation to ban the use of IQ tests in schools on the grounds that they are culturally biased and do not accurately measure intelligence. The Association of Black Psychologists (Williams, 1970) has urged a complete moratorium on testing until more is known about what IQ tests measure and how suitable they are for black students. In some instances, a ban or moratorium has been directed specifically against large-scale group testing — for example, a resolution passed by the National Education Association in 1972 — though the use of individual tests for clinical diagnostic purposes has been allowed to continue. But even this restricted use has been attacked, and some school psychologists have been forced to replace such tests with, for example, the Illinois Test of Psycholinguistic Abilities or tests of concept formation or of Piaget stages, which measure — rather less effectively and conveniently — much the same thing as the prohibited tests measure, but which avoid the controversial word *intelligence*.

Cronbach (1975) has pointed out that the very success of intelligence and educational achievement testing has contributed to their downfall. With the increasing complexity and specialization of postwar society, there have been increasing demands for highly intelligent individuals and increasing competition among schools and universities to pick out the most able, largely on the basis of test scores. The public feels threatened because so many educational and career decisions are based on impersonal instruments that they do not fully understand, and many would prefer that high-grade personnel be selected in the old-fashioned way: on the basis of academic and occupational record and the interview. Despite the proven subjectivity and inaccuracy of these methods, they are familiar and, therefore, more generally trusted.

Another growing trend in the 1960s and 1970s is suspicion of invasions of privacy, largely because the government, corporations, hospitals,and schools collect, and often computerize, so much personal information on parents and their children, and there is very little control over possible prejudicial use of these data (see Tyler and Wolf, 1974). Parents generally admit the rights of schools to maintain files of examination marks and other relevant data concerning their offspring, but many have pressed successfully that they should have access to such records, including the results of any IQ or other tests or psychologists' reports. Obviously, this would greatly hamper the work of psychologists, who regard their findings as being as confidential as a doctor's files. A psychologist could hardly examine or treat a retarded or emotionally maladjusted child without recording comments about the home that the parents might resent. It has been an almost universal policy that parents should *not* be told their children's IQs, because they are liable to misinterpret them. In addition, open access would seriously interfere with the conduct of any psychological research in schools—though I would agree that children should not be impressed into research projects, just because they are a captive audience, especially those using personality scales or questionnaires concerning home upbringing, unless the parents have been consulted (see Amrine et al., 1965).

Compared to trends in the United States, the reaction against intelligence testing has been much less marked in the United Kingdom and other technologically advanced countries. But, during the 1950s and 1960s, there was sustained and vehement criticism of the eleven-plus selection by some politicians and educationists, and it has by now been largely abolished. Tests may still be used occasionally for grading and grouping of students—for example, at the beginning of secondary schooling—and they are retained for selection and allocation of adults in the civil service and armed forces. So far, no restrictions appear to be imposed on the work of school psychologists with individual handicapped pupils or on their record keeping.

In light of the strong feelings on both sides of the issue, it is the object of this book to analyze the evidence for and against testing, and to attempt to reach a rational verdict.

SUMMARY

1 A brief outline is given of the origins of mental testing in the nineteenth century, including the statistical contributions of Galton, quantitative experiments on mental processes by early psychologists, and evolutionary studies of animals and the development of the higher brain centers.

2 Binet's approach was based chiefly on observation of children's mental growth, leading to the construction of an age scale of abilities. This was complemented by Spearman's Two Factor Theory, showing that a combination of varied items or subtests would measure an underlying general intelligence, or g factor.

3 Terman much extended the Binet scale and introduced the Intelligence Quotient. Various inadequacies in the IQ concept led to the substitution of Deviation Quotients. Following the development of group tests of educational achievement, the Army Alpha and other group intelligence tests came into widespread use.

4 Major assumptions underlying the mental testing movement, which came under criticism in the 1920s and 1930s, include the notions that intelligence is a homogenous mental entity, is genetically determined, and is therefore predictive of educational and vocational success throughout life. Observed ethnic differences, the effects of deprived or improved upbringing, and the variability of IQs measured over long periods indicated important environmental effects.

5 With Hebb's theories of neurological functioning and the developmental work of Piaget, the interactionist position won wide acceptance. This view (well argued by Hunt) holds that intelligence has a genetic basis but that the individual's effective ability depends on stimulation by, or interaction with, the physical and social environment.

6 A strong environmentalist trend dominated United States psychology and sociology in the 1950s and 1960s, as instanced by the belief that compensatory early schooling could overcome the effects of deprived environments on children's educational achievement. The general failure of Head Start programs touched off the reaction by Jensen, who reemphasized the importance of genetic differences, not only within white society but possibly also between ethnic groups, such as blacks and whites.

7 Other critics in the 1960s pointed out weaknesses in intelligence tests and their liability to be overused and misinterpreted. These criticisms, combined with the violent counterreaction to Jensen's writings, have produced in the present decade widespread suspicions of intelligence testing, and legal restrictions on its applications.

2

Criticisms of Intelligence Tests

WHAT THE CRITICS SAY

Almost all published intelligence tests contain particular items that appear to be defective in various ways. Some are ambiguous, and the critic can think of alternative answers not allowed for in the manual, or can claim that one or more of the wrong answers to a multiple-choice item is better than the right one. Many critics find some items actually humorous (see Gross, 1962) or criticize them because they appear to involve ideas quite beyond the range of most normal children. Others look trivial or silly, though quite possibly they are meaningful to children of the age for which they are intended. Some may well have become obsolete if the test has been used for many years, yet they continue to be used, owing to the high costs of replacement or revision and restandardization. The critics usually ignore the fact that in any good test the items have been tried out beforehand and the apparently unsuitable ones actually have been answered correctly more often by those with high total scores (or high M.A.'s) than by those with lower scores. In other words, Spearman's criterion (p. 4) has shown that they are good measures of the underlying general factor, even though they also contain irrelevant specific elements.

However, more difficult to answer are assertions that a particular item measures not intelligence but memory, motor skill, perception, verbal knowledge, or the like. Because there is no clear consensus as to the nature of intelligence, it is obviously difficult to prove that any particular item is a good or poor one. A test item or group of items is merely a sample of children's intellectual growth, as Binet pointed out, and the fact that test scores have been shown to increase with age or are higher among children judged bright than among those judged dull cannot prove that better items could not be found. Again, Spearman comes to our aid, because his theory implies that any kinds of items that correlate well with other items generally would have a large g component. And his own investigations indicated that the best measures of g were those involving grasping of relations ("eduction of relations and correlates"), as typified in abstracting, generalizing, reasoning, and problem solving (that is, the higher mental processes); whereas items mainly requiring simple memory or motor skills or specialized talents would show relatively low g content.

Unfortunately, later work (see Chapter 4) showed that Spearman's theory was oversimplified—that abilities common only to certain types of items but not present in other types could be distinguished. Hence, different intelligence tests, though constructed on much the same principles, could yield considerably different results. Thus, nonverbal tests based on grasping relations in figures or designs do not correlate more than 0.6 to 0.7 with verbal tests similarly aimed at intelligent thinking. Such a correlation is also typical for the Verbal and performance IQs of the Wechsler scales. Again, individual tests, such as Terman-Merrill or Wechsler, seldom correlate more than about 0.8 with group tests based on multiple-choice items that have to be answered within a fixed time limit. In fact, IQs from different tests given to the same individuals at about the same time can occasionally differ by as much as 20 to 30 points (though smaller differences of 5 to 10 points are much more common). Fine (1975) and others quote even more horrendous stories of extreme variations, though without indicating how frequently they occur. In fact, much of the variation may be caused by differences in test content or materials; by differences in the norms, one test being standardized on a more recent and representative sample than the other; or by differences in the spreads or Standard Deviations of IQs (see Chapter 5). Hence, it can be highly misleading for a school to apply a group test to all students at a certain grade level and merely enter the IQs on the children's record cards without indicating which test was used, implying that these IQs will remain constant for several years to come.

Block and Dworkin (1974), Williams (1970), Daniels (1976), and other critics state that current intelligence tests are not good tests of "real" intelligence; but they fail to indicate how real intelligence can be defined, let alone measured. Because intelligence is admittedly a rather vague construct, there is little hope of getting aggrement among psychologists on just what sort of tasks best represent it. This is why the empirical approach through factor analysis is preferable, though it, too, has its weaknesses (see Chapter 4).

Commenting on this point, Loehlin, Lindzey, and Spuhler (1975) suggest that the intelligence measured by well-constructed tests does come close to intelligence as it would normally be defined within white culture. I would agree with this verdict in respect to the results of individual tests given from about 5 to 12 years and some group tests from about 10 to 16 years. Such tests seem to correspond pretty closely to Intelligence B as manifested by brightness or cleverness in daily life or at school. But the scores or quotients obtained from very young children or preschoolers are a very different matter, as will be seen in Chapter 5; and beyond about 16 years the kinds of tasks included in most group tests become less and less representative of the thinking capacities of intelligent older adolescents or adults.[1] Such tests appear to involve a kind of mental slickness rather than the wisdom and grasp of the really able thinker. They usually give quite low correlations with occupational success or with nonacademic (e.g., commercial or social) competences.[2] But this is just one psychologist's judgment, and it is unlikely that others would agree on what kinds of items would be more suitable.

Elsewhere (Vernon, 1955), I have suggested that we should add a third usage to Hebb's Intelligence A and B, namely Intelligence C, which stands for the score or IQ obtained from a par-

[1] Even in senior high school, intelligence tests are of some value for entry to college, although they generally have lower correlations with college grades than do achievement tests or examinations. They are useful because they can reveal differences between schools, whereas grading standards are apt to vary widely among schools.

[2] The wide differences between mean IQs of people in different occupations are often cited as evidence of the predictive value of intelligence tests. But these differences could be artifactual insofar as different occupations demand different levels of schooling, and the level of schooling attained correlates substantially with IQ. The range of IQs in any one occupation is remarkably wide; for example, professors might range in IQ from 110 to 180, and chimney sweepers from 60 to 130. However, although the range is the same in both cases, the averages differ by 50 points.

ticular test. Different tests yield different Intelligence Cs because each test is only a rather narrow sample of the immense range of cognitive skills. Tests are also liable to be distorted samples insofar as they measure familiarity with the particular type of items or instructions or other variables called *extrinsic factors* (see Chapter 16). Far too many writers talk about intelligence without making clear whether they mean scores on a particular test or tests, the more general construct B, or the hypothetical genetic basis A.

It would be a reasonable criticism of intelligence tests to say that their tasks or items have developed haphazardly, rather than being based on any clear theory. The Stanford-Binet and Terman-Merrill tests extended the same sort of collection as Binet and Simon had formulated. McNemar (1942) showed, in fact, that the items at any one age level were rather heterogeneous, not measuring the same combination of abilities consistently. The various types of group test items were devised partly for convenience of format; a large number of items could be printed on one page, with fairly simple instructions, and could be answered in a fairly short time. Later these tests also became amenable to machine scoring.

But there seems to have been remarkably little progress in item types since the original Army Alpha. For example, Guilford's work (1967) is more theory-based than previous attempts and does extend the range of intellectual faculties that are sampled. But Guilford has deliberately not produced a "general intelligence" test (see Chapter 4). However, there seems to have been little or no impact on intelligence testing from, for example, Chomsky's linguistic theories, Piaget's analysis of developmental stages, or information theory.[3] And although IQ is so often regarded as showing ability to learn, no test includes any learning as such, apart from the retention of digits and sentences and a couple of other Terman-Merrill items.

DO INTELLIGENCE TESTS MEASURE "ACQUIRED SKILLS"?

One of the commonest criticisms — reiterated, for example, by Fine (1975), Daniels (1976), and even by Kagan (1974) — is that most intelligence test items consist of learned information and skills. Some examples quoted are:

[3] Some Piaget-based items are included in the new British Intelligence Test (see Warburton, 1970). Learning tests have been experimented with and generally found too unreliable to justify the time they require (see MacKay and Vernon, 1963).

1   Who wrote Romeo and Juliet?
2   What is a hieroglyphic?
3   What is the meaning of catacomb?
4   What is the thing to do if another boy (or girl) hits you without meaning to?

The obvious objection is that children from deprived environments are quite unlikely to have been exposed to such knowledge as the first three items require. The last item mainly elicits knowledge of moral conventions in middle-class society, and the normal response from lower-class children might be very different. Though such objections are plausible, they cannot justify the inference that intelligence, as measured by IQ tests, is acquired. True, children hear words and moral conventions from adults or peers, or read them in books and elsewhere; but, in fact, attempts to *teach* vocabulary have quite limited success, because children do not readily retain and use unfamiliar words unless they have reached sufficient mental maturity to understand the concepts the words stand for. One might as well say that walking is a learned or acquired skill, because children build it up slowly, usually with much adult assistance and practice. But we know perfectly well that walking is an innate skill that matures when children are ready for it. Verbal skills no doubt do depend on environmental stimulation to a greater extent than walking, but it is incorrect to say that verbal skills are acquired, a statement which implies that anybody could acquire them if taught. Rather, they are *developed,* like any other aspect of Intelligence B. (We return to this issue at the end of Chapter 3).

Actually, scores on vocabulary tests correlate so highly with scores on tests of reasoning, which involve very little advanced vocabulary, that they can hardly be distinguished by correlational analysis. Thus, vocabulary level and general information constitute some of the best tests of intelligence we possess, though it is true that most test constructors nowadays do try to avoid such items as those quoted, which particularly lay themselves open to charges of cultural bias, and substitute less obscure, though equally difficult or complex, items.

As far back as 1927, Thorndike, E. O. Bregman, and M. V. Cobb sought to examine specifically differences between informational items, or associative thinking, and reasoning items, or inferential thinking. In one of their experiments, 250 eighth-grade boys took six tests, three being chosen as informational—Vocabulary, Routine Arithmetic, and Information; and three as reasoning—Sentence Completion, Arithmetic Problems, and Analogies. The mean correlation among the first three was .602; among the second three, .544; and between the first three and the second three, .601. Thorndike concluded that the more informational subtests were as good measures of intelligence as those depending more on reasoning, and this conclusion supported his theory of intelligence as the total number of connections in the mind, whether innate or acquired or a combination of both. It is unwise, then, to judge, from just speculating about them, what intelligence tests measure.

We will return to the issue of cultural bias in intelligence tests in Chapter 20, for, despite evidence such as Thorndike's, psychologists with environmentalist views would naturally deny that children from disadvantaged environments have had the opportunities to build up vocabulary, information, or other mental skills to the same extent as children from privileged backgrounds.

SOURCES OF INACCURACY
IN TEST SCORES

Another, more reasonable criticism of group tests is that, when applied by teachers in schools, they are often inexpertly administered. For example, the teacher may fail to follow the directions adequately, may mistime the working periods allowed, or may give extra help to students in difficulty. Distractions can easily occur, such as intercom messages or noisy activity outside. It is seldom possible to prevent some students from copying their neighbors' answers. Misscoring or wrong totaling of scores is not infrequent. Misinterpretation of the psychological or educational significance of results can be egregious. There is no evidence of how often such errors of procedure or scoring occur, but they persist despite sustained efforts by test publishers, textbooks, university courses, and workshops to improve the efficiency of test usage and interpretation among teachers.

Even in individual testing, normally administered by school psychologists who have received thorough training in test procedures and scoring, we know that considerable discrepancies can occur—for example, in the scoring of borderline responses in the Terman-Miller or WISC (Wechsler Children's Scale). Some testers are consistently more severe, others more permissive in their styles of administration and scoring. A study by Cohen (1965) of 13 testers showed that, when differences in total scores were held constant, that is, with children of the same overall IQ, some testers gave scores on particular WISC subtests that were significantly higher than scores on other subtests. Sattler (1974) draws attention to other common errors, such as failing to continue testing far enough up the scale or, in the WISC, continuing to test beyond the limits laid down by the manual.

One of the commonest sources of error is the halo effect, or expectancies based on pretest information about the child (see Goodenough, 1949). For example, the teacher may have told the psychologist that the child is bright or dull, or that he or she comes from a middle- or lower-class background; or the tester jumps to conclusions from initial appearance and conversation. Such expectancies, which are similar to those pointed out by Rosenthal (1966) in psychological experimentation, are especially likely to occur with inexperienced student testers. Nevertheless, in most school testing departments, when two testers independently test the same children, using the same or equivalent tests, close similarities between the two IQs are far more frequently observed than marked discrepancies.

Effects of Practice and Coaching

It has long been known that previous practice or familiarization with the same or similar tests help children to score better. This was a particularly controversial issue in Britain at the time of the eleven-plus examination, where it was shown that children (or adults) who are sophisticated or trained in tackling multiple-choice items, following instructions, and working at speed have on average about a 10-point advantage in intelligence or educational quotients over those who are unfamiliar with objective tests (see Vernon, 1960). The problem has not aroused as much concern in the United States, where children tend to be introduced to objective tests and become thoroughly accustomed to them in early grades. However, it is probable that some students living in remote areas, where tests are seldom used, may be handicapped. This is particularly true of cross-cultural testing in non-Western countries. According to Goslin (1963), coaching, even for intelligence tests, is quite widespread in the United States. The Educational Testing Service has carried out some studies showing that the effects of coaching on their Scholastic Aptitude Test are negligible. However, they try to offset any such effects by providing ample information regarding the Scholastic Aptitude and Achievement Tests for all candidates to study beforehand.

Even repetition of the Terman-Merrill or WISC within less than about one year produces a distinct practice rise, especially on the performance subtests. Often the educational or clinical tester knows, from the records or from the child's own comments, when a child has been tested before, and either makes some allowance for practice effect or uses a different instrument for retesting. But in group testing the degree of familiarization is less likely to be known. Teachers and parents are highly disturbed when they realize that intelligence test performance is susceptible to practice or coaching, because they still believe that the tests are supposed to measure innate potentiality. In so doing, they have confused Intelligence B with Intelligence A, whereas what in fact improves through training or familiarization is Intelligence C. The training is highly specific to the kind of items practiced and has little or no spread or transfer to general mental efficiency. Moreover, the effects are limited: Excessive coaching seems to lead to irregularity in performance rather than to further consistent gains. However, when important educational decisions rest on differences of a few IQ points, special care must certainly be taken to obviate distortions from unequal practice.

Coaching or practice on educational achievement tests might seem less objectionable, because improvements in students' scores presumably mean that they have learned more about the particular topic. Nevertheless, there is substantial evidence that "test-wiseness" affects student performance on most educational tests, some students being more practiced than others in making good use of their time, guessing the tester's intentions, spotting any flaws in the items that give them additional clues, guessing when there is no penalty for wrong guesses, and so on. Millman, Bishop, and Ebel (1965) give a detailed analysis of the components of test-wiseness, though they do not attempt to estimate how far the scores obtained on commonly used tests are influenced by this factor or factors.

Another serious consequence of test sophistication is that students are known to adapt their methods of study to the type of test they know will be used. Thus, they may neglect more thoughtful uses of textbooks and lecture notes, because they realize that these are unlikely to help in the conventional objective achievement test.

Teachers' Expectations

A further reason for public distrust of intelligence tests arose from the wide publicity given by the press (and even by many psychological textbooks) to Rosenthal and Jacobson's study published in 1968. But no publicity was given either to later reports by psychologists that the study was technically faulty and did not prove what was claimed, or to replications by other researchers that disconfirmed the results.

Rosenthal and Jackson claimed that when certain children (actually chosen at random) are reported to their teachers as bright and likely to show unusual gains in ability, their IQs rise, presumably because the teachers pay them more attention and stimulate them better. In fact, significant gains on retesting after 8 months were obtained only with first- and second-grade children, not with those in the third to sixth grades. Also, the authors did not mention until after the press publicity had appeared that retests after 4 and after 12 months showed better results in the later grades than in the early ones. Competent reviewers pointed out various other reasons for distrusting the findings, and Elashoff and Snow (1971) summarize nine other studies, all of which entirely failed to demonstrate any teacher expectancy effects. Considering the failure of Head Start programs, where the teachers consciously tried to improve the intelligence of disadvantaged children, it seems highly improbably that teachers' unconscious biases would be any more effective. Moreover, teachers generally tend to give more individual attention to the dull and backward than to the bright.

It is, of course, quite likely that self-fulfilling prophecies play a prominent part in children's school *achievements*. For example, many teachers would have higher expectations of neatly dressed, well-spoken middle-class children than of less well dressed and less articulate lower-class children. It may well happen, then, that teachers do stimulate the former more, and that the children tend to live up to what teachers expect of them. Rist (1970) records a horrifying example of how this took place in a kindergarten and elementary school with students who came mostly from poor families. It was observed that the teachers classified children into good, medium, and dull groups on the basis of quite unreliable preentry information and a week's classwork. They then treated these groups so differently that the lowest groups never had a chance to improve. Though this is only one instance, it may be all too typical of what happens when homogeneous grouping is imposed prematurely (as we shall see later in this chapter). Nevertheless, there is as yet no evidence that teachers' expectations likewise affect children's intelligence quotients.

Motivational Factors

Another aspect of intelligence testing that draws unfavorable criticism is that scores must depend not only on the child's cognitive skills, but also on his motivation to succeed. A child who is extremely anxious, distractible, fatigued, or obsessed by some traumatic incident cannot perform optimally (and most people taking tests on which a lot depends suffer from anxiety). A child who is self-confident and keen to cooperate and concentrate will surpass those less motivated.

Despite the plausibility of these contentions, it has proved difficult to show that such factors significantly affect intelligence scores, except in the case of seriously maladjusted children, mental patients, or among children in cultures in which testing is a totally unfamiliar experience. The individual tester of maladjusted or retarded children takes considerable trouble to build up good rapport with each child before testing is begun and can usually recognize whether emotional conditions, unwillingness to concentrate, fatigue, or sickness is detracting from the child's performance. The tester then either postpones testing or draws attention, in the accompanying report, to the abnormal circumstances that make the score unreliable. If maladjusted children are retested after a period of treatment has ameliorated their emotional blocks, they commonly show considerable score gains.

A study by Zigler and Butterfield (1968) did demonstrate, however, that testing conditions significantly affected the Terman-Merrill IQs of 40 nursery school children aged 3 to 5 years (about two-thirds of them blacks). One-half took Forms L and M according to standard procedure, the tester being friendly but neutral. The other half took one form under standard conditions but for the second form received greater encouragement and reinforcement, easier sequencing of items, and so on. The mean gain in the first group (i.e., due only to practice) was 4.2 points; in the second group it reached 10.7 points. The children were further retested some months later and compared with another small but similar group of children who had not attended nursery school; the results showed that nursery school attendance also tended to help them adjust better to the testing situation. Exner (1966) reports a rather similar comparison with respect to WISC: One member of each of 33 matched pairs of children was treated formally, with a minimum of preliminary conversation and no reinforcement of responses; the other member was treated more warmly, with general conversation and much encouragement to increase rapport. The subtests were given in the regular order to some of the pairs, in reverse order to the remainder. In both groups, scores were significantly affected by the difference in rapport. The Arithmetic, Digit Span, and Picture Completion subtests were most seriously affected by poor rapport; other subtests yielded more irregular or else negligible differences. Arithmetic and Digit Span (though not Picture Completion) have often been noted as particularly susceptible to anxiety or distractibility.

We have to realize that individual testing is not merely a matter of applying standard procedures to a child but a complex process of social interaction. Many children react defensively if taken out of class by a strange adult, though most can be won over to cooperate by preliminary conversational exchanges. Sattler (1974) surveys a number of studies purporting to show that scores are raised when better rapport is built up (e.g., Feldman and Sullivan, 1971). However, the results of other studies are by no means unanimous, or they vary with the child's age, sex, or race. It is difficult also to separate the effects of the tester's personality or manner from the halo effects of the teacher's perceptions of the child.

Many experienced testers using the Stanford-Binet or Terman-Merrill tests like to adapt the order of the test items to the particular child — for example, starting with easy, interesting items and inserting another easy one after there has been an obvious failure on a more difficult one. Another alteration is to give all the forward and backward items in the Digit Span together to avoid repeating tiresome instructions; likewise with other items that appear at several levels. This practice is now generally frowned on, but Hutt (1947) was able to show that it made no difference to the final scores of normal children, though it did help to raise the scores of unstable children.

Testers may also be insufficiently aware that young children are highly susceptible to unintentional changes of facial expression or tone of voice. They may, therefore, be able to pick up cues as to whether their first response is right or wrong and correct themselves accordingly.

Testers of young infants, such as Bayley (Jones et al., 1971), admit that performance on developmental tests in the first 2 to 3 years of life is particularly affected by the child's social outgoingness, fear of strangers, temporary moods, and so on; hence the scores are less reliable than among older children and are also less valid indicators of later intelligence. But by the time children have settled down in school for a couple of years and are used to being asked questions by teachers and thinking out answers themselves, it seems unlikely that normal children will be much affected by the testing situation or require special motivation.

Motivational differences are more difficult to discern or make allowance for in group test performances. Sarason et al. (1960) found rather consistent, though small, negative correlations between scores on Sarason's Test Anxiety or General Anxiety scales, and intelligence or achievement tests. But, obviously, this does not prove that the anxiety causes lower cognitive test performance; one could equally claim that children of below-average ability are more likely to become anxious when faced with tests. Though there is no evidence, it seems quite possible that some teachers giving tests are too authoritarian and threatening, others too permissive and lax, to motivate students optimally.

Some investigators have tried to throw further light on the topic by measuring the effects of additional motivation on group test scores. Burt and Williams (1962) compared the IQs of several groups of 11-year-old children and of adult students in two different situations: (1) when the test was applied as a trial run or in the course of a research in which the results were of no concern to the testees; and (2) when the test was given competitively and would determine entry to secondary school or college. The authors claim that in the strongly motivating condition increases averaged some 3 to 6 points, but it is not clear how far these might have resulted from ordinary practice effects. In one study of 131 children, monetary rewards were offered to those who increased their scores at a second testing; an average rise of 7.5 points was obtained. Here Burt estimates that 3 points of the increase could be practice effect, the other 4.5 points being attributable to motivation. However, similar studies have indicated that when children are strongly motivated, they attempt more items, but they do not get more of them right. According to Sattler, also, it does not seem that children's results are improved by offering rewards of candy for correct responses in individual tests or by giving additional praise.

As regards health and fatigue, some large-scale experiments were carried out in the British Army in World War II (Vernon and Parry, 1949). Over 1,000 women recruits who took a standard battery of tests were asked to record their present stage in the menstrual cycle. Another group was asked to say whether they thought they had failed to do themselves justice because they were suffering from colds or other minor ailments. No significant differences on any of the tests were found between those who were in poorer health or were menstruating and the rest of the groups.

Even if motivational factors were of much greater importance in intelligence test performance than I have stated here, the tests would not necessarily correlate any less well with future educational achievement, because similar motivations are likely to be involved in doing well at school work.

I have not attempted to discuss here the problems of motivational effects on the scores of United States black children, though it is widely believed that they tend to score lower than white children partly because of anxiety or negative self-concepts, or because they feel threatened by a white tester. We will turn to this issue which is also particularly important in cross-cultural testing of other ethnic groups, in Chapter 20.

HARMFUL EDUCATIONAL AND SOCIAL CONSEQUENCES OF TESTING

Ebel (1966) has pointed out some of the consequences of applying and interpreting tests with insufficient caution. He is referring mainly to standardized tests of achievement, but many of his remarks are relevant to intelligence testing (see also Kirkland, 1971):

1 Tests place an indelible stamp of inferiority on testees who do badly, which affects their feelings of self-worth and motivation, and thus may adversely affect their later careers. Tests should be used more for counseling individuals on present strengths and weaknesses than for long-term prediction.
2 Tests foster a narrow conception of ability and neglect many talents or skills in which testees might have scored more highly.
3 Test constructors and publishers have an undue influence on curriculum and teaching through what they choose to include in, or exclude from, their tests.
4 Tests suggest a mechanistic concept of evaluation, implying that each individual can be summed up in a few scores, even though some scores may well be inaccurate. Thus, they restrict the freedom of individuals to plan their future careers.

Other, subsidiary effects, according to Ebel, are that tests favor conformity as against creativity or innovation; they emphasize competition and individual success as against cooperative endeavor; and they may reward those individuals who possess specious test-taking skills and penalize those who lack them. Ebel also mentions their liability to cultural bias and their high cost both in money and in time. Furthermore, some kinds of test constitute unwarranted invasions of personal and family privacy.

Though admitting that there is some substance in all these criticisms, Ebel concludes that there would be greater biases and social and educational losses if testing were abolished and we had to fall back on teachers' or other subjective evaluations. A striking instance of socially valuable testing is that of the U.S. Civil Service, which selects employees largely by objective tests, thus avoiding the dangers of nepotism and political patronage.

Let us expand on some of Ebel's points. With respect to the first, Fine (1975), for example, claims that children are often damaged for life by getting a low IQ early in their school careers. Not only do teachers think of them as permanently dull, but the children themselves realize that they are so regarded and give up trying, or rebel against scholastic values. Parents, too, are apt to find out that scores are disappointing, even if specific IQ figures are withheld. To an undue extent, they regard such results as important and accept their finality. Thus, such information tends to kill their ambitions for their children, to lower family morale, and to reduce the amount of help and encouragement they give. The children's peers soon pick up, from the way the teacher treats the low scorer, that he is "dumb." Even the referral of a child to see the school psychologist suggests to the child and his peers that there is something wrong with him. However, Fine neglects to add that some students, and their families as well, become more strongly motivated if they know that they have done well and, for example, that they might win a scholarship to college. Many gifted children, including some from relatively deprived backgrounds, might never have been discovered other than by intelligence testing. There is a growing trend to provide high-IQ children with enrichment, acceleration, or other measures that help them realize their potential (see Vernon, Adamson, and Vernon, 1977). Moreover, it has often been to children's advantage to have their low ability identified. For example, parents or teachers may have been pushing such children unduly, thus causing their compensatory delinquent behavior. But on the basis of the psychologist's report, the children can be shifted to a less stressful curriculum that they can handle adequately.

Thus, not all labeling of children with IQs is undesirable, though, admittedly, misuse of this practice is far too frequent. The same can be said of homogeneous grouping by ability, which is widely practiced in North American and British schools but is strongly attacked by more progressive educationists. It has even been made illegal in some areas of the United States on the grounds that it is racially discriminatory, because larger proportions of ethnic minority children are apt to end up in the less able tracks.[4] The main danger, again, is that duller children tend to get pigeonholed at too early an age, even before they have had a chance to demonstrate their educational capabilities; once they are fixed in a slower track, it becomes increasingly difficult for them to be promoted to a faster one. Their work and their morale suffer. Conversely, those (usually from middle-class backgrounds) who get good IQs and make a good impression on entry are much more likely to be placed in the faster track and to receive better teaching and reinforcement. Thus, initial IQs show an inflated predictive validity, because they often act as self-fulfilling prophecies. Nevertheless, many teachers prefer this type of class organization because it somewhat reduces the range of ability in their classes. According to several summaries, the achievements of homogeneously grouped children tend to show no overall superiority to those of heterogeneous classes. But as Ekstrom (1959), Esposito (1973), and others point out, such negative findings often arise because teachers have made no effort to differentiate their curricula and methods to suit the brighter, average, and duller groups, respectively.

There is one criticism of educational testing with which I would agree: Mass application of standardized achievement tests inevitably tempts teachers to teach "to" the tests—that is, to coach children to do well on the kinds of items in the tests to be used, at the expense of other, probably more valuable educational activities—and in so doing, they rigidify the curriculum. Goslin (1963) and Kirkland (1971) note that although most teachers deny that they practice such coaching, it is nevertheless almost universal, especially when the teacher's competence or the school district's efficiency are liable to be judged by comparison with national standards. The advocates of "creativity" in the late 1950s and early 1960s had a sound point, though the tests of "divergent" thinking they proposed to substitute for "convergent" intelligence and achievement tests are disappointing in many respects as criteria of pupil or school ability, and seem to be losing popularity (see Vernon, Adamson, and Vernon, 1977).

I have not attempted in this chapter to cover the criticisms that intelligence testing is culturally or politically biased and discriminates against children from deprived homes or from ethnic

---

[4] The pros and cons are discussed more fully by Vernon, Adamson, and Vernon (1977). I would suggest that it does more harm to force a uniform educational step-ladder on all children than to educate them according to their different capacities.

minority groups. Such criticisms cannot be taken up until we have gone more deeply into the heredity—environment controversy. The existence, already admitted above, of so many possible sources of error and bias in intelligence tests results might seem to undermine the whole testing movement. Yet most professional psychologists are themselves aware of and highly critical of shortcomings in tests or testing, and concerned about overcoming them. Many of the widely used textbooks — for example, those of Cronbach (1970), Anastasi (1968), and Sattler (1974) — draw attention to such weaknesses and attempt to show how they can be avoided.

CRITICISMS BY PSYCHOLOGISTS

It is said that Jean Piaget started work on mental tests in 1919, but he soon became interested not in how many children passed or failed various items but in why those who failed did so. He thus embarked on his lifelong study of the nature of children's understandings and misunderstandings at different ages, using his so-called clinical method rather than a psychometric approach. Nonpsychometric psychologists have made the same kind of criticism of psychometric tests more frequently in recent years. Mental testing, they claim, implies a static view of the individual child as a bundle of fixed abilities and traits rather than as a dynamic, growing, and ever-changing organism. Tests merely measure the end-products of intellectual development and acheivements up to a given time, without throwing any light on the processes whereby this stage was reached or what progress there will be beyond it. Sigel (1963) suggests that tests limit rather than increase our understanding of the individual: They merely score the person right or wrong on each item instead of inquiring into the method of solution or the difference in cognitive styles or personality that led the individual to prefer a wrong answer to the conventionally right one (see also Riessman, 1962; Ginsburg, 1972).

Now one would agree that developmental studies like Piaget's, or experimental studies of information processing, perception, retention, and thinking, should be highly relevant to the assessment of intelligence. Any techniques that promise to throw further light on children's intellectual development are of obvious theoretical importance. But it does not seem that current work — with Piagetian tasks, with concept formation and learning, or with cognitive styles (which could be applied within the rather brief period that the psychometrist can afford to spend with an individual child)—is capable of yielding much more diagnostically useful information than present intelligence tests. Perhaps Uzgiris and Hunt's (1975) ordinal scales of infant development are a good beginning to the improvement of testing. They are claimed to provide information directly usable by teachers, though, at the moment, they do not extend beyond Piaget's preoperational stage. Kagan's (1967) studies of reflective and impulsive styles are also relevant (see p. 126). The trouble with most of such work is that we know so little about the generalizability of the tasks employed, i.e., how far they transfer to thinking in general (see Messer, 1976). For example, although Piagetian conservation is believed to be basic to the development of number sense and rational thinking generally, it is well known that children who conserve in certain tasks do not necessarily do so in other tasks, and there seems to be no clear demonstration that conservation measures tell us more about a child's readiness for arithmetic than does his or her Binet Mental Age.

It is unfair, also to state that the school psychologist is uninterested in "processes" and merely assesses "products." When applying Terman-Merrill, WISC, educational tests, the good psychologist has the opportunity to observe a great deal about the child's lapses in attention, inefficiencies in thinking, or sources of difficulty in reading or number that can then be passed on to the teacher. The psychologist is also well aware of the importance of motivational factors and personality in educational retardation. Admittedly, however, many inferences drawn from qualitative observations are fragmentary and subjective, and there is certainly room for better diagnostic tests.

A further type of criticism is well expressed by Stott (1971), who entirely rejects the notion that backwardness in school may arise from insufficient genetic potentiality or from such other global causes as "a perceptual deficit." He sees retardation in terms of specific patterns or strategies of cognitive inefficiencies, induced by early environment, or linked to personality weaknesses. Among the 14 common maladaptive strategies that he lists are impulsiveness (failure to stop to think), high distractibility, and avoidance difficulties by withdrawal or by "playing dumb." The same children, he claims, are often quite well adapted and able in everyday situations outside the school. But although such syndromes may be pragmatically useful to the tester, there is little or no evidence to demonstrate that the assumed temperamental factors affect cognitive performance.

Stott further believes that the syndromes can be overcome by providing carefully regulated experiences and reinforcing manifestations of more adaptive behavior. Some support for this approach can be derived from such findings as those of Bereiter and Engelmann (1966); their compensatory educational program, aimed at specific linguistic and study skills, was more successful than Head Start in general. Harlow's (1949) well-known work on learning sets in monkeys is likewise relevant. But however useful professionally planned behavior modification techniques could often be, it seems unlikely that many teachers could devise and carry them out while coping with the varied needs of a class of 30 children. Moreover, it would seem unwise to ignore basic individual differences in learning capacities. After all, any good school teacher already does try to train pupils to attend, to interpret what they hear or read, to classify and rehearse experiences; yet most teachers clearly have little success with some children — usually, though not always, those having low IQs.

THE IMPACT OF INDIVIDUALIZED EDUCATION

Recent attempts to make education more individualized or adaptive also represent a break with the traditional psychometric evaluation of children's abilities and achievements. Such education is based on behavioral objectives and is evaluated by criterion-referenced, rather than norm-referenced, tests. A notable example is the work of Glaser (1977) at the Learning, Research and Development Center at the University of Pittsburgh. It is claimed that with the aid of a panel of expert teachers, any academic discipline can be reduced to a sequence of instructional steps or behavioral objectives; likewise, teaching materials for pupil study can be produced that match any individual's particular level of proficiency. (These materials may include computerized or programed learning units but are more commonly based on audio-cassettes or printed instructions.) The pupil learns a unit either by individual study or with teacher assistance and, after satisfying a certain criterion of proficiency, moves on to the next step. In some experiments, computers have been used to record the stages that pupils have reached and to decide what should come next. These decisions can also be left to the teacher.

Individualized learning materials, or modules, are not to be regarded as "cookbooks" that any teacher can apply. Their aim is, rather, to supply several alternative routes, or branching programs, to suit children with varied capabilities. Children can enter at whichever of various points befits their previous achievement in the topic, and they are encouraged to plan their own activities as far as possible, though the teacher or an aide is always present to advise and provide remediation if necessary.

Criterion-referenced tests are designed to show what stage of accomplishment with respect to a sequence of processes or skills the pupil has reached. Neither ordinary school grades nor conventional test scores tell us what students can actually do. Criterion-referenced tests do not need norms that show how students stand relative to their age or grade group. Instead, the level reached is defined operationally by the skills mastered (see Airasian and Madaus, 1974). The use of such tests is strongly supported by Bloom (1976) and Block (1974), whose work on mastery learning is discussed in Chapter 10.

Glaser does not deny that intelligence tests are predictive of scholastic achievement in the conventional school. Such tests work well because of the very inefficiency of our teaching methods: School instruction so often fails to get across new ideas or principles that it is mostly the children with high IQs who can bridge the gaps and understand what is being taught. But with adaptive instruction, IQ becomes less relevant, because students can progress at their own individual rates through the successive stages of mastery. The traditional view that individual differences in intelligence govern the child's present and future rate of learning stands in the way of more adaptive kinds of instruction.

Individualized learning has been applied to the early stages of reading and arithmetic, but apparently it is less successful for developing reading comprehension, for which it is more difficult to define a sequence of operational stages. It also works well in elementary school science but, naturally, becomes less applicable as the complexity and breadth of topics increase.

Although individualized learning is clearly an important breakthrough in educational technology, it has its limitations. It is also very costly, having to be formulated and applied by specially trained teachers. Though it would appear to bypass the need for intelligence tests, it is still highly probable that some children will consistently progress through the stages and attain more complex achievements than others. Indeed, most current or future improvements in education are likely to benefit the bright more than the dull. Thus, it would be foolish for educationists to ignore the existence of basic individual differences in learning capacities, whether of genetic or of environmental origin. The changes in educational techniques and psychological views that have been outlined above (and will be discussed further in Chapter 3) should not conflict with the continued use of intelligence tests for diagnosing learning difficulties, or predicting future promise. They are complementary, rather than opposed.

It is interesting to note, in conclusion, that Jensen himself has admitted (1973b) that the abolition of IQ tests would make very little difference to the world at large. If psychologists preferred to observe processes rather than measurable products, or used Piagetian or criterion-referenced tests or tests based — as Layzer (1972) suggests — on "bits" of information, the results would be very similar to those for IQ tests; that is, they would measure much the same thing, though the scores or findings would be much more awkward to handle. The same problems of nature and nurture would persist, but it would be more difficult to investigate them. The IQ is a useful term for quantifying individual differences that everybody — whether teachers, parents, or employers — observes when people are faced with complex thinking tasks. It is unfortunate that controversy has centered so much around the IQ, just because it has become so strongly identified in the public mind with superiority and inferiority. In fact, a number of steps are already being taken to dispense with the term. The Moray House testing unit at Edinburgh long ago ceased calling its tests intelligence tests and calls them instead verbal reasoning tests — an apt description that carries no implications as to how far the ability is innate or acquired. The same is true of the Scholastic Aptitude tests produced by the Educational Testing Service.

SUMMARY

1   Critics often characterize particular test items as trivial, culture-bound, or obsolete, ignoring the fact that they have usually been tried out beforehand and shown to be effective. However, the rejoinder that they all measure the same g, or general intelligence, is weakened by Spearman's disregard of group factors in abilities. Such factors mean that, to quite an extent, different intelligence tests do measure different skills.

2   Other critics suggest that tests don't measure "real" intelligence. Admittedly, the conventional types of items have evolved haphazardly, without a clear theoretical basis. But that they measure only "acquired knowledge" is fallacious. Thus, vocabulary cannot readily be expanded by training, and there is evidence that vocabulary tests measure much the same ability as verbal reasoning tests.

3   The extent to which test scores are affected by testing conditions, the tester's expectations, or the testees' motivation is often exaggerated, though admittedly care is needed in administering and interpreting tests. Greater difficulties occur in testing children in other cultural groups and the very young.

4 Large-scale group testing is much more liable to such weaknesses and to unreliability than is individual testing by a trained psychologist, though the latter kind of testing involves more subjective judgment.

5 The claim that children's IQs are affected by teachers' expectations is entirely discredited, though their achievements may be much affected by self-fulfilling prophecies.

6 There is some substance in the criticisms that testing lowers children's self-esteem, unduly influences the curriculum, and narrows the range of abilities to be inculcated. But the abolition of relatively objective intelligence testing would result in greater bias in making educational decisions about pupils.

7 Psychologists themselves are critical of tests as giving an overly static view of children and yielding little information about the processes of learning or development. Alternative types of tests, however, have not yet shown much advantage. Kagan's learning styles are helpful, and Stott emphasizes that much educational backwardness results not from general mental backwardness but from maladaptive learning strategies, which can sometimes be remediated.

8 The approach of Glaser and others, using behavioral objectives and criterion-referenced testing, is promising, though it seems unlikely to overcome the basic individual differences in learning abilities.

3

Theories of Intelligence

The word *intelligence,* according to Burt (1955), goes back to Aristotle, who distinguished *orexis,* the emotional and moral functions, from *dianoia,* the cognitive and intellectual functions. Cicero translated the latter word as *intelligentia* (*inter* — within, *leger* — to bring together, choose, discriminate). Although psychologists are well aware than every animal or human action or thought combines affective and cognitive aspects, the two domains are sufficiently distinct to be studied separately. Nevertheless, the historical origins of the term have been partly responsible for many dissensions and misunderstandings. They have led us to reify intelligence as some kind of thing or monolithic entity in the mind. As Ryle (1949) has pointed out, attempts to describe or define intelligence are futile, since they involve the fallacy of "the ghost in the machine." We can never observe it directly; all we can observe is that some actions, words, or thoughts are more intelligent, clever, complex, or efficient than others.

Burt (1975) argued that it does not help us to state that intelligence is an adjective or adverb rather than a noun. There are plenty of examples of what he calls *dispositional properties,* which likewise are not "things" — for instance, solubility of a chemical substance, or the conductivity of an electric circuit. Surely, though, there is a difference, in that we have agreed methods of measurement of these properties; they can be defined in terms of specific operations, whereas there is no such consensus for operationalizing intelligence. Nevertheless, it can be a useful construct, something that helps us to explain behavior, despite its lack of observability and its ambiguity. Goslin (1963) points out that ability at baseball is also a construct, but it is much easier to specify the actions covered by it than in the case of intelligence. In fact, a large proportion of psychological theory is based on hypothetical constructs such as perception, associations, images, instinct or drive, and so forth. But we have to be aware of what we are doing when we use these terms and always endeavor to translate them back into the operations or observable behavior to which they refer. Jensen (1969) indeed argues that intelligence, or *g*, is as valid a construct for explaining behavior as are genes in biology or atoms in physics.

Fourteen psychologists (Thorndike et al.) contributed to a symposium in 1921 on intelligence and its measurement, and put forward 14 different views. Ideas about the essential faculty or quality of mind involved overlapped a good deal, but different writers have variously stressed abstract thinking (e.g., Terman); problem solving, planning capacity (e.g., Porteus); and attention, adaptability, educability or learning capacity, insight, and grasping of relations (e.g., Spearman). But none of these descriptions is sufficiently explicit to tell us whether a certain kind of behavior or test response is a good or a poor instance of intelligence. Binet regarded intelligence as a complex set of qualities, including: (1) the appreciation of a problem and the direction of the mind toward its execution; (2) the capacity for making the necessary adaptations to reach a definite end; (3) the power of self-criticism. And elsewhere he writes that the fundamental quality is "judgment, otherwise called good sense, practical sense, initiative, the faculty of adapting oneself to circumstances. To judge well, to comprehend well, to reason well, these are the essential activities of intelligence" (Binet and Simon, 1905).

Note that Binet makes some reference to motivational as well as cognitive traits; and in this he was followed by Wechsler (1958), who defined intelligence as "the aggregate or global capacity of the individual to act purposefully, to think rationally and to deal effectively with his environment." As we shall see later, more modern views of intelligence are less speculative; they derive more from developmental, experimental, and statistical research.

BIOLOGICAL ASPECTS
OF INTELLIGENCE

First, let us consider what we can learn from physiology and from the evolution of intelligence. The work of biologists, comparative psychologists, and ethologists has shown that the connection between adaptability of behavior and size or complexity of the brain is less simple than it first appeared. True, innate mechanisms, universal to all members of a particular species, play a major part in behavior at lower evolutionary levels; but even at quite simple stages, there is already considerable variability and spontaneity. Moreover, the distinction between innate mechanisms and acquired habits is not clear-cut. For example, as described by Lorenz, imprinting involves innate patterns, but they appear only under conditions of appropriate environmental stimulation. Even among insects, we can observe quite complex levels of adaptability; for example, spiders in siting their webs, bees in mapping their territory, ants in learning mazes, are displaying accomplishments comparable to those of rats, which have far larger brains. Likewise, some of the apparently human thinking capacities of generalizing, grasping relations, and problem solving by insight occur in rudimentary form in rats and birds, and much more clearly in apes, who can even acquire many of the functions of language.

Stenhouse (1974) has pointed out that the evolution of human intelligence could scarcely be ascribed to some fortuitous set of genetic mutations (which are more often disadvantageous than helpful). He attempts to trace the gradual development of four main factors or attributes necessary for intelligence in higher animals and humans, all of which are likely to have survival value and, therefore, to have evolved by natural selection:

1   Increased variety and capacity of sensory and motor equipment. (These were vastly improved with human adoption of erect posture, making possible better vision and distance reception, and use of the hand for manipulation and the larynx for speech.)

2   Greater retention of previous experiences and organization or coding of such experience for flexible retrieval.

3   The capacity for generalizing and abstracting from experience, seeing relations.

4   The capacity to delay immediate instinctual responses — shown in delayed and latent learning in rats,

exploratory behavior and curiosity, ability to unlearn and modify previous learnings, and reflection in creative problem solving.

A general statement, which accords with modern biological and psychological research, is that in lower species, the animal's behavior is more directly and immediately determined by its organic structure (innate neural and biochemical mechanisms), by external stimulation to which it becomes conditioned, or both; whereas in higher species, intervening processes occur to a much greater extent in the central nervous system. This view not only links up with the work of Hebb and Piaget, described later in this chapter, but it is also relevant to practical intelligence testing, since the more complex intellectual problems that humans, apes, or rats can solve are those that require most internal thinking.

The anatomy and physiology of the brain also give us little help. Within the human species, there appears to be very little correlation between intelligence and brain size, complexity of convolutions, or other identifiable features. Only in some pathological cases of idiocy or in senility does microscopic examination of brain structures reveal any noticeable abnormalities. And, although the enormous growth of the cerebral cortex is obviously associated with superior mental abilities in human beings, it is not possible to identify particular areas or lobes with particular functions, apart from the motor and sensory areas and the tendency for aphasia or other language defects to be associated with Broca's and neighboring areas of the left hemisphere (see Penfield, 1959). Recent work (see Nebes, 1974) has indicated that there is considerable differentiation of function between the hemispheres, the left being more responsible for verbal and temporal processes, the right for spatial and visual processes. But it is well known that large sections of the brain can be removed or damaged without leaving permanent effects on specific capacities and that the electrical stimulation of points on the surface can produce very variable motor or sensory responses. Penfield (1958) has shown that stimulation of parts of the temporal lobe can sometimes resuscitate forgotten past experiences with almost hallucinatory vividness, though, again, there is no uniformity of evidence. Even the motor cortex of monkeys can be removed without loss of skilled movements. Thus, it is clearly untrue that particular percepts, ideas, and so on are located in particular neurones.

With the recording of electric potentials from the brains of normal human subjects, a new avenue of study appeared to open up. Certain abnormal wave forms have been shown to be diagnostic—for instance, in epilepsy. The predominant alpha waves are generally lacking in young infants; they increase in amplitude and rate up till about age 13, and thus they do correlate to some extent with Mental Age, though apparently not with IQ, that is, with differences in intelligence among normals at any one age. However, the latencies of electroencephalographic waves, that is, the speed of response of electric potentials induced by external stimulation, seemed to be more promising. Ertl (1966) claimed correlations as high as 0.6 with measured IQ, and Eysenck (1973) has followed up this work and confirmed the existence of positive correlations, though usually nearer 0.3. In a study by Shucard and Horn (1972), where response latencies were correlated with a variety of ability tests, the coefficients were mostly below 0.25; and those with nonverbal tests, which Cattell (1971a) regards as measures of "fluid" intelligence, were no higher than those with verbal tests, which he identifies with "crystallized" intelligence (see p. 47).

We should not expect to get very high correlations even if the EEG measures genuinely represent innate brain potential, because the intelligence measures with which they are compared are, as we have seen, much affected by environment. Thus, the correlation, whether high or low, would not prove that the EEG or other aspects of brain function correspond to the physical basis of Intelligence A. It is obviously possible that upbringing in a stimulating environment might foster neuronic growth. In other words, superior brain characteristics might be a result, as much as a cause, of superior Intelligence B.

PSYCHOLOGICAL THEORIES OF INTELLIGENCE

At one time, Spearman suggested that g represented general mental energy, which activates the various mechanisms or engines of the mind corresponding to the s, or specific, factors. The former he considered to be mainly innate, the latter acquired. However, this theory won little favor, and more attention was paid to his detailed analysis of the kinds of relations and correlates that g was capable of "educing" (Spearman, 1923). One of his strongest critics was Godfrey Thomson, who claimed (1939) that the observed tendency for all ability tests to correlate positively did not necessitate the notion of a general underlying power of the mind. Rather, Thomson followed Thorndike's view of the mind as made up of very large numbers of bonds or connections (see p. 23). Any one mental test item would involve the operation of many such bonds, and two or more tests would tend to correlate because they drew on the same total "pool" of bonds. Such a theory, he showed, could equally well account for the overall positive correlations without invoking Spearman's g factor. Also, insofar as certain groups of bonds (e.g., those concerned with verbal, or number, or spatial thinking) might tend to cluster more closely, he was willing to accept the appearance of additional, partly distinguishable, mental factors (e.g., verbal, number, and spatial), which Burt, in England, called group factors and Thurstone, in America, called primary factors (see Chapter 4).

However, by the 1930s, most experimental psychologists were realizing that the traditional view of mental processes as built up from associations or stimulus-response (S-R) bonds was quite inadequate, especially in light of the work of Gestalt psychologists. Moreover, the notion of neurological functioning as a kind of telephone switchboard, with each bond dependent on the synapses between particular neurones, had proved untenable.

A more promising basic unit of mental activity was provided by Head and Bartlett's notion of the schema (see Bartlett, 1932). The *schema* is a flexible mental structure or template that brings to bear the totality of relevant experience on any percept or concept. For example, a schema enables us to recognize a white plate as a white plate, regardless of the distance and angle of viewing or the lighting conditions. Similarly, Piaget adopted *schemes* to refer to the reflex responses or habits, the percepts and concepts built up by assimilating incoming experience to existing structures and the accommodation or modification of existing structures by new experience. The same notion appeared in a new guise in Miller, Galanter, and Pribram's (1960) discussion of *plans* as the underlying mechanisms of human responses and thoughts. Reflexes and instincts are inherited plans that permit more adaptive and flexible behavior than the simple S-R bond. As new plans are acquired, they operate more like hypotheses that the organism tries out and tests against the outcome. (These are referred to as TOTES,[1] or feedback loops.) In the course of mental development, more and more complex plans are learned or built up and organized hierarchically in the form of strategies or generalized skills, which can be applied in a wide range of learning or problem-solving situations. Clearly, this theory is quite similar to that of Piaget.

[1] A psychological acronym that stands for Test Operate Test Exit.

Hebb and Piaget

I will make no attempt to set out fully the implications for intelligence theory of the work of D. O. Hebb and Jean Piaget, since these are so well covered by Hunt (1961). I will touch on only a few major points. It is remarkable that although their approaches were so different — Hebb being interested primarily in animal psychology and neurology, Piaget in child psychology and epistemology — their conclusions are so concordant. Both were concerned to show how the infant, whose primitive consciousness is only partially differentiated, comes to perceive a world of objects independent of itself, that is, to build up percepts and, later, concepts and logical thinking skills.

As a behaviorist, Hebb hypothesized that many types of animal learning require brain mechanisms to account for autonomous, internal processing. He thus envisaged groupings, or *assemblies,* of neurones in the association areas of the brain, giving rise to reverbatory discharges. The more complex systems underlying perceptions of objects are referred to as *phase sequences;* the same kind of mechanisms might be involved in what we have called perceptual schemata. Hebb believed that much of the infant's first year or two of life is spent in the building up of phase sequences as a result of rich and varied visual, tactile, and other experiences. His work on apes brought up in the dark, and reports of the great difficulties that people who are born blind, because of cataracts, have in acquiring visual perception after gaining sight through operations, led him to suggest that there are certain critical periods for laying down these basic elements of perception. If they are not acquired within the usual period, it may be impossible for them to develop later. Hebb and his colleagues carried out further experiments on rats and dogs. Some were brought up in very restricted caged environments, others in more varied and stimulating environments; the latter were found to be more intelligent and better at maze learning when they reached maturity. Hebb's laboratory at McGill University was also responsible for much of the work demonstrating the severe emotional and other effects of prolonged sensory deprivation on normal adults, which, again, suggested the need of the organism for varied perceptual stimulation in intellectual development. These findings have obvious implications for Hebb's view that effective intelligence — Intelligence B — depends on appropriate environmental stimulation as well as on genetic predispositions.

Piaget's early work of the 1920s was greeted with suspicion, not only because he rejected psychometric concepts and techniques, but also because he appeared to be claiming that all children pass through a series of qualitatively different stages in the development of their thinking — sensorimotor, preoperational and egocentric, concrete, and finally formal operations. His linking of these stages to particular ages suggested that he attributed them wholly to maturation. Later, however, he specifically pointed out that intellectual progress depends not only on cerebral growth but also on interaction of the child with the physical and social environment and the process he called *equilibration,* that is, the building up of a hierarchy of more and more effective schemata or mental structures. This view (Piaget, 1950) was typified in his careful observation of successive substages of sensorimotor development and of the beginnings of imagery and internalization of thought in his own children from 0 to 2 years. He showed that early problem solving was largely overt trial and error, but this became progressively abbreviated into internal mental processing. Language was assigned a rather secondary role: Children do not acquire new schemata or concepts by being told or taught them so much as by discovery through their own interactions with their environment. Later, however, language serves for labeling of schemata and for carrying out more rapid and flexible thinking.

For Piaget, then, intelligence is not a causal or distinctive faculty of mind but an extension of the biological processes of adaptation, which can be observed throughout animal evolution. As in Hebb's theory, behavior becomes progressively more intelligent the more complex the lines of interaction between organism and environment, and the more inclusive and logical children's conceptions of the world and their thought processes.

Another misunderstanding arose from Piaget's apparent claim that all children progress to all the characteristics of a given stage almost simultaneously; in fact, he admits that there are considerable variations in different situations. For example, conservation of area and volume do not usually develop until some time after the acquisition of conservation of amount and number. Like Hebb, also, Piaget stresses the need for a rich and varied environment if the full implications of a new concept, structure, or schema are to be realized and stabilized. Hunt (1961) indicates that the acquisition of a new structure or stage depends on matching the environmental stimulation or new experience to already available structures; that is, they should be in advance, but not too much in advance, of the child's present stage. At the same time, it would appear that Hunt is too apt to assimilate Piaget's work to American learning theory and to assume his support for the view that children's cognitive development can be manipulated or improved just by appropriate provision of stimulating experiences and modifications of environment. Piaget, however, insists that the building up of a new structure is a process of assimilation and accommodation involving the interaction of the child with the learning situation. Several investigators had little success in accelerating the development of a particular process, for instance, conservation; or, if there were progress, it was apt to be unstable and failed to transfer to other conservation situations. However, Piaget's colleagues, Inhelder, Sinclair, and Bovet (1974) have shown that, under certain conditions, children who are approaching the transition from preoperational to concrete thinking can be trained by appropriate exercises to the stage of full conservation.

Harlow's work on developing learning sets, or training monkeys "to learn how to learn," is often cited in this connection. However, he too was dealing with a rather narrow range of problem solving. Thus, a good deal of caution is needed in accepting the view that intelligence can be raised by training children in transferable strategies.

More Recent Theoretical Discussions of Intelligence

There are at least two other theories that have attracted a good deal of interest. First, Ferguson (1954) considered intelligence as the generalized techniques of learning, comprehending, problem solving, and thinking, and the all-round conceptual level, which have crystallized out of cognitive experiences during the individual's home and school upbringing. Such habits and strategies have broad transfer value to a variety of problems or to new learning; they become overlearned and thus achieve considerable consistency and stability. Humphreys (1971) defined intelligence along the same lines: "the entire repertoire of acquired skills, knowledge, learning sets, and generalization tendencies considered intellectual in nature, that are available at any one period of time."

Second, Cattell's formulation (1963a, 1971a) is particularly important, since he links up factorial work such as Spearman's and Thurstone's (see Chapter 4) with a plausible theory of heredity and environment. He suggests that the prominent general factor that emerges from most studies of the correlations between cognitive tests consists of two components — fluid intelligence or G_f, and crystallized intelligence, or G_c. G_f is "the total associational or combining mass" of the brain; that is, the biologically determined aspect of intellectual functioning that enables us to solve new problems and grasp new relationships, whereas G_c represents the concepts, skills, and strategies we have acquired under the influence of our cultural environment and education. Normally both are involved to varying extents in any intellectual operation; hence, the difficulty of distinguishing their contributions (they are oblique or correlated factors; see p. 56). However, Cattell claims that his nonverbal or culture-fair tests, based on reasoning with abstract shapes, measure primarily G_f, whereas conventional verbal individual or group tests of intelligence and achievement are much more dependent on G_c.

Note that these are not the same constructs as Hebb's Intelligence A and Intelligence B. Both can be measured and, with appropriate batteries of tests, can be shown to be factorially distinct. Moreover, G_f does not correspond exactly to genetically determined ability; it is constitutional rather than purely innate. For example, a child who is born brain-damaged due to adverse conditions during pregnancy or parturition and the senile patient whose brain structures are breaking down both have poorer G_f, or constitutional equipment. On the other hand, performance in verbal tests such as vocabulary does not simply represent acquired learnings; the subject must have reached the present vocabulary level through the interaction of G_f with cultural pressures and experience. Clinical psychologists have often observed that seniles and some psychotics can continue to perform well on vocabulary and some other subtests in the Wechsler–Bellevue Scale or WAIS that "Hold," but score much lower on "Don't Hold" tests, such as Kohs Blocks and Similarities, which require the comprehension of new relationshiops. Their G_c is relatively stable, though their G_f has declined (see p. 60). The main difficulty with this view, which is further elaborated below, is that most psychologists would be reluctant to agree that any test is culture-fair or culture-free. Performance on nonverbal tests such as Cattell's own battery, or Raven's Progressive Matrices, is dependent to a considerable extent on the stimulus or lack of stimulus provided by the environment, even if less obviously than in the case of tests involving verbal concepts and skills.

One might have expected some effects on intelligence theory following the current popularity of information theory models of cognitive processing. L. B. Resnick has edited a book called *The Nature of Intelligence* (1976), which brings together the views of a number of contemporary psychologists with different backgrounds and interests. The general theme is that conventional intelligence testing seems to have reached a dead end, and that, after some 70 years of independent development, it is high time that a rapprochement should be effected with experimental psychology. Several of the authors suggest that tests should be based on experimental investigations of information processing and cognitive psychology. Others draw attention to the relevance of computer models of problem solving, of ethology, and of cross-cultural studies.

I would suggest that, so far, there has been little integration, partly because experimentalists have not shown much concern with individual differences in processing. Moreover, there are considerable difficulties in observing and measuring separately the various stages involved between input and output of information—the initial filtering, short-term rehearsal, chunking and storage, coding and long-term storage, retrieval and decoding; not to speak of the "controls," partly motivational, partly sets or strategies derived from past experience, that determine what information is accepted and coded. It would seem that intelligence is involved at every stage; thus, the familiar Digit Memory tests correlates quite well with other intelligence tests, although it involves no coding. But Digits Backward, which does require more mental manipulation, always has a higher g loading. The chunking, coding, and relating to previous structures before entering long-term storage obviously correspond to Spearman's eduction of relations. Success in reasoning, or solution of intelligence test problems, must depend on efficient organization of previously acquired relevant information in the long-term store, and ability to retrieve required concepts and skills.

Guilford (1967) is one psychometrist who claims that his psychology is *operational–informational,* but he uses the term mainly to show his preference for cognitive learning theories, such as that of Miller, Galanter, and Pribram (1960), over the classical S-R theory. His classification of factors of intellect (see p. 59) implies that there are 24 types of information to be processed. But his attempts to show that his Structure of Intellect factors fit into the current work of information theorists seem rather farfetched.

A more radical departure is that of Carroll (1974), who attempted to analyze the cognitive structures and processes involved in 48 of the ETS Kit of Reference Tests for Cognitive Factors (French, Ekstrom, and Price, 1963). He does not aim at a taxonomic classification of factors as Guilford or Cattell do but tries to specify the characteristics of the stimuli and the test responses, the nature of the "productive systems" or "task sets," and of the LTM components involved. For example, the V, or verbal comprehension, factor probably depends mainly on richness and variety of the "lexicosemantic" store. He points out that practically all tests are complex, that is, composed of many elements that often overlap. This accounts for the tendency of all cognitive tests to correlate positively, and for the correlations between tests and such external criteria as school achievement, which requires similar processing. So far, Carroll's analysis is speculative, but it provides a basis for fruitful experimentation. Intelligence as such does not appear in his model, but the analysis should increase our understanding of the underlying cognitive processes and, thus, go some way toward answering the criticisms of intelligence testing by psychologists (see Chapter 2; also Estes, 1974).

However, another of Resnick's collaborators, L. G. Humphreys, expresses a word of caution, since the variables that experimental psychologists most often work with tend to be confined to rather narrow and specific tasks that can be strictly controlled and measured. Thus, he sees a continuing need for tests based on large numbers of items, as these are likely to be more valid indicators of major dimensions of information processing.

CONCLUSIONS

Several writers have criticized intelligence testing, and genetic studies of intelligence in particular, on the grounds that there is no clear theory of intelligence. I would suggest that there is no lack of theorizing and that there is a considerable consensus among psychologists regarding the kinds of cognitive processes that deserve to be called intelligent. But intelligence comprises a collection of very varied skills rather than a clear-cut entity; hence, the precise selection of skills the tester decides to include in an individual or group test is, admittedly, arbitrary and subjective. As will appear in the next chapter, factor analysis can contribute toward making a rational choice, though it does not by any means provide a decisive answer to what skills should be included.

Let us return to the problem, raised in Chapter 2, of the difference, if any, between intelligence and achievements. It is certainly untrue to state that the former is purely maturational, the latter acquired, or that intelligence is the ability to acquire education rather than education actually received. Both intelligence and achievement, in my view, depend on genetic potentiality and on environmental stimulation, and it is often quite difficult to classify certain skills as dependent on one or the other factor. Thus, vocabulary often turns up either in intelligence or in English achievement tests; and mathematical reasoning is accepted by Guilford and others as one of the best tests of a general reasoning factor, though obviously it is also assisted by appropriate schooling. Humphreys (1971) suggests that aptitude and intelligence tend to refer to earlier acquired skills, achievement to more recent ones; also, intelligence tests are used more for predicting future capacity, achievement tests for evaluating present accomplishment.

I would say, rather, that intelligence refers to the more generalized skills, strategies of thinking, and overall conceptual level, which apply in a wide range of cognitive activities or in new learning and which are built up primarily from interacting with everyday environmental experiences in the home or in leisure pursuits, and only secondarily by stimulation at school. Achievements, on the other hand, are more specific and more directly dependent both on the nature of the instruction provided at school and on the individual's interest in, or motivation to learn, the particular subject matter. IQ helps to predict future achievement, since, in most cases, a child should be able to apply the reasoning powers built up elsewhere to studying a new school subject. But high intelligence is no longer seen as a cause of success in school, nor is low intelligence the cause of failure. Generally, there is quite a high correlation between IQ as tested individually or by a reliable battery of group tests and average or all-round school achievement (probably as high as 0.7 to 0.8 in a heterogeneous group, such as a complete age group, though often lower in more selected, or in postadolescent, groups). But even this figure implies considerable discrepancies in individual cases, often for motivational reasons or because of ineffective teaching or nonsupportive home environment. Hence, as we will see later, the influence of genetic factors on school achievement is considerably lower than it is on general intelligence.

The above interpretation of the nature of intelligence and achievement has been widely accepted for at least 20 years. Yet, unfortunately, it is still quite common to find clinical or school psychologists regarding the IQ as innate ability and educational achievement as wholly acquired.

SUMMARY

1   It is much more difficult to define mental traits, such as intelligence, in terms of observable operations than physical traits. Thus, attempts to specify the essential quality of intelligence lead to little more than semantic arguments, which fail to

provide any clear criterion of what performances are or are not representative of intelligence.

2 The approach through phylogeny shows some correspondence between brain size or complexity in the species and adaptability. At lower evolutionary levels, behavior is determined mainly by built-in mechanisms or conditioned habits. In more evolved species, an increasing dependence on internal cerebration between input and output is associated with larger brains, as in human beings. But plasticity or adaptability of behavior and the rudiments of thinking occur at earlier stages of evolution than is generally realized.

3 Within humans, neither brain size or structure nor measurable properties such as EEG waves appear to correlate with differences in intelligence (though speed of "evoked potentials" shows some promise). Some functions, such as language, tend to be localized in particular areas of the brain, but there is no specific localization of percepts, movements, ideas, and so forth.

4 Spearman's theory of general mental energy, and Thorndike's and Thomson's opposed theories of bonds are outlined. Though the classical S-R bond is unacceptable as the basic unit of intellectual thinking, the schemata of Bartlett and Piaget, Hebb's phase sequences, and Miller, Galanter, and Pribram's plans, all of which have much in common, are more promising.

5 The major contribusions of Hebb and Piaget in explaining the development from infant sensorimotor capacities to perception of a world of objects and hierarchically organized conceptual skills are outlined. Both writers emphasize the need for external stimulation and experience in the growth of thinking capacities.

6 Ferguson's contribution is recognized. Cattell's distinction between fluid and crystallized ability provides a valuable link between heredity–environment theory and factor analytic findings, though many psychologists would question his claim to be able to measure the former—the constitutional bases of intelligence—by nonverbal, culture-fair tests.

7 The integration of intelligence theory with information theory has made little progress, since all stages of input, processing, and output appear to involve intelligence. But Carroll's recent attempt to analyze the processes involved in commonly used factor tests is notable.

8 Criticisms of psychometrists for neglecting theoretical aspects of intelligence are unjustified. But it should be recognized that the term *intelligence* covers a very varied range of cognitive skills, so the choice of which to include involves subjective judgment.

9   The notion of intelligence as a cause of good or poor achievement must be discarded. Both intelligence and achievement depend on genetic and environmental factors, and the distinction between them derives mainly from the greater generality of intellectual skills and their lesser dependence on deliberate teaching.

4

Operational and Factorial Conceptions of Intelligence

Operationalism

Some of the authors of the (Thorndike et al.) 1921 symposium, and several later writers, have rejected the need for any theory of the nature of intelligence, stating in so many words: "Intelligence is what intelligence tests measure." An analogy is sometimes drawn with electricity, which we also cannot observe, but whose effects we can measure with great accuracy. A similar argument is that we know that intelligence exists because intelligence tests work, and they enable us to make useful predictions of behavior.

However, there are numerous flaws in such arguments. To begin with, psychologists could not have constructed the first intelligence tests unless they had some conception of the mental skills they were trying to sample. Moreover, Block and Dworkin (1974) add, the view that intelligence is what tests measure implies that intelligence tests are already perfect; there is no room for modification or improvement. Second, the comparison with electricity is inadmissible, just as Burt's comparison with solubility was (p. 39). We can measure electricity because there is a perfectly clear theory linking the manifestations of electricity with its measurable effects; whereas we had to admit, in the previous chapter, that the theory of intelligence is relatively vague and is unable to specify just what operations are to be accepted as manifestations of intelligence. Third, the claim that tests work is only approximately true. IQs give moderate correlations with educational and other types of achievement, but so does, for example, socioeconomic status and parents' education, or some of the variables measured by personality and attitude tests.

Hence, the argument that intelligence tests are valid because they measure what they set out to is quite a weak one. Nevertheless, the criticisms of validity studies by Block and Dworkin and others ignore the enormous weight of evidence of substantial correlations between intelligence tests and a very wide range of cognitive skills, besides general educational achievement (see also p. 210). It is perfectly possible to set up formal hypotheses, for instance, that intelligence is involved to a greater extent as the information load becomes heavier, and to test this out by showing higher correlations of IQ with complex choice reaction times than with simple reaction times. In other words, intelligence is a viable construct because of a variety of indirect evidence, not just because current tests correlate with some external criterion of what people generally mean by intelligence.

Another obvious rejoinder to the naive statement that intelligence is what intelligence tests measure is that different tests, to a considerable extent, measure different things (see Chapter 2). It is here that we must look at the implications of Spearman's (1927) work, and of the various later factor-analytic studies. Since, from his own small-scale experiments, Spearman satisfied himself that all correlations between cognitive abilities could be accounted for by the same g factor, it followed that g was invariant in the sense that we would arrive at virtually the same individual g scores even if we started out from many different test batteries.

Group Factor Analyses

Unfortunately, this claim was soon shown to be untrue, for example, by Cyril Burt in much of his work in the second decade of this century. Burt demonstrated the presence of additional group factors running through clusters of similar tests, which were not accountable for by g. For example, a set of verbal tests, number tests, memory tests, or spatial tests intercorrelated among themselves more highly than would be expected from their g content. One might be able to explain the correlations within the verbal battery by a single underlying factor, and one might do the same with the other sets of tests; but the resulting gs would not be identical. This meant that, although Spearman's emphasis on a general factor was justified, it was not possible to rely on his approach to tell objectively just what tests are the best measures of g.

The recognition of additional group factors opened the door to such criticisms as that intelligence is not unitary or global, since there are many other kinds of talent, and we have no satisfactory way of deciding whether or not to regard them as parts of intelligence or as distinct faculties. The kind of hierarchical model of abilities proposed by Burt (1949) and by myself (Vernon, 1961), which allows for both a general factor and partially distinguishable group factors that might be of major or minor importance, gave a better fit with the correlational data. But it was less mathematically precise than the centroid approach of Thurstone and the Principal Components technique of Hotelling and later writers, and has, therefore, been generally abandoned. Hence, the view that intelligence is multiple, consisting of a series of distinct faculties, became more widely accepted, although practical mental testers in education and industry still rely mainly on Binet, Wechsler, or group tests that provide only a global or general factor measure of IQ, or, at most, break it down into verbal and nonverbal IQs.

Multiple Factor Analyses

Thurstone's (1938) first factorial study of abilities accounted for the correlations between 56 tests in terms of seven or eight independent, primary, or multiple factors. This finding appeared to contradict flatly the existence of any general or g factor. However, Thurstone was working with college students who constituted a highly selected group; and, in any such relatively homogeneous sample, all test intercorrelations are reduced, particularly those between verbal and reasoning tests, which would be most likely to be loaded with g. When the all-round level of correlation is lowered, this necessarily lowers the variance of any general factor, but it has less effect on correlations between tests within any group factor; hence, the group or primary factors stand out more clearly than they do in a heterogeneous sample.

Later, Thurstone and Thurstone (1941) applied similar batteries of tests to younger students and children, who would be more representative of complete age groups; although much the same patterning of primary factors reappeared, it was found that the factors were oblique (i.e., correlated) instead of orthogonal (independent). This implied that there was a super- or second-order factor, or factors, running through all the primary factors.

Thurstone readily admitted that such a second-order factor corresponded to Spearman's g; that is, that there was generality among all his tests in addition to their primary-factor content. His V (verbal comprehension) and R (reasoning) or I (inductive) factors had the highest second-order factor loadings and thus corresponded most closely to verbal and nonverbal g.

Thus, a substantial rapprochement was achieved between the g plus group factor and Thurstone's multiple factor models, although the techniques of analysis are different.[1] But it is still true that the British school of factorists tend to retain a large g and then to categorize what is left over into group or primary factors, whereas Americans extract the primaries first and treat second-order factors (if they bother about them at all) as secondary. Americans sometimes accuse British factorists of underfactoring, that is, failing to bring out all the diversity that exists in a given battery of tests; whereas the British consider Americans too apt to overfactor, that is, to accept too many small factors, which are consequently low in statistical reliability and are psychologically nonmeaningful.

Another explanation of the difference between studies that appear to reveal, and those that deny, the general factor is that the former have been based mainly on children, the latter on college students. Garrett (1946) proposed the quite plausible theory that there is increasing differentiation between abilities with age. Young children's performances in different areas tend to be relatively uniform, whereas adults might, for example, be quite high on verbal ability and low on number ability, or vice versa. This theory is substantially supported by Burt (1949). However, it is difficult to prove, because, if we contrast different age groups of children, we can never be sure that our tests are measuring the same abilities at different ages, and with equal reliability. Even in a vocabulary test, for example, the child's response to *regard* or *tolerate* is surely qualitatively different from his or her response to *orange* and *puddle*.

Among the most extensive of many comparative studies of factors obtained from the same tests given to different age groups are those of Dye and Very (1968). Their tests were designed to measure each of nine factors; they were given to students ranging from grade 4 to college level. Although there were no very clear-cut trends and results differed between the sexes,

---

[1] Burt (1939) has shown that it is quite possible to transform mathematically a matrix of multiple factor loadings into a general plus group factor model. or vice versa; that is, they are merely alternative ways of formulating the ability-structure of the factorized tests.

there certainly were changes in factorial structure with age, and some evidence of a larger number of distinguishable factors at later ages. For example, number and perceptual speed constituted a single factor up to grade 9, but subsequently became separated. Several other investigations, however, have failed to demonstrate any such age difference, even when designed to show what proportion of variance is general at different ages. Thus, I found at least as large a general factor in a varied battery of tests given to a heterogeneous adult population (army recruits) as commonly occurs among elementary school children taking equally varied tests (see Vernon, 1961). My findings suggested also that certain factors became clarified, or more distinct, with increased age or practice, whereas others may tend to fuse. For example, number and space may be relatively distinct around 9 to 11 years but then seem to coalesce to yield scientific or technical ability during adolescence. It may still be true that development during infancy is characterized by differentiation from global to more focused, analytic responses. But in older children and adults, any reduction in generality is certainly affected by, and may be wholly explicable by, the reduction in heterogeneity among the groups available for testing (see Vernon, 1965).

Fleishman's (1972) experiments, mainly in the psychomotor area, have contributed to our knowledge of the growth of new factors with training. He has shown that, typically, his subjects' approach to novel tasks made use of such already established factors as verbal and spatial. But as the subjects became more proficient, other psychomotor abilities became more important, and a new factor, specific to the learning task, emerged. This is why it is so difficult to predict ultimate proficiency in a task by selection tests or by performance in the early stages of training.

Later Developments of Multiple Factor Analysis

During the 1940s, Thurstone and his followers, including J. P. Guilford, carried out numerous studies that greatly extended the range of factors beyond Thurstone's original list of eight. Sometimes a Thurstonian factor was found to break down into several distinct abilities. For example, space appeared to involve visualization, $S1$, $S2$, and spatial orientation; likewise, there were at least four types of fluency. This kind of divisibility would be expected on Burt's or Vernon's hierarchical group factor approach, but it was somewhat disconcerting to American factorists that more and more factors presuming to be primary dimensions of ability should appear, and that the results of different studies (using somewhat different batteries or different populations) so often disagreed.

After World War II, Guilford initiated a long train of systematic analyses of all the major cognitive domains, and he linked his factorial approach with general psychological principles; with experimental studies; and with the contributions of Piaget, information processing, and clinical psychology (Guilford, 1967). This led him to a threefold categorization, or morphological model, which he called Structure of Intellect. This model has been published so frequently that I will merely list the three principles or dimensions of classification:

1 By materials or contents: verbal, figural, symbolic, behavioral.
2 By operations: cognition, memory, divergent thinking, convergent thinking, evaluation.
3 By products: units, classes, relations, systems, transformations, implications.

This model implies the existence of $4 \times 5 \times 6 = 120$ different intellectual factors; Guilford claims that his numerous large-scale investigations have confirmed 98 of these (Guilford and Hoepfner, 1971). Thus, he entirely rejected the notion of any general factor, partly because low or zero correlations occur quite frequently between tests designed to measure different factors, and partly because there is evidence to suggest that different factors show different curves of growth and decline and are differently affected by pathological conditions, drugs, or environment. Guilford also refuses to recognize hierarchy or obliquity among his factors. He is criticized on this count by Eysenck (1967; 1973) and Cattell (1971a), who believe that the Structure of Intellect model could be considerably simplified by amalgamating factors that overlap. They also argue that we would expect oblique or overlapping factors or hierarchy (i.e., some factors being more inclusive than others) in normal human functioning. Horn and Knapp (1973) further criticize the subjective element in Guilford's choice and rotation of factors, particularly where, as in Guilford and Hoepfner's (1971) study, "targeting" is used; that is, the factors are rotated to conform with a previously specified model.

No doubt Guilford is justified in arguing that intelligence is too rich and variegated, especially at the higher levels with which he usually worked (e.g., Air Force cadets), to be adequately covered by a single g score or IQ. But his own system is too elaborate to have won many followers; McNemar (1964) refers to its "fractionization and fragmentation of ability into more and more factors of less and less importance." My own objection to Guilford's approach is the lack of evidence to prove that his ingenious batteries of tests measure recognizably distinct abilities in daily life (apart from a few studies outlined in Guilford and Hoepfner's book). His factors are clusters among the tests that clever psychologists have thought up rather than dimensions of everyday cognitive and thinking processes. Indeed, they do not even cover many of the kinds of abilities or special talents that are of practical importance, such as mechanical, artistic, or musical abilities. However, Guilford's distinction between convergent and divergent thinking has been widely accepted. We will discuss later the question of the differences between intelligence and "creativity."

Certain alternative models deserve mention. Eysenck (1967) largely accepts Guilford's first two classifications, by materials and by mental functions or operations. But he substitutes a third principle, which classifies tests into those mainly dependent on speed and others more dependent on power, carefulness, and persistence. This enables him to link ability factors more closely with information theory and with personality differences.

Cattell (1971a; 1971b) has greatly elaborated his initial theory of fluid and crystallized intelligence (see pp. 47–48) and recognizes three or four levels of factors:

1   Neurologically organized *powers;* for example, visual, auditory, or motor abilities.
2   *Proficiencies,* or skills, in particular areas.
3   *Agencies,* or tools; that is, acquired strategies and cultural equipment that transfer (as in Ferguson's 1954 theory) to many situations. Thus, G_c has become an agency, since it represents the overall equipment, including language, educational achievements, modes of thinking, and the like, in which individuals have "invested" their stock of G_f.
4   Several general capacities (second- or third-order factors) are recognized besides the fundamental G_f; for example, general spatial ability, retrieval or fluency, cognitive speed, possibly carefulness, and memorizing.

While Cattell's book on *Abilities* (1971a) is wide-ranging and provocative, it is not yet clear how far these numerous factors can be measured and distinguished. Horn (1976) accepts

Cattell's list of general capacities, but admits that G_f is very much the same as general reasoning, or R, factor and that G_c is a swollen verbal ability, or V, factor; and he amalgamates memorizing with Thurstone's M and Jensen's Level I (see p. 66). He admits that fluency and spatial factors are relatively distinct, though each comprises several subtypes.

Discussion

We can now see that factor analysis does not yield any definitive solution to the problem of uni- or multi-dimensionality of intelligence, though there is more agreement than appears on the surface when account is taken of the effects of the heterogeneity of the population. For some purposes, and with some populations, a hierarchical model of g plus specialized group factors seems most appropriate; in other circumstances, multiple factors, showing little or no obliquity, are more effective. There is no necessary contradiction between these approaches, as can be seen by an analogy with school grades. School pupils can be classified in terms of average or all-round achievement or else in terms of their grades in each of the main subjects — English, mathematics, languages, science, and so on. Many pupils show considerable unevenness in their achievements. Thus, these school subjects are comparable to Thurstone's primary factors, which tend to show a good deal of obliquity. Further, we can readily break down these particular achievements to still more specialized skills — for instance, spelling, grammar, quality of composition, knowledge of literature, and the like within the major dimension of English.

Block and Dworkin (1974), Lewontin (1970), and other critics deny the relevance of factor analysis to defining intelligence because of the disagreement between different factor models. But I have tried to show that these discrepancies are exaggerated. One of Block's objections to Jensen's work is that he (Jensen) accepts a Spearmanian concept of a single intelligence or g as having a firm mathematical foundation and ignores the diversity of abilities revealed by Thurstone, Guilford, and others. While many psychologists might agree that this is a weakness in Jensen's approach, a majority would be likely to accept Terman-Merrill or WISC or WAIS IQs as suitable measures for heritability studies; and, in fact, these tests have most often been employed in such studies. In other words, psychologists are content to use such total scores, whether or not they are regarded as measuring g plus some minor group factors, or as chiefly measuring V plus R plus some small admixture of number, spatial, fluency, memory, or other components. For most predictive purposes, these general tests give as good indications of future ability as tests based on Thurstone's, Guilford's, or other models, or as so-called Differential Aptitude Tests (see McNemar, 1964; Vernon, 1965).

Block and Dworkin (1974) raise another objection, which is somewhat contradictory to their previous complaints about the factorial complexity of intelligence and the variations in what different tests measure. They assert that current tests are too homogeneous. If items for a test are selected because of high g content or because they correlate well with total score, a good many items that might provide a broader, more representative sampling of "real" intelligence are likely to be discarded. Hence, the validity of the IQs is lowered. This objection is rather unfair to the Terman-Merrill scale, where such a wide diversity of items is included (following Binet's lead), and where McNemar's (1942) factorial analyses show that the content is quite diverse. It might be more true of group tests, whose items do tend to represent a fairly narrow range of skills, and only those that correlate with total score are usually included. This narrowness of group tests is one reason the popular individual scales appear to give more valid indications of children's all-round intelligence. But it is difficult to prove their superiority in the absence of any acceptable external criterion of Intelligence B. Block and Dworkin would prefer a test that would sample such aspects of daily-life intelligence as creativity, capacity for sustained problem solving, and so on. Important as these everyday qualities may be, in my view, they would render intelligence an even more vague and imprecise construct.

It might seem preferable to study the genetic and environmental components of half a dozen or so of the most widely accepted factors on the grounds that these measure more distinctive and definable attributes than g does. Indeed, Royce (1958) goes so far as to claim that factors do tend to represent genetically determined entities, and Cattell regards what he calls *source traits* as largely genetic in origin. I would disagree with this position, first, because there would still be considerable room for subjective choice in selecting suitable subtests or items for any primary factor; and second, because the results so far obtained from heritability studies of Thurstone's primary factors have been generally contradictory (see p. 186). Hunt and Kirk (1971) add that Thurstone's and Guilford's models are as sterile as the Spearman—Burt type of theory; they limit, rather than extend, the growth of a psychology of intellectual development.

But the main reason for rejecting factorial analysis goes deeper. Spearman, Thurstone, Cattell, and Guilford have always tended to regard factors as revealing the basic dimensions of mind. They are comparable to chemical elements out of which more complex substances are built; that is, factors are real psychological entities. By contrast, Burt, Thomson, and I have been impressed by the variability in factors and factor loadings when somewhat different batteries of tests are studied in somewhat different populations by factorists who favor different models or techniques; hence, we have consistently thought of factors merely as groupings of different kinds of tests. Probably the difference is largely a semantic one; both sides are dealing with constructs that underlie functional unities in human behavior (see Coan, 1964). But certainly both Thomson and I would deny that the existence of even a stable and clearly definable factor tells us anything about its heritability. Many of the clusterings that occur among test results may just as likely, or even more likely, arise from cultural uniformities; that is, verbal, mechanical, number, or musical factors exist largely because these are different domains of experience in our society, each one reinforced by appropriate schooling and training. Of course, such talents may also depend on certain gene combinations, but the fact of their existence does not prove it. Guilford also admits that factors may arise partly from genetic, partly from environmental, causes.

SOME SUBSIDIARY PROBLEMS

We have argued that Stanford-Binet or Terman-Merrill and WISC IQs provide reasonable measures of intelligence for heritability studies among children, despite their heterogeneity of content and rather strong verbal bias. Wechsler's WAIS would probably be the preferred test for adults, although there are reliable group tests available that would likewise chiefly measure V plus R factors.

I have already suggested in Chapter 2 that overmuch importance has been attached to general intelligence. Can factor analysis help us to determine other major types of ability, which are of comparable importance in successful life adjustment but which play only a minor part in general intelligence tests, and which have received relatively little attention from psychologists? Obviously, health, physique, temperament, and personality are of crucial relevance to child development and adult careers, but here we are concerned only with intellectual functions that may be worthy of special attention in genetic and environmental studies of abilities. A thorough review of up-to-date literature on well-established factors is provided by Horn (1976).

Mathematics and musical talent are obvious candidates, since, although they have not been studied extensively, there is some evidence that these abilities tend to run in families and sometimes show themselves at a very early age. Note that mathematical ability is very different from Thurstone's N factor, which is based merely on facility in simple arithmetical operations.

The S spatial and visualization factor, which is much the same as Witkin's field independence (see Vernon, 1972), is another possibily heritable attribute, despite the tendency of Thurstone and his followers to break it down into several subfactors. This factor is, to some extent, predictive of engineering and physical-scientific achievement as well as ability in the visual arts. In addition to the marked sex difference on spatial and field independence tasks, there are considerable ethnic differences; hunting peoples, such as Eskimos and various American Indian tribes, score much higher than food-gathering Africans, for example (see p. 268). Elsewhere (Vernon, 1969a), I have discussed explanations of this difference in terms of ecological demands or of child-rearing practices. But there is also some evidence of genetic origin; that is, the distinction may depend on genes in the X chromosome (see Bock and Kolakowski, 1973).

Creativity

There are two other particularly controversial major areas — creativity, or divergent thinking, and memory, or associative learning. Guilford singles out each of these as one of his *operations,* and therefore regards it as comprising numerous different factors. Yet each one has also been treated by some psychologists as more or less unidimensional. Several psychologists did work with tests of "imagination" (e.g., Binet and Burt; also Hargreaves, 1927) or with fluency (e.g., Carroll, 1941) before Guilford. But it was his address on "Creativity" in 1950 that set off the flood of interest in the topic from the 1950s to the 1970s. Guilford pointed out that most ability tests devised by psychologists and most scholastic achievement tests are in multiple-choice form; each item calls for one right answer, and the student's thinking has to converge on this predetermined solution. However, there are other types of test that encourage a wide variety of responses. Guilford's criticism fitted in with a general indictment of the American educational system for favoring conventionality and conformity to the teacher's instruction and the textbook and for discouraging students with ideas of their own, who might become the creative scientists and artists of the next generation. Many tests of divergent thinking[2] were developed by Getzels and Jackson (1962), Torrance (1965), Wallach and Kogan (1965), and others, and it was claimed that these measured a faculty largely independent of ordinary convergent intelligence, though rivaling it in educational importance.

The literature on creativity has been discussed at length elsewhere (Vernon, Adamson, and Vernon, 1977), and tests of creativity, expecially verbal ones are shown to yield a clear factor; though its independence from, or overlapping with, V or verbal g depends largely on the heterogeneity of the sample. There is some evidence of nonlinear regression; that is, above an IQ of about 115, divergent scores become increasingly independent of convergent performance.

But the fact that unusual types of items measure something rather different from conventional tests does not prove that the "something" corresponds to creativity, as it is generally understood. Some interesting personality and other differences between high-divergers and high-convergers have been reported, as well as some correlations with miscellaneous variables, such as free composition writing at school, cultural leisure-time pursuits, and so on. But the creativity of outstanding artists and scientists is probably more a matter of personality and motivation than just of certain "styles" of thinking. As scores on divergent thinking tests are rather unreliable (i.e., unstable over time), it seems unlikely that they will reveal any strong genetic component.

Memory

The distinction between associative or rote learning and intelligent or meaningful learning goes back a long way in the history of psychology. Spearman regarded meaningful learning as depending almost wholly on g, and this view has received considerable confirmation, though some writers claim to have established meaningful learning factors. Jensen uses the terms

[2] Guilford did not identify creativity with divergent thinking alone but suggested several factors from other domains as relevant, too. Torrance (1965) also aimed to study fluency, flexibility, originality, and elaboration as separate aspects of creativity. However, the scores for these factors usually intercorrelate so highly, as did Wallach and Kogan's (1965) scores for fluency and uniqueness, that most psychologists have confined their investigations to a single general divergent thinking factor.

conceptual learning, intelligence, and *g* as more or less inter-changeable. Because rote learning tasks do not involve grasping relations, Spearman regarded them as low in *g*, in other words, almost totally specific; and he considered *retentivity* as a distinct psychological function. However, Anastasi (1932) and Thurstone (1938) have found a common rote memory (*M*) factor in several tests, such as Paired Associates and other simple learning tasks, though the memory factors that emerge in such studies depend considerably on the nature of the materials, the conditions of learning, and the type of recall (see Vernon and Mitchell, 1974).

In several studies carried out in the 1960s, Jensen showed that associative learning, unlike conceptual learning, bears little relation to socioeconomic class or ethnicity (e.g., black versus white). Indeed, children of low SES (socioeconomic status) with low IQs (e.g., 60 to 80) actually did better on memorization than did high-SES children of similar IQ. Jensen also noted that many children lacking in aptitude for conceptual learning may quickly learn everyday knowledge and skills outside school. Thus, he was led to his theory of two types, or levels, of learning, which have different genetic origins (Jensen 1969; 1973d). Jensen con-sidered Level I, associative learning, as basic, underlying most of children's early learning; whereas Level II develops more slowly and assumes greater importance as thinking becomes more rela-tional. In other words, Jensen assumed a hierarchical model, Level I being necessary, though not sufficient, for the emergence of Level II. The important practical implication was that some children who, through lack of *g* or Level II capacity, were likely to be permanently handicapped in conventional school learning, might develop more successfully if taught by methods that made greater use of their average or superior Level I ability. Horn called such learning (1976) *Short-term Acquisition Functions,* and thought it might represent "another form of intelligence."

The experimental studies arising out of the level theory are too intricate to detail here (see Humphreys and Dachler, 1969; Jensen, 1973d; Horn, 1976), and are only partially confirmatory. The hierarchical aspect of the theory does not seem to hold up, since some children are found with good Level II but relatively low Level I scores. But a major difficulty is that Level I is not, like Level II, a strong general factor that is common to a wide variety of tasks. The correlations among Paired Associates, Serial Learn-ing, Digit Span, and other measures that have been used to mea-sure Level I tend to be low (see Vernon and Mitchell, 1974), suggesting that associative learning tests may give little indication of a distinctive "faculty" that could be used as a basis for a differ-ent approach to education.

SUMMARY

1   Attempts to get around the problems of definition by claiming that intelligence is what intelligence tests measure are inadmissible. The precise operations involved in intelligence cannot be clearly specified, and the fact that tests correlate with such external criteria as educational achievement does not prove that they measure intelligence as usually understood. However, the reality of a general intelligence, or g, factor is strongly supported by the indirect kind of evidence normally used for construct validation. Much of this evidence comes from factorial studies.

2   Spearman's belief that g was invariant regardless of the battery of tests employed broke down when Burt demonstrated the existence of additional group factors. Thurstone's approach, based on centroid analysis, and Hotelling's Principal Components elevated group factors into multiple primary factors or components, thus eliminating any g factor. However, when the primaries are oblique rather than orthogonal, second-order factors are obtained that do indicate a general factor or factors.

3   The apparent conflict between the various models does not imply that factor analysis is worthless. Discrepancies arise mainly because heterogeneous samples are used in some studies, and selected, homogeneous groups in others. An alternative theory that factors tend to differentiate with age has received little support, though factor structures do tend to alter with practice.

4   Guilford's much more elaborate Structure of Intellect model is outlined, together with certain criticisms of it. Cattell's comprehensive theory makes the useful distinction between G_f (fluid, or constitutional) and G_c (crystallized, or acquired), and other second-order factors.

5   Some critics regard the strong emphasis on g and current techniques of test-item selection as unduly narrowing the range of abilities that psychologists should be concerned with. However, divergent thinking ability (as a possible indicator of creativity) has received much attention, probably more than it deserves. Jensen draws a fundamental distinction between associative learning, or Level I, and conceptual learning, or Level II (virtually the same as g). However, Level I seems to be based on rather specific skills, so it is not a strong enough factor to be of much educational relevance.

6   It has been suggested that genetic studies of abilities should concentrate on stable primary factors rather than on g, but attempts to do so thus far have been contradictory. However, there is some evidence of genetic influences in special talents (notably musical and mathematical) and possibly in spatial ability.

II

Child Development and Environmental Effects on Intelligence

5

Variability in the Growth and Decline of Intelligence

Naturally, there is no intention, in a book of this kind, to provide an abridged psychology of child development. I will dwell only on those aspects of the subject where there is fairly extensive research evidence of the effects of environmental factors on intellectual growth. Inevitably, my selection from the very large literature is subjective, but, I hope, not unrepresentative. The discussion may conveniently be started by recounting how far we have departed from the earlier view that intelligence is fixed by heredity, and stays constant throughout life, when measured in IQ units.

In early studies where the Stanford-Binet test was given to children twice, a few weeks or months apart, the reliability coefficients were indeed very high, about 0.90. However, R. L. Thorndike (1933) surveyed a number of retest investigations of miscellaneous intelligence tests and showed that correlations fell regularly over time, till they averaged only 0.70 at a 5-year gap. When adults are tested, the correlations tend to be higher: Jencks et al. (1972) estimate 0.80 to 0.90 even over 15 to 30 years. But the instability becomes far more noticeable the younger the children concerned. Thus, in the California Growth Studies,[1]

[1] These studies were carried out by a group of psychologists at Berkeley, California, and resulted in a large number of publications. They are usefully summarized in the book by Jones et al. (1971). However, special reference is made below to the articles by Honzik, MacFarlane, and Allen (1948) and Bayley (1949; 1955).

where some 200 children were followed through from birth till 18 years or later, there were not only negligible, but even slightly negative, correlations between early developmental or infant tests given in the first year of life and later IQ. Up till the age of 18 months, parental SES correlated more highly with 18-year IQ than did tests of the children themselves (see also McCall, Hogarty, and Hurlburt, 1972).

LOW PREDICTIVE VALUE OF EARLY DEVELOPMENTAL SCALES

Table 5.1, adapted by Cronbach (1970) from Bayley's (1949) data, gives a good survey of the findings. Note, for example, that tests given around 2 to 3 years correlate 0.6 to 0.7 with Stanford-Binet 1 year later, but only 0.3 to 0.4 with the same test 12 years later. Children tested for the first time at age 4 show greater stability, correlations with later IQ reaching 0.7; and 11-year-old tests provide correlations exceeding 0.9.

The results naturally vary with the particular samples of children and the particular tests used, but Table 5.2, from McCall, Hogarty, and Hurlburt (1972) summarizes similar findings for the later validity of preschool tests given during the first 2½ years.

One of the reasons for the low predictive value of infant tests is simply the variability of performance from day to day. Infants are apt to be highly distractible, and much depends on their general level of activity or passivity and on the social reactions of the infant to the tester. For example, Bayley noted a correlation of 0.57 between infant tests at 3-month intervals; whereas, for the identical group in elementary school, the correlation was 0.92 at 3-year intervals. Also, when the scores on tests given at 10, 11, and 12 months were averaged, they already gave a substantial positive correlation with 17-year IQ, although performance at a single testing had virtually no validity.

Some test items are more predictive of later intelligence than others, though there seems to be little consensus regarding which tests, or why. Bayley found vocalization items in the first year correlating 0.40 with IQ from 12 to 21 among girls though not among boys; and a similar difference has been confirmed by Kagan and McCall (see Lewis, 1976). Others have suggested that qualitative aspects of infant behavior, such as alertness and social responsiveness, are more predictive than performance on particular test items, though there seems to be no supporting evidence for this hypothesis.

TABLE 5.1

Correlations Between Developmental and Intelligence Quotients at Different Ages

Age at first test	Name of test*	Years until retest			
		1	3	6	12
3 months	CFY	0.10 (CFY)	0.05 (CPS)	−0.13 (SB)	0.02 (SB)
1 year	CFY	0.47 (CPS)	0.23 (SB)	0.13 (SB)	0.00 (SB)
2 years	CPS	0.74 (CPS)	0.55 (SB)	0.50 (SB)	0.42 (SB)
3 years	CPS	0.64 (SB)	— —	0.55 (SB)	0.33 (SB)
4 years	SB	— —	0.71 (SB)	0.73 (SB)	0.70 (SB)
6 years	SB	0.86 (SB)	0.84 (SB)	0.81 (SB)	0.77 (W)
7 years	SB	0.88 (SB)	0.87 (SB)	0.73 (SB)	0.80 (W)
9 years	SB	0.88 (SB)	0.82 (SB)	0.87 (SB)	— —
11 years	SB	0.93 (SB)	0.93 (SB)	0.92 (SB)	— —

*CFY = California First-Year Scale   CPS = California Preschool Scale
 SB = Stanford-Binet   W = Wechsler-Bellevue

Note: The name of the test used for retesting is given in parentheses after the correlation coefficient. Where no test was given, a dash (— —) is printed.

Source: From L. J. Cronbach, *Essentials of Psychological Testing,* 3rd ed., 1970. Reprinted by permission of Harper & Row.

But the main reason for the weak validity of most infant tests is that the test items selected as representative of children's developmental level in the early years are quite different in content from those given from about 5 years on. The former are largely psychomotor, including gross and fine movements, reactions to objects, imitation, and the beginnings of speech; the latter are mainly based on verbal reasoning. Hofstaetter (1954) factor analyzed the IQs of children included in the California Growth Studies from 2 to 13 years. Three major factors appeared: The first, which was most prominent in the tests given in infancy, was identified as sensorimotor; the second, called *persistence* or *rigidity,* loaded the tests given from 20 to 40 months; the third, appearing in tests from 4 years on, more nearly represented in the conventional *g* and *V.* To quote Bayley (1949):

> There was no evidence of a general factor of intelligence during the first three years, but the findings indicated, instead, a series of developing functions, or groups of functions, each growing out of, but not necessarily correlated with, previously matured behavior patterns.

TABLE 5.2
Correlations Between Infant Tests
and Later Individual IQs

Age of first testing	Age of follow-up		
	3– 4 years	5– 7 years	8– 18 years
1– 6 months	0.23	0.01	0.01
7– 12 months	0.33	0.06	0.20
13– 18 months	0.47	0.30	0.21
19– 30 months	0.54	0.41	0.49

The child seems to concentrate on the development of particular sets of skills at certain ages, and then moves on to largely new ones. There is an obvious resemblance here to Piaget's sensorimotor, preoperational, and operational stages, each stage representing a new reorganization of the child's schemata.

McCall, Hogarty, and Hurlburt (1972) note a similar tendency for certain types of skills to correlate quite highly over a few months or a year; some of these skills relate to later outgrowths, though others are almost entirely nonpredictive and lead, as it were, to a dead end. These researchers, too, carried out a factor analysis, this time of test items applied between 6 months and 11 years. They characterized the first factor as manipulation of objects leading to perceptual consequences, the second as concentrating on imitation and on simple social and verbal skills, and later factors on more complex usages of language. Thus, they also challenge "the belief in an unchanging, pervasive, general mental ability" (see also Yarrow and Pedersen, 1976).

Lewis (1976) gives detailed accounts of the various infant scales and shows similar specificity and low predictive validity in all of them. One point that does emerge, however, is that low scores are more diagnostic than high ones, since they often result from prematurity or brain damage (see Hunt, 1976). On the other hand, gifted children who obtained Binet IQs of 140 and over at 4 years showed virtually no differences from average children on the Bayley Infant Scale at 8 months (see McCall, 1976).

Psychologists in the 1920s and 1930s were probably overinfluenced by Gesell's demonstration of the regular sequence of growth in psychomotor, linguistic, and other skills, and thus believed that early childhood growth was mainly determined by internal maturation (although Gesell himself never claimed to be measuring general intelligence with his scales). Nowadays we are more aware of the trainability of many such skills (see Fowler, 1962) and their dependence on differences in child rearing. Moreover, the overall rate of maturation in young children is not necessarily continuous with, or predictive of, later mental growth, that is, IQ.

HONZIK'S, BLOOM'S, AND OTHER STUDIES

Instead of studying the stability of intelligence by correlations between successive retests, it is possible to chart the IQs of individual children who are tested repeatedly over several years. This was done by Honzik, MacFarlane, and Allen (1948) in the California Growth Studies, by Dearborn and Rothney (1941) in the Harvard Growth Study of later childhood and adolescence, and by others. Typically, such charts show three or more children with identical IQs at an early age, whose subsequent scores criss-cross and deviate as much as 30, even up to 50, IQ points. Alternatively, a few children identical at a later age, show astonishing variations when their records are traced back. Thus, Honzik found in her sample that, over the years of schooling, 15 percent of children varied in their IQs less than 10 points; 17 percent varied between 10 and 15 points; 58 percent varied more than 15 points up or down, and 9 percent changed by 30 points and over. She also described a few cases that fluctuated over as much as 4 Standard Deviations, that is, roughly 60 IQ points.

However, as I pointed out elsewhere (Vernon, 1957a), these and other such figures are likely to be exaggerated for a number of reasons, including:

1 Changes in test content, particularly when several different individual or group tests are used.
2 Uneven standardization; one test may give higher IQs all-round than another.
3 Differences in variance; one test may yield far more very high *and* very low IQs than another. In tests that employ classical, or ratio, IQs rather than deviation quotients, there are variations from one age level to another.
4 Low short-term reliability and internal consistency of the tests. This includes variations attributable to conditions of testing and motivation of testees.

TABLE 5.3
Correlations of Earlier Group Tests with Terminal IQ

Grade	Verbal	Nonverbal	Combined	Bloom
1	0.52	0.32	0.53	0.66
2	0.59	0.51	0.66	0.75
4	0.75	0.65	0.72	0.83
7	0.74	0.65	0.77	0.88
9	0.78	0.67	0.82	0.90

5 Practice effects, which can be quite considerable if the same or similar tests are given frequently (see Chapter 2).

6 The level of ability of the group. Terman and Merrill's (1937) results showed greater variations around IQ 120 than at IQ 80; and most follow-up groups have been of above-average ability.

7 When several tests are given, maximum differences are naturally larger than the median differences between any two testings, typically about 1½ times larger.

Only when we allow for these factors should we interpret alterations as due to developmental changes, environmental circumstances, personality adjustments, and so forth. Both Honzik's and other published studies indicate the correlation, for example, from 6 tp 10 years or from 10 to 17 years, to be approximately 0.70, as Thorndike concluded in 1933. This figure implies that only 17 percent of children vary 15 IQ points or more for single retests, whereas 63 percent stay within ± 10 points of the first IQ. (The remaining 20 percent vary between 10 and 15 points.) Thus, the statement by Fine (1975) that "the IQ is a yo-yo" is grossly exaggerated. However, with repeated retestings, 33 percent can vary 15 points or more, and 48 percent stay relatively stable (Again, the remainder vary from 10 to 15 points.)

Hopkins and Bracht (1975) have pointed out that the major longitudinal studies have relied chiefly on individual Binet or Wechsler tests; the stability of IQs obtained from some of the best available group tests is much poorer. They report results for some 20,000 students who were given the California Tests of Mental Maturity at grades 1 and 2, and the Lorge-Thorndike Tests at grades 4, 7, 9, and 11. Both of these tests yield verbal, nonverbal, and combined IQs. Table 5.3 shows the correlations of the earlier tests with grade 11, or terminal, IQs criterion.

The table shows that verbal test predictions do not exceed a correlation of 0.7 until grade 4, and nonverbal IQs at any age fail to reach even this modest level. Bloom (1964) has surveyed Bayley's and other follow-up studies of IQ and has attempted to correct for unreliability and some of the other weaknesses of available test results. The last column of Table 5.3 shows approximate figures from Bloom's graph (1964, p. 64); these clearly show the superiority of individual assessments, even as early as grade 2.

Bloom argues that the rising correlations among older children can well be accounted for by Anderson's (1940) Overlap Hypothesis. If a child's Mental Age or test score at a certain age is a_1, and at a later age (say after 1 year) it is a_2, there is no correlation between a_1 and the gain ($a_2 - a_1$). Nevertheless, a_2 correlates highly with a_1, simply because a_1 constitutes a considerable proportion of a_2. To quote Bloom: "In other words, Anderson was hypothesizing that the correlations in longitudinal data are a direct function of the per cent of the development at one age which has been obtained at an earlier age."

At first reading, we would surely expect a child with high IQ at age 9, for instance, to increase more in M.A. by age 10 than one of low IQ over the same period. But Bloom concludes that the correlations of initial with gain scores are low or zero, which implies that miscellaneous circumstances rather than maturation greatly affect growth over any limited period.

Nevertheless, Bloom's arguments are questionable, since three years earlier Pinneau (1961) had shown that there *is* a tendency for positive correlations between initial M.A. and later gains. Moreover, insofar as Deviation IQs have fairly high reliability for several years ahead, the high-IQ children must surely gain more per year than the low-IQ children if they are to retain much the same IQ. According to the Overlap Hypothesis, all children, regardless of IQ, would gain in one year the same amount — namely, 1 year of M.A. — apart from chance fluctuations.

Bloom proceeded to use the Overlap Hypothesis and the IQ retest data he had collected to estimate what percentage of 17-year intelligence is already determined by certain ages. His findings are summarized as follows:

Age	Percent
1.0	20
4.0	50
8.0	80
13.0	92

These results are sometimes interpreted to mean that people complete half their total intellectual growth by age 4, and so on. What it actually says is that half of the variance, or the individual differences present at 17 years, are already present at 4 years. Also, of course, the figures tell us nothing about the relative influence of heredity and environment, other than the obvious point that intelligence is not a fixed trait from birth onward.

In the light of interactionist theory (see Chapter 1), we would expect variations as children meet and absorb new experiences from their environment. The results we have quoted suggest that it would be unwise to make any judgment of a child's intelligence until at least age 2, and we should not expect performance to be fairly predictive of ability in later life until at least 6 years.

I would also question whether Bloom does not actually overestimate the stability of the IQ, expecially during the adolescent years. First, his correlations were corrected for attenuation, which boosts them above the level normally obtainable in practice. Second, I will cite in Chapter 10 definite evidence that environmental factors can make substantial differences in intellectual growth after 11 years. What Bloom's figures show is that variations in IQ attributable to chance environmental or other influences, favorable in some adolescents and unfavorable in others, do not bring about large changes overall between ages 13 and 18. But they do not imply that systematic influences (such as type of home) that tend to raise the ability of a certain group or to depress the growth of another group are ineffective.

DIFFICULTIES IN LONGITUDINAL STUDIES

The data surveyed so far are based purely on the extent to which a group of children retain, or do not retain, the same rank order of ability as they grow from birth to maturity. It is much more difficult to delineate the actual gains made by any one child, or a group, than it is in the case of a physical measurement like height because our units for psychological measurements do not constitute a ratio scale. Since there is no zero point, we can only assess children as high or low in relation to the mean and variance for their age-peers. Though we are generally entitled to assume that the test scores of any single age group give us an interval scale, this is certainly not true of Mental Ages, where the growth from, say, 2 to 3 years is likely to be much greater than that from 12 to 13. In this case, the units are far from equal.

Another major difficulty is that it is never possible to obtain and study a representative sample over a long period. In addition to attrition due to death, which mainly affects those initially least healthy, families move away and it becomes more and more costly to keep in touch with them. On the whole, the poorer socioeconomic strata are more likely to drop out through lack of interest or to become untraceable. In Terman and Oden's (1959) follow-up of highly gifted children, mostly from upper-middle-class families, over 90 percent of the cases were retained from middle childhood till over 30 years later. By contrast, in Douglas, Ross, and Simpson's (1968) follow-up from birth of a representative sample of 5,362 British children in the National Survey of Health and Development, full data up to 16½ years were obtained only on 68 percent. In consequence, a good deal of our developmental information is collected on different groups at different ages, and the comparability may be dubious. This difficulty applies also to groups used for test standardization, such as the 10- to 60-year-old subjects for the Wechsler-Bellevue Scale, and to the various school-age samples studied by Piaget.

Several attempts have been made to arrive at "absolute" scales of intelligence, with a true zero and equal intervals. Thurstone (1928) postulated a linear relationship between score (e.g., M.A.) and variations around the mean, and this enabled him to extrapolate to a hypothetical zero point at birth or shortly before. At one time, Heinis' (1926) "Personal Constant," based on a logarithmic curve for mental growth, offered promise, but it has now dropped out of use. Rasch (1960) claims to have devised a technique for absolute (i.e., "person-free") scaling of test difficulty; though so far it has had little practical application, it is being used in the new British Intelligence Scale (Warburton, 1970).

Bayley (1955) worked out conversion tables for the Mental Ages given by the various tests used in the Berkeley study, from shortly after birth up to 17 years. All scores could be expressed in what she called a *D scale*, consisting of the number of standard score units below the mean performance at 16 years. When this scale was extrapolated at the bottom end, it reached zero at 1 month chronological age.

Such attempts at devising absolute scales mostly agree in showing a negatively accelerated, or slightly S-shaped, curve for the growth of intelligence in childhood, which supports Bloom's view that growth rate is maximum in the early years. However, such curves are not very meaningful, both because they refer to different psychological functions at different ages and because they represent group or average tendencies only. Any one child's growth curve is likely to fluctuate quite widely and to be characterized by spurts and plateaus (see Honzik, 1957). Little can be said regarding the causes of rapid, slow, or changeable growth, though some data on associated personality and environmental factors will be cited later in this volume.

One might think that comparing growth on specific factors instead of just on the general component of successive individual tests would give a clearer picture. Thurstone (1955) analyzed cross-sectional (not longitudinal) data on his Primary Mental Abilities tests, plotting the percentages of adult performance reached at different ages. Apparently *P*, Perceptual Speed, was the fastest growing of his factors, reaching 80 percent of adult level by 12 years. Space and Reasoning came next, reaching 80 percent at 13 and 14 years; then Number, Rote Memory, and Verbal, which reached 80 percent level by 16 to 18 years; Word Fluency was slower still. However, other types of data seem to yield quite inconsistent results. Thus, it is known that nonverbal (classical) IQs tend to have larger Standard Deviations than verbal IQs (Cattell, 1963a), which would seem to indicate nonverbal performance increases more slowly with age than verbal performance. This difference is plausibly explained by Cattell's fluid and crystallized *g* theory, since social and educational pressures would stimulate growth in verbal abilities.

AGE OF MAXIMUM GROWTH AND DECLINE OF ABILITY

The difficulties in deciding at what age maturity in intelligence is reached, and the various devices adopted for obtaining an average IQ of 100 at all ages, have already been mentioned in Chapter 1. With more recent investigation, it became clear that, even if growth slowed somewhat after about 14 years, scores, at least on some tests, continued to increase up to 20 years or beyond. However, several investigations indicated decreasing scores beyond that age. For example, Vincent (1952) standardized a group verbal test on 7,000 civil servants and obtained an almost linear decline with age from the 20- to 25-year group to the 55- to 60-year group, amounting to 0.3 of a Standard Deviation per decade (i.e., 9 IQ points per 20 years). When Wechsler standardized the Bellevue Scale, maximal scores occurred in the 20- to 24-year group. Thereafter, there was fairly rapid decline on some subtests, for instance, Kohs Blocks, Similarities, and Digit Memory, but tests such as Information and Vocabulary held up considerably longer (see p. 48). Foulds and Raven

(1948) gave the Progressive Matrices and Mill Hill Vocabulary tests to comparable groups of employees in a large firm, covering a wide age range. Performance on the Matrices was highest at approximately 18 years; on the Vocabulary not till 37 (indeed, the highest scorers went on rising till 50 years). These and other studies indicate earlier decline in reasoning (especially nonverbal) ability and in tests that Cattell classifies as G_f, also in spatial tests and tests markedly dependent on speed, than on most verbal tests. By contrasting these scores with vocabulary (a good measure of G_c), it is possible to derive an index of mental deterioration.

However, one might anticipate from Hebb's theory of Intelligence B that continued mental growth in adulthood, as in the developing years of childhood, would depend considerably on educational and other environmental stimulation. The astonishingly low average adult M.A. of 13 years was found in 1918 because, at that time, the majority of the population probably left school at, or soon after, that age. In 1949, J. B. Parry and I published the scores on the Progressive Matrices test of 90,000 naval recruits of different ages and occupational backgrounds. These showed a tendency to decline even as early as 18 years among men who came from unskilled and laboring jobs, which presumably made little call on their "brains"; whereas the scores of skilled tradesmen and clerical workers went on increasing till a later age and then decline much more slowly.

Research in the 1960s began to show that the above cross-sectional studies of successive age groups could be seriously misleading. When the same individuals were tested in early and later adulthood, scores on verbal tests tended to increase up to 50 to 60 years, and even on spatial and reasoning tests up to 40 or beyond. An ingenious study by Schaie and Strother (1968) provided both longitudinal and cross-sectional data, which illustrated the same contrast. They collected samples aged 25, 30, and at 5-year intervals up to age 70, and then retested each of these 5 years later. Hence, they were able to calculate the rise or fall over successive 5-year periods without having to compare one sample with another nor to keep in touch with the same groups over a very long period.

Why the cross-sectional and longitudinal approaches yield different results has not been satisfactorily explained, though one relevant factor is likely to lie in intergenerational differences. For example, people who are now aged 50 to 70 would mostly have had a shorter and perhaps less stimulating education than do present-day adolescents and young adults. In addition, living conditions nowadays may help more people to keep their intelligence "alive" than previously—for instance, exposure to television, easier access to books and periodicals, better medical care, and so on. Horn (1976) discusses at length the differing results and draws attention to the many biases likely to arise from death and attrition, from using volunteer samples, and from possible practice effects. But he accepts the notion of a general decline of mental power with aging, in contrast to W. K. Schaie and his coworkers (Baltes and Schaie, 1976), who argue that this decline is a myth. Other writers have suggested that there is no inevitable decay, though losses may often occur merely because people aged over 60 and their acquaintances expect them to occur or because of the changes in life-style on retirement.

In fact, there is now neurological evidence of decline in brain weight and considerable loss in sheer numbers of neurones, which accompany the general decay of bodily tissues with age. Much experimental work has shown that information processing does tend to become less efficient from middle-age onward. The qualities most affected are those that characterize Cattell's G_f, such as organizing and perceiving relations with unfamiliar inputs, flexibility, and ease of shifting from one task to another. Reitan (1966) regards problem solving with novel materials as particularly sensitive to brain impairment. At the same time, it is very probable that some individuals retain such skills longer than others, in part, perhaps, because there are genetic differences in longevity, but also because their attitudes are more positive, and they continue to make good use of their minds.

The greater stability of G_c implies that mature and older adults can continue to acquire concepts and strategies useful in their occupations and avocations. With their extensive and rich long-term storage, they may show what we call superior wisdom. But there are also losses through interference; the availability of previous or recent memories becomes much less reliable. Here, too, then, biological change is involved, which can only be offset to a limited extent by practice, motivation, and a favorable environment.

SUMMARY

1   Early workers in the field of mental measurement exaggerated the reliability of the IQ and its predictive power from childhood to adulthood. Well-conducted longitudinal studies have shown clearly that developmental quotients obtained in the first two years of life, though fairly stable over short periods, give zero correlations with later childhood and adult IQs.

2   This change in correlation occurs largely because tests that sample early development are based mainly on sensorimotor and language skills; not until about 4 years, when children have begun to develop internal symbolic thinking, do tests of their mental capacities begin to provide fairly valid indicators of later reasoning and conceptual capacities.

3   As Bayley, McCall, and others have pointed out, these findings imply that no general intellectual capacity is revealed in the first few years, but rather the progressive emergence of discrete series or hierarchies of skills.

4   In plots of successive IQs of individuals over many years, considerable instability of growth is found. However, the reported variabilities tend to be exaggerated on account of changes in test content, norms and variances, repeated retesting or practice effects, use of above-average samples, and so on. A typical repeat reliability figure of 0.70 over 5 to 10 years implies that five-sixths of retested children obtain the same IQ within ± 15 points, though some of the remaining one-sixth may fluctuate much more widely. Group tests, especially nonverbal, give much less valid predictions than individual scales.

5   Bloom, following Anderson's Overlap Hypothesis, believes there is no correlation between initial IQ and gain or loss in IQ over a succeeding period. His amalgamated figures for IQ retests indicate that late adolescent IQ is already determined to the extent of 50 percent by 4 years, 80 percent by 8 years. However, reasons are given for doubting Bloom's conclusions.

6   Special difficulties occur in longitudinal studies of ability development, because we have no absolute units (or ratio scales) of measurement and because of sampling biases. Attempts to arrive at an absolute meaure do suggest, as Bloom claimed, that the most rapid mental growth occurs in the early years. Such growth slows down, but does not cease, in the teens or young adulthood.

7   Many contradictory claims have been made regarding the age to which intellectual growth continues or when decline sets in. The contradictions arise partly because continuing growth depends on continuing education and "use of the brains," and partly because the G_f type of ability seems to reach a limit and start declining considerably earlier than the G_c type. Thus, some cross-sectional comparisons have suggested declines beginning by age 25 or earlier, whereas other longitudinal studies have indicated increases, at least on some tests, to age 50 and beyond. Cross-sectional studies are less reliable, probably because of differences in background (e.g., educational opportunity) between samples tested at different ages.

8   Although decline may not set in until later ages than previously thought, and it may be influenced by the degree of activity or depression experienced by the retired adult, there is no reason to doubt that a decrease in the efficiency of information processing does eventually result from breakdown of neurones and brain structures with age.

6

Effects of Prenatal, Perinatal, and Other Constitutional Factors

T he development of children's intelligence is affected not only by genetic factors and the physical, social, and educational environments in which they are reared but also by a number of physiological conditions operating during pregnancy or parturition or in the early months after birth. For example, if the mother takes excessive alcohol or certain drugs such as thalidomide, or suffers from such diseases as rubella or syphilis, the fetal blood supply can be infiltrated and fetal growth adversely affected. Physical injury or anoxia at the time of delivery can cause permanent brain damage. Inadequate nutrition or severe stress experienced by the mother before birth also may be injurious to the offspring. Such factors, which are usually present at or shortly after birth and which have lasting effects, are not inherited or genetic, but neither are they environmental in the ordinary sense. Rather, they should be recognized as *constitutional*. This term includes all the basic biological equipment, whether genetic or resulting from special physiological conditions.

It is surprisingly difficult to obtain adequate evidence proving the effects of this miscellaneous and ill-defined collection of conditions. Much of the information on pregnancy or delivery complications, for example, has been obtained by questioning the mothers, sometimes many years later. Because such recollections are extremely unreliable, it would be preferable to use only those cases where full hospital records are available. Frequently the available health statistics are inadequate or based on unrepresentative samples (see Birch and Gussow, 1970). However, Broman, Nichols, and Kennedy's Collaborative Prenatal Project (1975) included over 25,000 births, about half white, half black. Detailed records were kept from the mothers' first appearance at clinics in 14 hospitals, and all the data were correlated with the children's Terman-Merrill IQs at 4.0 years.

Contradictory findings can also occur because different investigators make use of different maternal and child variables. The direction of causation — what causes what — is far from straightforward, since we normally find a whole syndrome of cultural background conditions, maternal health, and child deficiencies. For example, pregnancy and delivery abnormalities cannot be attributed simply to conditions of poverty, because they also occur in higher SES families, even if less frequently. And much the same pattern of symptoms could result from genetic weaknesses in the child or from postnatal upbringing, rather than from pre- and perinatal factors.

Because it is seldom possible to control adequately the relevant factors in humans, much more extensive experimental work has been done with rats. This is well summarized by Joffe (1969), who pays particular attention to methodological problems. In such research it is possible to subject mother rats to various forms of stress before or during pregnancy, for instance, audiogenic seizures, and to control for postnatal differences by transferring the offspring to foster mothers during rearing. The offspring of different genetic strains who have undergone the same, or different, prenatal conditions can be measured for weight, maze-running ability, or activity and defecation in the open-field tests, which are thought to indicate some kind of emotionality. Significant effects on the offspring have been shown to result from handling the mothers during their own infancy or from stressing them during pregnancy by preventing them from reacting to previously conditioned stimuli. However, the results of these experiments are quite complex and characterized by numerous interactions between genetic strain and type of treatment. Hence, they throw little light on what to expect at the human level.

PASAMANICK'S CONTINUUM OF REPRODUCTIVE CASUALTY

Let us turn now to the broad syndrome of associated characteristics commonly found in humans. Mothers with poor health are more liable to incur diseases or to undergo complications or emotional stress during pregnancy. Most frequently, such women come from lower economic class families, which are often poorly nourished, and they are less likely to receive good prenatal and postnatal care. Premature or difficult births occur more frequently among this group; birth weights are low, and infant mortality is greater than normal. The surviving children are likely to be less healthy and susceptible to various physical ailments; they tend to be mentally backward and to show later neuropsychiatric symptoms and behavior disorders.

Much of the evidence in this area comes from researches by Pasamanick and Knobloch (1966) and their colleagues, who have made numerous studies of what they refer to as the *continuum of reproductive casualty*. They show, for example, that mental defect, epilepsy, cerebral palsy, and reading disability and certain behavior disorders tend to occur more frequently in the children of mothers who have pregnancy complications or premature births. Such conditions also occur with much greater frequency among blacks than among whites (see Lilienfeld and Pasamanick, 1955). In addition, mothers who are much above average child-bearing age are more seriously at risk. As H. Birch puts it, mothers living in poverty often have children "too young, too old, and too often."

Birch and Gussow (1970) provide extensive documentation for a similar concept, that of a continuing cycle of poverty, prenatal and perinatal abnormalities, and children who fail at school and are, therefore, fit only for low-grade employment; and so the cycle repeats itself (see also Amante et al., 1970). Some commentators simplistically ascribe this vicious circle to innate genetic inferiority; others take the equally simplistic position that economic and welfare measures and educational reform would eliminate it. In other words, both sides ignore the important interaction between physiological conditions and poverty. With their current resources, the wealthier nations should certainly be able to break the chain, but there is too much ignorance among the public and lack of coordinated planning for this to happen easily. The situation in the United States is actually worse, in many respects, than in European countries, since nonwhites frequently live in far more impoverished conditions and there is less access to free medical care. Despite recent enormous improvements in public health, reduced infant mortality, and so on, the differential between different SES or racial-ethnic groups has not been reduced. If anything, the handicapped are relatively worse off now than they were, say, 20 years ago. Obviously, the problems of poverty and ill-health are magnified still further in underdeveloped countries.

Though carried out on a much smaller scale than Pas-amanick's work, Stott's (1957) studies are of particular psy-chological interest. Stott consulted the medical records and interviewed the mothers of 105 subnormal or mentally defective children. He found among 49 percent of them more maternal illness and/or emotionally stressful conditions, such as matrimo-nial problems, housing difficulties, or illness in the family, during pregnancy. The mothers of control groups of mentally normal children, including siblings of the subnormals, were similarly questioned; only some 15 to 20 percent of these women had comparable pregnancy difficulties. The difference in incidence could not be accounted for simply by differences in poverty be-tween the two groups; the difference in conditions of stress was crucial. Nevertheless, Stott's data and his interpretations are open to doubt on account of the unreliability of the mothers' recollec-tions. Moreover, other investigations in the United Kingdom, such as Barker's (1966) study of 600 subnormal children, indi-cated that "complications of pregnancy and labour play little part in the aetiology of intelligence." However, Barker's work was concerned more with effects of maternal illnesses than with the psychological factors emphasized by Stott.

McKeown and Record (1971), after surveying early en-vironmental influences, likewise conclude that perinatal condi-tions and abnormalities of pregnancy and labor make very little difference to children's intelligence. Broman, Nichols, and Ken-nedy's (1975) follow-up of 25,000 children yielded multiple cor-relations averaging 0.44 among whites and 0.30 among blacks between prenatal data and 4-year IQ. By far the most important predictors, however, were mother's education and SES not mother's health. Significant, but smaller, contributions were made by mother's age (under 20 or over 30), number of clinic visits, and any kind of brain abnormality at birth. The correla-tions rose to 0.51 in whites and 0.39 in blacks when other in-fancy data, such as delayed motor development and scores on the Bayley Mental and Motor scales at 8 months were included. In other words, some 26 percent and 16 percent of variance in 4-year IQ was predictable. In addition, particular abnormalities, such as Down's syndrome and cerebral palsy, led to low IQs in a small number of cases.

Although they do not directly support Stott's view, investi-gations such as that of Davids and De Vault (1962) provide some additional evidence showing that women with abnormalities of pregnancy and delivery tend to get higher anxiety scores on personality tests, including the MMPI and the Manifest Anxiety Scale. This does not, of course, tell us whether the mother's anxiety was responsible for the abnormalities, or vice versa, or whether both are due to some other, presumably genetic, factor. Sontag (1966) found that severe emotional shock among pregnant women was associated with feeding and gastrointestinal problems in the offspring.

EFFECTS OF TWINNING

It is well known that twins, whether mono- or dizygotic, average some 5 points below normal in IQ (see Record, McKeown, and Edwards, 1970). This difference has been plausibly attributed to the unusual intrauterine conditions that subject one or both fetuses to abnormal physical pressures. Husén (1959) obtained group intelligence test scores for some 3,000 male twins and 200,000 singletons who were called up for military service in Sweden. The mean among the twins was lower by the equivalent of about 4 points of IQ. But there was very little difference in the above-average distributions; the deficit occurred primarily because of the much greater numbers of twins obtaining very low scores. These data suggest that constitutional factors particularly affected the bottom 5 percent or so of the twin distribution.

On the other hand, the recent work of Record, McKeown, and Edwards (1970); Broman, Nichols, and Kennedy (1975); and Lytton, Conway, and Sauvé (1977) indicates that postnatal rearing conditions are more important than constitutional factors. The major factor seems to be that the parents can give less attention and speech to each twin than they could to singletons.

Nevertheless, several writers stress the importance of uterine conditions among identical or monozygotic twins. According to Darlington (1976) the splitting of the ovum often damages one or both fetuses. The babies are apt to be born prematurely, with low birth weights. It has been claimed by Price (1950), Munsinger (1977a), and others that, when one member of a pair of monozygotes has a considerably higher birth weight than the other, he or she will be likely to show a higher IQ when tested at a later age. However, the evidence for this association is mixed, and Fujikura and Froehlich (1974) present data that contradict it.

Munsinger (1977a) describes a condition believed to affect monozygotes particularly. Some two-thirds of these are monochorionic; that is, they share the same placenta. This condition, called the transfusion syndrome, is believed to occur when there is a blood leakage; it results in one fetus getting much less hemoglobin than the other and thus brings about weight differences and IQ differences. However, as mentioned later (p. 177), Munsinger's data and methods of analysis were open to doubt. Indeed, Kamin (1977c) has claimed that greater birth weight differences are found among dizygotic than monozygotic twins, which clearly indicates that monochorionic conditions are not responsible.

PREMATURE AND DIFFICULT BIRTHS

Prematurity was one of Pasamanick's main causes of constitutional handicap in children. It can arise from a variety of reproductive complications and is associated with high birthrate, high infant mortality, and low birth weight. However, there are considerable difficulties in pinning down the date of conception, especially among less educated parents, and therefore in gauging the degree of prematurity.

Some writers (Knehr and Sobol, 1949; Guilford, 1967) have denied that the prematurely born differ from normals in intelligence when differences in SES are allowed for. However, both Douglas (1960), in his follow-up of some 300 premature children in the United Kingdom, and Knobloch, Pasamanick, and Lilienfeld (1959), in the United States, found among prematures a deficiency of some 5 points of IQ at later ages, which was also reflected in low educational achievement, even when the premature and the normal-birth controls were matched for SES and other factors. Douglas attributes this deficiency mainly to the poorer standards of maternal care and disinterest in the children's education in the families of premature children.

Anoxia, or oxygen deficiency, frequently results from difficulties of delivery or delay in starting to breathe. Here, too, there are many questions about its effects. As Gottfried (1973) points out, it is often difficult to assess whether anoxia has occurred or for how long, though several clinical signs are commonly employed. Some 5 to 10 percent of children are affected in greater or lesser degree. Cutting off the oxygen supply to the brain is well known to have severe and irremediable effects in later life, but it is possible that many infants, though temporarily affected, nevertheless develop normally. Gottfried agrees with Pasamanick that an excess number of mentally deficient children have been affected by anoxia, and there is some tendency for their performance on the Gesell and other infant scales to be low. But later IQ distributions often show these children to be no different from normal. As in so much research on perinatal factors, the results are apt to vary according to the particular kind of control groups with which the anoxic children are compared. A survey by Hunt (1976) of fetal and neonatal "insults," including anoxia and hypoxia and anesthetization during delivery, brings out the complexities of investigation in this area. It concludes that these conditions seldom have any clear effects on later ability.

BRAIN DAMAGE AND LEARNING DISABILITIES

Brain Damage

While most likely to occur at delivery, brain damage may also arise during pregnancy, or postnatally from brain disease, injury, and so on. Amante et al. (1970) point out that it may also result from chromosomal anomalies, malnutrition, and other biochemical conditions. They stress that is is far from randomly distributed among the population; it is much more common in lower SES and in black families.

In such an immensely complex field, it is hardly possible to make any useful generalizations other than that certain degrees of damage to certain parts of the cortex produce a wide variety of defects, ranging from the cerebral palsies to the agnosias and aphasias. At the same time, there are scarcely any one-to-one correlations between specifiable injuries and specific symptoms (see p. 42). We cannot even make the claim that intelligence, in the sense used in this book, is impaired by particular kinds of damage; though the disorders of speech functions in different types of aphasia, which can, to some extent, be identified with certain cortical areas (see Penfield, 1959), do include inability to recognize, comprehend, and produce words, and thus incapacitate thinking. Goldstein and Scheerer's (1941) early study suggested that their brain-damaged patients were able to think "concretely," but were deficient in "abstracting" ability. However, Reitan (1959) showed that deficient abstraction is a matter of degree rather than of type of thinking. His tests of Halstead's Abstraction factor did indeed differentiate significantly between 52 brain-damaged and 52 nondamaged adults, though there was much overlapping.

Guilford (1967) argues that it would be more profitable to study the effects of different injuries on different Structure of

Intellect factors, but the examples he quotes are almost wholly hypothetical. However, there are some specially devised tests, such as those initiated by Halstead and developed by Reitan, that do yield more diagnostic information on brain damage (see Reitan and Davison, 1974).

Much of the difficulty in this field arises because we seldom know the exact location and extent of brain injury, other than through autopsies, and, of course, these are rarely available for children with birth injuries. Moreover, any effects differ considerably according to the age at which damage occurs (see the useful survey by Hutt, 1976). The EEG and X rays can provide some relevant information; hence, a thorough neurological and psychological examination is of value in cases of suspected damage not because this can point the way to any cure, but because it can give guidance as to remedial exercises and training that may minimize the effects of the handicap. In general, the younger the child at the time of damage, the greater the chance that other parts of the brain can take over and function vicariously.

It has been claimed that some 10 percent of mentally defective children are brain-injured, but naturally the range of severity is very wide, and much larger numbers of children, some even with normal or superior intelligence, who show various learning disabilities may have suffered minor damage. Unfortunately, the term *minimal brain damage* (M.B.D.) has tended to become a catch-all to explain almost any disability for which there exists no obvious educational, environmental, or motivational explanation. Many such cases show no evidence of physical injury (except perhaps a medical record of a difficult delivery), merely the inexplicably inadequate test performance. It has been suggested that a better term than minimal would be *undetermined* brain damage. The same symptoms may arise from general retardation of cortical maturation rather than from specific damage.

Dyslexia is a particularly controversial and frequently misused term. Undoubtedly, there are cases of children who have quite unusual difficulties in learning to read (generally also in spelling and writing) despite, in many instances, average or superior IQs and even good number ability. They are not "word-blind" (as they used to be diagnosed), since some of them do improve with sufficiently patient and elaborate individual coaching. But dyslexia takes many forms, and the stereotype of the nonreader with perceptuomotor difficulties who also tends to show distractibility and hyperkinetic behavior—the so-called

Strauss syndrome — is far from typical. Reitan points out that all these symptoms can be found in normal children, where there is no suspicion of cerebral damage. They may also originate in neurotic or psychotic, rather than constitutional, conditions.

Learning Disabilities

Currently, there is widespread interest in children with "specific learning disabilities," though very little consensus on how to classify or treat the conditions. There is even disagreement on their incidence, estimates ranging from 1 to 15 percent of children (see Wallace and McLoughlin, 1975; Rourke, 1976). Another common euphemism is "children with perceptual problems," which may console some parents, but which is usually misleading because learning disabilities may, in fact, occur much more frequently in other areas, such as listening, speech, reading, language, writing, arithmetic, retention, or organized thinking; even in psychomotor coordination. And yet these cases cannot be attributed to ordinary mental retardation, sensory or environmental deprivation, or emotional causes; and few of them are likely to involve brain damage. Most writers de-emphasize the diagnosis of causation; they carry out very extensive testing, but mainly with a view to recommending possible rehabilitative measures.

Rourke denies that such children are incurable because their disabilities are probably constitutional in origin, since they can often be trained in compensatory skills. Moreover, the extent of the disability varies greatly with feelings of security or anxiety; hence the child can cope adequately in some situations but not in others. Recent studies by the American Institutes for Research (A.I.R., 1971) have shown that the common belief that learning disabilities are associated with later delinquent tendencies is unfounded. In sum, while genetic factors may underlie some disabilities, it is also very necessary to explore how parents and teachers have handled the child's condition.

MATERNAL AND CHILD NUTRITION

A maternal diet that is inadequate in quantity or lacks important constituents, such as proteins and vitamins, might be expected to affect the growth of the fetus and the breast-fed infant, or it might render the mother more vulnerable to disease. A crucial period occurs from about 3 months before birth to 6 months after, when the brain structures and neurones are being laid down (see Scrimshaw and Gordon, 1968). By the end of the first year of life, the infant has attained 70 percent of adult brain weight, hence, the importance of the early growth period. However, myelination of brain tissues is not complete by this age, and children may be seriously affected by protein-calorie deficiencies up to 4 years or so.

Most of the well-controlled work in this area has been done with animals (see Joffe, 1969). McCance and his colleagues (Dobbing, 1968) have demonstrated the effects of chronic undernourishment and of ill-balanced diets in pigs and rats not only on body growth but on brain development. Cowley and Griesel's (1966) investigations merit special mention, as they show strong intergenerational effects: Malnourishment of mothers affects the development of offspring, and even if the second generation is rehabilitated, the third generation may still show deficiencies. This finding supports Birch and Gussow's claim that the cycle of poverty, malnutrition, and ill-health cannot readily be broken just by intervention at some single stage. Although considerable efforts and expenditure have been put into experimental improvements of human diet, Birch and Gussow admit that most of the published work is conflicting and confusing, often owing to methodological inadequacies. Nevertheless, they conclude that something like 10 million children in the United States — perhaps half of the families living below the recognized poverty line — are malnourished. Often this is due as much to ignorance regarding suitable choice of foodstuffs as to sheer lack of quantity.

One large-scale study of the effects of dietary supplements on poorly nourished mothers and their children has been carried out by Harrell, Woodyard, and Gates (1955). Some 2,400 pregnant mothers were involved, half of them poor whites living in a rural area of Kentucky, the others a depressed urban group in Virginia, of whom the majority were blacks. During later pregnancy and early nursing, they were given one of three kinds of supplementary vitamin pills, or else placebos. Their children were tested with Terman-Merrill at 3 years, and a large proportion of the Virginia group was retested at 4 years. In the latter group, the children whose mothers received the diet supplement scored 3.7 IQ points higher at 3 years and 5.2 at 4 years than the control (placebo group) children. (There was no significant difference among those taking the three types of supplement.) In the Kentucky group, there were no significant differences between any of the 4 subgroups. Although these mothers were as impoverished as those in Virginia, it is possible that, living in the countryside, they did obtain more adequate diets.

A number of other studies are surveyed by Kaplan (1972). But Warren (1973) strongly criticizes the weaknesses of design in most of these studies and the absence of suitable control groups, and concludes that there is no convincing evidence for effects of nutrition on mental development.

Investigations by both Harrell and Pasamanick, Knobloch, and Lilienfeld raise the question whether the difference in intelligence scores between blacks and whites might not be attributable to inferior diet among the former or to greater likelihood of physical or emotional stress. Loehlin, Lindzey, and Spuhler (1975) discuss this problem and show that black diets in the United States are often defective, but they conclude that the deficiencies are not sufficiently serious or widespread to account for more than a fraction of the IQ difference. Dietary inadequacies also tend to be more severe among American Indians. In his 1969 article, Jensen indicated that a substantial proportion of the environmental differences between whites and blacks might be constitutional or nutritional in origin, but now he argues against this position (1973a). He points out that maternal malnutrition would be most likely to influence the early physical development of psychomotor behavior of young children; whereas, it is well known that, on average, black infants are more advanced than whites in such behavior, and it is not until 3 or 4 years that the black children's developmental and intelligence quotients tend to fall behind. Beyond that age, malnutrition probably ceases to have any further effects on brain growth.

A very different study in Holland, by Stein et al. (1972), appears to contradict Harrell's findings. These authors tabulated the test scores at age 19 of some 20,000 Dutch army recruits whose mothers had been subjected to severe undernourishment during the crucial perinatal months, at the time of the German occupation in 1944–1945. Compared with 100,000 recruits whose mothers had not so suffered, there was a slight suggestion of increased incidence of low-grade mental defect, and there may have been unusually high infant mortality. But the scores of the surviving recruits on the Progressive Matrices nonverbal test showed no general and lasting retardation. It is conceivable, of course, that the mothers carried some nutritional reserve despite their temporary starvation; hence, their condition would not be comparable to that of chronically undernourished black families.

A report issued by the World Health Organization states that:

> There is practically no evidence of a relationship between ... mild and moderate forms of malnutrition and mental retardation. What seems more probable is that there is an interaction between malnutrition and other environ-

mental factors, especially social stimulation, and that the child's ultimate status is the result of this interaction (WHO, 1974).

Similarly, Birch and Gussow (1970) hold that "children who have been acutely and chronically undernourished are retarded in mental development," yet they agree that the effects are difficult to substantiate as they are always liable to be complicated by other aspects of poverty and maternal or child ill health. Nevertheless, Birch and Gussow consider that many of the differences in height and physique among different racial or ethnic groups are attributable more to nutritional and health conditions than to genetic differences. They further stress the frequency with which socioeconomic class or poverty and racial-ethnic background interact in their effects on nutrition and health. That is, nonwhites (excluding Orientals) tend to be more handicapped in the areas we have considered than whites; however, the lower SES and less educated classes, with race or ethnic group held constant, are also more affected. For example, the infantile mortality rate (from conception till 1 year after birth) is a pretty good index of poor health in surviving children. This rate is twice as great in the lowest as in the highest SES groups in the United States; in nonwhite groups, the ratio is nearly 4 to 1.

Although we must conclude that malnutrition has little, if any, effect on intellectual growth among Caucasian children, the situation is very different if we turn to underdeveloped countries, such as those studied by Cravioto et al. (1967; see also Vernon, 1969a). Here we commonly find a vicious circle of technological backwardness and low purchasing power, inefficient agriculture and inadequate diet, large families and poor health care, deficient education, and so forth. Such conditions are associated with low weight gain among babies, and low socres on Birch's tests of intersensory integration, which probably represents a relatively culture-fair test of general intelligence. Often the staple diet is deficient in proteins and vitamins. Although women do much of the heavy agricultural labor, they get even poorer food than men do; hence, the nourishment available for the fetus or breast-fed infant is seriously deficient at the most crucial phase, when damage to neural structures is likely to be irreversible (i.e., it cannot be made up by better feeding later). Particularly in African countries, malnutrition may lead to deficiency diseases such as marasmus and kwashiorkor. According to Rose (1972), it is probable that half or more of all black African children are affected in some degree by protein deficiency. After weaning, children's physical and mental growth may be further impaired by the change from mother's milk to the staple diet.

But at later ages, chronic malnutrition seems to be less harmful to mental development insofar as the brain is well insulated against health hazards and susceptible only to a few diseases, such as meningitis, that attack the actual brain membranes.

The effects of severe perinatal food deficiencies have been demonstrated by Stoch (1967) in South Africa. For over 5 years, she followed up colored children who were badly malnourished in the first two years of life and compared them with a group of adequately nourished children matched for socioeconomic level. The former group scored 15.7 IQ points below the latter on a South African adaptation of the WISC scale.[1] Their performances on verbal and nonverbal subtests were quite similar in pattern to those of brain-damaged children. Jensen (1973a) points out that, in several other similar studies in different parts of the world, the number of cases of severe malnutrition affecting mental development are quite small; even in such cases, it is difficult to demonstrate that mental retardation does arise from inadequate nutrition rather than from many other conditions often associated with it.

Glutamic Acid

It was frequently argued in the 1940s that glutamic acid is an amino acid essential to neural growth that may be deficient in mentally defective patients, and significant gains in IQ were reported following supplementary administration of glutamic acid. However, Astin and Ross (1960) showed that, in the majority of investigations, there was either no control group or the results were negative.

General Ill Health

There is little convincing evidence that ill health or inadequate nutrition have any consistent effects on mental development after the first year of life. True, it has been found in such investigations as Burt's (1937) and Douglas' (1964) that children who are backward in school achievement tend to show a lot of minor illnesses and that their retardation is not due merely to their missing school. Apart from the fact that low socioeconomic class, backwardness, and poor health tend to be associated, it does seem probable that poor health conditions reduce the

---

[1] Birch and Gussow estimate the deficiency at 22 points. They also point out some inadequacies in Stoch's control group, which are further criticized by Warren (1973).

physical strength of growing children and therefore reduce the amount of energy they can put into school learning. Birch and Gussow mention apathy, lack of responsiveness and concentration, and irritability as the main consequences of poor nutrition, but they are probably inferring more from the extreme cases mentioned above, or from animal studies, where the undernourishment is very severe, than from evidence collected over the normal range in white societies. Here, too, it is extremely difficult to disentangle causes and effects.

Smoking Parents

It has often been claimed that heavy smoking by the mother during pregnancy increases the prematurity rate and the risk of perinatal mortality (Butler and Alberman, 1969). As usual, there are difficulties in controlling other variables, such as SES. But Davie, Butler, and Goldstein (1972) developed an ingenious multiple regression technique for holding these factors constant. On applying their method to a large and representative sample of some 10,000 British children, they found among children of smoking mothers a small but significant deficit in reading achievement at 7 years; it was equivalent to 4 months of Reading Age. However, the interpretation is greatly complicated by Yerushalmy's (1962) finding that low birth weight and prematurity are more closely related to the father's than the mother's smoking, and are most frequent when both are smokers. These facts would contradict the obvious explanation that nicotine in the mother affects the fetus and would support, instead, the notion that smokers generally are somewhat different kinds of people from nonsmokers, and they carry some genetic influence adverse to fetal growth. In the largest study of its kind, that of Broman, Nichols, and Kennedy (1975), the mother's smoking was related to low birth weight. Although smoking gave no significant correlation with white children's IQs at 4 years, the mean IQ of black children in the sample was significantly lower.

FAMILY CONDITIONS

Month and Order of Birth

Much has been written on intellectual differences, in very large populations, between children born in different months of the year. The claims are often contradictory, and, in any case, the differences seldom amount to more than 2 or 3 points of IQ. If there is any such consistent tendency, it seems more likely to arise from more intelligent parents choosing, say, spring and early summer birth dates than from physiological effects of particular seasons. More sizeable differences in achievement do occur when children are admitted to first grade only once a year, on the basis of when their birthdays fall, since this means that some children have 11 more months school experience than others nearly the same age.

Birth order has also been a popular area of research, though it, too, has generally yielded inconsistent findings. Several studies suggest that first-borns tend to have IQs from 1½ to 3 points higher than later siblings; and there is even stronger evidence that more first-borns become high achievers, as shown by college grades, eminence in later life, and so on. (This fact was noted in Galton's and other early studies of genius.) But, as Schooler (1972) points out, the difference could be partly or wholly due to the fact that the ratio of first-borns to later children is greater in small than in large families, and this means that more of them come from middle- and upper-class families. Sometimes, too, there are population changes that temporarily affect birth rates in particular geographical areas. Schooler admits that differences between first- and later-born children may have occurred in some societies over some periods, but he concludes that, in the United States in the 1960s, there is insufficient evidence of any reliable trends, once SES is controlled.

Personality differences between first- and later-born children have also been claimed, though first-borns seem to show a rather contradictory pattern of greater dependence, more anxiety, yet also more need for autonomy. Altus (1966) states that first-borns show stronger development of conscience and other traits likely to gain teacher approval. Over and above any social-class difference, it would seem very plausible that first-borns should receive more talking to, stimulation, and attention from parents, and that parental aspirations for their education and careers would be stronger. This, of course, would point to an environmental, not a constitutional, effect.

Breland (1974), in his analyses of birth order and ability among many thousands of candidates for National Merit Scholarships, draws attention to the fact that only children actually score less well than first-borns in families of two or more children. The explanation he suggests is that the first-born is given greater responsibility in caring for younger siblings, whereas the only child gets no such experience.

Size of Family

Small correlations of -0.2 to -0.3 are consistently found between child intelligence and size of family (i.e., number of siblings), since, in most Western societies, lower SES parents tend to have more children than middle- or upper-class parents. In my survey of Army recruits (Vernon, 1951), the mean IQs of men from one- to two-child families was 106, and there was a regular decline until, for families of 13 and over, the mean was only 87. This difference was as great on measures of *g* as on more verbally loaded tests. The study had an advantage over several others where younger children were tested, since most of the families of recruits, aged 17 and over, would be complete.

Such findings caused a great deal of concern in the United Kingdom in the 1930s to 1940s, when Burt (1946), Cattell (1950), and others argued that the greater fertility of the less intelligent families would produce a progressive, even catastrophic, decline in national intelligence. However, the Scottish Council for Research in Education (1933; 1949) carried out two surveys of the whole 11-year-old population of Scotland but found no decline in mean IQ over a 15-year period; in fact, there was a small rise. A similar result was obtained in Cattell's (1950) study of the 10-year-old population of an English city, using nonverbal tests 13 years apart.

The reasons for this negative finding are complex: Probably children in Britain were more accustomed to, and sophisticated at, tests at the later date. Improvements in child health and education over the period might mask any small genetic decline. A further environmental explanation is the tendency for children in larger families to receive less parental attention and stimulation. Thus, in the National Child Development Study in England, Davie, Butler, and Goldstein (1972) found that, even when SES was held constant, children from larger families were significantly inferior both in physical growth and in reading ability. Similarly, Douglas' (1964) follow-up showed poorer reading and arithmetic scores among children from large families at 8 and 10 years. Davie believes that the difference was due to the parents' having less time for each child or being less concerned for the intellectual achievement of each than the parents of small families. A multiple regression analysis by Marjoribanks, Walberg, and Barger (1975) likewise showed verbal ability among 11-year-old boys to be best predicted by father's occupation and numbers of children; they saw the inverse relation between number of children and verbal ability as an indicator of the amount of attention available for each child (see also Zajonc and Markus, 1975).

The fact that adults of very low IQ are low in fertility would tend to compensate for anticipated declines in intelligence and keep the overall population level stable. This is stressed by Bajema (1963), who also points out that social class differences in family size can vary quite considerably in different countries at different periods. Currently in the United States, the highest IQ group of parents shows the greatest fertility, followed closely by those with IQs 80– 94; those with IQs under 80 are the least fertile.

SUMMARY

1   Many conditions during the child's prenatal and early post-natal life, or at the time of delivery, are liable to create constitutional handicaps. However, it is difficult to prove specific effects, owing to inadequate maternal reports or medical records and unrepresentative samples. Moreover, such conditions and symptoms are always mixed up with social class or other factors. Experiments with animals can be better controlled, and these have provided evidence of maternal conditions affecting the growth and later ability of the offspring. Studies of pigs, for example, have demonstrated the effects of severe malnutrition on brain development.

2   Pasamanick's continuum of reproductive casualty describes the widespread syndrome of poverty, maternal ill-health, and pregnancy and delivery abnormalities associated with poor growth and intellectual and emotional disorders in the children. Birch and Gussow point out the vicious cycle of such a syndrome, leading to failure in school and low employment level. The importance of such physiological factors is often neglected in view of the interest of psychologists in genetic and environmental influences. The syndrome tends to be more frequent in blacks than in whites.

3   The average IQ of twins is consistently below normal, suggesting the effects of prenatal and biochemical difficulties. However, recent studies indicate that differences in rearing, such as the amount of care and conversation that parents can bestow on each of the two babies, is a major factor.

4   Evidence for the effects of maternal stress during pregnancy and of anoxia at delivery is controversial. Prematurity of birth does seem to be associated with mental defect and lowered intelligence.

5 Brain damage at delivery, or from other causes, may underlie a wide range of abnormalities from cerebral palsy to aphasia. But "minimal brain damage" is too often assumed in cases of dyslexia and other learning disabilities, without direct evidence of physiological impairment, merely because these conditions cannot be attributed readily to ordinary genetic, environmental, or emotional causes. However, comprehensive neuropsychological testing can often provide a basis for planning remedial and compensatory measures.

6 Malnutrition of mother or infant is another condition bound up with a complex of social and economic factors. Though malnutrition is widespread among low-SES groups and ethnic minorities, there is little convincing evidence of the effectiveness of dietary supplementation. Under more severe conditions of malnutrition occurring in underdeveloped countries, particularly in the few months before and after birth when brain cells are being laid down, deficiency diseases such as kwashiorkor occur, which certainly impair mental development. Together with poor health conditions generally, malnutrition tends to produce apathy toward, and failure in, school learning. Heavy smoking in either parent has some deleterious effects. Lack of glutamic acid as a factor in mental deficiency is nowadays discredited.

7 First-born children are usually found to be a little above average in intelligence and more likely to achieve well, presumably because of the greater parental stimulation they receive. But it is uncertain whether the difference does not derive largely from social class differences between smaller and larger families.

8 Size of family consistently correlates negatively with mean IQs of children, leading to predictions of decline in national intelligence level, which have been disconfirmed by experimental surveys. Many factors may be involved in this discrepancy—the low fertility rate of mentally defective adults, the improvements in education and medical care, swings of fashion in the differential birthrate, and the probability that children in large families get less parental stimulation.

7

Studies of Development in Infancy

There is currently a great deal of interest and research activity in the early stages of cognitive growth, following the lead given by Piaget, Bruner (1975), and Schaffer (1971). It is difficult to provide a lucid summary of the present position, or even to list the most significant books and articles.[1] The object of this chapter is simply to search for solid evidence that the manner in which parents treat young children affects their cognitive and intellectual growth.

A great variety of research techniques have been used, ranging from high-speed photography of infant behavior to long-term follow-up from birth to adulthood. The first is particularly valuable in providing information on the sensorimotor, cognitive, affectional, and social behavior of first-year infants and their mothers. Under appropriate conditions, various functions have been shown to be present much earlier than previous observers had claimed; for example, discriminating the loudness and location of sounds in the first week after birth. The ingenious experiments devised to elicit the various stages of development of, for instance, the concept of an object, are well described by Bower (1974).

---

[1] I have relied chiefly on Schaffer's (1977) book, *Mothering*. Attention may also be drawn to the comprehensive survey of cognitive development by Hamilton and Vernon (1976).

MOTHER–CHILD INTERACTIONS

The main finding has been the extent to which infants are active in their own cognitive and linguistic growth and their socialization. While much depends on the parents' providing appropriate stimulation and reinforcement at different ages, the child is certainly not just molded into a perceiving, sentient, and social being. More often, he — and, of course, *she* should also be understood throughout — is the initiator of each new stage, and the mother follows his lead. She seldom directly teaches but rather facilitates the conditions for incidental and discovery learning. Although Gesell's notion of natural maturation of motor and cognitive skills is no longer acceptable, Schaffer (1977) suggests that the infant has inborn dispositions to be selectively attentive to human visual and auditory stimuli; to organize activities such as sucking, sleeping, and intercommunication in periodic cycles; and to interact with people. We can no longer agree with William James' description of the infant consciousness as "a big, booming, buzzing confusion." The infant is responsive to many kinds of stimuli at birth and, in a few weeks, shows a preference for patterned, complex, and moving visual stimuli over static, simple ones. According to Trevarthen (1974), the infant reacts differently to the sights and sounds of his mother than to objects. Within a few months of birth, much of his waking time is spent in actively looking for people and objects, and his eye movements in following people around are coordinated with turning his head or reaching with his hand in the same direction.

The most interesting phenomenon, brought out by Richards (1974), Schaffer (1974), Trevarthen (1974), and Newson and Newson (1975), is the development of mutual "conversations" long before the child can speak. Crying is, of course, one of the first kinds of signaling behavior to appear, and sensitive mothers soon learn to discriminate to some extent between different crying sounds indicating different needs. Mutual communication occurs also through the tactile contacts in feeding, cuddling, lifting, and rocking. Thus, the infant finds that he can produce effects by crying or cooing, and later babbling, or by gestures. (On the other hand, for the infant reared in an institution or by an apathetic or rejecting mother, the absence of such effects shows him he is helpless.) From about 2 to 3 months, alternating activities can be observed. The child signals by noises, hand waving, or reaching, and switching his eyes to an object. The mother can follow his line of sight, that is, what he is fixating on, and then talks to him or displays the object. The infant appears to listen to her and watch what she is doing, and this initiates a further oral or gestural communication. By the end of the first year, the mother and child have developed a whole series of alternating or synchronized activities, including pointing, reaching, vocalization, and imitation games; and each of these interactions is characterized by a large amount of repetition and reinforcement. Gordon (1975) refers to this as verbal ping-pong, which he contrasts with the mother's just talking to the child.

It also is noticeable that, when pointing at something, the mother makes sure that she has caught the child's attention. In other words, her behavior is continuously reactive to his state of mind. However, this synchronization does not occur if she is lacking in sensitivity, either through temporary fatigue or preoccupation, or if she is less concerned with facilitating the child's communications than with the imposition of her own wishes.

It would seem quite plausible that such mother– child interactions (or transactions, to use Gordon's term) provide elementary training in attending, observing, and listening, which are basic to the growth of information processing and intelligence and the acquisition of language skills. But some caution is necessary, since it is shown in Chapter 5 that there is remarkably little correlation between any measurable features of sensorimotor development in the first 1½ years and either family SES or later child IQ. There has not yet been sufficient follow-up to show how far children who are advanced in prevocal communication are superior later in cognitive or linguistic skills, nor what kinds of maternal sensitivities or strategies, or lack of these, affect the rate and effectiveness of cognitive growth.

Several writers, such as Yarrow and Pedersen (1972) and Gordon (1975), follow Erikson (1950) in regarding the establishment in the child of a feeling of basic trust, or attachment-dependency, as the necessary first step in mental growth. Up till about 5 months, the infant is fairly indiscriminate in his smiling, babbling, and social responsiveness. But soon after he clearly displays a particular attachment to the mother and may be disturbed if she is absent. People are no longer interchangeable, and many children show fearfulness of strangers. That the child is distinguishing self from environment is shown by active searching for a previously seen toy (see Schaffer and Emerson, 1964). In other words, there are the beginnings both of object permanence and of the realization that his actions can cause or change things, so that he has some control over his environment. Later, when he has this secure base and when he becomes mobile, the child sets out to explore the world around him and thus embarks on the next of Erikson's stages, the attainment of autonomy.

Curiously, there do not seem to be differences among mothers of different socioeconomic classes in the establishment of this initial security. Some mothers of every class are not sufficiently aware of their baby's needs to be responsive to his communications or to reinforce affection by fondling and playful interchanges. Probably this is partly a matter of the mother's own happy or unhappy childhood upbringing. Harlow's female monkeys, brought up in complete isolation, made very poor mothers, rejecting or even attacking their babies. However, it is not simply a matter of the mother's personality; some children seem to seek much more cuddling than others, just as some have a higher all-round activity level, and others are more passive, and the mother has to allow for these characteristics. Thus, mother and child affect each other.

A surprising finding is that it does not seem essential that there be a one-to-one relationship, so long as the child has a particular caretaker during a substantial part of his waking life. Caldwell and Richmond (1968) found no ill effects when infants of 6 to 15 months spent half of each day at a day-care center, and those from 15 to 48 months underwent a full-day program, approximating that of a nursery school. If anything, this group showed more trustful and flexible behavior and more autonomy than children who spent all their early years with their mothers. Schaffer concludes that the mother-figure need not be the biological mother; a foster mother who adopts a young infant, or even a father, can meet the same needs. Similarly, Yudkin and Holme (1963) found that children of working mothers who spent most of their day in care were, if anything, more self-reliant and less anxious than home-reared children, according to a questionnaire filled in by the mothers when their children were 6 years old. However, a further comparison was made by those authors between a group whose mothers had started work when they were infants (mean age 1 year, 2 weeks) and a group whose mothers started work after the children reached 3 years. Here, the first group of children was assessed as more insecure and more anxious for affection. The groups studied were small (15 to 16 children), but the results do suggest that better adjustment occurs when very young children are cared for by their own mothers; after 2 or 3 years, stable day care in a nursery school or with private individuals is superior (other evidence is cited on p. 141).

On the other hand, a study by Yarrow (1963) of 40 6-month infants did provide empirical evidence of the relation of the mother's behavior to the child's characteristics. A number of maternal variables, falling into the following three groupings, were carefully defined, and each mother was rated after a period of observation and an interview:

1 Adequacy as need gratifier and tension reducer (e.g., responding to expressions of need, amount of physical contact, etc.).
2 Adequacy as a source of sensory and social stimulation and provider of conditions of learning.
3 Emotional involvement and affection.

The children were rated on six developmental or personality characteristics (though, unfortunately, it is not clear whether this was done independently of the assessment of the mothers). Substantial correlations in the 0.40s to 0.60s were found between mother variables and the children's developmental quotients, exploratory-manipulative development, handling of stress, and social initiative (though not between mother variables and child autonomy or adaptability).

The relation of mother–child interactions in the first year to the development of language is also obscure, though it would seem plausible that their "conversations" lead on to the child's attaching names he hears to familiar people, objects, actions, and concepts. McCall (1976) suggests that language arises out of the child's need to communicate and develops through exploratory and imitative activities. Early speech is mainly a continuation of child–adult interchanges rather than the maturation of an innate Language Acquisition Device or a universal generative grammar. However, in my view, we should allow that the growth from pre-linguistic to vocal communication implies a species-specific potentiality, since this appears only at the human level. Interestingly, also, it seems to function at quite low grades of intelligence — for example, in many imbeciles.

The building up of vocabulary and of relatively complex sentence structures from about the age of 2.0 does appear to be linked more closely with social class. Well-educated and high-SES mothers not only talk more to their children but vary their speech from time to time to adapt better to the child's current developmental level and emotional state. They use simple sentences, and name things, combining this with demonstration, and reinforce the child's vocalizations. They make much more use of questions, much less of commands. They avoid distracting conditions; in particular, they do not expose the child to high-intensity background noises. Wachs, Uzgiris, and Hunt (1971) applied four of their ordinal scales of psychological development to 102 infants ranging in age from 7 months to 22 months; half were from middle-class, half from low-SES (mostly black) homes. The scales covered object permanence, means for obtaining events, development of schemas for relating to objects, and vocal imitation. SES and qualities of maternal verbalization similar to those listed above tended to correlate with scores on these scales, especially vocal imitation, whereas high ambient noise from which the child could not escape gave negative correlations. Therefore, we need to be wary of the term *stimulation*, since it may vary so much in types, amount, duration, and so on.

AFFECTIONAL-MOTIVATIONAL FACTORS AND LATER COGNITIVE DEVELOPMENT

I have mentioned earlier that part of the difficulty of isolating and measuring intellectual development in young children is that their performance depends so much on affectional factors such as current mood, on temperamental qualities, and on their reactions to an unfamiliar tester. It is only to be expected that research in this area should be particularly complex; and, indeed, it is almost surprising how much progress has been made in linking child and parent personality characteristics, aspects of parental handling or upbringing, and later intellectual capacities. Various techniques of obtaining information have been used (see Mussen, 1960) and, as Yarrow, Campbell, and Burton (1968) show, each has its weaknesses; hence, there are often low or negligible correlations between the parental methods of handling and the traits, attitudes, and abilities, and the like that they are supposed to encourage.

The main approaches, with their advantages and disadvantages, may be described as follows:

1   Perhaps the most popular source of information, because of ease of administration, but also the least reliable, is the answers of one or both parents to a questionnaire regarding their attitudes or their practices in socializing their children. What they say they do or believe should be done (e.g., in disciplining a child) may differ widely from direct observation of what they actually do in disciplinary situations. From factorizing responses to various scales or items, Schaefer and Bayley (1963) suggest that differences in parental attitudes fall along two main dimensions — Warmth versus Rejection and Autonomy versus Control — though other writers prefer rather different classifications. Probably these dimensions are so general as to have little

concrete meaning; nevertheless, they have been found to relate, to some extent, to child characteristics.

2   A social worker or other trained interviewer carries out a more unstructured enquiry with one or both parents, encouraging them to express themselves freely and to give concrete examples. However, the questioner is covering particular variables laid down in a schedule and will generally end up with a series of ratings of parental warmth, dominance, and other characteristics. Naturally, the validity of the results will vary with the skill and insight of the interviewer and rapport achieved with the parents.

3   Mother and child are brought to a playroom or laboratory where various activities are arranged, and an observer can record or rate the behavior of one or both in concrete situations; for example, how much help of what kind does the mother give when the child is required to solve some performance test? Presumably because of differences between this relatively controlled setting and the home, the behavior shown may differ considerably from that observed in a natural home setting (see Lytton, 1974). A variant of this method occurs when a psychologist is applying individual Binet or other standard tests and can often make useful ratings of the child's personality characteristics in tackling difficult tasks.

4   Direct observation of parent–child interactions over a considerable period (e.g., 2 hours) in the home. Some kind of time-sampling or detailed coding on a previously prepared schedule of the behaviors is recorded; hence, the technique is necessarily limited by the range of different behaviors that the observer has time to record accurately. Very considerable training and practice are required if two independent observers are to achieve reasonable agreement (e.g., 85 percent correspondence) in their categorizations. It is a moot point how far natural responses tend to be inhibited by the presence of an observer who is obviously keeping records of what occurs. But, on the whole, children below 3 or 4 are little, if at all, affected, and their parents soon become accustomed to the unusual conditions. Lytton (1974) compared methods 2, 3, and 4 with the same group of 2½-year-old boys and their mothers and concluded that method 4 provided the greatest amount of information that yielded substantial correlations with other personality variables.

5   A further source is the children's own impressions of their home environments and parents, which may, of course, differ considerably from independent observers' home ratings or from parental beliefs about their own behavior. This technique has probably been used infrequently, partly because one can hardly obtain reliable written questionnaire responses from children till at least 11 years (see G. W. Miller, 1970), and partly because both older children and their parents object to invasions of privacy. However, in individual intelligence testing, a clinical psychologist can elicit a good deal of significant information orally about home background and the child's attitudes that complements or contradicts what the teacher or parents have volunteered.

Particularly useful results have emerged from the long-term studies at Berkeley and at the Fels Institute, where the same subjects have been observed and assessed frequently from infancy to adulthood. The results are complex and, given the rather small numbers, quite variable. Also, they tend to differ considerably for boys and girls and fathers and mothers and at different ages. (One notices, also, a regrettable tendency to pick out for quotation the most favorable and most consistent sets of correlations from hundreds of comparisons and to ignore the much larger number that are negligible or more difficult to interpret.) However, the relevance of Schaefer and Bayley's warmth and autonomy variables is suggested by rather consistent negative correlations, around −0.4, between mother Irritability, Punitiveness, and Ignoring with boy's intelligence from 5 to 18 years; Egalitarian Treatment, Positive Evaluation, and Achievement Demand yield positive correlations. In girls, however, mother's Intrusiveness gave the highest (negative) correlations. On the whole, a warm, sympathetic emotional climate, but one that stresses independence and demands for achievement, seems the most encouraging to development of intelligence (see Jones et al., 1971). A more recent study by Bradley and Caldwell (1976) of 49 infants (mixed sex and race) was generally confirmatory. Six main maternal variables were rated on the basis of observation in the home plus interviews with the mothers, both when the children were aged 6 months and again at 24 months. Terman-Merrill IQs at 4½ years gave substantial correlations for the three following variables: (1) emotional and verbal responsiveness of mother; (2) maternal involvement with the child; and (3) provision of appropriate play materials.

The average coefficient between 6-month ratings and later IQ was 0.33; for the 2-year ratings, 0.54. Thus, the quality of the environment and mother–child interactions strongly influence childhood cognitive growth. Similarly, Wulbert et al. (1975) compared 20 children who were backward in language development with 20 matched normals, aged 2½ to 6 years. Maternal characteristics were rated in the homes and the mothers of the language-retarded were found to be poorer in emotional and verbal responsiveness, less involved with the child, and more apt to punish. The retarded were much lower in verbal IQ, though not in performance tests. There was no SES difference.

The relevance of Schaefer's dimensions of Autonomy versus Control is more doubtful. Coopersmith (1967) brings this question out in an investigation that was concerned not with ability or achievement but with self-esteem. He found that the families of boys with positive self-concepts did encourage independence and democracy in the home, but within a context of consistent and demanding standards. In other words, autonomy should be distinguished from lax indulgence and control from authoritarianism. Another study, by Kent and Davis (1957), did use ability measures as dependent variables, namely Verbal and Performance IQs. On the basis of home interviews, the mothers of 118 8-year-old boys were classified as Normal, Demanding, Overanxious, or Unconcerned. The highest mean child IQs, especially on verbal tests, were found in the Demanding group. The Overanxious were also above average on verbal tests, but only average on performance tests; the Unconcerned were low on both, but particularly on verbal. It is possible, of course, that there were genetic differences between the groups, for instance, high-IQ parents may be more likely to be Demanding, low-IQ parents to be Unconcerned. Thus, caution is needed in interpreting this study as one of environmental effect.

Similarly, Baumrind (1971) classified the homes of 134 nursery-school-age children on the basis of parental interviews into several types, which distinguished Authoritative (controlling, firm, rational) from Authoritarian (more distrustful, less warm). Observations of the behavior at school showed the boys from the former type of home to be more socially responsible, confident, and independent than those from the latter type. This finding was not confirmed in the case of girls.

In another recent review of the literature on "Motivation and Personality in Cognitive Development," Hamilton (1976) concludes that, although most correlations are low, they rather consistently indicate that a warm, accepting, tolerant, and stimulating mother makes for good social and cognitive development and lack of anxiety in her children. She is sensitive to their needs, communicates her affection, and encourages interactions between the child and the environment, while also maintaining strict controls that enhance both personal safety and family cohesion. Crandall, Preston, and Rabson (1960) and other researches at the Fels Institute likewise emphasize the mother's rewarding behavior and fostering of independence rather than dependence as affecting children's motivation and achievement in nursery school.

OTHER STUDIES OF FACTORS IN UPBRINGING

Witkin's (1962) extensive studies of field dependence and field independence included a largely interview-based analysis of mothers' upbringing of their sons, suggesting that those mothers who were overprotective and who emphasized conformity to social conventions and respectability tended to foster dependency, and such boys were apt to be superior in verbal abilities; whereas those whose mothers encouraged autonomy, resourcefulness, and independence were more likely to show independent perception and good performance on spatial and flexibility of closure tests. Again, the results were much less clear-cut with girls, and some researchers (Bock and Kolakowski, 1973) show closer resemblance in field independence of mothers to sons and fathers to daughters than vice versa, thus suggesting sex-linked inheritance. Elsewhere (Vernon, 1969a; 1972) I have argued that the construct of field independence overlaps to some extent with general intelligence, or g, as well as with S-factor, and that the conditions said to favor it are often similar to those associated with upper-middle as opposed to lower-class homes. Bing (1963) also attempted to explore the influence of home upbringing in Verbal, Number, and Spatial factor scores of fifth-grade boys and girls. The mothers were interviewed and were observed helping their children with verbal and nonverbal test problems. Bing claims to have shown a relation between verbal ability and close dependency on adults, between number ability and tendency to concentrate on the task and carry it out without help, and between spatial ability and interest in exploration of the physical rather than the interpersonal world. But her numbers were small and even when the hypothesized relations were confirmed, they seldom applied to both sexes.

Abnormal family circumstances such as a "broken" home have long been associated with delinquency, maladjustment, and school failure. The most recent large-scale research, carried out by Davie, Butler, and Goldstein (1972) with a representative sample of 11,000 English children, was more successful than most in holding constant such related variables as SES. They found significant effects of broken home on the achievement of 7-year-old children in the middle and upper classes, but not in the lower-class groups. Presumably, this finding indicates that other handicaps in these social classes are already so pronounced that the addition of disturbed family relations adds nothing.

An interesting series of studies has correlated background home influences with changes in IQ accompanying growth rather than with intelligence at any particular age. Baldwin, Kalhorn, and Breese (1945) obtained visiting interviewers' ratings of home climate and found that children who increased in IQ over a 3-year period tended to come from homes rated as Acceptant-Democratic or Acceptant-Democratic-Indulgent rather than from those classified as Rejectant Casual, or Autocratic. This accords well with Kent's and Davis' study mentioned above.

Moss and Kagan (1961) reported correlations between IQ gains from 6 to 10 years with mother's Concern for Cognitive–Motor Development of 0.49 for boys and 0.42 for girls; while Sontag, Baker, and Nelson (1958) found that children who are aggressive, competitive, nonconforming, and actively exploring tend to show most IQ rise. Where there is lower need for achievement and the child is highly dependent on the mother, IQs tend to drop. However, more recently Kagan (1976), stated that there is little relation between maternal handling and later personality characteristics.

Although the above researches make relatively little mention of the effects of father characteristics, other studies suggest that the father plays a particularly crucial role in the personality and ability development of boys, presumably because he provides, or fails to provide, a model of the masculine role. Lynn and Sawrey (1959) interviewed the mothers of 40 Norwegian boys and 40 girls aged 8 to 9½ and applied a structured doll-play projective technique to the children. Half the children had fathers who were whalers or fishermen liable to be absent from 9 months to 2 years at a time; the fathers of the other half were normally at home. The father-absent boys showed some signs of immaturity, compensatory masculinity, strong father idealization, and poorer peer acceptance than the control group. They did not show signs of greater mother dependence; however, the girls did so.

A very different study pointing in the same direction was that reported by Carlsmith (1964) on the Scholastic Aptitude Test results of male Harvard undergraduates. Normally, male scores were well above the national norms on both the verbal and mathematics sections of the Educational Testing Service's Scholastic Aptitude Test; female students scored markedly lower on the mathematical than the verbal section. Carlsmith tested considerable numbers of males born between 1941 and 1945. The scores of those whose fathers had been absent on war service for 1 to 3 or more years tended to resemble the female pattern, the drop on mathematics being greater the earlier and longer the period of father absence. Twenty students with fathers absent for 2+ years and 20 with no absence were matched for SES and academic background. The numbers with verbal scores (V) higher or lower than mathematical scores (M) were as follows:

	V > M	M > V
Father absent	13	7
Father present	2	18

It seems a reasonable inference that fathers supply something in the early cognitive development of boys that contributes to their spatial and mathematical abilities, that is, abilities that normally show considerable sex difference.

However, a word of caution is suggested by Conrad and Jones' early survey (1940) of the intelligence of all parents and children in certain New England communities. They found almost identical correlations between parents and children of either sex. That is, there was no evidence of stronger mother–daughter and father–son resemblance than in opposite-sex pairs; also, there was no stronger resemblance between same-sex siblings than between brothers and sisters. Interfamilial relations, therefore, seem to have little or no consistent effect on intellectual growth as measured by the verbal intelligence tests employed, namely Stanford-Binet for the children and Army Alpha for the parents.

Jones et al. (1971) provide an interesting discussion of personality and ability in their summing up of the California Growth Study results. After reiterating the variability of IQs from infancy to adulthood, they ask why it is that many children of rather consistently average ability during childhood, whose school careers are also undistinguished, nevertheless end up as highly successful adults in creative professions or business; whereas others, who generally showed high intelligence and came from strongly supportive homes, turn out as "brittle, discontented and puzzled adults whose potentialities have not been actualized." Their evidence is impressionistic rather than statistical, but they point out various reasons why people are nonpredictable.[2] Many children react unexpectedly to family, school, and environmental pressures because of differences in temperament or in level of maturity. During their childhood and particularly their adolescent growth, they meet many frustrations and traumatic problems and learn to cope with these more or less successfully. Those who succeed are better fitted to deal with future difficulties and thus build up well-adjusted personalities; experiences of failure lead to more negative self-concepts. Throughout this process their cognitive skills may be enhanced or depressed and, although we can sometimes observe this happening and find plausible explanations in individual cases, we do not know enough about the interplay of individual dynamics with life experiences to be able to control or predict cognitive development or retardation, apart from a few rather vague generalizations.

SUMMARY

1   Recent work on development during the first year of life demonstrates the active role of children in building up prelinguistic interchanges and communications with the mother. These are probably basic to the development of speech, but the extent of their contribution to intellectual development is unclear.

2   Personality and ability development are closely linked in young children. Some progress has been made in tracing the effects of parental characteristics and home climate on children's psychological growth, despite the extreme complexity of the relationships and the methodological difficulties of research.

3   A warm, encouraging manner, not overprotective but demanding of achievement, seems to give substantial correlations with later ability and achievement in boys, though the picture is less clear-cut for girls. The influence of the father as a model is also particularly important for boys in stimulating the growth of mathematical and spatial abilities. Some of the work of the California Growth Study, the Fels Institute, and Witkin and others, is outlined.

[2] A possibility not discussed by the Berkeley group is that intelligence and school achievement tests do not take sufficient account of special talents or creativity, which come to the fore in adulthood.

8

Environmental Factors in Intellectual Development: Socioeconomic Advantage and Disadvantage

The role of socioeconomic status (SES) in intellectual differences is a complex one and is often misunderstood. In Western societies there is a positive correlation between parental SES and child IQ of about 0.30 to 0.35 (Neff, 1938); and, in general, the children of the top professional and business executive fathers tend to average about 1 Standard Deviation above the mean—115—while children of the lowest laboring and unskilled fathers average about half a Standard Deviation below the mean—92½ (see Terman and Merrill, 1937). The means for adults themselves within such occupations tend to show much wider differences, as seen, for example, in the data published for the American Army General Classification Test (see Tyler, 1965). This variation would be expected on the grounds of filial regression. Since the correlation of parent with child IQ is typically 0.5, we would expect the upper and lower groups of parents to be twice as far from the mean, that is, 130 and 85, respectively; although there are considerable variations in different studies using different tests, these estimates are fairly close.

It is usually taken for granted by most American psychologists that the superior IQs of upper- and middle-class children are completely explained by the superior environment in which they are reared and that, conversely, the more deprived or disadvantaged conditions of lower SES homes account for the poorer average IQ of their children. However, without disputing in any way the importance of such environmental differences, we will see later (see Chapter 16) that there is also very strong evidence that socioeconomic classes do, to some extent, differ in their genetic makeup. In consequence, it becomes extremely difficult to sort out cause and effect in studies of the influences of what would appear to be environmental factors on intellectual development.

For example, books and periodicals in the home generally yield a substantial correlation with child IQ. But we cannot infer that they provide an independent stimulus to mental growth, since it may be merely that the possession of reading matter is more common among well-educated and well-off parents, and such parents are more likely to stimulate their children's growth in many other ways. Alternately, such parents are probably superior in intelligence themselves and pass on better genes to their offspring.

There are further complications in that parental SES gives different correlations with different kinds of tests, usually higher with verbally loaded tests than with nonverbal. It seems reasonable that parental influence should be greater on tests having linguistic and educational content; that is, on tests of Cattell's G_c than of his G_f. There are also age differences: For example, Jones et al. (1971), taking parental education as predictor, obtained negative correlations with children's developmental scores below 6 months; zero at 1 year; and +0.40 and over by 3 years, rising to +0.60 and over by 6 years. This increase could be accounted for in terms of the successive maturation, with age, first of sensorimotor functions and later of linguistic and reasoning abilities. Or it might be explained by the cumulative effects of home upbringing, though this explanation seems less likely as there was little increase in correlation after 6 years. Further evidence is provided by Willerman, Broman, and Fiedler's (1970) study. They tested over 3,000 babies at 8 months with the Bayley Mental and Motor scales and retested them at 4 years with Terman-Merrill. Children in high-SES homes who scored low on the infant scales obtained a normal IQ distribution later. But children in low-SES families with similar scores showed much lower 4-year IQs.

It certainly seems remarkable that there are virtually no behavioral characteristic differences on Gesell, Bayley, or other tests between higher and lower social class children until nearly 2 years of age. A few isolated instances mentioned in Lewis (1976) seem, if anything, to favor lower SES children. For example, when observed in a laboratory situation at 3 months, low-SES children tend to vocalize and smile more and fret less than high-SES children. We might expect to find rather more cases of poor psychomotor development among children from poor backgrounds on account of the association between poverty and fetal or perinatal risk (see Chapter 6). But very likely the children chosen for intensive studies by psychologists would tend to exclude any with brain damage or very poor health.

THE COMPLEXITY OF SES

Bronfenbrenner (1961) suggests that there have been considerable changes in class differences as they affect child rearing since the late 1920s, when investigations of SES and intelligence first started. In addition to changes in fashion, such as in feeding on demand, middle- and working-class families have become more alike in many respects. Thus, the father nowadays is more often an affectionate helper than the dominant autocrat he used to be. With such alterations we might expect to obtain rather different correlations between SES and child ability or personality than those reported in the earlier literature. Similarly, in England (see Bernstein, 1971), the traditional working-class family hierarchy has become much eroded through changes in economic, housing, and educational conditions.

The assessment of SES is less straightforward than it might seem. Father's occupation alone is a rather crude measure of the favorableness of the home to intellectual development, and information about the nature and level of his job is often unreliable. Sometimes information on father's or both parents' length of education is also given, and it tends to be considerably more predictive of child characteristics than does job status, income, or other material aspects of SES. Alternatively, a composite index may be based on family income and education, type of housing (e.g., rooms per member of family), and the like. Or a questionnaire is given to children, such as the Sims Score Card, which chiefly covers family possession of equipment, books, cars, and so forth.

All these indices are fairly highly correlated, but obviously they do not measure exactly the same thing. Hoffman and Lippitt (1960) point out that we sadly lack an agreed taxonomy of the major family parameters that have most influence on children's abilities and personalities, though some progress has been made (see Chapter 7). Probably the most reliable technique is for a home visitor to ask a standard series of questions regarding parental status, education, home furnishings, and the like, as in Burks' (1928) survey of good and poor foster homes and in several other researches mentioned below. It is then possible to correlate either separate items or a total weighted score with child characteristics.

Freeberg and Payne (1967) point out that psychologists nowadays are less interested in the effects of global variables, such as enriched versus deprived environments, and more concerned to differentiate particular aspects of child rearing. Cronbach (1969) adds that different kinds of environment may suit different individuals at different ages. There is no reason to suppose that all infants and children benefit from the same kind of environment.

Van Alstyne's (1929) study was one of the first to compare specific home characteristics with child's M.A. at 3 years, with the following results:

Mother education	0.60
Father education	0.51
Opportunities for use of constructive play materials	0.50
Hours spent by adults with child daily	0.32
Number of playmates in the home	0.16
Father reading to child	0.60
Nutritional index	−0.03

Wolf (see Bloom, 1964; Wolf, 1966) obtained a multiple correlation as high as 0.76 when 13 variables assessed in the homes were compared with group test IQs of 60 fifth-grade children. These variables chiefly emphasized parental intellectual aspirations and provision of linguistic stimulation, learning opportunities, and materials. Wolf's aim was to assess what parents do in relation to the child rather than just status variables. Though this study is much quoted, it does not prove the very strong influence of good environment, since it is entirely possible that parents with superior genes would be more likely to display such characteristics; furthermore, children with superior intelligence might provoke parents to provide more stimulation of this kind.

Similarly, Dave (see Bloom, 1964) obtained a correlation of 0.80 with overall school achievement. In Scotland, Fraser (1959) found among 400 12-year-olds a multiple correlation of 0.69 between home variables and child IQ. The major contributions were made by parental encouragement, parental education, small family size, and general family atmosphere of emotional security. With school achievement the figure was 0.75.

The work of the Chicago group (Bloom, Wolf, and Dave) has been criticized by Williams (1974) on two grounds. First, it seems to picture the child's development as resulting merely from the "presses" to which he or she is subjected by parents and home environment. Second, the measurement of the strength of each "press" is based on summing ratings of several detailed items, and when these items are factorized, they often fail to group under the hypothesized general categories or presses. Williams himself believes that greater progress in isolating the main family variables would be obtained by classifying them under:

1   Opportunities and stimuli that parents provide for the child to interact with a wide range of situations.
2   Reinforcements that are given for appropriate performance in such interactions.
3   The expectations that parents hold out for good performance. Research on the validity of this approach is currently in progress.

FURTHER STUDIES OF THE EFFECTS OF PARENTAL SES ON ACHIEVEMENTS OF OFFSPRING

Several other socioeconomic indices, such as rooms per family member, likewise give significant, though lower, correlations with child ability (see, for example, Scottish Council for Research in Education, 1953). However, Wiseman (1964), in Manchester, England, noted that sociological variables such as bad housing area, overcrowding, and infant mortality rate have less association with intelligence and achievement than they did when Burt carried out his investigations of different areas of London in the 1920s. More important now than economic conditions seemed to be morale versus social disorganization of the neighborhood, standards of maternal care, and quality of schooling. J. W. B Douglas and his colleagues (1964; 1968) have published exhaustive follow-up studies of the British sample referred to earlier (p. 78), which indicated the cumulative effects of environmental and educational handicap not merely in early childhood but from 8 to 11 and from 11 to 15 years. The achievement and intelligence scores of upper and lower SES groups tend to diverge further during these periods.[1]

A number of recent studies have shown that SES, as evaluated by parental occupation, is less important than other factors of home upbringing in influencing IQ and achievement. Miller (1970) applied a questionnaire on home characteristics and attitudes to 480 students aged about 11 years in the United Kingdom and compared the responses with summed Verbal Reasoning, English and Arithmetic quotients. SES as such correlated only 0.35 and 0.29 with his criterion in boys and girls, respectively. But 72 questionnaire items that correlated significantly were factor analyzed, and it was found that the following factors gave correlations of up to 0.6 with ability:

1   High educational aspirations; aiming at university.
2   Preference for jobs requiring intellectual effort.
3   Autonomy and freedom in decision making at home.
4   Confident self-concept and parental support.
5   Cultural, intellectual, and socioeconomic deprivation (negative).
6   Parents domineering or overprotective (negative).

Such factors strongly suggest middle-class as opposed to lower- or working-class values. But here, too, one should not forget that at least some of these qualities might be as much the result of achieving well at school as a cause of it. Miller's results are supported by those of Morrow and Wilson (1961) at the high school level.

Duncan (1968) used path analysis to estimate the effects of boyhood IQ (tested mainly at sixth grade) and father's education and occupation on son's educational and occupational achievement and earnings. He used various sets of published statistics from large populations to arrive at best estimates of the relevant correlations. The son's educational level (number of years of schooling) depended to a greater extent on his IQ than on father's education and occupation or small size of family.[2] The findings were similar for son's occupational level, though the regression coefficients were smaller, since son's own education was the best predictor. Duncan concludes that it is untrue that

[1] It should be noted that Douglas' test scores were all expressed in standard score units, with a mean of 50 and S.D. of 10. Thus, they are not open to Jensen's objection to using raw scores to study "cumulative deficit" (see p. 300).

[2] This directly contradicts McClelland's (1973) attack on intelligence tests as being less predictive of attending college than the father's SES.

son's boyhood IQ merely helps to fixate him in the social class of his birth; on the contrary, it makes a large contribution over and above the SES of the family. However, its overall influence is rather small, as indicated by correlations of 0.28 with son's later earnings and 0.41 with his occupation.

Waller (1971) studied 131 fathers and 173 of their sons, the latter all aged 24 years and over. IQ results from tests given between 13 and 15 years were available. Social mobility, that is, the difference between father's and son's SES, was the dependent variable. SES was classified into five categories,[3] and 146 pairs were studied where the fathers fell into categories II, III, or IV. (The sons of those in categories I or V were omitted, since they could not show upward or downward mobility, respectively.) The correlation between differences in IQ and differences in SES was +0.368, which is not high but is surprising in view of the coarseness of the SES scale and the use of difference scores. Multiple regression analysis also showed that son's IQ made just about as large a contribution to his occupational achievement as did his father's SES.

Bowles and Gintis (1974) provide a clear statement of the opposite position, namely, that any relation found between IQ and success in later is life is spurious, arising simply because IQ is correlated with parental SES and education and with the educational level achieved the by the child and this educational level largely determines the child's occupational level. However, in the light of Duncan's findings, Bowles and Gintis' analysis of partial correlation coefficients does not justify the inference either that family variables are the primary cause of later success or that the contribution of intelligence is negligible.

It may seem somewhat of a digression to hark back to Terman's follow-up of gifted, or high-IQ, children (Terman et al., 1925; 1930; 1947; Terman and Oden, 1959). However, some writers have accepted this monumental study as striking proof that high childhood IQ presages high occupational success and productivity in later life — in other words, as evidence of the long-term validity of intelligence tests. Other critics have claimed that all the study shows is that children born in privileged homes are likely to score high on intelligence tests, to conform to the

[3] These categories are:
  I. Professional, upper business.
  II. Semiprofessional, lower business.
  III. Clerical and skilled.
  IV. Semiskilled.
  V. Unskilled labor.

values of the U.S. white middle and upper classes, and thus to end up in similarly privileged positions. In other words, it is merely a self-fulfilling prophecy.

There certainly were weaknesses in Terman's study. The sample was biased from the start in being selected first by teacher ratings and then by performance on group and individual intelligence tests. Not only was there an excess of white Anglo and Jewish families and very few blacks, Chicanos, or recent immigrants, but also many children who might later have development emotional maladjustment, undesirable character traits, or failure at school, college, or vocation, were screened out. In other words, a more truly representative sample of IQ 135+ children would not have turned out to be as generally superior in all respects as Terman claimed.

How far is it true that they all came from superior SES backgrounds? Actually, 31 percent of the parents were professional and 50 percent business or semi-professional, leaving only 19 percent clerical or manual. In one-quarter of the families, one or both parents were college graduates, and there were already many outstandingly successful adults among close relatives. But this does not prove that all children of superior IQ come from "privileged" families. The *proportion* of bright children of professional and executive parents is indeed much higher than the proportion of children of lower-middle-class and lower-class parents. But the actual *number* of children who come from non-privileged families may be as large or even larger, because, in the total population around the year 1920, there were far more clerical and working-class parents than higher-class parents in the total population.

I have shown (Vernon, 1957a) that among 11-year-olds who passed the English 11-plus examination, 61 percent came from the working class and only 39 percent from "white-collar" homes. Here, the IQ borderline (for admission to higher secondary schools) was approximately 113. But if we took a higher cut-off, like Terman's 135, the advantages of high social class would be greater. We might expect some 50 percent of such children to come from Terman's two top occupational categories, 30 percent from the clerical and skilled manual, and 20 percent from semiskilled and unskilled.[4] This means that there are quite

[4]These are rough figures, both because the total number of children with IQ 135 and over is small and because the distribution of socioeconomic classes in the general population has altered considerably since Terman began his work. However, there is some confirmation for this estimate from the report that 50 percent of National Merit Scholars come from professional- and business-class homes.

substantial numbers of high-IQ children who do not come from professional- and upper-business-class homes. It is, of course, particularly unfortunate that so many of them fail to be identified by their teachers, or are prevented by other reasons from reaching college or fulfilling their potential talent.

Thus, Terman's follow-up did show some influence of childhood IQ on later occupational success, but he exaggerated this, as did Burt, and Herrnstein (1973). Jensen (1969) suggested that IQ is highly relevant, basing his position on a correlation of approximately 0.80 between prestige ranking of occupations and the mean IQs of people within those occupations. He also draws attention to the substantial influence of IQ on assortative mating (which is discussed on p. 184). But these correlations, of course, do not prove that IQ has substantial predictive value for success within any specific occupation; numerous researches (e.g., Thorndike and Hagen, 1959) indicate that this is quite low. Additional confirmation is obtained from Baller's (1936) and Charles' (1953) follow-up of children who were diagnosed as mentally defective while at school but ended up in a considerable range of occupations, many of them skilled.

Jastak (1969) also has discussed this point, concluding that the importance of IQ in respect to adult achievement is generally overestimated. He suggests that it accounts for no more than about 15 percent of variance in educational or vocational success, or "total life adjustment." Moreover, he was talking of phenotypic intelligence; the proportion attributable to genetic factors in abilities would obviously be less. On the other hand, occupational success also involves qualities of physique, temperament, and other abilities, which likewise have genetic components. Hence, the total genetic contribution might well be distinctly higher.

Social critics frequently complain that intelligence tests exist largely to preserve social class privileges (e.g., Bowles and Gintis, 1974) forgetting that these tests first became popular in educational assessment in the hope that they would pick out the able, regardless of parental wealth or superior home conditions. Jencks et al. (1972) specifically deny this popular accusation and argue that the effects of both childhood IQ and parental SES on eventual occupational achievement and income have been exaggerated. We would naturally expect the correlations of parental status with child's school achievement and later occupational level to be greater than the 0.35 found with IQ. For no one would deny that well-off and educated parents are more likely to provide a more extended and better education for their children and be better able to help them up the occupational ladder. By contrast, a school-leaver from a poor background, especially from a minority group, is undoubtedly handicapped in gaining access to tertiary education and to high-level employment, however able he or she may be. Nevertheless, the correlation is still quite moderate — probably no more than 0.5 — which means that parental status accounts for only one-quarter of the variations in offspring status. Thus, it is absurd to try to explain the successful careers of Terman's gifted group, or other high-IQ children, purely in terms of social class advantages.

Despite the changes in social class behavior patterns, it is still obvious that white middle- and upper-class children, on first arrival at school, differ fundamentally from lower-working-class children and especially from those children who are further differentiated by ethnic or racial origins, such as blacks, Chicanos, and American Indians in the United States, or West Indians, Indians, Pakistanis, and Cypriots in Britain. Middle-class children are advantaged not merely in such surface characteristics as better clothing or a different speech accent; they are also much more fluent and grammatical in expressing ideas, they have had a lot of experience at home in school-type tasks, and they are generally more cooperative with teachers and accepting of school aims; they will, therefore, settle down to learning more readily.

Bernstein's Work

One of the major contributors to the topic of how these differences arise is Bernstein (1961), who has described the different language usages that tend to characterize upper-middle and working classes — which he calls the formal or elaborated code and the public or restricted code. The elaborated code is more impersonal and analytic and thus makes possible precise description and analysis of experiences and their relationships; the restricted code uses more ungrammatical phrases and simple vocabulary, largely supplemented by gestures, and is particularly adapted to expressing emotions and personal relations. Middle-class children can understand and use both codes, but their parents usually employ the formal language for explaining concepts, giving information, problem solving, and showing the child what conduct is acceptable or undesirable; for the most part, school teachers follow the same approach. But lower-class children are handicapped in intellectual and educational development and apt to be confused and frustrated at school because they are accustomed to the restricted mode of discourse and are faced with learning what is almost a new language. The middle-class child is encouraged to plan and organize rationally; the working-class child lives more in the present and is often subjected to arbitrary and inconsistent rewards and punishments. In other words, the linguistic differences are not merely intellectual; they are closely bound up with differences in values, family living, and socialization processes, and these are culturally, not genetically transmitted from one generation to the next.

Bernstein and his colleagues (1971) have greatly expanded this analysis and published an extensive series of related researches. One that is relevant here is the study by Bernstein and Young (1966) of the contrast in attitudes between middle- and working-class mothers to children's toys. The former emphasize that toys help children to find out about things, whereas the latter see them more as a means of keeping children occupied while the mothers get on with their chores. A similar study by Lewis (1976) found that, in reading stories to 2- and 3-year-olds, middle-class mothers explain and discuss the story more than working-class mothers and relate it to the accompanying pictures.

On the basis of their observational studies of 4-year-olds, Hess and Shipman (1965) draw attention to the relative poverty of mother- child interactions and instruction in lower-class families. They contrast the cognitive environment of the middle-class child, which focuses on the intrinsic demands of the task, with that of disadvantaged children, whose behavior is controlled more by imperative commands. The middle-class mother helps the child who is engaged on some problem-solving task to organize his or her approach by showing how language is used as a mediator in planning, and thus she fashions the information-processing skills that the child will need for intellectual and educational growth at.school. The low-SES mother is probably at least as affectionate to her young child as the middle-class mother, but she sees no point in beginning to educate a child who is too young to benefit. Deutsch (1965) also points out the lack of reinforcement of cognitive and linguistic achievement of disadvantaged children at home, adding that they actually learn to be inattentive by living in a noisy and disorganized environment.

Other Analyses of Cognitive Difficulties

Meichenbaum, Turk, and Rogers (1972) state that lower-class or deprived children are more concerned with the "here and now" and less accepting of delayed gratification. They respond better to concrete rewards than to abstract reinforcers such as adult praise. These authors go on to criticize most preschool programs, ranging from Sesame Street to Bereiter and Engelmann's (1966) verbal bombardment, since they do so little to integrate verbalization with action. For example, Sesame Street does not (as the middle-class mother does) encourage the internal manipulation of experience through language nor teach children to reflect on situations and produce organized, adaptive responses, to employ spontaneously their own verbal mediators, or to regulate their own behavior by verbal decisions.

A different but related approach to cognitive development is that of Kagan (1967), who has investigated what he calls reflective and impulsive styles of thinking in preschool and school children. He uses chiefly a matching test, where the subject has to match a given drawing with one out of six quite similar figures. Children are found to vary widely in speed of response and number of errors. To a considerable extent, reflectiveness depends on age; younger children are generally impulsive, whereas older ones are more apt to stop and think before giving their answers. Reflectiveness correlates moderately with Witkin's dimension of field independence (see p. 111). It also relates to SES: Middle-class children are more concerned about mistakes or anxious over failures; that is, they have learned to inhibit immediate, impulsive responses. Yet this difference has very little relation to IQ (see Campbell and Douglas, 1972). In a study by Pedersen and Wender (1968), 30 boys aged 2½ were rated in nursery school for several traits, including Attention Seeking and Sustained Play Activity. Four years later, they were tested with WISC and a version of Kagan's Categorization test. High ratings for Sustained Play and low ratings for Attention Seeking correlated with WISC Performance IQ and with inferential categorizations. The authors regard these scores as aspects of reflectiveness and thus claim a considerable degree of consistency for this cognitive style in early childhood.

Impulsivity may also be linked to the hyperactivity syndrome, which is commonly attributed to minimal brain damage (see p. 91), but which may represent merely the low-SES child's reluctance to sit quietly, to listen, and to think about school tasks. The school psychologist frequently comes across such cases of impulsiveness in individual intelligence testing and can usually keep them in check. It seems very likely, though, that such children would tend to do badly on any kind of group test.

Bernstein's formulation of the relation between SES and language has been attacked, partly because he exaggerated the differences between the two types of language and values rather than regarding elaborated coding as different from restricted coding only in degree. Obviously, a great many working-class children either acquire enough of the elaborated code at home or at school to be able to become high achievers and upwardly mobile in their careers. In his later writings, Bernstein (1971) does stress that all families, regardless of SES, can and do use both restricted and elaborated codes, depending on the context; however, elaborated speech occurs much more frequently in middle-class homes and in school classrooms. He agrees that social classes are not homogeneous categories and that his earlier formulations tended to encourage a stereotyped picture of class differences.

A more basic objection has been raised by Labov (1970), Ginsburg (1972), Baratz and Baratz (1970), and Cole and Bruner (1971); namely, that lower SES or disadvantaged ethnic group children should not be regarded as less competent in speech and language than middle-class children. Their natural speech is different from standard English; yet, in their own social contexts, it is as grammatical and fluent. These authors maintain that all languages are of roughly similar syntactical complexity and are acquired at about the same age in different cultural groups. Ghetto dialects are coherent wholes, well adapted to the needs of the inhabitants even if unacceptable to teachers and middle-class employers (see also Swift, 1972). Meichenbaum, Turk and Rogers (1972) follow Labov in distinguishing *performance* from *competency*. Disadvantaged children may show poor performance when forced to use teacher-English and yet be entirely competent linguistically with family or friends. And Tizard (1974) claims that working-class children possess the same language structures middle-class children do, though they have not been trained to apply them to the same extent in recalling, anticipating, or analyzing experiences. Some supporting evidence comes from a study by Francis (1974) with 50 middle- or upper-class and 24 lower-class English children ranging from 5.9 to 7.3 years. The lower-class children were somewhat poorer in vocabulary, sentence length (when retelling a story), and grammatical errors; but they were not defective in linguistic competence, that is, the use of complex sentence structures.

However, I would agree with Hunt and Kirk (1971) that speech differences are of greater psychological significance than merely differences in usage and application. It is surely rather obtuse to argue that standard English and Bernstein's elaborated code are not more effective in building up abstract ideas and thinking skills, and therefore more characteristic of intelligence, than the restricted code or various dialects, such as "black English." Hunt notes that the mother tongue used in the homes of most U.S. Chinese and Japanese families differs even more from standard English than does black English; yet their speech must be more nearly equivalent in elaboration, since the children's IQs and achievements are equal to, or even higher than, those of whites.

Black English constitutes a special problem in that it is so often used by black children and adolescents as a form of rebellion against the white middle-class values of the school. The extent to which it handicaps school or test performance is discussed later (see Chapter 20).

In conclusion, we need to be cautious about the distinction drawn between *competence* and *performance*. Competence has no useful meaning beyond the maximal performance that can be elicited under appropriate conditions, and performance is often inferior to competence merely because it is measured by an inadequate test given under inappropriate conditions. The relation between these terms is the same as that between Intelligence B and Intelligence C (see p. 20). I will point out in Chapter 16 that test results (i.e., performance) of members of some disadvantaged cultural groups are often lower than they should be because of the influence of various "extrinsic" factors.

SUMMARY

1   A moderate correlation is consistently found between parental socioeconomic class (SES) and child intelligence. This is generally attributed purely to the more favorable environment in which upper- and middle-class children are reared and the deprived environment of lower-class children. Evidence will be given later that genetic differences are also involved to some extent. The degree of correlation differs for different types of ability and with age. Thus, higher-class children show little or no advantage at the sensorimotor stage of development (0 to 1½ years).

2   Parental education and intellectual stimulation in the home are generally more predictive of child ability than are material circumstances. Several studies, including Terman's follow-up of gifted children, show that educational and career achievement are not merely dependent on parental SES; child IQ makes a significant positive contribution.

3   Many of the observed differences in educability of middle- and lower-class (or ethnic minority) children have been attributed by Bernstein to the different language "codes" commonly used in the homes, which reflect not only the efficiency of information processing but also the values of middle-class versus lower-class parents. This finding is supported by the observational studies of Hess and Shipman, Deutsch, and others, and relates to some extent to Kagan's reflective versus impulsive styles of thinking.

4   Bernstein's classification has been criticized on various grounds, particularly by such writers as Labov, who see middle-class, lower-class, or other dialects as distinctive but not as varying in efficiency when used in their appropriate social contexts.

9

Studies of Deprivation and Remediation

$\mathbf{A}$s mentioned in the previous chapter, some writers object to any notion that deficits in ability or achievement arise from poor social conditions. This they refer to as a *social pathology* theory. However, most psychologists still do tend to attribute low intelligence and scholastic failure mainly to the deprived upbringing of children in the lower socioeconomic classes or from ethnic minority groups. Fewer writers admit the likelihood that genetic factors are also involved. However, the notion of environmental deprivation resulting from poverty or from inadequate stimulation in the homes of less intelligent and educated parents is, in fact, very complex and varied in its content and effects. Naturally, scientific evidence on the consequences of different kinds of deprivation is more readily obtainable in research with animals; mention has already been made of the work of Hebb and his colleagues, which supported the view that reduction of stimulation adversely affects the growth of the phase sequences and mediating processes that provide the substratum for higher mental development.

Further studies by Krech, Rosenzweig, and Bennett (1962) have shown that stimulation of baby rats through handling not only improves their later maze learning but also brings about anatomical and biochemical changes in the brain; the ratio of brain to body weight and the thickness of the cerebral cortex increase. Similarly, Levine (1960) found that handling, and even painful stimulation, of rats brought about greater weight gain, less timidity, and quicker learning. However, the evidence is often contradictory, and a critical review by Daly (1973) concluded that there is no consistent or "typcial" effect of additional early stimulation.

SEVERE DEPRIVATION OF CHILDREN

Eysenck (1973) observes that the kinds of deprivation imposed in animal experiments are in an entirely different category from those to which children are exposed in all but the most abnormal environments. Nevertheless, there have been several reports on children who have survived under conditions where they received little or no human contacts, for example, Itard's wild boy of Aveyron. There are many doubts regarding the authenticity of so-called feral children, who are supposed to have grown up among wolves, monkeys, and so on; for obvious reasons, their previous backgrounds are unknown. According to Zingg (1940), they usually turn out to be almost untrainable in speech and human social behavior, a fact which suggests that the absence of normal brain growth in early childhood is irremediable. Another possibility is that they were mostly low-grade defectives or psychotics.

Nevertheless, in cases where isolated children have had some, even if very limited, human contacts, they have proved remediable. Davis (1947) describes a girl who lived with a deaf-mute mother and thus developed no speech until she was removed from this environment; but when transferred at the age of 6 to a more normal environment, she improved from an IQ of about 30 to average level (see also Stone, 1954). Equally striking is an account by Koluchova (1972) of two twin boys who, up to the age of 7, were brought up almost like animals, with scarcely any human contacts. When first rescued, they were severely subnormal, with IQs — insofar as they were testable — of about 40. But after 4 years of normal upbringing by understanding foster parents, they tested at 93 and 95, suggesting a rise of over 50 points; by 14 years, both had reached 100 IQ (see Clarke and Clarke, 1976). Possibly the fact that the boys had experienced one another's company meant that they had sufficient perceptual and social stimulation to build up the basic structures for communication. Jensen (1969) reminds us that Harlow's monkeys, reared initially in complete isolation, did not show subsequent defects of ability, although their social adjustment to other monkeys was greatly impaired.

Spitz (1946) has described the appalling effects of early upbringing in a hospital with a minimum of adult care. The infants he studied simply lay in cribs with very little to look at except when they were fed or cleaned. They appeared to regress into a state of complete apathy; they made no progress in psychomotor maturation, and many failed to survive. Though his report has been criticized, quite similar observations were made by Dennis and Narjarian (1957) in a Lebanese children's hospital. Here, too, there was a very homogeneous and dimly lighted visual environment, and the children up to 1 year were seriously retarded in motor and mental development. On Cattell's scale, their mean developmental quotient was only 63. However, the effects of this experience appear to have been only temporary. After the age of 1 year, the children spent most of their time in small play groups, and, although the equipment and numbers of adult helpers were very limited, there was presumably enough interaction with adults, with other children, and with objects to allow relatively normal development. By the age of 4½ – 6 years, children who had been thus institutionalized in their first year were scoring close to American norms on three performance tests, though their Stanford-Binet IQs remained considerably lower. Dennis claims also that, among children who were fostered out from the institution, those adopted before the age of 2.0 made much more rapid progress towards normal intelligence than those adopted later.[1]

An illuminating cross-cultural study of children in remote Guatemalan villages was reported by Kagan and Klein (1973; see also Kagan, 1976). At the age of about 1 year, the children were far more quiet and passive and retarded in object permanence and in speech development than U.S. children. This might be partly attributable to mild malnutrition, but probably the lack of variety in their environment and of adult attention and stimulation were mainly responsible. A few months later, the children were able to leave their huts and mix with other children, and they became increasingly alert, though still retarded on some cognitive tests. By the age of 8, they were assigned responsibilities by their parents, and by about 11, they were typically active, gay, and intellectually competent. Such evidence, the authors argue, runs contrary to the conventional American view that cognitive development is wholly molded by environment and that early stimulation is particularly important. Though re-

[1] Clarke and Clarke (1976) give more detailed accounts and evaluations of this, and of Skeels' (1966) investigation.

jecting the notion of an innately maturing intelligence, they do suggest that the mind has its own "blueprint" for growth, which may be delayed, but not irremediably, by unfavorable circumstances.

In most of the work so far cited, there was not any adequately matched control group. However, Skeels' (1966) long-term follow-up of 24 orphaned children, originally diagnosed as mentally retarded, did meet this objection. The children were first tested at around 1½ years when living in a highly unstimulating orphanage. Thirteen of them were transferred to another home, where they were cared for and played with by older mentally defective girls, and Skodak claims that they showed a considerable increase in IQ. Those who were not moved decreased further in IQ. Subsequently, most of the first group were adopted into average (not specially superior) foster homes. When traced 25 years later, the 13 transferred cases were normal, self-supporting adults, holding quite highly skilled jobs, or married women. But the other 11, who had been left in the original hospital, were still institutionalized or in very low-grade jobs. I would be disinclined to place much credence in the IQ results with children so young; but the later adjustment of the transferred as against the nontransferred certainly bears out Skeels' claim of an average rise in the former of 30 IQ points or more.

There have, of course, been a great many other studies of foster children, from Burks (1928) and Freeman, Holzinger, and Mitchell (1928) onward, as the approach appears to give evidence of environmental effects unencumbered by genetic influences of parents on children. The adoptees usually show a significant IQ rise in good foster homes (though much smaller than that claimed by Skeels), that is, of the order of about 10 points of IQ. But this source of evidence is fraught with difficulties (see Munsinger, 1975a); a fuller discussion will be postponed to Chapter 14.

HEBER AND GARBER'S INVESTIGATION

The most striking study of the effects of improved environment in early childhood is that of Heber and Garber (1975) in Milwaukee (see also Garber and Heber, 1977). They observed that, in the poorer core areas of the city, there were large numbers of seriously retarded children, mostly black. Their condition was probably the result of a combination of low intelligence among the mothers (IQ 80 or below) and their disadvantaged environment; so that, although they tested normally on preschool tests, their IQs at school sank steadily to about 65 by the age of 14, and they became more and more antagonistic to education. Forty children of such background were selected at birth, avoiding any who showed physical anomalies, and divided into 20 experimentals and 20 controls. The control children took all the tests but received no special treatment. The experimentals were submitted to an all-out effort to improve their sensorimotor, language, and thinking skills. From 3 months on, for 7 hours a day, 5 days a week, they attended a University Training Center for the Mentally Retarded, where a planned, stimulating environment was provided. Adequate medical care and nutrition were also attended to. Simultaneously, the mothers were given an educational program including homemaking, childrearing, and vocational training. An assessment of the children was made every 3 weeks, either by a standard test or experimental learning task, or by measures of language and social development.

Up to about 14 months, the experimental (E) and control (C) groups remained closely parallel on the Gesell scale, but the Cs began to fall behind after 18 months. On preschool scales applied between 2 and 4½ years, Heber found a mean IQ of 122.6 in the Es, 95.2 in the Cs—a difference of 27.4 points. Up to the age of 6, the Es stayed between 110 and 120, whereas the Cs dropped to around 85. The special program then ceased when the children entered first grade. At ages 8–9, the Es dropped to an approximate average of 104, while the Cs by now averaged 80; however, this still represents a substantial lead over the controls of 24 points. (At the time of the report, not all the children had reached this age; hence some revisions in these figures are to be expected.) Moreover, when a sample of siblings of the Es was tested as an additional control, their mean was 80. The Es appear to have stabilized, though Heber admits that they may drop further, perhaps to 100, now that they have no special stimulation.

In school achievement, also, there was a very wide gap between the two groups and rather little overlapping. Similar differences emerged on other tests. On learning tasks from age 2½ to 6½, the Cs tended to perseverate with wrong responses, whereas the Es more readily adjusted their behavior in the light of feedback. In other words, they had developed a more efficient learning style. The Illinois Test of Psycholinguistic Abilities and other indices of language showed some of the biggest differences between the groups. Observation of mother–child interactions suggested that the E children communicated more, and the mothers were providing better information and reinforcement; each, as it were, was training the other.

The investigation has been criticized, partly because little detailed information on the training program and the test results has been published, and partly because it is doubtful whether the Es and Cs were adequately matched, despite random assignment (see Page, 1972). Heber admits that much of the training might contribute directly to success on the tests employed and that, with such frequent testing, a certain amount of test sophistication would be acquired, which would be likely to help the brighter children, the Es, more than the duller Cs. He agrees, too, that we do not know how far the abilities that have been built up will transfer to other cognitive skills or school learning, though, with such a wide variety of assessments, it seems likely that they will spread to other aspects of Intelligence B.

Until the subsequent progress of the two groups has been followed through several more years, it is not possible to decide the extent to which genetic lack has been overcome by additional stimulation in infancy. My own guess is that the Es' average after another 10 years of slum living may well drop below 100. However, Heber himself interprets his work as showing that the cycle of poverty, deprivation, low IQ, and school failure is cultural rather than genetic in origin. In his view, the most crucial feature of deprivation is the ignorance among poor lower-class mothers of how to provide a good learning environment in early life, which will stimulate children's cognitive growth; and this, he believes, can now be remedied. Although his findings are of great theoretical importance, we should realize that a "total immersion" program such as he suggests is immensely costly; it would be quite impracticable to try to supply similar treatment to all deprived children.

We have, then, several studies, such as Koluchova's, Skeels', and Heber's, indicating that environmental changes can bring about some 30 or more points of increase in IQs. However, I shall argue later that there is no necessary incompatibility between these findings and the claim that genetic factors play a major part in ability differences.

REMEDIATION THROUGH IMPROVED SCHOOLING OR INTERVENTIONS

As early as the 1930s, it was asserted by some psychologists—notably the Iowa group (Wellman, Skeels, and Skodak)—that attendance at nursery school or kindergarten before the age of 5 to 6 led to significant rises in IQ. Studies yielding positive evidence were reported by Stoddard and Wellman (1940), but these were contradicted by other writers, such as

Goodenough (1940). It seemed likely that the gains associated with attendance might be largely, if not wholly, explained by the greater cooperation and sophistication of nursery school children in taking tests, or by the training effects of nursery school activities on materials very similar to those included in the tests. Selective differences between attenders and nonattenders are also extremely difficult to control. In some instances where attenders did show initial superiority to nonattenders, the difference disappeared by the end of first grade (see Kirk, 1958).

More recently, there have been a number of studies (e.g., Robinson and Robinson, 1971) showing striking IQ differences at 2½ to 4½ years between children attending day-care centers and supposedly matched controls. Bee (1974) accepts these findings, but admits that the programs of the centers were exceptionally well planned and financed. Also, we do not know how far the criticisms mentioned in the preceding paragraph were met. Kagan, Kearsley, and Zelazo (1976) report no differences in IQs at 2½ years between children reared largely in day-care centers and others reared at home. Clarke and Clarke (1976) state that there is no support in the literature for the alleged harmful effects of day nurseries, though naturally these vary considerably in quality.

The most extensive scheme for preschool education was the Head Start experiment in the 1960s, which, as described in Chapter 1, proved to be a virtual failure. Nevertheless, it did stimulate psychologists to look more closely at just what they were trying to train and to push the training back to much earlier ages than the year before entry to elementary school. In addition to Heber's elaborate investigation, a number of simpler but quite promising intervention experiments were carried out. These, likewise, worked considerably better than Head Start. Useful surveys of such programs are provided by Bronfenbrenner (1974), Gordon (1975), and Golden and Birns (1976).

There are differences of opinion as to how early preschool programs should start, but probably 2.0 years is sufficient. The crucial element is to involve the mother in the process; indeed, the main aim is to make her a better teacher of, and reactor to, her child. (Involvement of the father has been ignored by almost all investigations.) There is no one best way of bringing this about; several methods have been tried with comparable success, for example, bringing mothers to a center or sending out trained tutors to help them at home. But simply counseling or advising the mother on cognitive and linguistic stimulation seems to be ineffective. The tutor should demonstrate to her how to participate in play and other mutual activities with the infant or preschooler, how to accompany this by verbal explanation of what is happening, and how to reinforce the child's own accompanying speech. The process should not be thought of as one of instruction but as incidental learning taking place during ongoing activities in the home, and the mother is encouraged to carry this out consistently, not merely while the tutor is present.

Karnes et al.'s (1970) study of 15 children from disadvantaged backgrounds involved weekly meetings of the mothers over a 2-year period, where they were trained in methods of stimulating and interacting verbally with their children and supplied with suitable materials. Occasional visits were made to the home by the staff to ensure that the mothers were carrying out the agreed methods. The children were initially aged 12–24 months, and no pretest was given. But the Terman-Merrill IQs at the end averaged 106.3; while another group approximately matched with the experimental children averaged 90.6. Thus, a 16-point gain is claimed, though there is no evidence yet as to its permanence.

Levenstein's (1970) Mother–Child Home Program (see also Madden, Levenstein, and Levenstein, 1976) seems to be one of the most successful intervention programs; it has been applied from 1965 onward and has been replicated by other psychologists with similar results. Its theoretical background derives largely from Bernstein's elaborated code; that is, it tries to show mothers how to use language to increase childhood cognitive awareness and information processing. Bronfenbrenner (1974) has also suggested that "highly structured, cognitively oriented programs" are generally the most effective. Levenstein's method developed out of the work of Gordon (1975) in Florida, which included infants starting at 3 months, 12 months, or 24 months. The actual age of starting seemed less important than the length of time over which the program was continued, which should generally be at least two years. The actual training is carried out in the mothers' own homes by weekly visitors, either social workers or paraprofessionals. Quite a number of carefully conducted experiments along Levenstein's lines have resulted in increases on the Cattell or other scales equivalent to 10 to 20 IQ points; some experimental groups that have been followed up 3 to 4 years later indicate that the gain is maintained at least into the early elementary years. As usual, it is difficult to secure adequate control groups, but comparisons with the children's older siblings (who were reared before the intervention started) tend to show striking differences.

Guinagh and Gordon (1976) report on a follow-up of 91 children who had been included in the Florida program for 2 years before the age of 3.0. When they were tested at 6 years, their IQs averaged 7 or 8 points higher than those of a control group. And, in grades 2–4 (i.e., 6 years after the original program), they were above average in achievement and very few had been assigned to special education.

In contrasting these gains of about 10 IQ points with Skeels' improvement of over 30 points, it is worth pointing out that Skeels' intervention was lifelong, whereas the present schemes occupy only a few years. In comparison with Heber's study, there is no doubt that the home-visiting schemes are far less costly; indeed, they are probably more economical than the special classes set up under the Head Start scheme. At the same time, too much should not be expected of any short-term schemes, unless they can be followed up by better provision in the schools, as Bronfenbrenner also emphasizes.

Tizard (1974) describes several other experiments in Britain and states that child psychologists are generally agreed that the typical nursery school programs and play groups have no effect whatever on later progress, or prevention of failure, in the primary school. She is less insistent than most American writers on intervention by "education visitors" (comparable to visiting health workers) in the home. Promising work has been done with mothers who attend day-care centers with their children. But any scheme that is likely to be worthwhile must be expertly planned to focus on clearly defined skills and must be followed through into later schooling not regarded as just a single intensive stimulatory boost.

FACTORS INFLUENCING GROWTH OF INTELLIGENCE

The Primacy of Early Experience

Clarke and Clarke (1976) discuss the evidence cited here and other investigations and conclude that the widely held belief in the primacy of the first 2 years of life is unjustified. Both psychoanalytic writers and learning theorists have accepted the dogma that what happens in early infancy largely lays down basic cognitive and affective structures, which permanently influence the child's later development and even adult personality. There is a common tendency among clinical and developmental psychologists to ascribe abnormal behavior (e.g., delinquency and maladjustment) to the effects of adverse early upbringing and to ignore the possibility that later environment, or current circumstances, may be at least as influential. Clarke and Clarke claim that early learning in a particular environment (e.g., unstimulating or deprived) can be unlearned in a more propitious environment, and that what happens before the age of 2, or some other alleged critical period, is not irremediable. They further criticize those writers who stress the harmful results of separation from the mother or of upbringing in institutions. Golden and Birns (1976), in their extensive survey of infant development and intervention experiments, also conclude that early deprivation does less irreparable damage than is generally believed. The more we learn about young children, the more we are impressed by their flexibility and their extraordinary resilience to a very wide range of environmental insults.

Thus, although severe deprivation can undoubtedly retard the development of Intelligence B, it does not appear that the notion of critical periods, which Hebb inferred mainly from work on sensorimotor capacities, especially in lower animals, is applicable to human cognitive skills.

Jensen (1969) has suggested that the relation of environmental stimulation or deprivation to intellectual growth is non-linear. At the lower extreme, it may produce catastrophic effects, reducing potentially normal children to imbecile level, with IQs in the 30 to 40 range; but, above a certain minimum, further improvements produce relatively little further increase. He compares the situation to that of nutrition and diet, which, when seriously defective, obviously impair health and physical growth. But, beyond a certain threshold, further improvements in quantity and quality of diet make relatively little difference (see p. 195). I would agree that the contributions of environmental differences to human intellectual growth within the more normal range are relatively limited, and the evidence suggests maximum average improvements of 15 to 20 points or less, rather than 40 to 50 points or more. But, in view of the evidence cited in the next chapter, I would not accept the conclusion that above-average intellectual and educational environments do not continue to add to intelligence.

Perceptual Deprivation

Several writers regard perceptual deprivation, in the sense of meagerness of environment, as explaining the difference in intelligence between white middle-class children and lower-SES or ethnic minority children (see Deutsch, 1968). While this connection seems plausible, there is little positive evidence, for at the time when young children are building up such schemata as object constancy and three-dimensional space, there is likely to be plenty of the required type of stimulation, even in quite poor environments. Whether in New York ghettos or in African villages, children still interact with one another and with adults, and common observation shows that they readily make use of sticks, stones, rags, and the like as materials for manipulation and play when toy cars, dolls, or building blocks are lacking. Indeed, as mentioned earlier (p. 107), lower-class children may be over-stimulated by their noisy, crowded, environment, rather than deprived by absence of objects and people.

It may be that conceptual deprivation is more important than perceptual deprivation; that is, the lack of suitable experiences and of the elaborated language code in lower-class homes at the period when children are moving on to the operational and concrete stages of thinking. Eysenck (1973) also casts doubt on the notion of perceptual deprivation: "... the perceptual environment of Eskimo children in the Arctic is surely much more limited than that of, say, native Africans, or black children in Harlem." Yet the performance of the former children on tests of spatial and nonverbal reasoning ability certainly tends to be superior to that of the latter.

It has generally been found that children brought up over long periods in institutions are below average in intelligence and achievement (see Thompson and Grusec, 1970; Kellmer Pringle, 1975). The institutional environment is often drab and monotonous, and there is little or no opportunity to build affectional bonds with a mother or mother-substitute. Goldfarb (1947) has compared adolescents who had been institutionalized during their first 3 years of life with others who lived in foster homes over the same period and claims that the former were considerably lower in intelligence, language, and conceptual development and showed more distractibility, greater passivity, and other signs of emotional disturbance. However, Clarke and Clarke (1976) query the comparability of Goldfarb's two groups.

Particularly in institutions for mental defectives, it has been observed that inmates tend to become more retarded and even to drop in IQ as they get older. However, Tizard (1964) found that such patients, when living in small family units with a foster mother and, where possible, given the opportunity to undertake paid employment at a suitably simple level, showed much better progress. Thus, even at IQ levels of about 40 to 70, there is more modifiability with changed environment than is usually supposed. This holds, too, with young adult defectives. Clarke and Clarke (1974) studied a group of hospital patients whose mean initial IQ was 66.2. Those coming from very poor family backgrounds gained 9.7 points when retested 2 years later; those from more normal homes gained 4.1 points, which probably represents ordinary practice effect. Thus, the disadvantaged group gained 5.6 points more.

Another study of an orphan institution by Tizard and Rees (1974) showed that in foster homes where there were plenty of adult contacts, materials, and so on, the children's mean IQ at 4 years was at least average. Nevertheless, other children from the same institution who were adopted into foster homes before the age of 2 averaged some 10 points higher and were more talkative and cooperative. Thus, this investigation seems to give some support to the conventional view regarding the importance of early home environment.

Mother Separation

Deprivation involving separation from the mother has been a controversial issue. At one time, John Bowlby argued that prolonged separation during infancy produced intellectual impairment and abnormalities of emotional adjustment, in particular the "affectionless" character. However, his own follow-up study (Bowlby et al., 1956) of children hospitalized for considerable periods in infancy on account of tuberculosis yielded very little evidence of ill effects when the children were examined 5 to 10 years later. As Yarrow (1961) points out, much depends on the age at which the separation occurs, for how long it continues, and other circumstances, such as availability of substitute figures. Temporary separation through hospitalization of either mother or child does often lead to considerable anxiety, apathy, and even regression, but these characteristics generally seem to be overcome rapidly. Possibly more serious than just physical separation is the deprivation that arises when the child is rejected and either badly treated or ignored by one or both parents.[2] Clarke and Clarke (1976) reject the commonly heard opinion that "a bad mother is better than a good institution."

It is relevant here to refer to Israeli kibbutzim, where most of the caretaking of young children right from the start is in the hands of a nurse, and children spend only a few hours every day

[2] Recent discussions may be found in Rutter (1972) and Dunn (1977).

with their parents. Since nurses look after several children, they could hardly have the time to give each one a great deal of personal interaction, a fact which suggests that such interaction may not perform any very essential function. However, this type of upbringing certainly does not amount to maternal deprivation. Moreover, it appears that the system is today changing in the direction of allowing a greater role to the parents and family (see Thompson and Grusec, 1970; Bee, 1974). Schaffer (1977) suggests that kibbutz children grow up to be less dependent on a parent or parents and to show a greater sense of belonging to their peer group.

Other Sources of Isolation

There are other groups often subjected to unusual isolation, such as the aged and the severely deaf. A great many old people, especially women, are forced to live by themselves or in unstimulating residential nursing homes when they retire from employment, relatives move away, and friends die off, and they become progressively less mobile. While we have little evidence regarding the effects of such increased isolation, it is reasonable to suppose that this is a major factor in their loss of intellectual efficiency (referred to on p. 81); those who can maintain more social contacts and a richer environment are less likely to deteriorate (see Suedfeld, 1975). In the case of the deaf, the lack of hearing obviously restricts an important source of stimulation and affects their social interactions. Evidence regarding their abilities is somewhat contradictory; they certainly tend to be retarded in educational achievements and linguistic skills. Yet some psychologists, such as Furth (1971) and Oléron (1957), claim that they are very little different from normals on nonverbal tests such as Matrices, Concept Formation, or Piaget-type tasks. If they do perform poorly compared with their age peers, they tend to catch up later; in other words, there is merely a developmental delay. Lewis (1963) has discussed the issues and concludes that the severely deaf are more handicapped socially than in intellectual development; for instance, they tend to be irritable and solitary and poorly adjusted. Many, of course, have sufficient residual hearing to develop fair verbal competence, and older children can become fluent in sign-language or lip-reading, so that they are somehow able to develop their own symbols for the encoding of experience. Thus, despite the reduction in external stimulation, they can, to some extent, compensate so far as intellectual development is concerned.

SUMMARY

1   The deprivation commonly thought to handicap low-SES children is a highly complex and varied phenomenon. The effects of extreme conditions, as demonstrated in animal studies, are occasionally found among children reared with severe lack of social contacts and physical stimulation. Though such children are highly retarded, they can usually be brought up to normal by removing them to a suitable environment, even in middle childhood. Skeels' long-term follow-up study showed that the fostering of children from a very poor environment can produce IQ gains of 30 points and over.

2   The major experiment on remediation of intellectually and educationally disadvantaged children — that of Heber — resulted in consistent IQ differences between experimental and control groups of 20 to 30 points between 2 and 7 years. The experiment involved training mothers to interact more effectively with their preschool children, as well as intensive stimulation of the children's cognitive and linguistic skills. Though the program ceased on entry to elementary school, the experimental group still scores over 20 points higher than the controls.

3   Many additional intervention experiments with young children, usually involving mother– child interactions, have shown substantial, and apparently lasting, gains, though ordinary nursery or preschool classes for children below 5 are quite ineffective.

4   Clarke and Clarke argue from this and other evidence that undue credence has been given to the primacy of early experiences over later learning. It appears that Hebb's "critical period" phenomenon has little, if any, application at the human level.

5   Though the alleged effects of perceptual deprivation on mental growth are doubtful, it is probable that children reared in typical institutional surroundings tend to be somewhat retarded. Likewise, part of the decline in ability among the aged and certain psychological characteristics of deaf children may arise from restrictions of stimulation that they experience.

6   The very serious long-term effects attributed to separation of the infant from its mother have not been confirmed, either by follow-up studies or by observations of Israeli children reared in the kibbutz.

10

The Effects of Education and the Problem of Social Inequality

EFFECTS OF LENGTH OF SCHOOLING

One might anticipate that the mental stimulation most children get at school would be as important an influence as that of the home in the development of their intelligence from 5–6 years onward. In fact, the research findings are very puzzling, for, while sheer quantity of schooling — the number of years children or students stay on in school or college — seems to affect strongly their adult ability level and achievement, the quality or kind of schooling apparently makes very little consistent difference. Some scattered cross-cultural evidence suggests that complete absence of schooling seriously retards mental growth. The work of Bruner et al. (1966) in developing countries indicated that children who received even poor-quality education performed better on Piaget-type tests than those who got none. I have cited a well-controlled study by Ramphal of Indian children in South Africa (see Vernon, 1969a). Many of these were unable to obtain entry to school till later than the normal age because of the shortages of schools and teachers (*not* because they were lower in ability). The investigation showed that lack of schooling during ages 7 to 9 brought about a retardation in mental growth (as measured by the Matrices, or by verbal tests) equivalent to 5 IQ points a year.

Much earlier, Gordon's (1923) investigation of canal-boat and gypsy children (which was mentioned in Chapter 1) pointed in the same direction. Weil (1958), in Brazil, gave a test similar to the Raven Matrices to a wide range of unschooled peasants and found no improvement in performance with age beyond 6 years.

During World War II, education in Holland was severely disrupted by the German occupation; De Groot (1951) was able to show, by postwar tests, that this had resulted in an average IQ drop of approximately 7 points. There is also evidence (cited by Jencks et al., 1972) that children tend to drop appreciably in ability over the long summer holiday period, though this effect is more marked among low-SES and black children than among white middle-class children.

In Chapter 5, I pointed out that intellectual growth tends to continue as long as students continue their schooling, or enter jobs that "use their brains." When these conditions are lacking, the age at which they reach maximum ability and start to decline occur earlier. Husén (1951), in Sweden, found that Army recruits tested at 20 years averaged 12 points higher in IQ if they had completed secondary schooling and matriculation than those who had had no secondary schooling. Their 10-year IQs were used as controls; in other words, the finding was not due to the initially brighter students staying on longer. Similar results were obtained by Lorge (1945) in the United States. Jencks interprets Husén and Lorge's findings as equivalent to a rise of about 2½ IQ points for each additional year of schooling, though he casts some doubts on the adequacy of controlling for initial differences in ability.

I have found (Vernon, 1957b) that the type or conditions of secondary schooling made a difference. At 11 years, all the boys in a large city in Britain were tested, and the brightest and most able ones proceeded to secondary grammar schools, which involve a strenuous academic curriculum; the average and duller students went to secondary modern schools, where there was less pressure and usually less favorable attitudes to schooling. The group was retested for verbal IQ 3 years later and, after controlling for initial IQ differences, the grammar school group averaged 7 points higher than the modern school boys. The difference between students in the best grammar school and the poorest modern school amounted to 12 points. However, the more rapid progress of the more stimulated students should not be attributed to type of schooling alone; naturally, those in the better schools tended to come more often from homes where there were more favorable attitudes and pressure toward academic achievement. In any case, the result shows that environmental factors can produce considerable differences over the 11- to 14-year age range, thus contradicting Bloom's statement that very little change occurs in IQs from about 13 to 17 years (see p. 76).

There are ample U.S. statistics to prove that length of secondary and tertiary education correlates highly both with adult intelligence and with occupational level and income achieved. But the interpretation of this finding is difficult, since it is obvious that employers normally require their employees to have certain educational credentials. For example, a university expects its professors to hold a Ph.D., but this does not prove that a person without this educational qualification might not be an excellent university teacher. As Jencks points out, the educational system largely exists to act as a selection and certifying agency; and it is natural that persons with higher IQs or with socioeconomic advantages, should progress further up the educational ladder. But this does not prove that more education, or better education, actually has any direct effects on success.[1]

ATTEMPTS TO REDUCE SCHOOL FAILURE AND SOCIAL INEQUITY BY IMPROVED EDUCATION

The failure of Head Start and other compensatory educational programs, on which several billion dollars of federal funds were spent, was described in Chapter 1; in Chapter 9, the similar ineffectiveness of nursery school programs for increasing achievement in the elementary school was pointed out.[2] It is true that we lack an adequate criterion for the skills such programs are supposed to train and that failure to raise the IQ should not be taken to mean that nothing has been affected. The sponsors of the Head Start schemes had, indeed, set themselves an almost impossible task. Consider, for instance, a 5½-year-old girl with IQ 75. She will normally gain 0.375 Mental Age years in the next 6 months. But if one aimed to push her up to IQ 85, so that she would be better fitted to learn in first grade, she would have to gain 1 year of M.A. in the 6 months, or more than twice as much as the normal gain. Another reason for criticizing the use of in-

---

[1] No attempt will be made here to sketch current investigations by sociologists and economists into the effects of education, family background, and the like on subsequent earnings—for instance, the work of J. Mincer, W. H. Sewell, R. M. Hauser, and P. Taubman. A useful review of three recent books has been published by Bowman (1976).

[2] But see footnote, p. 12.

telligence tests as criteria for improvement is that the items for these tests were chosen partly because the responses are fairly stable and unlikely to be modified much by the context in which testing takes place or by recent learning experiences.

A further defect of the compensatory schemes is that most of them provide programs similar to those of the typical nursery school or kindergarten for middle-class children, that is, for children who seldom have language problems when they first attend school. There was little attempt to analyze just what sort of remediation was appropriate to lower-class or minority group children. This probably explains why the more highly structured approaches like Bereiter's, which did not aim to improve general intelligence, were more successful. However, the advantages even of this type of program may be only temporary. Miller and Dyer (1975) compared 14 nursery schools for 4-year-olds that were following one of four contrasted approaches: Bereiter-Engelmann, Peabody Early Intervention, Montessori, and "traditional" Head Start. In all, 214 children were involved; a control group consisted of 34 children from moderately disadvantaged homes, mostly black. The first two, relatively structured, approaches seemed to bring about the highest rises in Binet IQs and school achievement when the children were tested at the end of 1 year's training. But, when the children were retested 3 years later (at the end of second grade), there were no significant differences between the groups in ability or personality tests and ratings, though, on the whole, the Montessori children were the most successful and the Bereiter children had dropped back 11½ IQ points.

Hunt and Kirk (1971) conclude that the original Head Start scheme was initiated before any adequate technology of early childhood education had evolved; and it is true that the later attempts, with younger children, outlined in Chapter 9, seem more promising.

However, an even greater shock to those who believe that improved education and greater equality of educational provision would help to close the gap between disadvantaged and advantaged children was dealt by the famous Coleman Report (Coleman et al., 1966). It revealed a lack of effectiveness of higher-quality over poorer-quality schooling so surprising that the data and findings were critically evaluated by Mosteller and Moynihan in 1972, with almost complete confirmation of the original conclusions. Differences between schools, it seems, have quite negligible effects on achievement compared with differences between home backgrounds. No particular educational resource, such as curricular reform, desegregation, district expenditure on schools, not even teacher qualifications and experience, seem to have any consistently significant effect on achievement levels. When students at one school achieve better mean scores than those at another, this is attributable to the abilities and the attitudes that the students bring with them rather than to more effective instruction. Another incidental, but important, finding was that the quality of schooling available to blacks, which has so often been blamed for their low scholastic achievement, was by now as good as that provided for whites in most parts of the country. Note that this report, and other studies that will be referred to below, were almost wholly concerned with the scores on achievement tests; they tell us nothing further regarding effects on IQ or other intellectual capacities.

Jencks et al. (1972) made use of an additional source of evidence, namely the gains in achievement on Project Talent tests between ninth- and twelfth-grade classes. Here, again, no association was found between smaller or larger gains and differences between schools. Jencks did find some evidence of differences in quality and effectiveness between elementary schools, but these were generally unstable from one year to another. He concluded that no general educational policy introduced by a school board is likely to have any effect on raising achievement in that board's schools. Nor would eliminating the remaining differences between schools do anything to make adults more equal in economic status and income.

A very clear demonstration of the lack of effect of type of schooling on children was provided by the Office of Economic Opportunity's (1972) report on "performance contracting." Special programs were instituted in 18 school systems in different parts of the United States, covering 25,000 students, at an overall cost of $6 million. These programs were planned by experts making use of up-to-date knowledge of educational psychology and technology, and the contractors genuinely believed that they were capable of bringing about improved achievement. Motivating the children was stressed, and rewards were given to those who achieved the best; audio-visual aids and teaching machines were freely used; the numbers of staff members were increased to allow for more individual attention. And yet no improvement beyond that of control schools in general reading and mathematical skills occurred over the 6 months of the trial programs. An interesting comment made by Eysenck (1973) is that the O.E.O. investigation, like other similar studies, made the mistake of assuming that all children are alike and that all will react in the same way to a particular method—a mistake classroom teachers are less likely to make. He is referring particularly to differences in personality types between different pupils; but the same applies, of course, to differences in ability levels, attitudes, and interests. At the same time, we must remember that many educational researchers have attempted to isolate ATIs — Aptitude Treatment Interactions[3] — with remarkably little success.

However, these negative findings appear to apply much more to schools in the United States than to those in most other countries. A series of comparative studies has been carried out by the International Educational Achievement Project, under the chairmanship of T. Husén (1967). Tests in each of the main school subjects were constructed to cover the instruction given in both elementary and secondary schools and applied to, as far as possible, representative samples of students in from 8 to 21 countries.

In most of the countries, differences in achievement were attributable largely to differences in the initial abilities of the children and their home backgrounds. There were differences associated with different types of educational organization in the various countries (e.g., the proportion of students admitted to higher secondary education), or with the amount of instruction given in the particular subject, that is, the opportunity to learn. However, in most countries, a number of school factors gave significant correlations with achievement — for instance, size of class and school, length of school week, expenditure per student, qualifications of teachers. But there was little consistency in the effects of such factors across subjects, student ages, or countries. For example, in exploring achievement in the native language, Thorndike (1973b) observed that many of the factors commonly assumed to bring about improvements, such as smaller classes, employment of counselors or psychologists, and the like, gave negative correlations with achievement. As he points out, this association might arise because classes tend to be smaller and counselors more numerous in schools for backward or maladjusted children. When the progressive measures do appear to favor achievement, it is usually because better qualified pupils are more likely to gain entry to the more favored schools.

The results obtained by Husén and his collaborators are difficult to interpret, since the correlations cannot readily show the direction of causation. Deprived home conditions and poor intellectual development among the children are usually associ-

[3] An Aptitude Treatment Interaction is based on a statistical analysis of test scores aiming to show that children with different aptitudes are better taught by different methods of instruction. See page 183 for further discussion.

ated with inferior schooling. Thus, the biggest difference on most of the tests was that between Western-type countries and less developed countries such as Chile, Iran, and India. But who is to say which of the environmental differences between these groups of countries is to be regarded as primary? Another point is that the correlation between various conditions and the mean scores for each country are usually quite different from correlations within countries. The lack of any clear-cut effects of school differences probably arises because so many complex factors, which may well differ from one country to another, are involved, and we have made little progress in sorting out the most crucial ones.

Nevertheless, some rather consistent differences between schools have been reported in the United Kingdom, including my own study (Vernon, 1975b) mentioned above (p. 145). For example, Douglas (1964) found that some primary schools in England regularly obtained higher pass-rates in the 11-plus examination than others did, even when SES differences were allowed for. But one should remember the coarseness of current indices of SES (in this instance, father's job plus parents' education). Parents are also apt to differ in the strength of their aspirations for high achievement in their children and in the amount of stimulation they provide at home. Thus, it might well be that the parents who are particularly ambitious, as well as being in upper-SES brackets, would be more apt to send their children to such schools with a high reputation for academic success and so provide these schools with a superior sample of pupils.

SOME UNFOUNDED BELIEFS ABOUT EDUCATION

The size of class, or teacher–pupil ratio, is one of the commonest educational "myths." Most teachers, and many parents and administrators, believe that much better instruction could be given if teachers had fewer children to cope with at a time. Several researches in England have, in fact, found no difference, or even a slight advantage to larger classes, the most recent study being that of Davie, Butler, and Goldstein (1972). The question is a complex one, since there is a tendency for more modern urban schools to be relatively large, and to have the best qualified staff and also larger classes, whereas smaller classes tend to be found more often in small, older, schools, often in rural areas. In their follow-up of 16,000 children at the age of 7, Davie and his colleagues tried to allow for such extraneous factors by multiple regression, and still found slightly higher scores in larger classes on a test of reading, though this did not amount to more than 3 months of Reading Age. Actually, sex differences—the average superiority of girls to boys—produced about twice as great an effect.[4] This finding does not, of course, necessarily apply to highly disturbed or physically handicapped children, where much more individual attention is essential, and classes more often have around 10 children than 30. Nor would we deny that teachers would find classes of, say, 20, less of a strain to handle than classes of 30 and over. But the available evidence definitely contradicts the view that children in smaller classes learn better than those in large classes.

Another hotly contested issue is whether homogeneously grouped, or tracked, classes produce better results than heterogeneous ones. The arguments were outlined in Chapter 2, and it was shown that, although tracking may have some advantages in allowing bright children to progress more rapidly, it also tends to undermine seriously the morale of duller groups. Obviously, homogeneous grouping must be introduced at some stage before tertiary education starts, but there is little agreement as to when. Moreover, the whole issue is complicated by sociopolitical attitudes regarding the desirability or undesirability of segregating by ability, so that no simple answer regarding its educational effectiveness can be given.

One might well expect to find differences between schools that are more traditional or formal and those that are more progressive and up-to-date. But such a dimension is far from clear-cut, and these differing school climates may take very varying forms according to the particular principal, staff, and parents concerned. Moreover, the results would vary with the criterion. If standardized tests of achievement are used, the more formal schools would very likely do better; with more broadly ranging criteria—as in the famous New York Eight-Year Study (Aikin, 1942)—the students from more progressive schools do show an advantage over those from more formal schools on a variety of tests. In an investigation of Canadian elementary schools, Bell, Zipursky, and Switzer (1976) compared children attending formal schools with others in informal, open-area schools. At the end of third grade, the formal children were approximately half

---

[4]A further follow-up of this group to 11 years has been completed, yielding results generally parallel to those obtained at 7; but it has not been published at the time of writing (see Kellmer Pringle, 1975).

a year superior in vocabulary and problem solving. However, Cattell's Children's Personality Questionnaire, given in grade 4, showed that the informal children were more mature, adventurous, relaxed, less anxious, and better leaders.

An investigation that has received a great deal of publicity in England is that by Bennett et al. (1976). They claim to have shown that achievement was significantly higher at junior 4 (or sixth grade) level in reading, mathematics, and English in 12 classes taught by more formal teachers than in 13 classes taught by informal teachers. There were also 12 classes classified as mixed, where teachers showed varying approaches. (These showed even smaller differences.) However, critics such as Gray and Satterly (1976) point out that the gains were quite small and sometimes of dubious significance; that the children in formal classes would naturally have more experience with standardized tests; and that the teachers were classified on the basis of their answers to 19 questions regarding their educational practices, not on the basis of observed behavior.

Most parents and teachers will probably still find it difficult to accept the proposition that some schools are not "better" than others, in the sense of producing higher grades or stimulating (or inhibiting) their pupils' intellectual growth. I am not saying that schooling has no effects. All children within a given culture tend to receive a fairly standardized schooling, and the amount of this certainly does affect their intellectual development. What the American researches do show is that differences in type, or methods, of education between different schools or groups of schools bring about very little consistent difference in achievement, except insofar as they draw on pupils with different intelligence and home background. Any one school may, of course, have some exceptionally able and inspiring teachers who stimulate better than usual achievement, conceptual development, and thinking skills in at least some of their students; however, other students may be put off by them. Moreover, all students meet many teachers in the course of their school careers. Thus, the effects of some particular person, educational resource, or curricular change on average performance may be quite small. Furthermore, any research is hampered by the difficulty of finding criteria on which a large number of schools can be graded, other than just standardized achievement and intelligence tests.

We must bear in mind, too, that, by the time children arrive at school, at about age 5 or 6, their capacity for future learning has already been largely fixed by the home background in which they have been reared. Hence, it is usually found that variations in achievement depend far more on differences in SES and IQ that the students bring with them than on school differences. I would also argue that a good deal of the fairly high stability in intelligence and achievement scores that we find in most children's performance should be attributed more to their ingrained habits of study and attitudes to schooling than to the constancy of their genetic potential for mental growth.

A further very important point is that any new resource or method is likely to have greater effects on the already more intelligent and those with favorable motivation to learn than it is on the relatively disadvantaged. In other words, the initially superior tend to benefit most. Take, for example, the contrast among schools that succeed in introducing a good deal of individualization of instruction—for example, using the Open Plan effectively to let all students progress more nearly at their own pace. Such measures are much more likely to benefit intelligent middleclass children than below-average working-class children, because the former have already been trained at home in self-directed, autonomous activities. The latter children are more likely to flounder because they are more used to being directed by adults, and they usually work better with peers who are all doing the same thing.

We should recall here Piaget's view that conceptual development and thinking skills depend more on the child's own exploration and discovery, much of which takes place at home or in leisure activities, than they do on what is taught at school. He claims that direct instruction in verbalized concepts and skills is relatively ineffective in extending a child's understanding or capacity to use concrete and formal operations. Here, too, the more intelligent and advantaged children are more likely to explore and discover than the less intelligent and deprived children.

A point that is habitually ignored by writers who believe that the home and school environments entirely determine children's intellectual growth is that, to a large extent, children fashion or shape their own environments. Those with favorable genes and early development are more likely to explore and experiment and to seek stimulation by questioning adults or from books, toys, and the like; whereas initially dull children are more often passive and restricted in their interests. Again, the parents of the former, who realize their potentialities, are more likely to provide opportunities, together with more extended or higher quality education. Thus, it is true not only that education stimulates ability but also that high ability provokes better education (see p. 181).

MASTERY LEARNING

A new approach to individual differences and school learning has been put forward by B. S. Bloom. The basic idea was proposed by J. B. Carroll in 1963, but most of the theory and applications have been developed by Bloom (1976) and Block (1974). These writers accept the existence of wide individual differences in rate of learning and in school achievements, but they reject the conventional explanations that the differences are due either to inborn ability or to home environment, or both. Such explanations provide a useful scapegoat for the ineffectiveness of a great deal of school teaching. The authors believe that the range of such differences can be greatly reduced by changes in the objectives and methods of instruction and evaluation in schools. At present, o ly about one-fifth of school pupils, on the average, reach a reasonable mastery of the subjects they are taught, but Bloom and Block claim that this can be raised to four-fifths without expenditure of more than about 10–20 percent of additional learning time. At present, most schools are, to a large extent, creating the wide range of differences by paying insufficient attention to the difficulties experienced by some incoming pupils; and the process is cumulative—the initially weaker ones get left more and more behind. The main features of mastery learning are as follows:

1 The teachers of a particular subject in a particular grade, either individually or in collaboration, draw up a clear formulation of the basic objectives of their course and divide this up into a series of subtopics or units, each likely to require perhaps 2 weeks or so of instruction and assessment. Note that, although there is much in common between Glaser's approach (p. 35) and Bloom's, there are also some crucial differences. Glaser aims to provide any teacher with all the materials required for individualized learning. But Bloom's scheme is designed for teaching a class as a group, and he expects teachers, individually or in collaboration, to work out their own objectives and materials.

2 Also needed are a series of "formative" tests to show proficiency at each stage in the unit, and a final overall or "summative" test. Also, "correctives" must be prepared; that is, additional and easier exercises for those who fail to reach a chosen criterion of success on any test. It is commonly demanded that 85 percent of test items should be answered correctly. All tests are criterion-referenced; that is, pupils are scored according to the specific skills acquired not in terms of competitive marks or grades (see p. 36).

3 The pupils who are about to start on the unit probably differ considerably in "entry characteristics," both cognitive (prerequisite knowledge or skill) and affective (positive or negative self-concepts and attitudes to the school subject, etc.). But generalized predictors such as intelligence tests are less useful in revealing adequate or inadequate entry behaviors than a test designed to show the extent of prior knowledge. The teacher attempts to bring the weaker students up to the same level as the majority by some preliminary teaching or tutoring and by restructuring the instruction in the early stages.

4 After each stage has been covered, a formative test gives the teacher feedback regarding which pupils have failed and what their difficulties are. Such pupils are provided with correctives, preferably in out-of-class time or possibly by arranging for the more able pupils to tutor the less able.

5 Once the more backward children find that they *can* achieve success, their attitudes change and they develop better habits of attention and studying, so that their entry characteristics for the next stage or unit improve, and the range of differences in the class is further reduced.

Bloom admits that a small percentage of severely retarded or maladjusted children cannot be expected to succeed with this plan. A number of attempts have been made to validate Bloom's claims for the effectiveness of his scheme, though, as so often happens in research on teaching methods, the results fail to give definitive answers. Many of the studies were small-scale ones, where the Hawthorne effect (see Glossary) may well have operated. Though the results are generally favorable, they are apt to be irregular and less strongly positive than Bloom expected. However, mastery learning is being introduced on a large scale in certain school districts of the United States and abroad (in South Korea).

Generally with mastery learning, the proportion of pupils reaching the criterion scores is increased, though the number is more likely to double than to increase four times. There is also quite strong evidence of the cumulative effect on student performance when a whole series of units or tasks are studied through mastery learning. On the other hand, studies of retention (i.e., summative testing two weeks or more later), of transfer of learning, and of personality or attitude change, are even more patchy.

In general, the additional time required to teach duller children seems likely to be considerably greater than Bloom's 10–20 percent. Bloom does not make clear where this extra time is to come from. If it involves work outside school hours, the weaker students are the least likely to have the necessary motivation. The use of coaching by brighter students may well be effective and make for good class spirit, but it also means that the brighter pupils use time that could have been better spent on enrichment activities, and they have to slow down their progress (to the pace of the weaker pupils) to an even greater extent than in ordinary class instruction.

Bloom and Block admit that the mastery approach works best with school subjects like mathematics and introductory science and that it would be more difficult to apply to arts subjects. One wonders also if the successful experiments have not usually been conducted by specially trained and interested teachers, and whether the bulk of average or poorer teachers are capable of making the necessary adjustments, let alone of developing their own materials. Another weakness is that experimental checks, and applications of mastery learning, have been carried out primarily in middle-class or lower-middle-class schools; there might be much more difficulty with lower-working-class children.

Nevertheless, the positive success of mastery learning does open up the possibility of more efficient instruction and learning than are currently regarded as adequate by educators and the general public. The wider implication is that the Intelligence B which pupils bring with them on entering school may be less crucial for learning than most psychologists believe. Bloom claims that, with mastery learning, the correlations between summative achievement and IQ drop from about 0.70 to 0.50. But the results so far obtained are insufficiently convincing to justify as much optimism as Bloom expresses. What we can reasonably hope is that the implementation of his plan would, to some extent, mitigate the problems of individual differences between children, but not abolish them.

CHILD UPBRINGING
AND SOCIAL INEQUALITY

The topics of this and the two preceding chapters raise highly controversial sociopolitical and ethical issues. As already mentioned, Labov, Ginsburg, Bowles, and Gintis, and many other critics, resent any view suggesting that the language or mental competence of working-class or ethnic-minority children are inferior to those of white middle-class children. Even when such differences are attributed by a psychologist to poverty and deprived conditions of upbringing (rather than to genetic differences), they would say that the psychologist is ethnocentrically assuming that we should try to eliminate such deficits by intervention programs; that is, trying to make the lower-class child as much like the middle-class as possible. Such intervention interferes not merely with the speech dialects of underprivileged families but, as Bernstein pointed out, with their values.

What right have we to assume that middle-class intelligence, manners, and morals are superior? To some extent, the psychologist might argue from history that white middle-class intelligence and values have been largely responsible for the growth of Western civilization, science, and technology. Children who, for any reason, are retarded at school are not merely falling below some quite arbitrary or artificial standards set by the middle class. When they fall much below average IQ, it is hardly possible that they can ever reach Piaget's formal operational type of thinking. This, to me at least, is a real deficit, since they usually want to attain the same living standards as those of the more advantaged middle-class families but are prevented from doing so by their less effective thinking skills. Yet, at the same time, one must recognize that Western civilization has many undesirable features and, according to the critics, its very existence rests largely on a hierarchical social system in which the majority of the population is relegated to an inferior status in order to support the successful and privileged middle- and upper-class minorities. Thus psychologists, with their tests and attempts at intervening, are accused of imputing retardation and educational and vocational failure to deficiencies in lower-class genes or in family rearing when it is the organization of Western society and its educational system that are at fault.

Ginsburg's book *The Myth of the Deprived Child* (1972) carries this argument further, stating that psychologists regard children as passive recipients of stimulation. Compensatory education programs assume that they can all be brought up to the conventional social norms by additional training and reinforcement. This runs counter to Piaget's view that children are active in shaping their growth, they are not just shaped by environment. Schools fail to recognize that children are capable of organizing their own learning, and they rely mainly on verbal instruction, despite Piaget's demonstration of the inferiority of this approach to practical discovery. Further, the schools disregard or repress the natural desire of children for social interaction.

However, as I pointed out earlier, a fuller application of Piagetian psychology would probably do most to help the already privileged.

Bernstein (1971) similarly criticizes compensatory education for ignoring the fact that a large proportion of the working-class population has never been offered an adequate education. Their children are regarded as inferior when they arrive at school, and no attempt is made by the teacher to understand their habitual language code. However, their speech and their culture are just as valid and significant as those of middle-class children.

Though I accept the "deficit" notion of retardation in children, I would certainly agree that the above criticisms should be taken seriously. Every psychologist's basic assumptions, theories, methods, and goals are apt to be biased, often unwittingly, by the particular culture in which he or she has grown up. The same is just as true of politically radical psychologists as it is of the more traditional majority, or of those accused of racist and fascist tendencies. But I do not accept the implication that any research undertaken by psychologists is thereby invalidated. To me, such questions of social and political reform are not really the psychologist's business per se; though, of course, as citizens, psychologists are entitled to advocate what they think best. It is their job to supply scientific data, collected as far as possible without prejudice and with due regard to the dangers, that will help the reformer and the politician to make wiser decisions.

Let us admit that the constructs of intelligence, "good" home environment, schooling, and compensatory education or intervention have been and still are unduly identified with the goals of the middle and upper classes — that is, with the cultural norms most psychologists themselves adhere to — and that there is a great deal of worth in the values of the poorer classes that researchers are apt to ignore or downgrade. The elaborated code and the attitudes of the middle class imply a certain distancing from, and rejection of, direct experience. The lower classes are, to a greater extent, more open to such experience; they are more concrete and practical, more self-reliant in many ways, more reactive and loyal to their families and peer groups. It should be possible to encourage and build on such attitudes as alternatives rather than as inferior to those of the middle class, though, unfortunately, this might not help much in the development of cognitive skills. Up till the industrial revolution, most children's education was carried out at home or in the community, and it was continuous with job training. Nowadays, however, we supply a "monocultural" educational system for all, which implies condemning the majority to failure, or only very moderate success, in a particular kind of abstract thinking. Perhaps the Chinese, the Soviet, and the Israeli experiments have a good deal to teach us about alternative routes to a better adjusted, less divisive and inequitable, society. (It should be realized, however, that Soviet education is at least as formal and abstract as Western education, even though Soviet schools do seem better at motivating and instructing their students.)

I have mentioned some of Jencks' contributions earlier and will describe his (1972) work on inequality more fully in Chapter 12. He argues that, in view of the differences between children and their homes, it is impossible to bring about equality of educational outcomes for all, though the provision of compensatory or special education does, to some extent, help the most handicapped. But any general improvements that we try to bring about in education are more likely to widen the gap between the more able and the more retarded.

A markedly different view is taken by Husén (1972), who writes from a consistently rational left-wing position. He admits that, under the present system, even when we try to provide equality of educational opportunity by family allowances, comprehensive rather than elitist education, scholarships, and the like, lower-class children will continue to achieve less well, on the average, on intelligence tests and scholastic examinations. He concludes that not only must we provide at least as good educational facilities for such children to make up for the handicaps of their upbringing, but we also must be willing to spend considerably more on educational reforms, such as compensatory schooling, remedial clinics, greater individualization, and so on. In other words, inequality should be imposed in the opposite direction in order to provide equality.[5] Bloom's mastery learning, likewise, aims to provide equality of outcome rather than just equality of opportunity, by giving more time and trouble to help-

[5] See also the contributions of Husén, S. M. Miller, and others to Ashline, Pezzullo, and Norris (1976).

There are, of course, several more radical revisionists, who follow the Marxist line in interpreting educational history. Thus, Bowles, Gintis, Karier, and others regard the liberal-democratic trend in American education (e.g., from Dewey onward) as a consciously devised and imposed instrument for reinforcing the capitalist class structure. But, in an extensive reivew, Ravich (1977) points out that these critics ignore or distort the evidence that liberal policies have brought about some desirable progress. Poverty and inequality have obviously not been banished, but they have been reduced; the income gap between black and white families has diminished; and the proportion of blacks receiving higher education has nearly caught up with that of whites.

ing the less able. Husén's solution seems even more radical, since it implies that children from more privileged homes should be accorded poorer facilities, and an inferior education, in order to promote greater social justice. Here, too, I cannot agree that we should deliberately downgrade those children and students who are likely (with a reasonable education) to make the major contributions to the technology, cultural achievements, and leadership, of the next generation. It is obvious that such conflicting positions can be argued ad infinitum; hence, my adherence to the view that they are not the psychologist's business.

SUMMARY

1   We might expect schooling to have as strong an influence on children's intellectual development as home background does. This is confirmed to some extent by cross-cultural studies indicating retarded development of intelligence when schooling is grossly deficient; and by studies in the United States, Sweden, and Britain showing rises in IQ the greater the quantity and the better the quality of secondary schooling.

2   However, the common finding of superior vocational success the greater the length of schooling may be spurious insofar as superior jobs generally demand superior educational credentials.

3   The ineffectiveness of compensatory educational programs, such as Head Start, in improving IQ and achievement may have been due partly to poorly chosen objectives and methods and to the lack of adequate criteria for evaluation.

4   The Coleman Report and several other large-scale studies have indicated that educational policies and resources or types of schooling have virtually negligible results compared with the effects of the home backgrounds of students and their childhood IQs. Sometimes apparently favorable measures actually show negative effects, presumably because they are provided more often to schools for disadvantaged students.

5   It is always difficult to isolate the effects of any particular curricular or policy change and, since its application will vary from school to school, much depends on the nature of the sample, the criteria employed, and other poorly controlled conditions. For example, "performance contracting," differences in size of classes, homogeneous versus heterogeneous grouping, progressive versus traditional approaches, and so on, have all given conflicting or negligible results.

6   Studies by Bloom and Block of mastery learning have succeeded in showing that the range of individual differences within a typical school grade can be considerably reduced by the application of Bloom's principles. This means that the intelligence and home background advantages or disadvantages of pupils and the cumulative retardation so often occurring among duller or deprived pupils can, to some extent, be overcome. But several limitations to Bloom's approach are pointed out.

7   A number of psychologists reject the notion of intellectual inferiority as resulting either from genetic differences or from deprivation in early upbringing. They criticize attempts to remediate such retardation by programs which, basically, involve trying to train lower-class children in middle-class skills and values. In their view, backwardness is being ascribed to genetic or environmental deficits in the child and his or her family rather than to the society and the educational system underlying the social class hierarchy. I admit the liability of psychological theories and methods to such cultural bias, but I reject the implication that psychologists as such should be committed to, or against, political reform.

III

Genetic Influences on Individual Differences in Intelligence

11

Introduction to Heritability Analysis: Twin Studies

The early work of geneticists on heredity in animals and plants dealt mainly with simple physical attributes that depended on the operation of particular genes and followed the classical Mendelian principles. That is, the likelihood of the appearance of such characteristics in the offspring could be predicted from the characteristics of the parents and grandparents. Only rather rarely do we find such simple examples of inheritance in humans—for example, blue eye color, color blindness, hemophilia, inability to digest milk or to taste phenylthiocarbamide, blood or serological groups, and some forms of pathological mental deficiency. Thus, PKU (phenylketonuria) is an inborn gene anomaly leading to defects of metabolism that are associated with damage to the brain; the children's IQs are usually under 50 unless their diet is suitably corrected. Mongolism (Down's syndrome), amaurotic idiocy, and numerous other rare syndromes are also attributed to major gene defects (see Lerner and Libby, 1976). Indeed, Gibson (1975) points out that Down's syndrome provides the best example of a specified chromosomal anomaly producing a rather consistent pattern of cognitive defects, though the degree of intellectual deficit shows wide variations.

Genes are no longer regarded as comparable to beads on a chromosome chain. Rather, we think of genetic information as coded on certain section of the DNA molecule, somewhat like the information on computer tapes. But it is still correct to think

Genetic Influences on Individual Differences

of genes as the fundamental particles of heredity, each gene being responsible for the production of a particular protein (see Loehlin, Lindzey, and Spuhler, 1975).

However, most human attributes in which we are interested, such as height or intelligence, are continuous rather than discrete variables. Insofar as they are genetic, they result from the cumulative and combined effects of large numbers of genes situated in different chromosomal loci. Since all individuals carry a very large number of genes on their 46 chromosomes, almost infinite genetic diversity is possible. In addition, many genes are polymorphic; that is, they have alternative expressions, known as alleles. This multifactorial or polygenetic type of inheritance would be expected to yield normally distributed traits. R. A. Fisher and his followers have shown that Mendelian principles can be extended to continuously graded characteristics and that the combination of genetic and other determinants can be studied by analysis of variance. But though they have formulated techniques for specifying the numbers of genes involved and their dominance, we are currently not in a position to identify specific gene frequencies or locations in individuals, or in groups such as races. Thus, the genotype, or pattern of genes, inherited by an offspring represents a random assortment of the parental genes, with an expected average of 50 percent from each parent.

I have already pointed out (Chapter 1) that the phenotype — that is, the observed characteristics of the individual, such as measurable intelligence — is never attributable to the genes alone. The genes realize their potentialities only insofar as the individual develops in an appropriate environment, and their effects can differ considerably in different environments. In other words, the phenotype depends on the interaction between genotype — the individual's overall gene pattern — and environmental conditions.

interaction

KINSHIP CORRELATIONS

The proportions of genes underlying intelligence that are held in common by two relatives enable us to predict the correlations between their IQs (assuming that there is no unreliability or errors of measurement, and no dominance or other sources of distortion). Identical twins, or monozygotes (MZ), have identical genes; hence, the intraclass correlation should be 1.0 if intelligence is determined wholly by heredity; and the extent to which the coefficient falls below 1.0 can plausibly be attributed to differences in their pre- and postnatal conditions, their upbringing or other environmental influences, or the imperfect statistical reliability of any test results. Likewise, the expected correlation, on genetic theory, between siblings or fraternal (dizygotic, or DZ) twins, or between one parent and one offspring, should be 0.50. The correlation between the offspring's intelligence and the average intelligence of both parents—referred to as the mid-parent—should be the square root of 0.50, namely 0.71.[1] Finally, the correlation between unrelated children, or between foster parent and adopted children, should be zero, and any departures from this prediction can generally be attributed to environmental influences, as when the mental growth of adoptees is affected by the type of foster home in which they are reared or the ability level of the foster parents.

Insofar as there are strong grounds for believing that such kinship resemblances are affected by dominance (which tends to reduce the correlations) and assortative mating (which tends to increase them), Burt and Howard (1956) have worked out a series of corrected figures, which appear in Table 11.1. Kamin (1974) objects that such corrections are largely guesswork and that other biometrical geneticists, employing different assumptions, might well arrive at somewhat different figures. However, Burt's are probably the best estimates we have and are likely to be better than the uncorrected genetic predictions of 1.0, 0.5, 0.25, and so on.

Table 11.1 lists the median correlations from some 52 investigations collected by Erlenmeyer-Kimling and Jarvik (1963). These have been amended to some extent on the basis of additional studies by Burt (Jarvik and Erlenmeyer-Kimling, 1967). Many critics have pointed out that the "EKJ" figures have various weaknesses, though they have been reproduced in numerous books and articles (including Jensen's 1969 article). There is a great deal of variability between the results of different studies of each kinship group, partly reflecting the tests used (e.g., group versus individual) and their unreliability, and partly sampling biases such as restricted range (which tends to lower any correlations). Some are corrected for such errors, others not.[2] Certain other published studies have not been included, because although the authors no doubt had their reasons for acceptance or

[1] The above figures assume that mating is random (nonassortative) and that there are no nonadditive gene effects (see Chapter 12).

[2] The parent–offspring (PO) correlations include some studies where the mid-parent correlation was used, and this would spuriously boost the results. On the other hand, all studies would involve parents of quite a wide age range, and almost all tests are inadequately standardized for age differences; these factors, then, would tend to attenuate any PO correlations. A more thorough survey of 17 reputable studies of PO resemblance by McAskie and Clarke (1976) revealed a range of variation from 0.80 to 0.05!

TABLE 11.1
Erlenmeyer-Kimling and Jarvik's, and Jensen's,
Median Correlations for Different Kinships

Kinship relation	Number of studies	Median r* obtained	Genetic expectation	Burt's corrected expectation
Monozygotic twins reared together (MZT)	14	0.87	1.00	1.00
Monozygotic twins reared apart (MZA)	4	0.75	1.00	1.00
Dizygotic like-sex twins reared together (DZT)	11	0.56	0.50	0.54
Dizygotic unlike-sex twins reared together (DZT)	9	0.49	0.50	0.50
Full siblings reared together (FST)	36	0.55	0.50	0.52
Siblings reared apart (FSA)	3	0.47	0.50	0.52
One parent with one child (PO)	12	0.50	0.50	0.49
Grandparent with child	3	0.27	0.25	0.31
Uncle or aunt with child	1	0.34	0.25	0.31
First cousins	3	0.26	0.125	0.18
Second cousins	1	0.16	0.063	0.14
Foster parent with adopted child	3	0.20	0.00	0.00
Unrelated children raised together (URT)	5	0.24	0.00	0.00
Unrelated children reared apart (URA)	4	−0.01	0.00	0.00

*r = correlation coefficient

Source: L. F. Jarvik and L. Erlenmeyer-Kimling, "Survey of Familial Correlations in Measured Intellectual Functions." In J. Zubin and G. A. Jervis (eds.), *Psychopathology of Mental Development.* New York: Grune and Stratton, 1967.

nonacceptance, their judgments were somewhat arbitrary. The use of median correlations is also questionable; weighted means might have been preferable and would certainly have given rather different results. The fact is, of course, that there just are not enough good data, especially on rather rare, but interesting, groups like identical twins or siblings reared in different families. The medians of several unsatisfactory investigations are somewhat more trustworthy than any one study, but we should be prepared to admit that any calculations based on them are liable to a good deal of uncertainty.

Introduction to Heritability Analyses   167

With this caution, we can agree that there is a rather striking similarity between the genetically expected and the obtained correlations. The biggest discrepancies occur for MZ twins, especially those reared apart, for the foster parent with adopted child, and for unrelated children reared together. All of these figures support the conclusion that, though heredity plays a major part, environmental differences between pairs of twins or similarities in the environment of foster children (or foster child with parent) appear to have a significant effect on intelligence. Nevertheless, it would be possible to argue (as does Kamin, 1974) that much the same degree of resemblance could be brought about by environmental factors alone; for siblings are more likely to be brought up alike than are cousins or adoptees, and twins tend to be treated still more alike than siblings who, of course, differ in age. However, it would be more difficult for environmentalist theory to explain why the DZ resemblances are much nearer to the sibling figures than they are to MZ. Also, fraternals or siblings in the same family (DZT and FST) should surely be more alike than identicals in different families (MZA). Again, parent–offspring should be no higher than foster parent–adoptee; except that the environmentalist might argue that children are more often adopted at the age of a few weeks or months rather than at birth and this might account for the difference between the correlations of 0.5 and 0.2.

Some writers point out that the kinship correlations for IQ are quite similar to those for height; and, although height obviously depends to a certain extent on nutrition and healthy upbringing, it is undoubtedly mainly genetic. Thus, it is claimed that intelligence is inherited in much the same way and to a similar degree. However, this would be a dubious inference, since it is quite possible that a correlation brought about by common genes in the case of height might be more or less duplicated by a combination of genetic and environmental factors in the case of intelligence. Vandenberg (1971) makes a more apposite point, namely that correlations between the heights of twins, for example, may vary quite markedly at different ages; hence, it is not surprising that IQ correlations are likewise very variable from one sample to another.

CLASSICAL ANALYSES: HOLZINGER'S *H*

An early attempt to arrive at an estimate of heritability or genetic variance was that by Karl Holzinger, based on the expectation that the genetic component for MZ twins should be twice that for DZ twins. He suggested the formula:

$$H = \frac{r_{MZ} - r_{DZ}}{1 - r_{DZ}}.$$

If we apply this formula to the correlations of 0.87 and 0.53 in Table 11.1, heritability (H) works out at 0.72. Vandenberg (1971) lists 16 comparative studies of MZ and DZ twins and shows that H ranges from 0.41 to 0.93, with a median value of 0.64.

However, Holzinger's H is no longer accepted as an appropriate statistic, and it is obviously open to the criticism that MZ twins brought up in the same home may have more similar environments than DZ twins.[3] Morton (1972) criticizes H as "a confusing statistic," and prefers the simple formulas for heritability:

$$2(r_{MZ} - r_{DZ}), \text{ and } 2(r_{FST} - r_{URT}).$$

Applied to Erlenmeyer-Kimling and Jarvik's medians, these formulas yield heritabilities of 0.68 and 0.52. But Morton points out that these formulas make the unjustified assumption that environment is equally similar for MZ and DZ, and the same for FS and foster children. Nichols (1976) has applied the same method to 756 published comparisons of MZ and DZ twins on various ability, personality, and interest tests. Heritability figures of about 0.40 to 0.50 were obtained rather consistently in all these areas.

IDENTICAL TWINS REARED APART

Particular interest has been taken in MZA, since they appear to provide information on individuals with identical heredity but different environments. Thus, they can be compared with URT, that is, individuals with different heredity but the same environment. In Table 11.1, the intraclass correlations are 0.75 for MZA and 0.24 for URT, and these can be interpreted as measuring directly the percentages of variance attributable to genes and environment.[4] Here they happen to add up almost exactly to 1.00, that is, the total phenotypic variance. Thus, it would certainly seem that the effect of the genes is much more powerful than

[3] At best, it represents only within-family variances, and it assumes, without justification, that differences between families are similar (see also Jinks and Fulker, 1970).

[4] Usually, we would expect the squares of correlations to give us the common variance, but Jensen (1971a) explains why, in this context, the correlations as they stand represent the heritable and environmental variances.

TABLE 11.2
Intraclass Correlations Between
Twins Reared Apart

Study	Number of cases	r_i
Newman, Freeman, and Holzinger	19	0.67
Burt	53	0.88
Shields	38	0.78
Juel-Neilsen	12	0.68
	Total 122	Average 0.82

that of the environment. However, the precise values are a matter of considerable dispute, to which we must now turn.

Cases of MZ twins reared apart are naturally rather rare, and only 122 have been reported on in four studies by Newman, Freeman, and Holzinger (1937); Burt (1966); Shields (1962); and Juel-Neilsen (1965). As shown in Table 11.2, the intraclass correlations differ considerably from study to study, though, according to Jensen, the differences are not statistically significant. For Table 11.2, the weighted average correlation is 0.82, though Erlenmeyer-Kimling and Jarvik's median is only 0.75.[5]

All of these figures are regarded by Kamin (1974) as more or less spurious for various reasons. I will attempt to summarize his main criticisms and to answer them in light of the comments made by Fulker (1975), Scarr-Salapatek (1976), and other reviewers.

Burt's Data

The largest single group of figures was collected by Burt, who was undoubtedly the leading figure in the development of mental measurement in Britain for nearly sixty years. He was also responsible (Burt and Howard, 1956) for perhaps the most extensive genetic analysis ever published of a number of different kinship groups, based on over 800 cases. In view of the immense value of Burt's contributions to child psychology and psychometrics, it is unpleasant to have to admit that he was often careless in reporting his data. In 1972, Kamin drew attention to

[5] There are surprising differences among the mean or median correlations tabulated by Erlenmeyer-Kimling and Jarvik, Vandenberg, Kamin, and others. The values listed here are regarded by Jensen (1970a) as the most acceptable.

certain discrepancies; and Jensen (1974b) published a complete list of these, based on an analysis of all Burt's articles together with any records left after his death in 1971. Some of the errors seem to be miscopyings, but others are more serious, such as reporting identical correlation coefficients for different-sized groups of twins. The latter situation suggests that Burt did not bother to recalculate when he gathered additional cases, and this fact makes it impossible to identify the true number of cases.

Another problem is that Burt habitually "adjusted" the IQs of the children whom he tested individually, partly by applying less culturally loaded performance tests and partly by incorporating teachers' judgments. (The latter is surprising, since elsewhere Burt (1943) criticized such judgments as quite untrustworthy.) Such adjustment, he claimed, provided scores that were more reliable and were better estimates of the children's genotypic intelligence. However, while such adjusted figures might be useful in clinical work with children, they are too subjective to yield replicable data for research purposes, where the psychologist is primarily concerned with analyzing actual phenotypes.

In other studies, Burt reports various correlations between rather unusual groups of adults and children, such as grandparents with children or uncles and aunts with children, yet he never makes clear how these adult IQs were assessed. He mentions that he sometimes employed "tests of the usual type" (unspecified); but often he relied simply on interview judgments or on "camouflaged tests" applied during interviews. It is quite probable that, when carrying out these interviews, he was aware of the obtained IQs of the children who were to be compared with the adults; in other words, that there may have been some contamination.

Kamin (1974) details these and other criticisms and concludes: "The numbers left behind by Professor Burt are simply not worthy of our current scientific attention." In this book, Kamin does not actually accuse Burt of "fudging" his data, but he does believe that Burt was so strongly committed to an hereditarian view of intelligence that he often unwittingly biased his collection and analyses of test scores.

However, in 1976, Kamin did accuse Burt of perpetrating systematic fraud. Daniels (1976) also refers to Burt's data as "faked," and, therefore, argues that most of Jensen's work—largely based on Burt's data—is worthless. Gillie (1976) published similar attacks in the British press and thus set in motion another violent and disgraceful controversy. In fact, Gillie's only evidence of such dishonesty was the set of errors Jensen had revealed two years previously.[6] In replying to Gillie and other critics, Jensen (1977c) made the point that the inconsistencies occur too haphazardly in Burt's tables of results to suggest that they were intentionally faked.

On the other hand, Kamin, who was the chief source of these attacks, was certainly a good deal more one-sided than Burt, in the opposite direction. Loehlin, Lindzey, and Spuhler (1975) criticize him for exaggerating Burt's inaccuracies and for making use himself of dubious techniques in analyzing discrepancies. Burt's inconsistencies certainly do not justify rejecting the whole of the enormous corpus of his contributions to mental measurement, though, of course, it is unfortunate that we cannot tell how frequently, or where, other errors occurred.

Fulker (1975) agrees that there are alarming discrepancies, though they actually amount to only some 20 instances out of hundreds or thousands of reported figures. He sees no reason to doubt the group test data and, in fact, these yield heritability figures much the same as those of Shields and Juel-Neilsen, and only a little higher than those of Newman, Freeman, and Holzinger (0.77 versus 0.73). True, the "adjusted" or "final" IQ results lead to higher estimates than those of other investigators — so much so that Jencks (1972) is led to suggest that IQ is more dependent on heredity among British children than it is under American conditions, where environments may well be more heterogeneous. However, Burt himself suggested a very plausible reason why his intertwin correlations are unusually high — namely, that all his cases were children, whereas most of the separated twins traced by others were adults whose intelligence tests scores would tend to be less reliable. It is also entirely possible that heritability of IQ is generally greater in children than in adults (and that environmental effects are greater in adults).[7]

Finally, while we regret Burt's reliance on subjectively adjusted IQs, it is reasonable to agree that he was, to some extent, able to allow for unusual environmental circumstances and that, therefore, his results *should* show greater genetic variances than those of others.

---

[6] Gillie also regarded it as shocking that Burt's collaborators, Howard and Conway, appear to have been imaginary persons who never existed. In fact, Howard's credentials were verified; but the style of Conway's (1958) article certainly suggests that Burt was the author. I cannot agree that this is heinous. The most likely reason for not acknowledging his authorship is that Burt could not get sufficient contributors to the *British Journal of Statistical Psychology,* which he edited, and, rather than appearing to write most of it himself, he did occasionally adopt pseudonyms.

[7] This is supported by Sewell Wright.

The sensible conclusion would seem to be that Burt's published results can be accepted only with considerable caution and that the figures for MZA would be better discarded. While it is true that much of the case for genetic influences was originally based on Burt's data, it is quite untrue that the rejection of these data would undermine the whole edifice; for, in fact, the main bulk of Burt's figures do *not* differ significantly from those published by other researchers. True, if we exclude Burt's figures from Table 11.2, the average MZA correlation for the other studies, representing 69 cases, drops from 0.82 to 0.74. While this is substantially lower, it is still greater than the figures for DZ or siblings reared together, let alone for unrelated children in the same home, thus still indicating a strong genetic component. One should, however, note that the 5 percent confidence limits for 0.74 are from 0.83 to 0.61, meaning that we could not expect a very accurate estimate of heritability from MZA evidence alone.

Weaknesses in Other Separated Twin Researches

A major criticism of all MZA research, raised by Kamin (1974) and Schwartz and Schwartz (1974), is that separated twins are never assigned randomly to the whole range of different environments. If, for example, the parents of twins are reluctant to rear both, but keep one themselves, they are very likely to place the other with relatives or acquaintances of a sociocultural level similar to their own. Likewise, if adoption agencies undertake placement, there is always a tendency to match the child to the foster home, which implies matching to some extent on the basis of true-parent intelligence, education, and SES. In the view of the critics, therefore, the high correlations between twins in different homes arise largely, or wholly, because of selective placement in similar homes. While I admit that there is a good point here, it is surely absurd to suggest that the similarity of environment is greater for MZ in *different* homes than it is for DZ reared together in the *same* home.

Burt attempted to answer this point in his 1966 article, by publishing a table of the socioeconomic levels of the two homes for his sample of 53 separated twins. This table shows no correlation whatever; however, I am inclined to agree with Kamin that the subjectivity of the judgments of home status and of adjusted IQs may well have affected this result. Also, SES alone is a rather poor index of the intellectual stimulation provided by a home, so that more detailed and impartial ratings (such as those used by

Burks (1928) in her research on foster children) might well have shown positive correlations.

This same factor was particularly marked in Shields' (1962) study, where 27 of his 40 pairs of twins were reared by relatives, and many of the sample lived in the same towns, attended the same schools, and had numerous contacts with their co-twins during childhood. Indeed, Shields included some pairs who had been reared together for a period, as long as they had been separated for 5 years or more. Kamin calculates that the inter-twin correlation for those reared by relatives was 0.83, whereas for the 13 pairs with unrelated foster parents, the correlation was 0.51. However, Fulker (1975) makes the point that first cousins are likewise reared by relatives and often have childhood con-tacts, yet their intercorrelation is 0.26, not 0.83. In addition, the group with more dissimilar environments, which gave the corre-lation of 0.51, happened to include 3 highly bizarre and abnor-mal pairs, and omitting these brings the correlation for the 10 remaining pairs up to the same level as for the 27. It should be mentioned, too, that in this study group intelligence tests were used, so criticisms of subjectivity in scoring are unwarranted.

In the Newman, Freeman, Holzinger research, Kamin again criticizes the selection of the sample. Pairs were included only if they looked strikingly alike (though it is difficult to see what kind of bias appearance would introduce). Some of them did have some contacts during childhood, and there was a tendency for their environments to be correlated (though certainly less than in Shields' study). Kamin's main complaint, however, is that the pairs showed a wide age range, from 12 to 59, and they were tested with the 1916 Stanford-Binet, whose adult IQs are liable to considerable distortion by age. For example, the pair that showed the biggest IQ discrepancy scored 92 and 116; had the procedure recommended by Terman for reducing age distor-tions been adopted, the IQs would have been 92 and 125, that is, a discrepancy of 33 points. By breaking down the sample of 19 pairs into several subsamples and applying ingenious corrections for the regression of IQ on age, Kamin claims to have explained away much, if not all, of the 0.67 intertwin correlation reported by the authors. Similar weaknesses are argued regarding Juel-Nielsen's data, where an unstandardized Danish version of WAIS was applied to twin pairs ranging in age from 22 to 77.

However, reviewers of Kamin's book, such as Scarr-Salapatek (1976), point out that his breakdowns into minute and often arbitrary subgroups are carried to extreme lengths. As Fulker (1975) puts it, he "obsessively overemphasizes idiosyncrat-ic detail." His nonlinear age regressions are quite implausible, and he neglects to point out that Newman's intertwin correlation for the Otis group test was 0.73 (i.e., higher than that for the Binet) and that, on this test, there was no significant age regression. Kamin himself agrees that Shields' data, also using group tests over a wide age range, did not display spurious age differences.

In summary, Kamin is justified in drawing attention to weaknesses in separated twin data and, in particular, to the likelihood of nonrandom placement in correlated environments. So far, no writer seems to have included this as a separate component in an analysis of variance. On the other hand, he has not demonstrated that a purely environmentalist hypothesis is tenable. The average resemblance of MZA still appears to be greater than that of DZT or FST. Thus, the higher genetic component in the former is more influential than the additional environmental component in the latter. Maybe the excess is not as large as we have supposed; the true figure for MZA might be nearer 0.65 than 0.75 to 0.80, as against 0.55 for DZT. Hence, the considerably higher correlation of 0.87 for monozygotes brought up together certainly indicates that similarity of environments does have a considerable effect. From Newman, Freeman, and Holzinger's results, and from Burt's, we can also see that genetic resemblance among twins is less marked in scholastic achievement, and that, here, environmental factors are relatively more powerful.

One of the most interesting findings of the Chicago study (Newman, Freeman, and Holzinger, 1937) was a correlation as high as 0.70 between *differences* in cultural level of the homes and education of the separated twins and their IQ differences. While this figure has not been replicated in other studies, Burt (1966) does report some relevant results on environmental differences between his 53 MZA twins—namely, correlations of 0.43 with differences on a group intelligence test; 0.26 with individual IQ differences and 0.15 for adjusted IQs; and 0.74 with differences in school attainments. Clearly, these data support the view that good measures of intelligence are much less affected by environmental differences than are more educationally loaded measures. However, a recent and thorough study by Martin and Martin (1975) found the same value of heritability for IQ and achievement examinations. This finding might be partly accounted for by the use of a group verbal intelligence test instead of individual tests; and the numbers of cases examined in some of the school subjects were quite small. In any case, I am still more inclined to accept the higher environmental variance in achievement measures as reported by Burt; Newman, Freeman, and Holzinger; Vandenburg (1971); and others.

TWINS BROUGHT UP TOGETHER

Kamin attacks some of the other median correlations in the EKJ table (Table 11.1) on the grounds that several studies have been neglected or that other less reliable ones were included. He argues, for example, that a better estimate for DZT is 0.63, rather than the EKJ figures of 0.56 for DZT, like-sex and 0.49 for DZT, unlike-sex. Such a high correlation would, of course, mean that DZ twins are considerably more alike than ordinary siblings because of greater environmental similarity, and that DZ do not differ so greatly from MZ as currently believed. However, Kamin's choice of "better" studies is arbitrary, as was EKJ's choice. Fulker, who differs again, concludes that the best estimates for DZT and siblings are 0.58 and 0.52. A difference as small as this might well arise because DZT are always tested at the same age with the same range of test items, whereas siblings are more likely to be tested at different ages and at different points on the Binet Mental Age scale.

Most writers agree that monozygotes are likely to experience more similar environments than dizygotes and that this partly accounts for their much higher resemblance. Parents and acquaintances treat them more alike, they are frequently dressed alike, and they seem to have a peculiarly close psychological bond or degree of empathy with one another. Dizygotes, on the other hand, are often as unlike as ordinary siblings and as liable to compete and quarrel with one another; there is empirical, as well as general observational, evidence to support this (e.g., Smith, 1965).

Kamin mentions, too, that the correlations of singletons with twins in the same family tend to be considerably lower—namely, around 0.26—than the usual coefficient of about 0.50 between siblings. If this point is confirmed by further research, it would suggest that the greater interaction between twins is accompanied by less interaction with the nontwins and, therefore, enhances environmental differences.

However, none of the above evidence proves that the high MZ correlation is explicable wholly by environment. Dobzhansky (1973) remarks that MZ twins are treated as more alike because they *are* more alike. Parents often do not know whether their same-sex twins are MZ or DZ; but if, in addition to closely similar appearance, they show very similar needs, capabilities, and development, they are naturally treated more similarly. This phenomenon might, then, be brought about by genetic similarity affecting environment, rather than by environmental conditions as such.[8] Confirmation is obtained from a recent observational

[8]This phenomenon is termed reactive G × E covariance by Plomin, De-Fries, and Loehlin (1977).

study (Lytton, Conway, and Sauvé, 1977), where the interactions of 2½-year-old twin boys with their parents were recorded in the homes. There were 17MZ and 29 DZ pairs. The study showed that parents do not initiate a greater number of similar actions toward MZ twins than they do toward DZ. The MZ are indeed treated more alike in certain respects, but this occurs because the MZ are, in fact, more alike, and therefore the parents more often respond to them similarly (at least at this age).

One of Kamin's objections to twin research is that the diagnosis of mono- or dizygoticity is often imprecise. However, this weakness would surely tend to reduce the differences between MZ and DZ correlations; hence, it runs counter to his environmentalist approach. If people often don't know whether twins are identical or not, it seems all the more unlikely that differences in treatments could raise the intertwin correlations from about 0.56 (DZ) to 0.87 (MZ).

Burt and Howard (1956) and Jensen (1975a) make the point that, in some respects, MZ twins may have a considerably different environment—namely, at the prenatal stage, when one is often in competition with the other for the placental blood supply. They occupy different positions in the womb and, not infrequently, they show physical reversals (for instance, in handedness and fingerprints). Price (1950) argues strongly that most twin-pair correlations underestimate their genetic similarity, since so many fetal conditions are apt to retard the prenatal development of one member of a pair more than the other. A recent study by Munsinger (1977a) appeared to confirm Price's view. He classified available monozygotic pairs according to similarity of birth weight and claimed to find a much higher correlation between IQs of pairs of similar weight than among those where one member was much lighter than the other, presumably on account of uterine disadvantage (see p. 89). However, Kamin (1977c) showed that Munsinger's classifications were often erroneous or arbitrary and subjective, and that his calculations were faulty; when these mistakes were corrected, the alleged differences in correlations disappear. Fujikara and Froehlich's (1974) study of 125 pairs of MZ twins, where there was no association between birth weight differences and later intelligence, led them to conclude that the brain is remarkably resistant to uterine deprivation.

An extensive investigation by Record, McKeown, and Edwards (1970) lends some support to an environmentalist interpretation of the low mean IQ of twins in general. They analyzed the IQs of 49,000 11-year-old British children and obtained the following means:

Singletons	100.1
Twins (2,164)	95.7
Triplets (33)	91.6
Twins with one survivor (148)	98.8

In 148 families, one twin was still-born or died within 4 weeks of birth, and it may be seen that the survivors approximated quite closely to normal singleton IQs. The explanation favored by the authors is that twin pairs tend to score below average because they cannot both get as much maternal attention as can a singleton or survivor. But a physiological explanation in terms of unfavorable fetal conditions might account equally well for this result. However, the issue is complicated; for example, it appears that dizygotes are more frequently born to mothers of low SES.

While I agree with Burt, Jensen, and Price that identical twins quite often experience different physical environments during pregnancy, I should point out that biochemical conditions are nevertheless much more similar for twins than they are for siblings or any other pairs of children. This would imply that comparisons between MZA IQs and those of unrelated children in the same home are questionable. The former not only inhabit the same womb, they are usually handled by the same mother for several days or weeks before they are separated, whereas the latter always have different prenatal and postnatal environments until several days or weeks after birth. At the same time, it does *not* appear that early-separated pairs develop more discrepant IQs than those separated after 1 year or more. Johnson (1963) actually found the opposite, although, as he was dealing with only 23 cases, his results cannot carry much weight. The mean IQ difference for 11 pairs separated before 6 months was 4.7; for the 12 cases separated at 1 year or over, it was 9.4.

Perhaps the safest general conclusion is that in many ways twins constitute a rather peculiar sample, so that we should not place as much confidence as earlier writers have on their being the outstanding source of evidence for heritability in the population at large. Nevertheless, the great bulk of the data clearly excludes any purely environmentalist explanation and thus reinforces my preference for the gene–environment interaction theory.

SIBLINGS REARED APART

Siblings reared apart constitute another interesting source of data, and many more of them than of MZA are available, although rather little has been published about them. EKJ's median of 0.47 is so close to 0.5 or 0.55 as to suggest that genetic resemblance is much stronger than environmental diversity. However, as usual, different studies differ, and Kamin readily finds some evidence of greater discrepancies between pairs in different homes. Freeman, Holzinger, and Mitchell (1928) quote correlations of 0.30 for siblings in different homes that were rated as similar, and only 0.19 for those in homes rated as dissimilar. Note that the average of these figures, 0.25, is no higher than that for unrelated children reared together. In another study, Sims (1931) compared 203 pairs of siblings reared in their own homes with 203 pairs of unrelated children in different homes who were, however, matched with the siblings for age, school attended, and SES (Sims Score Card). The intraclass (double-entry) correlations were 0.40 and 0.29, respectively, in these two groups, and the figures do not differ significantly. Like Sims, Kamin (1974) concludes that environmental similarity can bring about much the same resemblance as that found among genetically related pairs. However, it could also be argued that the matching of the environments for SES would, to some extent, match for genetic intelligence. Moreover, if age is held constant in both groups, the correlations rise to 0.48 and 0.34; and this difference does reach borderline significance at 0.10 level.

Another plausible comparison was proposed by Fehr (1969), who argued that we can never get rid of differences in upbringing either between MZ and DZ pairs or between MZA and MZT pairs. Thus, a better approach might be to contrast MZA with FSA—that is, monozygotes with siblings—both reared apart, since the differences in environment between separated pairs are likely to be much the same. Applying the appropriate formula to these groups, Fehr obtained a heritability of 0.53 for the aggregate of MZA, but it ranged from 0.38 in Newman's to 0.74 in Burt's data. This finding not only casts further doubt on heritability estimates of around 0.80, but also suggests that the available data for MZA have so many flaws that we cannot expect them to provide reliable and consistent evidence of heritability. However, modern behavior genetical theory does not rely solely on twin or kinship relations. There are several other sources of evidence, described in later chapters, and it is the concordance of these with analyses of kinship data that provides the most convincing demonstration of substantial genetic influence in IQ. This is disputed only by those who fly in the face of the established facts.

SUMMARY

1   A distinction is drawn between Mendelian-type studies of inheritance of particular attributes and polygentic inheritance of continuously distributed traits, such as height or intelligence.

2   On polygenetic theory, certain correlations can be predicted between the IQs of individuals who are related in varying degrees, such as mono- and dizygotic twins and siblings. Burt has somewhat modified these predicted values, allowing for dominance and assortative mating.

3   Erlenmeyer-Kimling and Jarvik have tabulated the available correlational results for such kinship groups and obtained rather striking agreement between their median coefficients and the predictions. But there are some notable exceptions, which are strongly suggestive of environmental influences.

4   Various techniques have been applied for calculating the genetic variance, or heritability, of IQ. Holzinger's H statistic is not regarded as satisfactory. The correlation between pairs of monozygotic twins brought up in different homes (MZA) gives another estimate, and, though this falls below the figure for those brought up together, it is still far larger than the correlation for unrelated children brought up in the same home.

5   However, the MZA data are open to many difficulties of interpretation. In particular, Kamin tries to show that they yield no sound evidence of genetic effects. Though some of his criticisms are rejected, it should be admitted that separated MZ pairs do tend to be placed in similar homes, which would tend to boost their IQ correlations.

6   The presence of certain inconsistencies in Burt's extensive data has to be recognized, though, again, some of the criticisms raised are unwarranted. Other difficulties with Newman, Freeman, and Holzinger's study of MZA, and with Shields' investigation, are considered.

7   Though monozygotics reared together clearly experience very similar postnatal environments, there are often gross physical differences in their prenatal environment that affect birth weight, health, and survival of the disadvantaged twin. But the claim that later intelligence is also affected is not supported. Hence, we must reject the argument that MZT or MZA correlations are under- rather than overestimated.

8   The generally low average IQ of all twins (about 95) may be due to these abnormalities in pregnancy or perhaps to the lesser amount of attention the mother can give to each of two babies.

9   In general, the data available on various categories of twins are less reliable, and more difficult to interpret, than psychologists have believed. Studies of siblings reared together and reared apart are also unsatisfactory.

12

Complex Analyses of Variance of Kinship Data

GENETIC – ENVIRONMENTAL COVARIANCE

One of the main reasons for the inconclusive findings from twins or other kinship correlations is that genes and environment do not operate as two distinct factors. Neither the breeding nor the upbringing of humans can be brought under experimental manipulation and control. We have to make do with what society happens to provide; hence, the results are inevitably "messy." In agricultural experiments, we can specify the genetic strains of wheat or the ancestry of cows, and subject them to specified environments and growth conditions. Following Fisher's analysis of variance designs, we would assign randomly chosen samples of each genetic group to each condition or combination of conditions. It would then be possible to partition the overall variance (e.g., in milk yield) and to determine the contribution of each independent condition and its statistical significance.

The application of this approach to human attributes is, however, much more complicated, since heredity and environment are apt to get mixed up, or to *covary.* For example, we referred to MZA pairs being placed in correlated environments, and earlier (p. 153) to the manner in which bright or dull children seek out and shape their own appropriate environments. Plomin, DeFries, and Loehlin (1977) refer to this as the *active* type of covariance, and distinguish two other types—*reactive* and *passive.*

Reactive covariance occurs when people respond differently to children with different genotypes (see p. 176). Jencks (1972) suggests that this behavior commences in early infancy, when mothers interact more with their babies and talk to them more if they are responsive and developmentally precocious. Passive covariance occurs when more intelligent parents provide healthier prenatal conditions, better education, and intellectual stimulation generally to their offspring, who probably possess superior genes. Jensen likewise suggests that we should distinguish self-selection or modification of environment by the individual from the imposition of an environment appropriate to the individual's abilities. But it is obviously difficult, if not impossible, to determine the direction of causation; usually, the covariation tends to be reciprocal or reactive.

Some critics of heritability studies, such as Layzer (1974), argue that this covariation, or overlapping, is always present and that it invalidates any attempt to analyze the separate contributions of genetic and environmental factors. In fact, most investigators from Burt onward have repeatedly drawn attention to the problem and have often included the joint, or overlapping, effects as a separate term or terms. But is must be admitted that there is no one satisfactory way of coping with the difficulty, and, therefore, different analyses have often yielded very diverse results. The most recent discussion by Plomin and his colleagues shows that the problem is statistically soluble, but that we require more adequate and complete data, for instance, on foster children, their natural and foster parents, and the foster environment. Meanwhile, these researchers do not attempt to make any quantitative estimates of covariation.

INTERACTION AND DOMINANCE

Another term in analysis of variance that has caused a lot of confusion is *interaction*. Critics frequently object to the whole notion of estimating the effects of genes and environment on the phenotype, on the grounds that genetic and environmental influences interact with one another from conception onward and therefore cannot be disentangled. In fact, there is virtually no dispute over "interactionist theory"; it is accepted by almost all recent authors, including Burt, Jensen, and Eysenck. Indeed, Jensen rejects the above criticism as merely stating the obvious. An "environment-free intelligence" is, to him, as inconceivable as a "nutrition-free weight." But it is still necessary to explore the effects of different conditions of upbringing, or nutrition, on individuals with different genotypes.

The kind of interaction important in this context refers to the possibility that different genotypes may respond differently to the same environmental factor; or, in other words, that certain gene patterns are fostered by one set of environmental conditions, other gene patterns by different sets of conditions. This is "interaction" in the statistical sense, and it can quite readily be studied in analyses of variance. For example, it could well be true that bright children benefit from different *kinds* of stimulation than do dull children, not merely from more extensive or complex stimulation. This can be demonstrated, as Jinks and Fulker (1970) point out, by finding if, within twin or sibling pairs, there is any correlation between the interpair differences and the pair means. Jensen (1970a) has examined the available data from this point of view, allowing for linear, quadratic, or higher-order interactions, but has been unable to find any results that are statistically significant.[1] Plomin, DeFries, and Loehlin (1977) similarly find no significant G × E interaction in Skodak and Skeels' or Munsinger's foster-child studies (see Chapter 14).

The finding, so far, that genetic – environmental interactions are negligible in humans is hardly surprising, in view of the difficulty educational psychologists are experiencing in discovering significant ATIs (aptitude – treatment interactions) that might help to adapt instruction or type of schooling to the potentialities of different children. Surveys such as that of Bracht (1970) have failed to reveal any consistent evidence of such interactions in cognitive growth. It seems that methods of teaching that work well for dull children also work well for bright ones, so the latter continue to show higher achievements and IQs than the former.

Quite another type of interaction occurs among the genes themselves, the most important example of which, in the present context, is *dominance* (D).[2] Dominance arises because each gene has two alternative forms (allelomorphs) at corresponding loci on the paired chromosomes. Assume that one allele, *A,* tends to increase intelligence, and the other, *a,* tends to reduce it. If *A* is dominant, then the *Aa* combination is as effective as *AA,* and only the *aa* combination is reductive. Dominance produces genetic differences between parents and offspring; thus, when it is present, parent – offspring correlations are reduced. It is also important in genetic change; for when the dominant gene

---

[1] It is not correct, as Light and Smith (1969) state, that Jensen attributed the 1 percent difference between 0.75 (MZA correlation) + 0.24 (URT) and 0.01, to genetic – environmental interaction.

[2] Epistasis, that is, interaction of genes at different loci, is ignored here, since there is no indication that it significantly affects genetic variance in intelligence.

favors a trait that is desirable in mating, that trait will tend to be strengthened through natural selection.

Few investigators have, in fact, attempted to calculate the component of variance attributable to dominance, but those who have provide positive evidence indicating that, in Western cultures at least, there is a certain amount of breeding for superior intelligence. As Jinks and Eaves (1974) put it, intelligence is a trait of biological relevance.

One other mechanism worth mentioning that affects the genetics of intelligence is *assortative mating* (AM). Clearly, there is a tendency, in our culture, for husbands and wives to select one another partly on a basis of similar intelligence, even if their cues consist mainly of similar socioeconomic and educational level rather than intelligence scores as such. In addition, of course, closely similar age and common religion and race are often sought. The average correlation between mates for years of education is found to exceed 0.60, both in whites and blacks, while the average of numerous studies of intelligence works out at 0.45 (Jensen, 1977a).

Such a correlation partly reflects similar environmental background, and this would not affect the genotype of the offspring; yet it must also imply some correlation between parental genotypes, and this enhances the between-families genetic variance. Assortive mating tends, then, to have the opposite effect to that of dominance, and, in practice (at least among whites), the two components tend to balance one another out. Hence, earlier analyses that neglected them were less distorted than might have been expected. One should note also that the presence of assortive mating in no way affects the average level of a trait, whereas dominance and selection do.

ANALYSIS OF VARIANCE MODELS

We are now in a position to specify a reasonably complete model for analysis of variance in place of the oversimplified techniques discussed in Chapter 11. Jinks and Fulker (1970) present as the basic formula:

$$\sigma^2_P = \sigma^2_G + \sigma^2_E + f(\sigma_G \sigma_E),$$

where

σ^2_P = total phenotypic variance in the population,
σ^2_G = genetic variance, and
σ^2_E = environmental variance.

$f(\sigma_G\sigma_E)$ refers to some function of the joint effects of genotype and environment, including both their covariance and any interaction. The correlational part, which we will refer to as GE–covariance, is given by

$$2r_{GE}\ (\sigma_G\sigma_E).$$

It will simplify our discussion to refer to the two main terms as G and E variances, which are expressed as proportions of 1.0, or as percentages. Many writers refer to G by the term h^2, that is, the hereditary variance. Note that in this context, G is entirely distinct from Spearman's g, or general intelligence factor.[3] E is that part of the phenotypic variance (excluding error) that is independent of the genotype; that is, it is $(1 - h^2)$.[4] E includes, of course, the prenatal and perinatal conditions, as well as differences between families in cultural level or in the rearing and education of their children.

A more complete list of the separable components that have been, or should be evaluated, is as follows:

G between families
G within families   additive variance or   broad
AM (assortative mating   narrow heritability   herita-
    between parents)   bility
D (dominance)
GE– covariance (effects of
    covariation between G and E)   f(GE)
GE– interaction
E between families
E within families   E
e (error or unreliability variance)

Note that it is possible, and often useful, to break down both genetic and environmental variances into differences between different families and differences between offspring within the same family. Cattell (1960) and Jinks recommend appropriate techniques. In general, twin data reveal within-family effects, whereas foster-child data are mostly indicators of between-family differences. Thus, Holzinger's contrast of MZ and DZ twins reflects only the within-family genetic differences. $G_{between}$ variance usually exceeds G_{within}, on account of the effects of assortative

[3] Burt and Howard use the letter G to refer to additive variance only, and H for broad heritability.

[4] If test reliability (r_{tt}) is allowed for, the formula becomes ($r_{tt} - h^2$/.

mating. The relative sizes of the environmental components is of considerable psychological interest; for example, we might expect E_{within} to be smaller among MZ twins than among DZ or siblings.

Next, it should be pointed out that geneticists distinguish "narrow" from "broad" heritability; some of the variations in published results are due to these being mixed. *Narrow heritability* includes only the additive effects of the genes that contribute to intelligence, together with their enhancement by assortative mating. This is the part of genetic variance that breeds true and accounts for genetic resemblances between parents and offspring, while *broad heritability* also includes the nonadditive dominance component; this is involved in the very high correlation between identical twins.

Like any statistical data, there is always some degree of unreliability, hence the error term, e. Some investigators correct their correlational data for attenuation, while others simply ignore the error component and calculate the other variance components as proportions of $(1 - e)$. Jencks, for example, assumed a reliability of 0.92 for Stanford-Binet IQs, but some tests that are popular in cross-cultural and genetic research (e.g., Raven's Progressive Matrices and Mill Hill Vocabulary) have rather lower stability and consistency.

Cattell (1971a), Jencks (1972), and Eaves and Jinks (1972) all admit that variance estimates tend to be far from reliable. This goes some way to explain the considerable variations in heritabilities reported by different authors or between studies using contrasted kinship groups. Cattell suggests that, in order to carry out a reasonably stable analysis of variance, it would be desirable to have no fewer than 100 MZA, 100 FSA, and nearer 300 of the other, less rare, types of kinship; that is, a total of some 2,500 subjects.

Another source of instability in genetic studies is that a number of different individual or group tests have been employed, but their results are interpreted as providing evidence on a uniform variable of "intelligence." Army Alpha, Otis, Matrices and Dominoes, Stanford-Binet, Terman-Merrill, and Wechsler IQs obviously do not measure the same thing. Even in a heterogeneous group, the correlations between verbal and nonverbal tests may be as low as 0.6. However, it is usual for the same test to have been applied throughout any one study, and there is scarcely any evidence to suggest that different tests consistently yield different heritability figures. Three studies have reported heritabilities for what were supposed to be pure factor tests (Blewett, 1954; Vandenberg, 1962; Nichols, 1965), but their findings show no coherent pattern, although one would surely

TABLE 12.1
Burt and Howard's Analyses of Variance

Sources of variance	Group test	Adjusted IQs
Genetic (additive)	40.5	47.9
Assortative mating	19.9	17.9
Dominance	16.7	21.7
Environmental (systematic), or GE– covariance	10.6	1.4
Environmental (random)	5.9	5.8
Unreliability	6.4	5.2
h^2	.77	.88
h^2 corrected for unreliability	.81	.93

Source: Data from Burt and Howard, 1956.

expect some factors, such as V and N to be lower in heritability than, say, S and I.

A further source of error or distortion in heritability research is that many of the samples studied could not be regarded as representative of the total white, or other, population. If there is restriction of range (i.e., the S.D. of IQ is less than 15), then all correlations are likely to be lowered. In any analysis of phenotypic variance, homogeneity of variance in the various subgroups is usually demanded, though fairly considerable departures seem to make little difference. Jinks and Fulker (1970) are careful to test their data for defects of this kind, but most authors seem to ignore the problem.

Burt and Howard's Analysis

The first full-scale attempt to assess the major components of variance in intelligence was that of Burt and Howard (1956; see also Burt, 1958). This study was based on 826 children in all, including MZT, MZA, DZT, FST, FSA, and URT, who were given group and individual tests, and whose "final" or "adjusted" IQs were assessed. These groups allowed the partitioning of six sources of variance, as shown in Table 12.1. Note that Burt distinguishes what he calls systematic environment from random effects. Systematic environment consists of environmental variations dependent on the genotype; that is, it corresponds to GE– covariance (and is so listed by Jensen (1969) in his reproduction of Burt's table). Random environment includes all the environmental effects uncorrelated with heredity; Burt claims that these amount only to 5.9 and 5.8 percent in the two analyses shown in

TABLE 12.2
Jinks and Fulker's Analysis
of Burt and Howard's Data

$G_{between}$	0.44 ± .04
G_{within}	0.39 ± .03
$E_{between}$	0.09 ± .03
E_{within}	0.08 ± .01
Total	1.00

Source: Data from Jinks and Fulker, 1970.

the table. The effect of adjusting the IQs, it will be seen, is to reduce the GE–covariance from 10.6 to 1.4 percent, with a corresponding rise in the (additive) G component. Jensen's original claim for a figure of approximately 80 percent for heritability was mainly based on Burt's group test analysis, corrected for unreliability.

It is hardly surprising that this table has aroused a good deal of incredulity, both because the environmental variance is very small and because GE–covariance appears to have been "carved out" from the environmental rather than the genotypical components. Note that the findings cannot be attributed wholly to the admitted weaknesses in Burt's MZA data, since the other kinship groups played a larger part in his calculations (only 30 MZA were included). However, Jensen (1974b) admits that there are ambiguities in some of the group test correlations also.

A further analysis of the final assessment correlations was published by Jinks and Fulker (1970; see also Jinks and Eaves, 1974), making use of all Burt's data instead of the more limited kinship comparisons carried out by Burt and Howard. Estimates from the various groups were weighted and combined by least squares. Their technique enabled them to partition the G and E variance into between and within families, but not to provide separate estimates of assortative mating or GE–covariance. Their results (see Table 12.2), which include standard errors, were as follows: Broad heritability is assessed as 0.83. Thus, this analysis has scaled down the G percentage from Burt's figure of 0.93. Presumably, had the more sophisticated technique of analysis been applied to the more objective group test data, the corresponding figure would have dropped to something like 0.70, which is much more in line with estimates subsequent to Burt's.

Jinks and Fulker do not supply AM and D estimates, but they agree that the excess of $G_{between}$ over G_{within} shows the presence of assortative mating and a considerable degree of dominance. They admit that their figure for narrow heritability of 0.71 could be exaggerated by correlated environments (e.g., among twins or siblings reared apart); but they consider both this effect and any GE– interaction to be negligible. It seems unfortunate that they did not attempt to calculate GE– covariance separately.

Cattell's Multiple Abstract Variance Analysis (MAVA)

Cattell (1960; 1963b) was one of the first writers to try to allow systematically for all the different sources of phenotypic variance, partitioning both genetic and environmental into between and within families, and recognizing the importance of GE– covariance and interaction. Earlier studies based only on MZ and DZ twins were incapable of revealing such covariance. The term *abstract* is used because his equations involve constructs that can be inferred from kinship correlations, although not directly observed. Cattell takes account also of the likelihood of different environmental components among sibs and among twins, among same-sex and opposite-sex children, and among foster and natural children. He further advocates using relatively pure factor scores rather than scores on single tests. However, although he has arrived at large numbers of equations, he admits that there are difficulties in covering all the variance and covariance components that he would wish to separate and that his solutions have large standard errors unless the samples representing different kinship groups are much larger than those usually available.

In one of the few published studies by Cattell, Stice, and Kristy (1957), an attempt was made to calculate the main sources of variance in 11 personality factors assessed by objective tests, including fluid intelligence as measured by Cattell's culture-fair battery. Over 600 children ranging from URA and URT to DZT and MZT were tested; corrections were made for age differences where necessary. Owing to the shortage of suitable data, the authors tried out likely ranges of values for certain variables, choosing those that yielded the most reasonable solutions. No final table for variance proportions in intelligence is given and the figures for environmental variance within families differed markedly between sibs and between twins. However, there was a substantial GE– covariance component, and (unlike Jinks and Fulker's study) the within-families G and E variances exceeded those between-families.

In his contribution to Cancro's symposium, Cattell (1971b) claims that his investigations yielded a heritability figure of 0.85. But in his book (1971a), he quotes 0.77 for G_f and 0.73 for G_c, as shown in Table 12.3. While the former estimate is in line with Burt's and Jinks and Fulker's (Tables 12.1 and 12.2), the size of h^2 for crystallized intelligence is surprising in view of Cattell's theory that this aspect of intelligence is the resultant of cultural and educational pressures. Cattell frequently criticizes studies that have used Stanford-Binet or verbal group tests, because they exaggerate the susceptibility of intelligence tests to environmental influence. He also suggests that crystallized intelligence might be expected to rise roughly 1 IQ point per decade in Western cultures and much more rapidly in developing countries; whereas fluid intelligence would be more readily altered by genetic intervention than by environmental change. Other questions suggested by Table 12.3 are why E_{within} should be much greater than $E_{between}$, and why almost the whole of the genetic component in crystallized intelligence should be within families and very little between families.

Jinks and Fulker

Jinks and Fulker (1970) criticize MAVA on the grounds that the choice of variance and covariance components depends too much on the subjective judgments of the investigator. They suggest a method, which they call biometrical-genetical technique, based on the principle of testing the statistical significance of any hypothesized component (e.g., GE– interaction) and thus arriving at the simplest model that fits the available data. They argue, however, that MAVA, like the earlier or "classical" forms of analysis such as Holzinger's H, are special cases of their own technique. They find simple additive ANOVA (analysis of variance) models usually give as good a fit as possible to the data.

In addition to reanalyzing Burt's figures, Jinks and Fulker applied their method to several other published sets of data, including Shields' scores for MZT and MZA on the Mill Hill Vocabulary and the nonverbal Dominoes test. They found some heterogeneity in the means and variances of the samples but, nevertheless, arrived at broad heritability figures of 0.73 and 0.71 for the two tests. With the Vocabulary (but not the Dominoes) test, there was an indication of GE– interaction, environmental variance being greater with below-average than above-average twins. Apart from this, none of the studies of intelligence they reanalyzed yielded any evidence of significant GE– covariance or interaction, or correlated environments, which leads one to wonder whether their sophisticated technique may not still be confounding these serious sources of distortion with the

TABLE 12.3
Cattell's Analysis for
Fluid and Crystallized Intelligence

	Fluid	Crystallized
G_{within}	0.46	0.66
$G_{between}$	0.31	0.07
E_{within}	0.20	0.22
$E_{between}$	0.03	0.05
h^2	0.77	0.73

Source: Data from Cattell, 1971a.

genotypic variance. Indeed, they admit to a preference for the "black box" view, which considers all genotype or genotype-correlated influences as genetic, and the rest as environmental.

Loehlin, Lindzey, and Spuhler

These authors (1975) accept Fulker's model as the most appropriate, and they have followed him in analyzing the Erlenmeyer-Kimling and Jarvik median correlations,[5] with the results shown in Table 12.4. Their environment within families figure includes some 5 percent attributable to unreliability; thus, differences between families are considerably more influential than between children in the same family. Their broad heritability of 0.75 is very similar to other analyses, although it is derived from a wider series of investigations than Burt and Howard's. While aware of the importance of GE– covariance and interaction, they do not include either as a separate term.

Morton

Morton (1972) applied his own technique of path analysis to the same EKJ figures, with the result shown in Table 12.5. He partitions E components very differently from other authors, though his specific resemblance among twins seems plausible. He does specify GE– covariance and, in consequence, obtains a lower G, or heritability estimate. He notes that it was necessary

---

[5] For correlations between spouses and between parents and offspring, they adopted Jencks' values of 0.52 and 0.48, respectively.

TABLE 12.4
Loehlin, Lindzey, and Spuhler's
Analysis of EKJ Correlations

G additive	0.52
AM	0.12
D	0.11
Broad Heritability	0.75
$E_{between}$	0.13
E_{within} (including error)	0.12
Broad Heritability	0.25

Source: Data from Loehlin, Lindzey, and Spuhler, 1975.

to assume equally similar environments for full siblings and fos-ter children, also the same for MZ as DZ. Both of these assump-tions are probably unjustified.

Jensen

Jensen (1977d) has also taken the EKJ data as his starting point, but he formulated a new set of equations for isolating relevant components of variance. Since there were too many var-iables to allow direct estimation from the data, he postulated a likely range of figures for some of these, and then solved for each combination. Thus, assortative mating coefficients of 0.00, 0.20, and 0.40 were tried out, and GE correlations of 0.04 to 0.40. Also the genetic correlation between DZ twins (referred to as $r_{GG'}$) was allowed to vary from 0.50 to 0.70.

Only one of the solutions obtained yielded rational values, where $r_{GG'} = 0.50$, $r_{GE} = 0.08$, and the effects of assortative mat-ing and a substantial degree of dominance cancelled one another out. The final resulting variances (excluding measurement error) are shown in Table 12.6. The G component is decidedly lower than the 80 percent Jensen proposed in 1969, though in line with his own later writings (1973a), which suggest that G is at least twice as large as E. His GE– covariance percentage still seems somewhat lower than we might anticipate, but he points out, as mentioned above, that environments are sometimes manipulated to compensate for genetic strengths and deficiencies; they do not always back them up.

It is interesting that the Loehlin and Jensen analyses, using the same basic data, yield apparently discrepant results, showing

TABLE 12.5
Morton's Analysis of EKJ Correlations

G	0.675
E_1 (common environment or GE– covariance)	0.139
E_2 (specific environmental resemblance in twins)	0.016
Random environment (plus error)	0.170
Total	1.000

Source: Data from Morton, 1972.

that the choice of model and analytic techniques makes a difference. But Jensen concludes that we should not expect to reach an exact percentage for G or h^2 but should think in terms of a range, depending on the extent of assortative mating, dominance, and other conditions present in the particular sample. Loehlin and his colleagues likewise state that the precise figure is not important; it is sufficient that most analyses tend to agree on something between 0.60 and 0.85, though a few dissenters still advocate much lower figures (Kamin, 1974; Layzer, 1974), Kamin in fact suggesting that intelligence test scores have zero heritability.

While there is some consensus among these three analyses of EKJ correlations that the value of h^2 is much lower than that claimed by Burt, one should note that EKJ's median correlations included many figures derived from Burt's investigations. Thus, it is conceivable that data derived from other authors might reduce the heritability estimate still further.

Jencks

Jencks' main concern was the extent to which social inequality or success and failure in life (income, status, etc.) depend on inequalities in family background, length or type of education, cognitive skills, and personality differences or chance factors that cannot readily be assessed or controlled (see Jencks et al., 1972). Thus, his thesis is, in effect, the reverse of Herrnstein's (1973) view of the important social relevance of IQ. In his broad treatment of these controversial issues, Jencks inquires whether "cognitive skills" are determined mainly by heredity or environment. He avoids the use of the term *intelligence* because of its political and moral overtones, but he accepts IQ as a widely recognized quantitative index of mental competence and intelligent behavior. Like other writers, he stresses the influence of genes on environment; for example, blacks tend to receive

TABLE 12.6
Jensen's Analysis of EKJ Correlations

G	0.65
E	0.28
GE– covariance	0.07
Total	1.00

Source: Data from Jensen, 1977d.

poorer schooling and poorer employment because of their black skin-color genes, and this effect tends to become confounded with genetic determination of their abilities.

Though critical of comparisons of correlations among MZ and DZ twins because the relative similarities of their environments are unknown, Jencks accepts the Newman, Freeman, and Holzinger data as yielding a heritability figure around 55 percent. He also reports Burt's and Shields' studies, but considers that their higher figures apply only in England (see p. 172). On the other hand, correlations among siblings, foster children, and natural or adoptive parents, when analyzed by path coefficients rather than analysis of variance, indicate a heritability amounting only to some 25 percent. (Note that Cattell, Stice, and Kristy were faced with a similar discrepancy.) However, his method led to an unusually high figure for GE– covariance, namely 20 percent. Thus, Jencks' overall conclusion is that genetic determination of cognitive skills amounts to some 45 percent; GE– covariance, 20 percent; E between families, 20 percent; E within families, 15 percent. But he admits that the confidence limits for all these figures are quite high, and later agreed that he had underestimated G– variance.

In regard to adult SES, Jencks apportions the variance of contributory factors as follows:

Cognitive potential (or innate intelligence)	5– 10%
Influence of home upbringing potential	10– 20%
Overall educational achievement	40– 50%
School differences	Insignificant
Uncertain (including luck, personality, etc.)	20– 45%

Note that the averages of these limiting figures add up to 100 percent. He concludes, therefore, that genetic differences in cognitive skills play quite a small role in the production of social inequality. Hence, the obsession that American (and British) parents have about their children's IQs, because they believe these to indicate achievement throughout life, is, in Jencks' view, quite unwarranted. Also, the common criticism that IQ tests serve mainly to preserve the privileges of the rich is greatly exaggerated (see p. 123).

Jencks' figure of 0.45 for genetic variance has been hailed by many reviewers because it is much smaller than earlier estimates of around 0.80 and, therefore, more in line with environmentalist theory. However, it represents little more than a compromise guess between the quite diverse estimates obtained form different kinship groups. Path coefficient analysis as such should not make much difference, though Jinks and Eaves regard it as less effective, statistically, than their own weighted least-squares approach. It would appear to involve a greater degree of subjective judgment of the most appropriate model. Loehlin, Lindzey, and Spuhler show that, with a few plausible amendments to Jencks' figures, the GE– covariance drops to 0.15, and they conclude that the best fit for his data would be G = 0.61 and E = 0.23. Jinks and Eaves have also applied their method to the correlations used by Jencks and arrive at a G estimate of 0.68 (with a possible range from 0.59 to 0.76). However, they find no evidence of GE– covariance and claim that inserting it as an additional parameter reduces the goodness of fit of the model. At least, though, there is a striking convergence in h^2 estimates among Jencks' revised figure of 0.61, Jinks' 0.68, and Jensen's 0.65.

Threshold Theory

A further possible complication is that the effects of heredity and environment may differ in relative importance at different levels of ability, or in different SES or racial– ethnic groups. Jensen drew attention to this in 1967, and I have outlined earlier (p. 139) his view of environment as a "threshold variable," which implies that gross deficiencies may seriously impair intellectual development, but improvements within the normal and above-average range make much less difference. If the heritability ratio should be larger at the top and lower at the bottom end of the scale, this might be missed by analyses of variance around the means of representative samples. Indeed, it would involve another form of GE– interaction, to which the additive model would not apply.

As far back as 1943, Burt obtained higher intersib correlations for scholastic achievement with children of above-average IQ (namely, 0.61) than with those whose IQs were below 100 (namely, 0.47). Jensen (1969) also pointed out that more high IQs tend to be found among low-SES children than low IQs among high-SES children, and this was confirmed in a study by Vernon and Mitchell (1974). One reason for expecting stronger hereditary variance among high-intelligence families is that they probably attach greater importance to assortative mating. There might also be differences in GE− covariance, insofar as above-average parents are more likely to adapt the environment appropriately to their own brighter and duller children. However, there is little relevant experimental evidence, and Jensen now tends to regard the threshold phenomenon as applying only to small numbers of children reared in exceptionally deprived environments, not as operating linearly throughout the whole range; thus, it would be of little relevance in comparing the mean IQ difference between blacks and whites (see Chapter 17).

In regard to cultural differences, Loehlin, Lindzey, and Spuhler outline four recent studies that provide some data on relative heritability of intelligence in blacks and whites. The results are somewhat conflicting, but, overall, they tend to show little or no difference.[6] Where there is lower heritability in blacks, it is usually associated with lower IQ variance, which is a common finding among black populations (see Kennedy, Van de Riet, and White, 1963). This might be due to their IQ distributions being somewhat skewed and possibly to poorer test reliability near the bottom end. However, one study by Scarr-Salapatek (1971b) is worth describing in some detail because she claimed lower heritability figures than most authors on the basis of somewhat unsatisfactory data.

Scarr-Salapatek

Scarr-Salapatek (1971b) begins by mentioning a study of MZ and DZ twins, 60 in all, where the intraclass correlation on an unspecified nonverbal intelligence test was 0.61 in both groups. She forebore to publish this because the absence of any difference would be unacceptable to readers who believe in substantial genetic variance. However, if the two groups each consisted of 30 pairs, their correlations might differ by as much as 0.30 (e.g., 0.75 and 0.45) without differing from 0.61 at more than

[6]Last (1976), working with L. J. Eaves, has recently completed the analysis of test scores of white twins and black twins living in Georgia. The broad heritabilities for the two races are almost identical, though the components of variance differ.

TABLE 12.7
Scarr-Salapatek's Analyses for
Different Ethnic and SES Groups of Twins

	Middle- and upper-SES whites		Middle- and upper-SES blacks		Lower-SES blacks
	V	V + NV	V	V + NV	V
G	43.6	39.0	72.3	26.0	34.3
E	56.4	61.0	27.7	74.0	65.7

Source: Data from Scarr-Salapatek, 1971b.

the 5 percent level; in other words, the absence of any MZ–DZ difference could well be due to chance.

Scarr-Salapatek's major study was an attempt to show that heritability is lower, and environmental variance higher, among blacks than among whites, and among lower SES than among average and higher-class children. She tested 506 pairs of black and 282 pairs of white twins in second to twelfth grade in Philadelphia schools, using verbal and nonverbal group tests that differed for different grade levels. The mean total IQs were 97 for whites, 84 for blacks. She was not able to pick out MZ from DZ twins, but by contrasting same-sex (MZ and DZ) with opposite-sex (all DZ), obtained approximate figures for MZ. The two groups were also classified into top, middle, and bottom thirds for SES on the basis of the city districts in which they resided. Heritability was calculated from

$$\frac{2(r_{MZ} - r_{DZ})}{1 - \sigma^2_{error}}$$

with a modification to allow for assortative mating.

The results for different subgroups are difficult to follow because of so many instances where the opposite-sex pairs yielded higher correlations than the same-sex pairs, but Table 12.7 seems representative. Clearly, the figures for whites both on verbal and total tests (V + NV) are much lower than in Burt's, Jensen's, and Jink's studies. But the results for blacks are too variable to carry any conviction. However, some simpler statistics seem to support Scarr-Salapatek's hypotheses. First, the mean score differences between upper- and lower-SES groups among whites was 14.5 points (on tests normed to a standard deviation of 20); whereas among blacks, the SES group difference amounted only to 5.2 points, indicating that IQ is less related to SES in blacks than whites. Second, among the middle- and upper-SES groups of both races, the same-sex correlations exceeded the opposite-sex on verbal, nonverbal, and combined tests. In the lower-class groups of both races, only 1 of the 6 differences was positive, thus suggesting no significant hereditary variance at this level. However, the latter finding might simply be due to the reliability of low-SES children's scores being too weak to prove anything. The author admits that the score distributions were often considerably skewed; moreover, the tests were routine ones applied by the pupils' own teachers, and such data are known to be less trustworthy than scores obtained by trained testers.

Eaves and Jinks (1972), and Loehlin, Lindzey, and Spuhler (1975) criticize the study on similar grounds. The former authors point out that Scarr-Salapatek's subgroup numbers were too small to support any conclusion other than that there exists some correlation between pairs of twins; however, this correlation does not vary significantly by race, SES, or MZ versus DZ, and does not demonstrate whether causation is genetic or otherwise. Some 4,000 of her pairs would have been necessary to prove even gross differences between races or SES groups as attributable to differences in heritability.

Despite these serious weaknesses, this study has been cited by such critics as Schwartz and Schwartz (1974) and Layzer (1972) as contradicting Jensen's and other claims for heritability of IQ. Even Dobzhansky (1973) refers to its findings of differential heritabilities as a promising breakthrough. In contrast, the editors of *Nature* (1972) remark that workers in the genetics of intelligence should lean over backward to ensure that inadequate data are not used to support unjustifiable conclusions.

GENERAL CONCLUSIONS

It would seem that all studies based on reasonably reliable data and fair-sized samples concur in indicating substantial genetic variance of at least 60 percent underlying individual differences in phenotypic IQ. However, the earlier studies, yielding heritability figures of 0.80 and over, should probably be discarded in that most of them derived partly or wholly from Burt's data, which, for one reason or another, yielded generally higher correlations than those reported by any other authors. Although Kamin's criticisms are, as we have seen, greatly exaggerated, he does point out weaknesses in many of the other studies that went to make up Erlenmeyer-Kimling and Jarvik's median correlations. Thus, it would not be surprising if the results from more satisfactory samples yielded h^2 percentages nearer 60 than 80, or even lower.

Another point brought out by our survey is that the use of different models or alternative techniques often produces quite widely varying figures; and, although there have been important advances in methodology and statistics since the early analyses such as Holzinger's, there is still no consensus as to the most appropriate. In particular, one feels dissatisfied with the treatment of genotype–environment covariance, which is sometimes deducted from environmental variance, sometimes from hereditary variance, and most often simply ignored. Probably, we should admit that mathematics alone cannot provide the answer; the causation of such covariance is so complex that it is difficult to treat it as a separate, additive component. Nevertheless, Jencks' 15 percent (as revised by Loehlin, Lindzey, and Spuhler), Morton's 14 percent, and Jensen's 7 percent suggest that an agreed definition, and method of estimation, may be possible.

SUMMARY

1   Many authors have attempted to analyze the relative contributions of genetic and environmental factors to variance in phenotypic intelligence. But the problem is greatly complicated by our inability to obtain human samples that meet the requirements of ANOVA designs. Different models and techniques of analysis, especially when applied to different samples or different intelligence tests, naturally yield discordant results.

2   Several plausible components of variance have been distinguished, including assortative mating between parents, dominance (or gene interaction), genetic–environmental covariance and interaction, and differences in effects between families and within families. The available data on different kinship groups are quite inadequate to sort out so many variables. GE–covariance would appear particularly important, but it has been ignored in some analyses.

3   The first large-scale study was that of Burt and Howard (1956), and this yielded the heritability coefficient (h^2 or G–variance) of 0.81, on which Jensen relied in 1969. Jinks and Fulker have developed more sophisticated "biometrical-genetical" techniques of analysis, which, when applied to the same data, yield a quite different pattern, though heritability is still very high. Cattell's Multiple Abstract Variance Analysis (MAVA) is also described.

4   Other analyses, by Loehlin, Lindzey, and Spuhler, by Morton, and by Jensen, have used the Erlenmeyer-Kimling and Jarvik median correlations. Again, the hypothesized components differ, but the broad heritability figures range from 0.75 to 0.65.

5   Jencks studied the factors contributing to social inequality among adults, including genetic differences in intellectual capacities, which he regards as far less important than most psychologists have supposed. With path analysis of previously published correlations, his hereditary variance dropped to 45 percent; but both Jinks and Fulker, and Loehlin, Lindzey, and Spuhler have reanalyzed his data, obtaining figures of 68 and 61 percent. These analyses do yield substantial covariance estimates.

6   Thus, there appears to be some convergence from the different researches on roughly 60 percent genetic, 30 percent environmental, and 10 percent GE– covariance. But in view of all the uncertainties, it is unlikely that general agreement will be reached on any precise figures.

7   There is some support for Jensen's suggestion of environment as a "threshold variable," having a greater influence at the lower end of the range of severely deprived environments. Genetic variance, then, would be relatively higher in the middle and upper classes.

8   ˙Similar claims have been made for lower heritability in black than in white samples, though a study by Scarr-Salapatek, designed to demonstrate this, provided only very limited support.

13

The Interpretation
of Heritability

I n this chapter, I will try to outline fairly and fully the many
published criticisms that, in effect, deny the applicability of
analysis of variance (or correlational analyses) to such complex
problems as the genetic and environmental determinants of intelligence. The meaningfulness of such investigations and the validity of their results have been questioned by several geneticists
and others; for example, Dobzhansky (1973), Lewontin (1970;
1976), Hirsch (1967), Gottesman (1968), Layzer (1972; 1974),
Block and Dworkin (1974), Cancro (1971), Morton (1972), and
Medawar (1977). While some of the writings contain a good deal
of abuse of "Jensenism," largely on ideological grounds, there
are also serious scientific and methodological arguments that deserve consideration, even if we disagree with them in the end.
The discussion will also show that the notion of heritability is
frequently misinterpreted and will attempt to clarify its actual
implications.

GENERAL OBJECTIONS

The basic objection might be expressed as the lack of determinacy between genotype and phenotype. The same genotype
can produce different phenotypes in different individuals depending on the particular sequence of their environmental ex-

periences; this is referred to as the range of reaction. Likewise, different genotypes can produce the same phenotype. Nature and nurture do not merely combine or interact; as Medawar puts it, "the contribution of nature is a function of nurture, and of nurture a function of nature." Dobzhansky states that no reasonable scientist denies the importance of genetic factors; but genes do not determine mental abilities, they merely specify a certain range of behavior in a population subjected to a certain range of environments. But the possible range of environments is infinitely varied, hence, our knowledge of genetics does not help us to make any useful predictions about psychological traits; each individual is a unique mosaic.

Lewontin points out that geneticists do not expect to find any simple gene–environment relations; a genotype may be relatively insensitive to a considerable range of environmental stimulation and then very sensitive outside this range. Moreover, gene interactions such as dominance nullify any additive model of genetic and environmental contributions such as the psychometrist relies on. Thus, the nature–nurture controversy is sterile and insoluble, since we can never hold either heredity or environment constant in order to discover their effects in isolation. Cancro adds that it is misleading to think of either genes or environment as being the more important; genes can only express themselves in an environment, and an environment has no effect except by evoking genotypes already present.

To talk of "high IQ genes" is a misnomer, in Rose's (1972) view, since the nature of the phenotype always depends on the particular environmental history. It is equally incorrect, according to Lerner and Libby (1976), to regard hereditary endowment as "setting the limits" of variation, though this has frequently been claimed in textbooks on individual differences. Hambley (1972) particularly criticizes such contentions as that genetic factors are four times as important as environmental, since this completely distorts the nature of their interaction. If $h^2 = 0.80$, all we are entitled to say is that four-fifths of the variation in the population is associated with genetic differences.

Both Lewontin (1976) and Savage (1975) object to the application of sophisticated statistical techniques to vague and unreliable raw materials. Investigations that rely on analysis of variance involve greatly oversimplified assumptions. The psychometrist does not, like the experienced geneticist, study natural biological units of physical structure or behavior, but, as Bijou (1971) points out, he is working with hypothetical constructs inferred from observations of twins and other similar data, and these are quite a different matter. While we must admit the force of these arguments, they are really objections to almost any kind of psychological research. For example, there is surely a good deal of scientific justification and practical utility in the construct of "reading ability" in children; yet our measurements are no more than rather crude end-products, which ignore the extreme complexity of the neurological and psychological processes involved in the development of reading skills. By extension, the physicist and chemist might be equally entitled to criticize the possibility of any kind of physiological or medical research.

Our criterion of the value of such psychological constructs and the applicability of quantitative analyses should not be the apparent amenability, or unsuitability, of the data, but the extent to which such work engenders predictions that can be tested out. Urbach (1974) argues convincingly that hypotheses regarding genetic influences on intelligence have produced stronger and better verified predictions than have the environmentalist-developmental constructs generally accepted in the 1960s. At the same time, we should certainly not ignore the concerns expressed by geneticists. Thus, even R. A. Fisher, who has done so much to advance biometric and psychometric studies, talks of heritability measures as "one of those unfortunate short-cuts which have emerged in biometry for lack of a more thorough analysis of the data" (see Hirsch, 1971). And Morton (1972) states: "Measures of heritability, when the environment is not randomized, are fraught with uncontrollable difficulties."

In a thoughtful critique of heritability studies, Poli (1976) agrees that neurological tissues, like other parts of the body, depend on the genes; therefore, all behavior must, to some extent, be under genetic control. However, genetic analyses of continuous variables are applicable only if those variables can be measured accurately and objectively and without gene – environment interactions.

Such criticisms would carry more weight if heritability analyses were still confined to simple additive models, as they were in the early days. But, as shown in Chapter 12, psychometrists nowadays try to cover all the main interactions that can be shown to have statistically significant effects. It is not so much the genetic psychometrist who oversimplifies the situation as it is the environmentalist, who attempts to explain all phenotypic variations in terms of a single variable of stimulation versus deprived environment.

HERITABILITY AS A POPULATION
STATISTIC, NOT A TRAIT PROPERTY

Burt, Jensen, and subsequent writers have emphasized that heritability refers to the particular population in which it is calculated. It is not an attribute of the trait as such, for example, intelligence or height. Nor does it tell us anything about the extent to which the trait of a particular individual or subgroup is inherited. Hirsch's accusation that psychologists mistakenly apply heritability studies to comparing different traits does have some justification. The generalization that height shows greater heritability than intelligence, and intelligence greater than scholastic achievement or than most personality traits happens to be true within white societies, but it would not necessarily apply elsewhere.

Heritability has no absolute value, in the sense that the ratio will always depend considerably on the variance and degree of heterogeneity of environmental conditions. The heritability of intelligence generally works out at about 60 percent or more in North America and Britain, largely because members of these cultures do experience fairly similar environments. Although some children obviously are reared in much more favorable circumstances than others, they all grow up seeing much the same world of people and objects; in the main, they speak the same language, and the great majority undergo a rather highly standardized education. But if it were possible to apply common tests and calculate heritabilities in a population ranging all the way from upper-middle-class U.S. whites to Australian aboriginals, we can be sure that the effects of different environments would be greatly magnified and that the heritability percentage would probably fall well below 50. No one would dissent from Lewontin's (1970) statement that "There is no such thing as *the* heritability of IQ, since heritability of a trait is different in different populations at different times."

It also follows, conversely, that the greater our success in equalizing environments through social and educational reform, the more will any remaining differences in ability depend on the genes; in other words, heritability will be raised. This paradox is discussed by Herrnstein (1973); however, he tends to exaggerate the dependence of real-life achievement on the IQ.

HERITABILITY IS PROBABILISTIC

As Hirsch has stated, heritability is an average figure for members of the group being studied. It does not indicate the extent of genetic determination in any one individual.[1] This in-

---

[1] An average figure could, of course, be quoted for any individual, but it would be likely to have a large Standard Error.

determinacy would also follow since we have admitted that genes and environment are inextricably entangled in the development of each individual. But the notion of heritability is not therefore meaningless, although Layzer, for example, goes so far as to state that the heritability of the IQ is a pseudo-concept, having no more reality than, say, "the sexuality of fractions." However, some of the examples quoted by Hirsch, Lewontin, Layzer, and Medawar in order to demonstrate that nature and nurture cannot be separated are based on the operations of particular genes. While the origins of polygenetic traits like intelligence are, doubtless, even more complex, they appear to be more amenable to variance analysis.

It is possible and meaningful to examine the extent to which differences in individual phenotypes are associated with differences in genetic endowment, and how far genetic potentialities are influenced by the variations in environment occurring in the population under consideration. In other words, we can make probabilistic statements. This is, of course, generally true in mental measurement: For example, a child with a high IQ and scholastic achievement in elementary school is more likely to be suited to a future college education and a professional career than a child with low IQ and achievement; yet there are many exceptions, as Terman frequently pointed out. Similarly, probabilistic knowledge of heritability ratios may assist many of our predictions about developmental potentialities and help to point the way to environmental modifications that might be more effective than those available at the present time. Cancro (1971) agrees that our ignorance of gene–environment interactions does not prevent us from studying the effects of heredity in a stable range of environments or the differences brought about by unusual changes.

The following simple example may help to show that the geneticist's forebodings about the inapplicability of variance analysis to heritability are less serious than they appear. In an ordinary analysis of variance design, suppose that four matched groups of children are taught arithmetic by two different teachers, each using two different methods. Obviously, the scores obtained on the dependent variable, achievement, will depend, in all kinds of complex and unknown ways, on the characteristics of the teachers, the individual children, and the methods, yet it is generally recognized as entirely legitimate to calculate the variance attributable to (1) teachers, (2) methods, (3) any interaction, and (4) individual differences and error. So why should analogous calculations not be applied to IQs, provided the greater complexity of the independent variables is borne in mind?

A good deal of confusion and controversy arises from failure to distinguish effects on mean performance from effects on variance contributions. Cattell (1971a) points out that developmental and social psychologists, who usually favor environmentalist theories, are characteristically interested in the extent to which particular environmental changes increase the effectiveness of children's intellectual, scholastic, or social functioning. Psychometrists, on the other hand, are concerned with individual differences, or rank orders, as it were, and the extent to which test scores correlate with one another in kinship or foster groups or correlate with measures of environment. Thus, heritability analyses, whether based on correlations or on analyses of variance, are basically weak in yielding information about causality, as was illustrated in the discussion of GE– covariance in Chapter 12. Again, it should be noted that analyses of variance are typically applied not to absolute values of a variable but to variations in values around the population mean.

HERITABILITY DOES NOT IMPLY FIXED INTELLIGENCE

Another commonly raised criticism is that high heritability means that an individual's intelligence is fixed for life. However, Jensen freely admits that heritability estimates hold only for the current range of environments within the population studied; they tell us nothing about what might happen if new environmental changes were introduced. Thus, Dobzhansky comments that knowledge of h^2 is of very little use to anyone, since environments are infinitely variable; and Elkind (1969) concludes that genotype and potential capacity are essentially meaningless, since they only represent expectancies under present conditions.

That high heritability does not imply immutability is well illustrated by height. Although h^2 is approximately 0.90, there has been a marked and continuous rise in the average height of people in Western cultures over the past hundred years — chiefly in the rate of growth in children, but also to some extent in adults. Presumably, this increase is attributable mainly to improved health and nutritional conditions; however, it might also result, to some extent, from genetic change due to heterosis, that is, outbreeding between different ethnic subgroups, for very little intermarriage occured between people living in different countries or separate communities until the development of mechanical modes of transport.

A similar increase has undoubtedly taken place in intelligence. The average intellectual level of the population of the U.S.S.R. must be far higher nowadays than in prerevolution days, when the bulk of the population consisted of uneducated peasant farmers. Many books on individual differences mention the remarkable improvement in average intelligence of Tennessee mountain children over 10 years, resulting from reduced isolation, improved health care, and particularly from improved education (Wheeler, 1942); and the rise equivalent to some 13 IQ points among U.S. Army recruits between World Wars I and II (Tuddenham, 1948). I have pointed out (Vernon, 1960) that the latter rise might be attributed partly to greater familiarization of young American adults with intelligence tests, but there is a general agreement that more extended school attendance in the 1930s than the 1910s was a major factor. Probably, also, adequate mastery of the English language became much more widespread over this period. There is good reason to believe that the average intelligence level of the human race will continue to rise as education improves in underdeveloped countries; and that, even in Western countries, further gains may occur as developments in our knowledge of child psychology and in educational technology increase what Bruner calls human amplifying systems.

It is not correct, as some critics believe, to interpret Jensen's writings as supporting innate limitations of intelligence, either in the individual or in ethnic minorities (apart from possible improvement through selective breeding). However, some earlier writers, such as Terman and Burt, did give the impression that an individual's g is a kind of static and unalterable personal possession, and that there exists in each racial-ethnic group a fixed "pool" of genes making for intelligence. For instance, it was often argued both that insufficient use was being made of this pool because so many high-IQ school-leavers did not go on to college, and, at the same time, that only a limited proportion of any population would be capable of benefiting from a college education (see Vernon, 1963). This view would certainly not be acceptable to modern genetic-interactionist theories of intelligence, such as Jensen's. Even if environmental variance is assessed at 20 percent, an improvement equivalent to 1σ on a scale of favorable versus unfavorable environments would increase a child's IQ by 5.8 points; and the differences between the very best and worst environments—say 5σ apart—could bring about an IQ difference of 29 points. If, however, environmental variance were reckoned at 40 percent, the differences would reach 8.9 and 44 points respectively.[2] These rises would readily cover the size of the gains reported in most studies of intervention, including the 24- to 27-point difference between Heber's experimental and control groups, and Skeels' gain of approximately 30 points. It would not cover Koluchova's gain from IQ 40 to 100, but such subjects as hers were so abnormally deprived that they can be regarded as falling outside the expected distribution.

It should also be remembered that, with the development of novel and more effective methods of childhood stimulation, still greater improvements can be anticipated. Hence, Jensen is much concerned with exploring new treatments and possible aptitude–treatment interactions, which would particularly help the growth of children who are handicapped by poor genes, poor background, or both. Though it is true that heritability analyses cannot tell us what would happen if more effective interventions are discovered, they do give us information about the effectiveness of currently existing manipulations of environment, which is surely what we want to know for immediate educational and social welfare decisions.

HERITABILITY AND TEACHABILITY

Hirsch complains that the title of Jensen's 1969 article ("How Much Can We Boost IQ and Scholastic Achievement?") suggests that the failure of Head Start was due to the much greater influence of genetic than of environmental factors on children's educability. Also, Medawar (1977) reiterates the hoary fallacy that high h^2 implies the uselessness of education and training. But Jensen does not claim that teachability is lowered, nor education unimportant, when heritability is high. What high h^2 does imply is that differences in learning in different school or other environments are small relative to the differences attributable to genetic factors. Even if the heritability of intelligence approximated 100 percent, the present average level and range of intelligence would not be achieved without the stimulation of intellectual growth that education supplies. Here again, I should emphasize the distinction between the population level

[2] These figures are calculated from:

$$\sigma_E = \sigma_P \sqrt{r_{xx} - \sigma^2_G},$$

where r_{xx} is the test reliability, taken as 0.95; σ_P, the phenotypic variance, is taken as 15; σ^2_G is the heritability; and σ_E is the Standard Deviation of environmental effects.

of a trait and the nature of individual differences in that trait. The factors that produce population changes are not the same as those producing the present range of phenotypes.

Population changes might be brought about either by genetic manipulation, such as selective breeding, or by the discovery of novel environmental stimuli that have not yet been tried out. What we can say is that change of either kind would by unlikely to bring about greater equality in achievement, since they would tend to help the bright as much as, or more than, the dull; hence, the present rank order of achievement would be little affected. (However, it is still possible that new interventions might be found that would be of particular benefit to those with relatively poor genetic endowment.) Some writers try to argue that the degree of heritability really makes very little practical difference, since, in any case, we would still wish to supply the best education for children that we can afford. Scarr-Salapatek (1971a) adds that, since all current authors allow some environmental variance, there is little reason for controversy; but she points out that the size of the heritability ratio is important, since, if it were low, we would aim mainly to extend present methods of education more effectively to deprived as well as to privileged children; if it were high, on the other hand, we should be more concerned to find new techniques of intervention. Again, the finding that scholastic achievement has lower heritability than intelligence means that we are perfectly justified in paying a good deal of attention to motivational factors and techniques of learning in the classroom. In contrast, we have few clear aims or agreed methods of trying to bring up children to be intelligent, although, as described in Chapter 7, considerable progress is now being made.

OPERATIONALISM

Both Block and Dworkin (1974) and Layzer (1972) criticize Jensen's acceptance of IQ as a suitable variable for genetic analysis in the absence of any sound theory as to just what it measures (see p. 55). He is arguing, they would say, that we do not need to know the biological or psychological significance of what we are measuring, provided the scores correlate with scholastic and occupational success. According to Layzer, Jensen and Herrnstein "would have us believe that we can gain important insights into human intelligence and its inheritance by subjecting measurements that we do not understand to a mathematical analysis that we cannot justify."

Layzer and other critics believe that this is a fallacious application of operationalism as the scientist employs it. The scientist's constructs always arise from a clear theoretical framework, so that further relationships can be hypothesized and tested; psychometrists reverse the procedure by trying to derive theories from measurements. Moreover, in trying to study intelligence operationally, they are content to use quite a variety of different tests that give somewhat different results and, therefore, should not be treated like height, for example, which is an objective measure of a defined trait. Over the years, psychologists have become so accustomed to reifying the notion of intelligence that they believe their tests are measuring the same thing in different individuals, even in different cultural groups. Another weakness of tests is that two or more people can get the same score, although their actual item passes or failures are very different. The IQ is a "black box" measure, whose constitution is largely unknown. Layzer advocates studying a more clearly defined operation, such as information processing, which could be objectively quantified; though even here there would, of course, be a mixture of genetic and environmental contributions as difficult to break down as the IQ.

It is for such reasons that the data on heritability are so inconsistent. Erlenmeyer-Kimling and Jarvik's table (see Table 11.1) does, on the whole, indicate genetic influence, but the ranges of correlations are so wide that they cannot be taken to prove the fit of the available data to an additive genetic–environmental model. Hirsch adds that such results, being population-specific, have very little general significance.

Layzer, like several other writers (e.g., Biesheuvel, 1972; Hudson, 1972; Rose, 1972), concludes that much more profitable than attempts to determine heritability would be further work like that of Skodak and Skeels, Klineberg, and Heber, to determine just what kinds of intervention work. This would save us from the fallacy that some children are so limited genetically that they are forever incapable of abstract reasoning or other complex mental skills.

In answer, I would reiterate that psychometry is quite entitled to use its own brand of operationalism, regardless of philosophical theories of scientific method, provided it works. This does not mean relying on the admittedly circular process of choosing intelligence test items that differentiate scholastically successful from less successful children and then claiming that the tests are measures of intelligence because they predict scholastic success. The critics generally ignore the whole corpus of factorial work from Spearman onward, which demonstrates that there is an underlying unity in different measures of intellectual performance, and that the nature of this variable is defined by the kinds of tests that load high or low on g. Block and Dworkin dismiss this argument on the grounds that different factorists prefer different models and techniques; but we have shown that there are no essential contradictions in the work of, say, Spearman, Burt, and Thurstone (see Chapter 4). Again, the calculation of g scores by the average of performances on a variety of item-types calling for diverse specific abilities is quite justifiable, providing the scores are sufficiently reliable or internally consistent. Obviously, it would be advantageous if we could deal with more homogeneous, or precisely defined, variables, but we have seen already that Thurstone factor scores yield quite variable heritabilities in different studies. Nevertheless, further research with these or other measures of more specialized cognitive capacities would be of great value, assuming that large enough samples, representing different kinships, could be reliably tested.

In similar vein, Medawar (1977) attacks the psychometrist's belief that so complex a set of variables as are involved in intelligence can be meaningfully expressed by a single number, the IQ. But this objection, too, has been generally admitted for some 50 years. We regard intelligence as a single linear variable only insofar as this is justified by the results of factorial studies.

There is a further reason for contesting Block and Dworkin's claim that theory should precede measurement — namely, that this does not seem to have happened often in the history of science. For example, much empirical information and measurement of heat and electricity were obtained before modern theories of their physical nature were formulated. Finally, as pointed out in Chapters 3 and 4, purely operational approaches to the definition of intelligence are inadequate, but it is by no means true that mental testing has developed without any regard for psychological theorizing.

ENVIRONMENT

There is probably more substance in criticisms of the way psychometrists have handled environment than in the attacks on the basic principles of mental testing. We simply do not know the most crucial environmental factors in mental development and, although earlier chapters described considerable progress, it is still very difficult to pin down and assess the major variables. Thus, we are apt to think of environment as a single, unitary variable and to measure it with crude indices such as father's occupation or parental education. One reason is that, in much genetic research, for instance, that using twins, the psychometrist does not usually attempt to evaluate environment as such, but treats it as the residual variance, that is, the totality of factors remaining after the various genetic contributions have been assessed (and sometimes, though not always, allowances made for the error component). Jensen agrees that $1 - h^2$, that is, the environmental variance contribution, does not correspond to the whole complex of prenatal, home background, and school conditions that would be included in the developmental psychologist's conception of environment as functional and dynamic (see Elkind, 1969). However, a large proportion of this broader conception of environment applies in common to all members of a cultural group. The psychometrist is interested only in environmental differences that can be shown to alter intellectual growth.

Bijou (1971) makes the point that we are too apt to think of environment as something "out there," which provokes or inhibits the growth of intelligence. In addition to current external stimulation and internal states (e.g., motivation), environment includes all of the individual's own past experiences influencing test responses. An important part, too, is played by "arrangers," such as parents and teachers, who design what they regard as appropriate stimulation for the growing child and reinforce or punish behavior. Other important components exist more in people's minds than in their observable behavior; for example, the different values of middle-class and lower-class parents, as described by Bernstein (also see Swift, 1972).

In some studies, particularly those of foster children (see Burks, 1928), attempts have been made to assess selected aspects of environment in more detail (see also Wolf, 1966; Miller, 1970). Generally, there is not a great deal of difference among the correlations from several variables (apart from the boosting that occurs in any multiple correlation, unless corrected for shrinkage or cross-validated). But there is always the possibility that we have neglected some particularly important factor that, if included, would have raised the correlation between environment and phenotype, and thus reduced the heritability ratio. This is an even greater problem in racial-ethnic group comparisons (see Part IV).

On the whole, the available studies, yielding correlations between child's IQ and environment of about 0.40 to 0.60, tally fairly well with genetic analyses of heritability, which ascribe from 20 to 35 percent of variance to environment. But there is certainly room for more direct studies of heredity and of major environmental variations in one and the same group, such as foster children.

SUMMARY

1   In addition to the violent attacks by environmental psychologists on Jensen's methods and conclusions, serious doubts have been expressed by many geneticists regarding the applicability of variance analysis to such complex phenomena as gene–environment interaction in the development of intelligence.

2   Genes cannot be thought of as causing particular attributes; rather, they have a wide range of effects in different environments. It is also argued that techniques used for analyzing precisely defined biological attributes are inappropriate when applied to vague constructs such as intelligence. However, it is suggested here that up-to-date methods of heritability analysis can cope with these difficulties to some extent.

3   Several other commonly raised criticisms and limitations are already admitted by Jensen; for example, that heritability is a population statistic, not a fixed property of any trait. It is reduced when the range of environments is large and increased when environments are relatively homogeneous.

4   The percentage attributed to genetic influences tell us little about the heritability of a trait in a particular individual (or subgroup). Like most mental measurements, heritability is probabilistic, yielding information relevant to educational or other decisions about people within a particular culture.

5   High heritability does not imply fixity of intelligence, since, with novel changes in environment, the population value of the phenotype can alter, as has already been demonstrated for height and for intelligence. Nor is there a fixed "pool" of intelligence available within a population.

6   High heritability does not imply that teaching and learning are unimportant, only that the range of variations in an ability brought about by currently available educational and child-rearing environments is limited. If the heritability of intelligence were low, more effective applications of current educational techniques should enable everyone to achieve better; if it were high, it would be necessary to search for novel approaches or different techniques that would be better adapted to children with different gene patterns.

7   Block and Dworkin have made a sustained attack on psychometric operationalism, that is, the notion that the IQ is a valid measure of human intelligence because it enables us to predict, for instance, educational achievement. They neglect the enormous amount of evidence from factorial and other studies of an underlying g factor in a wide range of measures of cognitive skills, and exaggerate the disagreements between different schools of factorists.

8   There are stronger grounds for criticizing the psychometrist's conception of environment, which is, at present, usually assessed merely by finding the residual variance in intelligence not accounted for by genetic components. Though progress has been made by developmental psychologists in delineating the major environmental variables in intellectual development, we have little understanding of the nature of their interactions with genetic influences.

14

Foster-Child Studies

The main evidence on the genetics of intelligence, apart from the studies of twins, derives from children brought up not by their natural parents but in a foster home or, occasionally, in an institution like an orphanage.[1] It is necessary, of course, to have some estimate of such children's basic intelligence before the new environment began to operate, but infant developmental quotients are too poor as predictors for this purpose. Therefore, the child's probable level is often estimated from records of the intelligence, education, and/or SES of the natural parents. After a few years, it is possible to see whether a gain in IQ has occurred in the foster home or whether there is some correlation with foster-parent ability or with the quality of the foster home. This should show the effectiveness of environmental influences that cannot be isolated when a child is brought up in the natural parents' home.

However, there are a great many complexities and disturbing factors that make the interpretation of such results highly dubious. Thus, many psychologists accept the view that a child's

---

[1] Some writers distinguish *fostering*, which is temporary, from *adoption*, which is permanent, the adoptee taking the adoptive parents' surname. I have followed the equally common practice of using the two terms interchangeably.

genetic intelligence has a greater effect on eventual IQ than the influence of foster home and parents; other writers — Kamin in particular — conclude the opposite; namely, that the foster child's genetic intelligence makes no difference, and later IQ can be accounted for entirely in terms of the kind of home or institution in which the child has been reared.

MUNSINGER'S SURVEY

Fortunately, an extensive survey of most of the published reports has been made recently by Munsinger (1975a; 1975b), and I will attempt to evaluate his somewhat genetically biased interpretations alongside Kamin's strongly environmentally biased criticisms.[2] Munsinger begins by listing the main sources of ambiguity and distortion that have entered, to varying extents, into all the published data.

1 *Atypicality of sampling of adoptees.* Adopted children tend to be atypical of the general population. Over the 1920s and 1930s, when many of the major studies were carried out, adoptees were mostly illegitimate children who were apt to be quite carefully selected. Those available for fostering were usually of good health; often attention was paid to the mother's educational level and the father's, if known, though admittedly the mothers were sometimes low in SES and education. Sometimes there was a trial period of 1 to 2 years, and foster parents could return children who did not appear to be progressing satisfactorily, which — despite the unreliability of judgments of intelligence of, say, 2-year-olds — would tend to bias the intelligence of those retained in an upward direction. In addition, some legitimate children were placed in foster homes, but usually they were older and more likely to have parents of low SES and education who had failed to care for them adequately.

2 *Attrition.* If cases are followed up after several years, there is almost always substantial attrition for one reason

[2] Since this chapter was written, Kamin (1977a) has published a commentary on Munsinger's review, claiming that it is inaccurate in several details, selective in stressing evidence that supports genetic theory, and neglecting evidence that supports environmental effects. My own review includes few of the points raised by Kamin; hence, I am letting it stand unaltered (apart from the comments on Munsinger's own research).

or another, and the remaining cases might differ somewhat in ability from the original group.

3 *Selective placement.* This almost always occurs, since the adoption agency tries to match the child to the foster home and to place healthier and brighter children, or those with well-educated natural mothers, in superior homes. The best way to discover this is to correlate natural parent intelligence, SES, or education with those of the foster parent, though this has seldom been done. Such placement will tend to boost any correlation between child IQ and foster-parent ability.

4 *Test unreliability.* The available mental tests for children below about 6 years are, as shown in Chapter 5, too poor in reliability and validity to provide a good indication of initial or present ability. In particular, it is impossible to assess children accurately at the time of, or shortly after, early adoption.

5 *Lack of information.* It is often impossible to obtain full information about the natural parents, especially the father, and this may further bias the sampling. When mothers have been tested, they have sometimes taken the 1916 Stanford-Binet, which is known to give unduly low adult IQs.

6 *Age of adopting.* Some adoptees are removed from their natural parents several weeks, months, even years after birth. In such cases, the natural parents may have had a substantial influence, and, therefore, any effects of the foster-home are restricted. However, in several studies, the children were removed very shortly after birth and kept in a fairly uniform institutional environment for a few weeks or months until adoption was completed. There seems to be no evidence that transfer to a foster home shortly after birth has any greater effect than after a few weeks or months.

7 *Parental age differences.* The typical age of natural parents is close to 20 years, whereas that for adopting parents is more likely to exceed 30. This may mean that the older foster parents handle the childrens' upbringing in a different manner. And it also means that there may be a spurious difference in SES between natural and foster parents, since the former are nearer the beginning of their occupational careers.

8 *Retest gains.* Some studies have involved repeated retesting of foster children. The resulting practice effects may produce apparent rises in IQ with age.

9   *Statistical difficulties.* A number of statistical problems may bias the results of foster-child studies. If the sample is restricted in range of ability, correlations with either natural or foster parents are lowered. Since the majority of foster homes are likely to be of average or superior quality, adopted children are exposed only to a limited range of environments. Then there are regression effects: A sample initially of below-average ability is likely to regress upward toward the mean when retested later. And, finally, if several variables, such as environmental indices, are combined to predict child IQ by multiple correlation techniques, the coefficient is likely to be boosted by chance errors in the correlation matrix unless corrected for shrinkage or applied to a fresh, cross-validation, sample.

Several of the major studies will now be examined, in order of their publication.

Freeman, Holzinger, and Mitchell (1928)

This study in Chicago included 401 foster children who came from low-SES backgrounds, but who, when tested with Stanford-Binet after some years in an average-to-good foster home, showed an almost normal distribution of intelligence. There is such a quantity of data, from subgroups that were legitimate or illegitimate and varied in age, race, time of placement, and the like, that we can pick out only a few of the results. Unfortunately, there was little information on the true parents, so the expected genetic IQ of the foster children cannot be calculated. Moreover, the average age at adoption was 4.2 (though there was a very wide range from 6 months to 17 years). The authors point out that 1916 Binet test IQs decline considerably with age, and this must have distorted many of the results.

The most thoroughly investigated group, tested at age 11 after an average of 6–7 years in a foster home, obtained a mean IQ of 97.5. However, in some 30 of these families, the foster parents had children of their own; the mean IQs for the natural and the foster children were 112.4 and 95.1, respectively, showing that, even if the foster children had improved on initial expectations, they had certainly not caught up with the natural children reared in the same home. This discrepancy could, of course, be due in part to the rather late age of adoption.

All the foster homes were rated on a scale comprising SES and foster-parent education, among other items; also, many of the foster parents had taken the Otis group test of intelligence.

The authors obtained a correlation of 0.48 between child IQ at 11 years and foster-home rating, and 0.39 with foster mid-parent IQ. For 156 children adopted before the age of 2 years, the even more striking correlation with foster-home rating of 0.52 was obtained. Although the authors claim that very little selective placement occured, a correlation as high as 0.34 was found in another subgroup of 74 between child IQ *before placement* at age 8 and home rating. Although this was an older group, it clearly suggests that part of the high correlation of foster-child IQ with foster-parent level was attributable to selective placement. Further, more of the younger adoptees, who were illegitimate and of higher IQ, tended to be placed in better homes.

The same group of 74 was retested 4 years later (around age 12); the mean initial and later IQs were 91.2 and 93.7, respectively. But the authors suggest that, if allowance is made for age effects on the scale, the second figure should be 98.7, indicating that an increase of 7½ IQ points had resulted from the improved foster-home environment. However, since ordinary regression effects would produce some rise, this argument does not seem very convincing. The initial correlation of 0.34 with the home rating had risen to 0.52, which does suggest some additional foster-home effect.

Other subgroups were made up of siblings in different foster homes. For 46 pairs separated before the oldest reached 6 years, the intraclass correlation was 0.25; for 38 pairs separated after the youngest reached 5 years, the correlation was 0.43. These results might suggest that the latter, who had lived together longer, intercorrelate about as highly as do normal siblings in their own homes, whereas the correlation drops when separation occurs at a fairly early age.

Kamin accepts the study as giving considerable support to environmental explanations, but admits that the results were likely to be affected by the unsatisfactory age norms of Binet IQs for older children. However, Munsinger regards as the only important findings: (1) the high degree of selective placement that affects any correlations between children and foster parents; and (2) the fact that the foster-children IQs were much lower than those of the natural children of the foster parents. In other respects, the study is quite inconclusive.

Burks (1928)

This California research, published in the same yearbook as that of Freeman, Holzinger, and Mitchell, was very much better controlled. The author studied 214 children, all adopted at less than 1 year (average age, 3 months), and compared them with a group of 105 children with the same sex and age distribution who were being reared by their own parents. The foster parents of the adoptees and the true parents of the comparison group were matched for occupation and locality. The children were given the Stanford-Binet test between 5 and 14 years, and their homes were carefully assessed for nine environmental characteristics, including the Stanford-Binet IQs of foster and control parents. Little is known of the ability level of the true parents of the adoptees, but they seem to have been of slightly above-average SES, and Woodworth (1941) suggests that the children's IQs would approximate 105, had they been brought up by their natural parents. Their Binet IQs averaged 107.4, suggesting little, if any, gain; whereas the mean for the control children was 115.4. Thus, the adoptees fell below the natural children, although brought up in parallel environments, much as happened in Freeman, Holzinger, and Mitchell's Chicago study.

Burk believes that there was little selective placement by the agency workers. Instead of relying on correlations between natural and adoptive parent characteristics, she and a colleague attempted to estimate the children's future IQs on the basis of agency records, and they achieved correlations of only 0.18 and 0.19 with the actual test results. The major findings of the study were correlations in the 0.20s between child IQ and foster-parent characteristics, whereas for the control group, the corresponding correlations were in the 0.50s. Multiple correlations were also calculated between child IQ and the best combination of home characteristics. These reached 0.42 in the foster-child group and 0.61 in the control group. Munsinger points out, as mentioned earlier, that these correlations would drop appreciably if corrected for shrinkage.

Burks goes on a stage further and regards her multiple correlation of 0.42 as showing the overall effect of environment on the IQ. She claims that the square of this figure, 17 percent, measures the proportion of variance in IQ attributable to environmental differences. Moreover, since the S.D. of IQ is around 15, then an environment 1 S.D. above the mean should raise the child's IQ by $0.42 \times 15 = 6.3$ IQ points. If we took the very best environments (1 in 1000), which were 3σ above the mean, the maximum effect would be to raise the IQ by 20 points. Similarly, an exceptionally poor environment could lower the IQ by 20 points.

Even if we accept these rather simplistic calculations, the result is not very convincing, since the correlation of 0.42 is dubious; on the one hand, it may be too high from lack of correction for shrinkage and because it is affected, to some extent, by selective placement. On the other hand, it may be too low,

TABLE 14.1
Lawrence's Correlation Ratios Between
Child IQ and Natural Father's SES

	Boys			Girls			
	Number	Mean IQ	S.D.	eta*	Number	Mean IQ	S.D.	eta*
Orphans	103	98.9	13.7	0.26	82	95.6	12.3	0.25
Control Group 1	211	100.7	15.8	0.27	228	100.9	14.1	0.22
Control Group 2	313	97.1	14.8	0.32	270	95.1	13.2	0.34

* eta = correlation ratio
Source: Data from Lawrence, 1931.

since there are likely to be other important aspects of environment that were not rated, including, for example, the prenatal and early postnatal influences.

Kamin's main criticism is that foster parents are always older than natural parents and differ from them in other respects. The fact that they are unusual tends to reduce any correlation between their own ability level and that of the foster children, or even of their natural children. We will take up this point later.

Lawrence (1931)

This English study is generally ignored by U.S. writers, but it provides valuable evidence on the resemblance of institutionalized children to their natural fathers. The main group of 269 was drawn from a home for illegitimate orphans, all of whom had been removed from their mothers between 1 month and 1 year and had had no contact at all with their fathers. However, the fathers' occupations were known. There were two main control groups, one consisting of children in a large elementary school and the other of children in a second institution who had, however, been admitted at various ages and spent, on the average, more than half their lives in their natural homes.

Correlation ratios between child IQ and father SES are shown in Table 14.1. The IQs were measured by the Simplex group test (verbal), which was given to all children aged 9 to 14 years, including 185 of the orphans. (Similar results were obtained by orphans on the Stanford-Binet, but these are not tabulated, since that test was not given to the elementary school control group.)

It can be seen that the mean IQs are all around 95 to 100. The mean correlation ratio for orphans of about 0.25 differs hardly at all from that for the elementary population (Control Group 1). However, the range of parental SES in the elementary group was rather restricted, and a fairer comparison can be made with the second group (although its members had spent part of their lives in an institution). Here, the mean of 0.33 is appreciably, though not significantly, higher than in the orphan group. We may conclude, then, that there is a small but significant correlation between the IQs of orphans and father's occupational level, but it is somewhat lower than the 0.33 obtained in a group reared mainly at home.

Burt (1943; 1958) claims to have found considerably correlations between the IQs of illegitimate children and those of their fathers with whom they have had no contact, but he gives no details. However, one study was based on 67 children of low-IQ mothers (range 70–85). These were separated into groups with high-IQ fathers (120–145) and those with average- or low-IQ (65–100) fathers. The mean IQs for the two sets of children were 103.2 and 88.6, respectively. This suggests a correlation of around 0.30, similar to Lawrence's, but it cannot, of course, be evaluated without further information.

Leahy (1935)

This study was similar to that of Burks, since the author compared a group of 194 adopted children with a control group of children in their own homes, matched for age, sex, education, and SES of foster and control parents. All the adoptees had been adopted by 6 months and had lived in the foster home for 5 years or more. The average Stanford-Binet IQ of adoptees was 110.5, that of natural children 109.7, suggesting that the foster children had gained in intelligence from the good environment. However, Leahy argues that the true parents of the adoptees were of above-average ability and the children were further selected for desirable attributes before placement. Both the foster and control parents were given the Otis S.A. Intelligence tests and Stanford-Binet vocabulary and answered a questionnaire on home background characteristics.

Leahy's major finding was a correlation averaging 0.56 between control children's IQ and mid-parent characteristics (IQ, vocabulary, education, general environmental status); for the adoptees and their foster parents, the corresponding figure was only 0.20, rising to 0.24 when corrected for rather smaller IQ range. Even this figure could be due in part to selective placement, despite Leahy's efforts to eliminate it; for there were correlations of about 0.20 between natural mother's education and adoptive parents' education, occupation, and intelligence. The correlation between adopted children's IQs and those of other children in the same family were even lower.

Kamin argues that, as in the Burks study, the low correlation of adopted-child IQs with foster-parent ability and home environment is due to some unusual feature of adopting families. Taking Freeman's, Burks', and Leahy's studies, he points out that the pooled mean correlation of IQs of true mid-parent with own child is 0.57, while that of adoptive mid-parent with adoptive child is 0.26. However, among parents who adopt *and* have children of their own, the correlation with own child drops to 0.35; Kamin concludes that this is very little larger than the 0.26 with adopted child. Fulker (1975) disagrees with this argument, and points out that, in foster families where there are also own children, the correlation between foster mid-parent and foster child drops to 0.18, which is considerably less than the 0.35 with own child. However, this figure of 0.18 is based only on 26 of Freeman's cases, so it is far from reliable. Considering the careful matching by Burks and Leahy of control with foster parents, it seems rather far-fetched to suppose that foster parents bring up both their own and any foster children in some peculiar way that reduces the normal parent– child resemblance. Certainly more evidence is required before we can dismiss the conclusion that foster children show lower resemblances to foster parents because they are genetically unrelated to them.

Snygg (1938)

Snygg studied 312 Canadian children, 90 percent of whom were placed in foster homes before the age of 2 years, the rest before 4 years. Nearly half were tested with Stanford-Binet at age 3 to 5+ and somewhat more than half at under 3 with Kuhlman-Binet. The mean IQ was 95.2. All the true mothers had been tested wtih Stanford-Binet and averaged 78.3 (using 16 years as divisor); they were generally below average in educational level. The foster children thus obtained IQs averaging 17 points higher than their natural mothers; but in view of the uncertainly of Stanford-Binet adult norms and the statistical regression effect, the real gain would be considerably lower, and Snygg does not try to argue that he has discovered a significant environmental effect. He is more concerned to show that knowledge of natural parent ability gives little or no indication of an adopted child's future intellectual development.

The correlation of child IQ with true-mother IQ was 0.13, most of this due to the cases with IQs below 70 rather than to a linear relationship between the two measures. No correlations were calculated with foster home or parent variables. Naturally, Kamin welcomes this result and points out, justifiably, that the study has been ignored by writers who claim a substantial genetic correlation between the intelligence of foster children and their natural parents.

However, there is the obvious weakness that the foster children were tested at a median age under 3 years. Even when children are brought up in their own homes, their IQs at this age show similarly low correlations with mother's intelligence or education (see Honzik, 1957). In Skodak and Skeels' somewhat parallel study, the correlation of true-mother IQ with child IQ at 2¼ years was 0.04; it rose to 0.44 by age 13½. However, the force of this objection is reduced, since 70 of Snygg's children were aged 5 and over when tested, and their correlation was 0.12, that is, no higher than for the total group. There was no trend for the correlations to increase with age. Thus, this research must be accepted as contradictory to genetic theory, though the very young age of most of the children and the rather small numbers in the older subgroups weaken the reliability of the evidence.

Skodak and Skeels (1945; 1949)

The most cited of all studies of foster children is that of Skodak and Skeels, who published a series of articles between 1936 and 1949. It is almost unique in providing information about the natural mothers as well as both foster parents, and test results for the children from age 2 to 13½. 180 white illegitimate children were involved, and these were placed in good foster homes before the age of 6 months. However, since there was a good deal of attrition, we will confine our attention to the last two reports, which dealt with 139 and 100 children, respectively.

The recorded education of the true mothers and of a smaller number of fathers was not much below normal; but the authors believe that the mothers' reports of grade completed in school were exaggerated by about one year. Stanford-Binet IQs were available for 88 mothers in 1945 and for 63 in 1949; these averaged 83 and 86, suggesting considerable inferiority. However, the adoptees were selected to some extent for good health, and a 2-year probationary period was imposed before adoption was finalized. That there was a considerable degree of selective placement is shown by a correlation of 0.27 between true mother education and foster mid-parent education. The avail-

TABLE 14.2
Skodak and Skeels' Results for Adopted Children

Mean age	Number	Mean IQ	Correlation with foster mid-parent education	Correlation with true mid-parent education	Correlation with true-mother IQ
2.2½	139	116	0.07	0.10	0.04
4.4	139	112	0.15	0.33	0.25
7.7	139	113	0.16	0.23	0.36
13.5	100	107– 108– 116	0.04	0.32 (mother only)	0.38 or 0.44

Source: Data from Skodak and Skeels, 1945; 1949.

able children were tested 4 times at the mean ages shown in Table 14.2.

Kuhlmann or Stanford-Binet was used on the first occasion, Stanford-Binet subsequently; Terman-Merrill Form L was added at 13½. The means at 13½ were 107 with standard scoring, 108 when IQs were calculated by Terman-Merrill tables, and 116 for Form L.

Thus, the authors claim that the children of low-IQ mothers, raised in a good environment, score some 20 to 30 points higher than their mothers, and this difference remains fairly stable up to adolescence. There would, however, be regression toward the mean among the children, and Jensen (1973c) calculates that on a genetic model the expected mean child IQ would be 93.6; that is, only 13.4 points lower than the obtained 13½-year figure of 107. Thus, the gain attributable to improved environment is much smaller than the authors claimed and, according to Jensen, it is what would be expected if the foster environment had been 1.7 Standard Deviations superior to the environment likely to be provided by the true parents—a very modest estimate considering the superiority of the foster homes.

However, there are difficulties: Jensen's calculation assumes a normal degree of assortative mating, which puts the true-father IQ at 94.5. But both the authors, and Kamin, consider the fathers to have been almost as backward as the mothers. Moreover, the Terman-Merrill is a better standardized test at 13½ than the Stanford-Binet, and it gave a mean of 116. On the other hand, this was probably boosted by practice effect and, indeed, Munsinger suspects that all the IQs after the first may have been raised by the repeated testing.

But it must be remembered also that the maternal Stanford-Binet IQs were reduced by using 16 as divisor; and, if 15 is substituted, the mean would be 91½. Then, too, the children were, to some extent, a selected group, as pointed out above. In view of all these ambiguities and biases, Munsinger concludes that no meaningful estimate of IQ gain can be made. On balance, I would agree with Jensen that there was some gain, but no more than could be expected from the 20 percent or so environmental component found in many heritability analyses.

A further difficulty in crediting any unusual environmental effect is that—as shown in column 4 of Table 14.2—there is scarcely any correlation between child IQ and foster-parent education; what there is could well be attributed wholly to the selective placement. If foster environment does have an important effect, surely the best foster homes should have more effect than the poorer ones (even if these are still above average). Skodak and Skeels, like Kamin, suggest that fostering families are atypical in showing low parent– child or foster child correlations. But if this is true, how can they produce overall gain?

By contrast, there is a clear tendency for child IQ from 4 years on to correlate with true-mother education and IQ. Honzik (1957) has compared the figures with those obtained in the Berkeley study (see Chapter 5) of children brought up by their natural parents and finds them virtually indistinguishable. Kamin attacks this finding, partly because the child with true mother correlations apply mainly to girls, not to boys. Furthermore, he claims that, at the 7-year testing, the correlation of child IQ with true-mother education was 0.24, with foster-mother education 0.20, which is very nearly the same. Naturally, there are variations in the correlations for different criteria (e.g., education and IQ) and varying, not very large samples (63 to 139). Kamin has picked out those figures most in line with his thesis. He objects also to the presence of selective placement, but Loehlin, Lindzey, and Spuhler (1975) point out the fallacies in that argument.

Munsinger (1975b)

The recent research by Munsinger was designed to overcome most of the weaknesses of previous studies. It was based on 21 children adopted into Anglo families and 20 into Mexican-American families, all before the age of 6 months. Complete data were available on the occupations and education of both natural and foster parents, though no intelligence scores were given. These data were combined into a SES + education index. The children took the Lorge-Thorndike group test at the average age of 8½. Details are not given, but it would appear that both sets of natural parents were close to average in SES + education index, the foster parents considerably above average. The latter also were older, by an average of 11 years. No attempt was made to estimate the children's initial or genetic IQ level from the true-parent characteristics. Their mean IQ at 8½ was 108, which could have arisen partly because the adoptees were fairly highly selected and partly because the foster parents provided a superior environment.

The correlations were very similar in the two ethnic groups, hence only the combined figures are quoted. The correlation between SES indices of natural and foster midparents was 0.07, showing no appreciable tendency to selective placement. Child IQ with foster mid-parent level correlated −0.14, but with natural midparent it was 0.70. Munsinger admits that, for children brought up in natural families, the correlation of child IQ with mid-parent index would be expected to reach only about 0.50. Hence, the obtained figure is surprisingly high. Kamin (1977c) claims that the parental indices were based on subjective ratings and were, therefore, unreliable. But this would surely lower the child–parent correlation rather than raising it. In his reply to Kamin's attack, Munsinger (1977b) states that he had the available information on true-parent and foster-parent education rated by an independent judge. He then ranked the children's IQs and classified them into 23 cases that showed closer resemblance to the natural-parent ability and 11 cases that were closer to the foster parents. (For the missing 7 cases, the data were incomplete, or the classification was neutral.) The probability of such a preponderance of natural-parent resemblances has a P-value of 0.034. But this further analysis clearly contradicts the original results, where there was zero resemblance to foster parents and very high resemblance to natural parents. A correlation coefficient having the same level of probability would be closer to 0.3 than to 0.7. Thus, the study does support the closer resemblance of adoptees to their natural parents, even though the correlation of 0.7 is an overestimate, for reasons unknown.

Texas Adoption Project

Munsinger gives an initial report on this project, which is being conducted by Horn, Loehlin, and Willerman. Results on 146 children separated from their natural parents at birth are available. The correlation of their WISC IQs with adoptive fathers' and mothers' Army Beta scores were 0.09 and 0.15, re-

TABLE 14.3
Correlations of Foster-Child IQ
with Foster-Parent Ability or Level of Home Situation

Authors	Number	Range of correlations	Measure of foster-parent(s) or foster-home
Freeman, Holzinger,	169	0.39	Foster mid-parent IQ
and Mitchell	156	0.52	Home rating
Burks	214	0.23	Foster mid-parent M.A.
	214	0.42	Overall home environment
Leahy	194	0.21	Foster mid-parent IQ
	194	0.24	Foster mid-parent education
Skodak and Skeels	100	0.04	Foster mid-parent education
	138	0.20	Foster-mother education
Horn and Loehlin	146	0.09	Foster-father IQ
	146	0.15	Foster-mother IQ
Munsinger	41	−0.14	Foster mid-parent SES + education
Approximate median		<0.23	

spectively, and these would be partly accounted for by a small degree of selective placement. However, the correlation of child IQ with natural-mother intelligence was 0.32. These figures may, of course, alter as further cases are tested.[3]

GENERAL CONCLUSION

Several studies suggest a tendency for children's IQs to rise following adoption into superior homes, but the true amount of the increase is always doubtful in view of the tendency for adoptees to be a select group and because of other distorting factors, such as attrition, practice effect, or unsatisfactory test norms. In no study has a rise been reported that would exceed what might be expected from the variance attributed to environment in heritability analyses.

The figures for correlation of child IQ with foster-home

[3] Since this section was written, Horn and his colleagues have circulated an unpublished report, based on results from 367 foster children. The correlations for different tests, and for the two sexes, are quite variable. However, the figures for all children and biological or adoptive parents who had taken the WISC or WAIS verbal scales come very close to those quoted in Tables 14.3 and 14.4.

TABLE 14.4
Correlations of Foster-Child IQs
with Ability of Biological Parent(s)

Authors	Number	Age of testees	Range of correlations	Measure of true-parent ability
Munsinger	41	8½	0.70 (?0.30)	Mid-parent SES + education
Skodak and Skeels	63	13½	0.38 to 0.44	Mother IQ; child test 1916 or 1937 Binet
Horn and Loehlin	146	?	0.32	Mother Army Beta score
Lawrence	185	9–14	0.26	Father SES
Skodak and Skeels	84	7½	0.23	Mid-parent education
Snygg	70	5+	0.12	Mother's Binet IQ
Approximate median			> 0.30	

rating or foster-parent ability range widely; Table 14.3 presents some that seem most representative. Obviously the median figure, estimated here as 0.23, has poor reliability; moreover, in most of the studies, there was considerable evidence of selective placement, so a more probably fair estimate might be under 0.20.

Table 14.4 gives correlations with true-parent ability. Insofar as the largest group (Lawrence's) would almost certainly have shown a higher correlation with mid-parent or mother education than with father SES, we may conclude that the best estimate from all the data in this table would be somewhat above 0.30. In other words, there is quite substantial genetic determination from the natural parents. At the same time, the correlation tends to be distinctly lower than that for children reared in their own homes (about 0.5), and there is clearly some tendency for correlation between foster child and foster parent. Hence, environmental factors are certainly of importance, though probably less influential than genetic. This accords rather closely with the suggested results from heritability analyses, namely G– variance, 60 percent; E– variance, 30 percent, GE– covariance, 10 percent.

SUMMARY

1   Because foster children are not reared by their natural parents, they provide a valuable source of data on effects of environment separated from effects of heredity. But there are serious complications in collecting unbiased data. Munsinger has analyzed these weaknesses and outlined most of the published studies.

2   A further summary of each of the main studies is given, together with Munsinger's and Kamin's differing evaluations and interpretations of their findings.

3   Freeman, Holzinger, and Mitchell's was one of the most extensive studies, but their samples were so miscellaneous that little emerges other than the importance of selective placement in fostering, and the failure of foster children to rise in IQ to the same level as that of the natural children of the foster parents.

4   Burks and Leahy both conducted well-controlled studies of smaller groups, which did show limited gains in IQ of foster children in good homes. They also found remarkably low correlations of foster-child IQ with foster-parent ability measures. Kamin's explanation of this finding is not acceptable.

5   Lawrence's study of orphans in an English institution revealed a significant correlation of child IQ with the SES of the true father, who had taken no part in the child's upbringing. Snygg obtained much lower correlations than most authors with true-parent ability, but his sample was too young for the finding to have much general significance.

6   Skodak and Skeels' long-term study showed considerable and consistent IQ gains among children fostered in good homes from 6 months, though part of the apparent improvement could be due to statistical regression, unreliable test norms, or even to practice effects. Correlations of child IQ from 2 to 13½ with foster-parent education were very small, whereas correlations with true-parent ability were approximately as high as among children brought up by their own parents.

7   A study by Munsinger of a small group of foster children gave an exceptionally low correlation between child IQ (at 8½ years) and foster mid-parent SES + education, and an exceptionally high correlation with the same index for true parents. The correctness of the latter figure is doubtful. A large-scale study in Texas is showing moderate correlation with true-parent test performance and much lower with foster-parent performance.

8   Though the results of different investigations vary widely, six studies of correlation between child and true-parent ability yield an approximate median coefficient of over 0.30; whereas 6 studies of child with foster-parent ability suggest a median of less than 0.20. This evidence of somewhat greater genetic than environmental correlation accords with the findings of twin and kinship studies in Chapter 11.

15

Additional Evidence of Genetic Factors in Intelligence

BIOGENETIC THEORY

An important argument for recognizing some genetic influence in human intelligence is that all attributes of, and variations in, structures and functions that have been studied in living organisms are considered by biologists and geneticists as having genetic origins, though they are also modifiable to varying degrees by the nature of the environment in which they develop. Undoubtedly, this applies to the number and types of neurones and other physical features of the human brain; and, since there is also complete agreement that mental functioning depends on the brain, it would seem illogical to disallow that mental skills also have a genetic basis. But this view can be, and has been, disputed on the grounds that humans are the only species whose mental development takes place over a lengthy period, mainly after birth; hence, it may depend chiefly on living in, and learning from, a social environment. A much greater proportion of cortical growth after birth occurs in humans than in any other species. Also, humans are the only species in which knowledge and skills can be passed on, cumulatively, to subsequent generations, without having to be built up afresh; and it is this that makes possible their intelligence. Thus, it could be argued that any variations in those mental skills that are found at the human level but not at subhuman level are attributable to variations in the stimulation provided by the environment not to variations in genetic neural structures. The genetic substrate would be the same in all members of the species, just as practically all its members are born with 2 arms and 10 fingers. Presumably, the growth of the dendrites or glial cells that subserve mental functioning results from stimulation and use of the brain not from maturation.

This seems a weak argument, not unlike that of the anti-evolutionists who regard human mental functioning as having no continuity with the evolutionary development of structures and behavior in subhuman species. It would be difficult to reconcile it with the large body of evidence showing that apes, dogs, rats, birds, and porpoises are capable of at least rudimentary concept formation, problem solving, insight, internal processing of information, latent learning, transfer, and other essentially mental functions, which must have evolved through Darwinian selection. The tests that psychologists have used to show cognitive development in animals can also be applied to young children, and it is claimed that they correlate well with the intelligence tests available for children of that age. In other words, g is not merely a cultural "invention" of Western civilization; it is something that is clearly beginning to emerge in subhuman species and is largely dependent on brain size.

ANIMAL BREEDING

It is well known that mammals can be bred to reinforce certain skills, for example, retrieving in dogs and racing capacity in horses. Furthermore, it seems highly probable that some subspecies of dogs are cleverer learners and more intelligent than others. Tryon's classical work on selective breeding of "bright" and "dull" strains of rats is often queried, since the animals were tested only at a specific type of maze. However, Thompson's (1954) replication did employ a test more similar to a general intelligence test, and he was able to produce, in a few generations, strains that differed in ability.

Crow, Neel, and Stern (1967) write that "animal experiments have shown that almost any trait can be changed by selection," and they conclude that human intelligence could analogously be raised or lowered, though probably rather slowly, over many generations. They also point out (in opposition to Shockley's eugenic proposals) that such breeding experiments cannot be tried, because humans would not tolerate any interference with their mating and reproductive habits. Dobzhansky (1973), however, rejects the analogy with dog breeding, where the genetic diversity of strains can be deliberately manipulated by the breeder. He agrees that human ability genes may have been reinforced through natural selection over a long period of time but states that our adaptations to the requirements of varied life situations are probably more cultural than genetic.

Again, we have a suggestion, though not very conclusive evidence, that abilities can be affected by genetic changes in the same way that physical attributes are.

NORMALITY OF DISTRIBUTION OF CONTINUOUS GENETIC TRAITS

I referred earlier to Burt's claim that normal distribution of intelligence test scores would be expected if intelligence results from the cumulative effect of numerous small, independent factors such as the genes. This is disputed by Lewontin (1970; 1976) on the grounds that the type of distribution is considerably affected by the presence of dominance or other gene interactions. Another counterargument on the environmental side would be that parental and other environmental stimuli also consist of numerous small influences, some of which favor, and others disfavor, the growing mental structures. These, too, might be expected to result in a normal distribution of intellectual abilities; hence, genetic theory has no advantage over environmental in this instance.

Kamin raises a different criticism of the widely accepted view that the distribution of intelligence is distorted at the bottom end by pathological low-grade cases attributable to major gene deficiencies or to diseased conditions or brain injury. It is generally accepted that the majority of defectives, whose condition depends on polygenetic inheritance and to some extent on environmental deprivation, do fall within the lower range of a normal distribution; but the pathological cases produce an additional bump, as it were, of IQs below 60, and especially below 45. Doubtless the two types overlap; thus, the general run of subnormals show an increasing incidence of pathological conditions the lower the IQ. However, the ordinary subnormals tend to occur much more frequently in low-SES families, and their relatives are mostly of below-average intelligence also; whereas pathological defectives, it is claimed, occur at all SES levels, and their parents and siblings show an intelligence distribution similar to the population in general.

Kamin ignores Penrose's (1938) survey of over a thousand institutionalized defectives in England and many other confirmatory studies (see Clarke and Clarke, 1974). Instead, he quotes a study by Roberts (1952) that appeared to give conflicting evidence. Roberts studied 271 defectives in the IQ range of 36 to 60 and also tested 562 of their siblings. He found it almost impossible to classify the defectives into feeble-minded (high-grade) and pathological or imbecile (low-grade) on the basis of clinical signs alone, and he also had to take into account their IQs and the distributions of their sibling's IQs. He believes that his difficulty was at least partly due to his cases' being closely bunched around the high- versus low-grade threshold. In view of this procedure, he could not, of course, draw any contrasts between the sibs of high- and low-grade defectives. Kamin takes this to mean that the alleged contrast has been falsified, but he neglects to mention that Roberts did find the low-grades to have parents of higher SES and better home conditions than those of high-grades. Moreover, Roberts continues to maintain that the subcultural or polygenetic feeble-minded are qualitatively different from the pathological who have major gene anomalies.

GENETICALLY CAUSED MENTAL DEFECT

Had it not been for Kamin's attack, it would hardly seem necessary to mention that some forms of mental subnormality clearly arise from genetic abnormalities. Many psychologists who generally favor environmentalist views seem to find little difficulty in allowing that such exceptional cases of genetic pathology do occur. There is nowadays virtually complete agreement that Down's syndrome (Mongolism) arises from chromosomal anomalies, though physiological conditions, such as the age of the mother, also contribute (see Gibson, 1975). PKU and amaurotic idiocy have been mentioned earlier, and several other rare diseases of genetic origin are associated with severe retardation of mental development (see Clarke and Clarke, 1974; Lerner and Libby, 1976). Medawar (1977) castigates those who criticize "karyotype screening" — that is, the genetical diagnosis of Down's Turner's and Klinefelter's syndromes, and of the 47 XYY type — because they cannot stomach this clear demonstration of inborn human inequalities.

One of the most interesting conditions is Turner's syndrome in females, since this chromosomal anomaly has been identified, and it is associated not with generalized defect but with deficiency primarily in spatial ability. Here, one chromosome is missing, so the count is 45 XO. Money (1964) tested 38 cases with WISC and WAIS and found them to average 17 points lower on Performance than on Verbal IQs. They were a little above average on verbal tests, but below average on Digit Span and Arithmetic and still more so on Block Design and Object Assembly. Similarly, Garron (1977) tested as many cases of Turner's syndrome as he could find in the Chicago area, using WISC for 37 children and WAIS for 37 adults. There was no significant difference from control groups on Verbal IQ, but on the "distractibility" and "perceptual organization" subtests, the scores were:

	Children	Adults
Distractibility	90.8	95.7
Perceptual Organization	89.0	87.4

However, as Hudson (1972) points out, we cannot go so far as to claim that a particular chromosomal defect, identified under the microscope, uniformly produces low spatial ability. Money's sample was, in fact, rather heterogeneous genetically; fewer than half were 45 XO. Their score patterns varied quite widely, and the fact that they were sexually and physically deformed might have something to do with their ability development. But Garron classified his cases into one-half who were 45 XO, and the other half who showed miscellaneous abnormalities of the X chromosome, and found no significant differences in score patterns.

It is relevant here to cite the evidence (summarized by Loehlin, Lindzey, and Spuhler, 1975) indicating that spatial visualization ability is, at least in part, dependent on the X chromosome and, therefore, genetically not merely culturally, sex-linked (see also p. 111).

INBREEDING DEPRESSION

What appeared at first sight to be one of the strongest pieces of evidence for the effects of dominant and recessive genes was obtained from studies of close inbreeding, though later work has cast considerable doubt on the interpretation of the results. It is probable that the almost universal taboo against incest is due to recognition of its harmful effects, which include high infant mortality, congenital malformations, and/or low intelligence in those who survive. Seemanova (1971) reported on 161 children of incestuous matings and found 40 cases of mental retardation, whereas there was no such retardation in a control group of half-sibs (i.e., children of the same mothers but unrelated fathers). However, it seems that most of these cases of mental defect were associated with congenital malformations, and it is unclear whether those who were not malformed did show below-average intelligence.

Much larger numbers of children of cousin marriages in Japan were tested with the WISC by Schull and Neel (1965). There were 486 first-cousin marriages and 379 second-cousin or cousin-once-removed, and a control group of 989 unrelated parents. The children of the former groups appear to have IQs averaging 8 points lower than the controls, but the published tables are difficult to follow, and Jinks and Eaves (1974) calculate that the inbreeding depression was 3.7 points. There were some differences in the SES distribution of inbred and control parents, and Kamin (1974) tries to attribute the lowered intelligence entirely to this factor. The authors claim to have held such differences constant by multiple regression analyses; both Vandenberg (1971) and Jensen (1977a) accept that the two groups of parents were effectively matched, though Loehlin, Lindzey, and Spuhler (1975) express some doubt. Kamin also mentions that the difference was statistically significant in girls but not in boys; however, it was in the same direction for boys, even if smaller than for girls.

Later, Schull and Neel (1972) tested other large samples in Hirado, Japan, and distinguished consanguinity—that is, children of related parents—from inbreeding—that is, children of parents who are themselves products of consanguineous marriages. (Their earlier work dealt with consanguinity rather than inbreeding.) Here, the difference in IQ attributable to consanguinity may have been confounded with differences between predominantly rural and urban families. There was some depression of scores, which was in line with the earlier findings, but is was not statistically significant with the available number of cases. The authors still claim that both studies support the existence of a depression effect, which would be expected from the effects of directional dominance on a polygenetic trait (see Jensen, 1977a). But in view of the uncertainty regarding SES and urban–rural biases, it seems that we cannot safely rule out the possibility of environmental differences.

One would also expect there to be evidence of the reverse phenomenon—namely, heterosis or hybrid vigor, which occurs when populations with different gene pools interbreed. This is familiar in animal and plant breeding, and Jensen argues that it accounts for the general increase in height among Caucasians over the past hundred years or so. However, Loehlin and his colleagues find the evidence for heterotic effects on stature contradictory, though they are willing to accept it as "a minor contributing factor." There have, of course, been numerous studies of the intelligence of children of hybrid—that is, interracial—mating (see p. 296), but they involve serious sampling and other difficulties and provide no support for the beneficial effects of outbreeding on intelligence. As already pointed out, the general intellectual level in Western countries may have risen considerably over the past hundred years. Selective mating and the decrease in inbreeding may have played a part, but clearly there have been many environmental changes that would account for this rise without genetic change.

REGRESSION PHENOMENA

Francis Galton was the first to show that, although offspring generally resemble their parents in height, they are less extreme. The mean height of sons of tall fathers is halfway nearer to the general mean than that of the fathers; likewise, the mean height of sons of short fathers "regresses" halfway up to the general mean. Regression works in both directions; that is, if tall or short sons are considered, their fathers average nearer to the general mean. From these regression coefficients the product—moment correlation technique later evolved, and the correlation between parent and offspring was close to 0.5, which would be the figure expected from genetic theory. However, the fact that other traits, such as intelligence, also show a correlation of close to 0.5 and regression to the mean cannot be taken as proof of the existence of hereditary resemblance. Regression is merely a statistical phenomenon that always appears when two variables are imperfectly correlated; in no way does it prove the nature of the causal factors underlying the partial resemblance.

It is curious that some writers, including Eysenck (1971; 1973) argue that the regression phenomenon demonstrates hereditary causation. The substance of Eysenck's claim seems to be that, if intelligence is entirely determined by environmental conditions, such conditions could not produce IQs *lower* than those of parents of *high* intelligence or *higher* than those of parents of *low* intelligence; whereas this would be expected on genetic theory.

In my own view, the proper question to ask is why parent—offspring and sib–sib correlations are only moderately high. It is well known that some extremely intelligent children are born of relatively dull and poorly educated parents; how could this be explained environmentally? Again, intelligent parents not infrequently give birth to one or more able children and also some quite dull ones. Surely they would be likely to provide very similar stimulation, commensurate with their own intelligence, to all the children in their family; if that were so, how could IQ differences of 20, even 30, points arise? Burt pointed out long ago that genetic theory is not necessary for explaining parent—offspring resemblances; they could well be attributed to environmental influences. But it is needed for explaining differences. One would expect children in a family to differ from one another or from parents on genetic grounds, just as cats produce variously colored or marked kittens in the same litter. It is this phenomenon, rather than regression to the mean, that can be accounted for more plausibly genetically than environmentally. Actually, parent—offspring or sib–sib differences could depend partly on environmental differences, since, obviously, the environmental factors influencing each child's growth arise from many sources, both in the home and outside it. But it seems unlikely that these factors would be so varied as to reduce the correlation to as low as 0.50, or to produce the same parent—child and sib–sib coefficients as predicted by genetic theory.

While the argument is a strong one, it could perhaps be overcome if we admit that prenatal environment and perinatal conditions (e.g., birth injury) have a considerable effect on children's intellectual potential. This aspect of environment is much less under parental control than is the intellectual stimulation provided in early and later childhood, and it might vary rather considerably from one child to another, thus producing constitutional, though not genetic, intersib differences. There is no good evidence either to support or to contradict this alternative hypothesis, but it should be possible to investigate it by making appropriate assessments of prenatal, perinatal, and postnatal environmental conditions.

VARIANCE

Another common misunderstanding of regression to the mean is that since, on the average, offspring always score nearer to the mean than their parents, one would expect a decrease in the range or spread of intelligence from one generation to the next, were it not for the diversification attributed to genetic mechanisms. This, of course, does not follow, since, as already pointed out, parents likewise average nearer to the mean than their offspring. Imperfect correlation always implies that there is considerable variability of offspring above and below the IQ of the parent; and the degree of correlation, whether high or low, makes no difference to the variance of the next or the preceding generations (see Li, 1971).

However, if environment is the main cause of intellectual differences, we should then expect that the range of such differences would be lowered if environments became more similar. One argument that Burt espoused in favor of genetic theory is that, when children are brought up in orphanages or institutional environments that are unusually homogeneous in the pressures they exert, this apparently does not result in any lowering of IQ variance. Hence, he concludes that it is genetic diversity that maintains the more or less constant range. Unfortunately, there seems to be little evidence to confirm the claim, other than Burt's own results, which are published in insufficient detail for evaluation. In Lawrence's study (p. 221), the S.D. of IQs among children in an orphan home was 13.0, compared with 14.5 in two control groups—a difference that is just significant at 0.05 level. In any further exploration, careful checks would have to be made on sampling, since orphaned children might well be drawn from a relatively restricted range of parental SES and education, and this would somewhat reduce the variance of their IQs.

Conway (1958) puts forward a related point, namely that there has been a tremendous decrease in differences between living conditions among upper and lower social classes over the past 50 years or so, that is, since the time that Burt related the incidence of delinquency and backwardness in different areas of London to demographic characteristics; and yet there has been no indication of reduction of IQ variance among British children. Although this decrease in the range of social conditions would have to be admitted, it is doubtful whether the argument is a convincing one, since, as mentioned previously, no one knows the crucial environmental conditions for intellectual development. Material poverty may be less frequent nowadays, but variations in intellectual stimulation between, or within, families may have altered little or not at all. However, so far as it goes, this argument to some extent suggests that genetically produced diversity is important.

GENERAL CONCLUSION

It will be seen that the case for genetic influences is by no means based solely on questionable evidence from twins and other kinship studies. The work on foster children tends to confirm the first approach rather neatly, though here, too, the data are very variable and their interpretation open to bias. Several other sources likewise point in the same direction. Thus, the combination of many lines of evidence carries conviction.

At the same time, we must not forget the rapidly accumulating evidence from developmental psychology that demonstrates the influence of constitutional differences (i.e., pre- and perinatal conditions) and mother–child interactions in babyhood, as well as of diverse conditions of rearing within the home, at school, and among peer groups, on the shaping of mental growth. Moreover, when one considers the enormous variety of cognitive skills and strategies in different individuals, which are so inadequately covered by the available mental tests, together with the much larger environmental contribution to variance in educational achievement than in intelligence tests, one wonders whether the high heritability of verbal IQ or g is of sufficient importance to deserve so much concern among psychologists and the public. Whatever is covered by intelligence tests constitutes only one of the major variables in each individual's educational, vocational, and social career. It is interesting that this generalized or all-round intellectual capacity, which samples children's most advanced and complex mental skills, should, according to the best evidence that I have been able to present, depend more on genetic endowment than on favorable or unfavorable environmental opportunities and learning, at least within white culture. But now that the findings of heritability researches and of environmental modifications are beginning to confirm or complement one another, we surely do not need to bother about which is the most important—genes or environment. Both are essential, and neither can be neglected if we are to plan children's upbringing and education wisely.

SUMMARY

1   Since biologists agree that all physical attributes of living organisms are genetically based (though also affected by environment), should not this apply also to the brain structures that underlie human intelligence? However, it is possible to argue that complex human cognitive traits are different in view of the lengthy period of childhood, during which mental capacities are built up.

2   Animal breeding experiments show that skills as well as physical features can be selectively bred. The same presumably holds for the human species, though, for obvious social reasons, it has not been possible to carry out controlled experiments for improving intelligence by intentional breeding.

3   The near-normality of the IQ distribution does not prove polygenetic inheritance, since it might also be anticipated on environmentalist theories, but the abnormal number of IQs below about 50 clearly point to pathological deficiencies over and above normal curve expectations. Unlike the higher-grade mental defectives, there is little or no association in low-grades with low SES or subaverage relatives.

4   Certain types of pathological mental defect are determined by chromosomal anomalies, for example, Down's syndrome and Turner's syndrome.

5   Inbreeding depression of intelligence commonly occurs with incestuous matings. This would be expected on genetic grounds and appears to admit no possible environmental explanation. A smaller amount of depression in intelligence has been found in first-cousin marriages, but there are difficulties in ensuring that these cases are not drawn from socioeconomically or otherwise biased samples.

6   The phenomenon of filial regression to the mean cannot be taken as evidence of genetic inheritance, since regression inevitably occurs when parent– child or sib– sib correlations are less than 1.0. However, while resemblances between such relatives seem readily explicable environmentally, the quite substantial differences that often occur can more readily be explained genetically.

7   Regression does not imply any restriction of variance in successive generations, but probably such reduction would be expected if children are brought up in unusually homogeneous environments. There seems to be no clear evidence of this occurring, nor has there been any reduction in range of general intelligence by social, economic, and educational improvements over the past 50 years.

8   In concluding Part III, I have pointed out that evidence from kinship and foster-child studies and that from miscellaneous other sources concur in demonstrating a strong genetic component in individual differences in intelligence. However, Part II also showed the importance of environmental factors. Thus, I have argued that these opposed views are complementary not irreconcilable.

IV

Genetic
Influences on
Group
Differences

16

The Testing of Racial, Ethnic, and Socioeconomic Groups

RACIAL AND ETHNIC GROUPS

It is abundantly clear that the different human groups, such as races, nations, and ethnic or socioeconomic subgroups within any country, differ tremendously in their degree of advancement and prosperity, educational achievement, and many practical and intellectual skills. To some extent, these differences reflect geographic and economic handicaps and advantages, including the prevalence of certain diseases and malnutrition. But external environment is, to a considerable extent, under human control; thus the inequalities lie much more in the psychological characteristics of different groups, their traditions and values, the way they rear and educate their children, and, possibly, their genetic potentialities. Considering the enormous and controversial literature on race and culture, it may seem rash to introduce it as a subsidiary topic in a book primarily concerned with intelligence. But the existence of genetic differences between individuals inevitably raises the question of differences between groups, and their origins and implications.

The concept of race is regarded by a number of writers (e.g., Klineberg, 1935a) as so complex and difficult to define, and so much bound up with racism, prejudice, and discrimination, that it would be better to ban it from scientific discussion. Although the term is still widely misused by laypeople, politicians, and even some social scientists, it does have a clear technical meaning that is generally accepted among geneticists (see Hirsch, 1967; Spuhler and Lindzey, 1967; Gottesman, 1968; Bodmer, 1972; Dobzhansky, 1973; Baker, 1974; Loehlin, Lindzey, and Spuhler, 1975).

Early writers tried to classify groups of people according to distinctive physical features, which were also found in different geographical areas; for example, Nordics were supposed to be tall, blond, and blue-eyed inhabitants of Northern Europe. But it soon became evident that a great diversity of features occurred in any one area and that such features did not always cluster together, as would be expected if there were distinct physical types of people. Anthropologists and archaeologists observed that skin color, shape of skull, type of hair, and blood groupings (when these were discovered) often gave very different distributions across the map. There might be a larger proportion of particular blood groups or skull shapes in one area than another, but also so much overlapping and such varied combinations of features that any classification of relatively distinct races was arbitrary. Different authors recognized anywhere from 3 to 30, even 150, races and, of course, named them differently. However, often cited as a reasonable compromise is Garn's (1971) ninefold division: Caucasian, Mongoloid, Negroid, Australoid, Amerindian, Polynesian, Micronesian, Melanesian-Papuan, and Indian.

To the geneticist, race is a kind of statistical concept. A race is a population that shares a common gene pool and is based on common ancestry; that is, its members possess more genes in common than they do with members of other racial groups. However, there is great genetic diversity within any race, much more so indeed than the differences between races. Every individual (apart from identical twins), regardless of race, is genetically unique. Thus, a race does not imply a typical genotype, only a sufficient similarity among its members to provide a basis for distinguishing them from another race. Needless to say, we do not know the precise genes involved, though blood groups and other biochemical measurements provide a beginning. Thus, we cannot diagnose a person's race from his genes, though we can from his ancestry; and we cannot determine scientifically how many, or what, races should be distinguished.

Members of a race usually breed with one another; but, since all races are subgroups of a single species, they can and sometimes do outbreed. When this occurs frequently, we have hybrids such as New Hawaiians, South African Cape Colored, and, even more obvious, American Negroes. It is generally stated that the last group carry, on the average, some 20 percent of their genes from white ancestors and 80 percent from African stock, though the figure varies widely in different parts of the country, the percentage of white genes being higher in Northern states than in Southern (see Reed, 1969). Moreover, there are many mulattoes with a much higher white percentage who are, nevertheless classed as Negro if they show enough of the usual distinguishing features of skin color, lips, and hair.

These facts point to a third definition of race, based on social acceptance: Members of a race are those who think of themselves as belonging to it and are so regarded by others. But this does not necessarily coincide with genetic race, as in the case of the Negro with, say, 3 out of 4 white grandparents. Indeed, American Negroes are generally classified almost entirely on skin color, which, as Baker (1974) points out, is almost as silly genetically as classifying all brown dogs as belonging to the same subspecies. This ready recognizability of most Negroes, whether in Africa, the West Indies, or the United States, has probably played a major part in the growth of the stereotyped and irrational attitudes that so many whites hold regarding blacks.[1] The same could be said of American Indians, Orientals, and Mexican Americans, but because of their smaller numbers in most areas of the United States, these groups have not been thought of as separate and threatening minorities to the same extent. Note that almost all the research on blacks reported by Shuey (1958; 1966), Jensen (1969), Dreger and Miller (1960; 1968), and others has been based on this visuosocial categorization rather than on genetic differentiation. However, such research is not invalid, since the gene pools of the vast majority of black and white subjects who have been tested are partially distinct.

A race usually shows demographic contiguity, all its members living in a definable area, since this is implied by inbreeding. But obviously, it is quite common for different racial groups to live in the same area and still largely retain their distinctiveness and inbreeding.

---

[1] The identification of white as good and black as bad goes back into the mists of time and is certainly not based merely on the observed (or imagined) characteristics of Caucasians and Negroids. It is more similar to Jung's archetypes, or universal symbols. In the middle ages, the devil was a black man, plague was the black death, and evil magic was black magic. Children are naturally afraid of the dark. One cannot assess how far the stereotype of Negroes arises from such psychodynamic sources, from the guilt that white Americans feel about the days of slavery, from a growing fear of black power, or from many other factors.

Cultural or ethnic groupings are distinguished from races by most writers. These groups refer to peoples who share common customs, traditions, language, values, beliefs, and the like, but not necessarily gene pools. As with races, the boundaries between ethnic groups are ill-defined and arbitrary and, though sometimes based on nationality or tribe, there are many overlapping cultures or subcultures. There may be common ancestry, since cultures, like racial groups, tend to practice endogamy and assortative mating. Indeed, it is often difficult to distinguish racial from ethnic groupings; hence we will frequently refer below to racial-ethnic groups, because we do not know how far the group differences are genetic, cultural, or both. The confusion is well illustrated by groups such as Jews or Celts, who are often referred to as races but should probably be regarded as ethnic groups—though opinions differ (see Baker, 1974). Jews certainly include subgroups that possess different gene pools.

The socioeconomic classes within a nation are subcultures, since they differ between themselves in certain customs, for example, though they also show many cultural features in common. SES is often associated with ethnic or racial grouping. In the United States, far greater proportions of blacks, American Indians, and Mexican Americans than of Anglos are confined to the lower-class occupations. Whereas substantial genetic diversity is obvious in any racial group, cultural characteristics tend to be accepted by all members of a cultural group, although a certain range of deviancy is generally tolerated. Although both genetic and cultural uniformities are highly resistant to change, on occasion some cultural characteristics alter rather rapidly (as in post-revolutionary Russia and China), whereas genetic change is inevitably slow.

Evolution of Races

An obvious next question is how different races emerged, since humanity, being a single species, must have had some kind of common origin.[2] The normal mechanisms of change and evolution are mutations, natural selection, migration, and genetic drift. Mutations are extremely rare and, as they affect single genes, they can hardly be of much importance in the modification of polygenetic traits such as intelligence. Natural selection implies that a trait that is advantageous for survival and procrea-

---

[2] Coon (1971) argues that the origins of partially separate races may have started as far back as 300,000 years ago. Thus, the present-day races may have evolved independently, though they are still capable of interbreeding.

tion will tend to be reinforced in the gene pool. However, it is often difficult to discern the survival value of most of the characteristics in which racial groups differ. One plausible example would be the strengthening of the genes for black skin pigmentation among Africans, who live in a hot climate; however, as Dobzhansky points out, this failed to occur among South Americans, who also live in tropical climates. Nevertheless, there could well have been genetic adaptation for some climatic or other conditions in the past. Thus, susceptibility to certain diseases may be reduced, as illustrated by the sickle-cell anemia gene in the Negro race.

Genetic drift refers to random variations that become fixed when populations are geographically isolated. Such drift has been observed under experimental conditions in *Drosophila* (see Gottesman, 1968), and, until fairly recent times, human groups have been very much isolated by geography, language, and cultural differences. Nowadays, the rate of genetic change may be increasing through more intensive selective mating for socially approved traits, by large-scale migration and racial cross-breeding, as well as by medical advances that allow more individuals with genetic abnormalities to survive. It may still be true, as Kuper (1975) claims in the UNESCO volume ᵒn *Race,* that social evolution has been much more influential in ᵘuman progress than biological or genetic changes. At the same ᵗime, it is worth remembering that the modern human brain size is some three times larger than that of the most advanced hominid.

In *The Evolution of Man and Society* (1969) C. D. Darlington makes a strong case for the importance of genetic differences in mental abilities in the development and decline of civilizations. A society with many members of superior ability would be more likely to adapt to its environment, to devise novel uses of natural resources, or to invent more effective tools and weapons, which would allow it to multiply more rapidly and to dominate less advanced societies. He illustrates from history how conquest, intermarriage and cross-breeding, absorption of foreign cultures, migrations, and the like have influenced the achievements of nations. He stresses the importance of genetic diversification, the rejection of incest, and the continuous fertility of women in the stabilization of some societies and the stagnation of others. But though he shows how a thorough-going genetic interpretation can help to make history more intelligible, his inferences are, of course, largely speculative. And it seems more probable that social change is chiefly due to cultural interactions within and between groups.

Genetic Differences Between Groups

How far are intelligence and other abilities likely to show genetic racial differences? It is quite possible that they might contribute to the survival and progress of particular groups, though it would be hard to prove it. For example, good visual perception and spatial judgment might well be more important to Eskimos in an arctic environment and other hunting peoples than to Negroes and other mainly agricultural peoples in a tropical environment (see p. 64); hence, the trait would be enhanced in the former groups by natural selection. I have argued already that the existence of innate physical differences suggests the existence of innate psychological differences. And yet, as mentioned by Scarr-Salapatek (1971a), almost all behavioral scientists vehemently reject any such notion, possibly because it might lend support to the widespread racial and ethnic prejudices and stereotypes that have done, and are doing, such harm to intergroup relations.

In 1951, expert consultants to UNESCO issued a declaration that was to become well known:

> According to present knowledge, there is no proof that the groups of mankind differ in their innate mental characteristics, whether in respect of intelligence or temperament. The scientific evidence indicates that the range of mental capacities in all groups is much the same (UNESCO, 1952).[3]

They should have added at least that there is also no proof that innate mental characteristics do *not* exist. However, their intention was probably not so much ⟩ deny genetic diversity as to emphasize that cultural and environmental differences between groups outweigh any known genetic differences; also, that there are far greater differences between members of any one race than there are between races.

In fact, not all the UNESCO advisors agreed; leading geneticists, such as Fisher, Darlington, Dobzhansky, and Medawar, have strongly criticized theories that deny or ignore genetic diversity. Fisher (1952) wrote: "Human groups differ profoundly in their innate capacity for intellectual and emotional development." And Dobzhansky regards as indefensible the position that the genetic basis of humanity is uniform everywhere, though this is seriously argued by Fried (1968). Humanity's main assets, Dobzhansky be-

[3] The term *range* is an ambiguous one: It gives little or no information as to the extent of group differences.

lieves, are its genetic diversity and trainability, which make humans far more adaptable and capable of further evolution than any other species (see also Hambley, 1972). The American National Academy of Sciences (Crow, Neel, and Stern, 1967) took the middle view that neither the purely genetic nor the purely environmental explanation of differences between human groups is scientifically established.

Although Medawar (1977) has already been quoted as a strong critic of the heritability of intelligence, he regards as even more objectionable the approach that attempts to discredit any genetic component and fails to realize that the ideal of sociopolitical equality is an entirely different matter from biological equality.

We will follow up this controversy further in Chapter 18.

ETHNIC AND SOCIAL CLASS DIFFERENCES IN INTELLIGENCE

Let us turn now to the question of cultural and SES differences in intelligence. There is overwhelming evidence of group differences when the same intelligence test is given to members of different ethnic groups, even when it has been translated in order to obviate linguistic difficulties. But referring to these differences as cultural naturally implies that they arise from differences in the upbringing, educational opportunity, acquired skills, and concepts of each group. Nevertheless, there are strong grounds for believing that SES groups do differ genetically as well as in acquired characteristics and environment. Assortative mating by social class and intelligence would tend to induce and reinforce genetic differentiation (see p. 184). We can also observe considerable social mobility, at least within white society, whereby the more intelligent members of any class are likely to move up in the occupational scale and the less intelligent to drop. As described earlier (p. 121), Waller (1971) found that sons who rise above the paternal SES are, on average, more intelligent than sons whose SES is lower than that of their fathers. Halsey (1958) and many other sociologists and psychologists still maintain that SES differences are wholly environmental, but Burt and Conway (1959) make a convincing case that assortative mating and social mobility must lead to an equilibrium of genetic differences among upper, middle, and lower classes.[4] Loehlin,

---

[4]One of the most convincing pieces of direct evidence comes from the study by Lawrence (see p. 221), where there was a correlation of 0.26 between children's IQs and the SES level of the true fathers who had never seen them.

Lindzey, and Spuhler (1975) agree that there is clearer justification for genetic differences in ability between SES than between racial groups (see also Eckland, 1967; Jensen, 1967; Cavalli-Sforza and Bodmer, 1971). This in no way denies the fact that upper-class children tend to be brought up under conditions far more conducive to intellectual and educational growth than are lower-class children.

Dobzhansky (1973) makes the interesting point that, if social class differences in ability were wholly environmental, the social hierarchy would probably be much more rigid than is now the case. It is because of genetic variability that a large pool of high-ability children is produced by lower-class families, many of whom rise in the occupational scale and displace the less able children of upper-class parents. The caste system that used to be enforced in India allowed no such mobility. There was rigid segregation, and the position and type of job of the offspring were wholly determined by the caste of the parents. This resulted in a serious waste of talent. It has been suggested that minority groups in the United States, such as blacks, native Americans and Mexican-Americans, to some extent resemble castes; they used to be, and often still are, restricted to relatively menial occupations, though greater mobility is now developing. The same could be said of the position of women. Finally, it follows that we should not rule out of consideration the possibility of some genetic difference between ethnic groups. Thus, Jews are commonly regarded as more intelligent than Anglo-Americans, Irish less so; however, the ability levels of these groups could be partly, or maybe wholly, transmitted culturally.

In view of the considerable overlap between racial-ethnic grouping and SES, there is a common tendency among psychologists and sociologists, when studying racial differences, to try to hold SES constant or to adjust for SES differences. Thus, commentators on the black–white difference in the United States of some 15 IQ points often claim that this is, at least in part, explained by the preponderance of blacks in the lower SES classes, and that the racial difference is much smaller when SES is allowed for. Shuey and others accept the average difference as 11 points, when adjusted for SES. It seems to be assumed that this residual difference does represent actual racial inferiority; though, more usually nowadays, it is inferred that SES combined with other environmental differences accounts for the entire 15-point deficit. The same point can be made about studies of Welsh-speaking school children (e.g., Jones, 1960). When their scores on group tests tend to fall below the English norms, it is attributed mainly to the fact that children who habitually speak Welsh come predominantly from rural families of low SES.

However, this tactic is fallacious and misleading, once we ~~nit~~ that there are genetic differences in intelligence between ~~er~~ and lower social classes. Holding SES constant means that ~~e~~ of the genetic, as well as the environmental, influences are ~~alled~~ out (i.e., eliminated). Minority groups tend to concen- ~~in~~ lower social classes partly because they are, in fact, lower ~~in~~ intelligence. Of course, no one would deny that the biased socioeconomic distribution of U.S. blacks is also largely due to racial discrimination among employers or to the persisting tradition in American culture that blacks can do only unskilled jobs. The same situation holds for American Indians in the United States and Canada, though here there is the added complication that the traditions and values of these peoples lead them to prefer rural occupations to work more highly rated by whites.

Dimensions of Racial-Ethnic Group Differences

Leaving aside the question of how far such differences are genetic or cultural, we must consider what are some of the main dimensions, or qualities, in which they differ. In Chapter 1, I pointed out that Intelligence B is culture-bound and determined by the values and modes of thought of a given cultural group; it is not a universal human dimension, such as height, that can be measured by the same ruler in different countries of the world. There is good experimental evidence (e.g., Segall, Campbell, and Herskovits, 1963) that different peoples show differences in cognitive "styles," that is, the ways they perceive and categorize their worlds. Though less is known about differences in thinking, it is highly probable that, say, the Chinese or the Indian conceptions of the most advanced forms of cognitive skills and reasoning differ from the Euro-American conception. Nevertheless, we can observe a fairly general tendency for more primitive and underdeveloped cultural groups to show lower capabilities in most cognitive functions than do members of developing countries, which appear to be aiming, through their education systems, to produce an intelligence more like the Western model. But there is no natural law that all cultures must follow the same path and try to produce the same kind of higher mental processes that we find most useful in the Western world. Lévi-Strauss (1956), in particular, insists that cultures differ in a variety of ways, not merely in degree of advancement, and that cultures are not static — they are constantly changing in different directions.

Anthropologists have long rejected Levy-Bruhl's conception of the "prelogical mentality" (of Africans, for instance) and Werner's (1940) attempt to equate the cognitive processes of primitive peoples with those of immature Western children. Yet it does seem possible to recognize a very general dimension of civilized versus primitive, and to define it in terms of fairly objective criteria. True, there is the danger that one is merely projecting ethnocentric bias by taking Western technological civilization as the ideal, and denigrating other groups according to the extent that they deviate from it. However, the criteria suggested here do not imply that groups described as more civilized are morally superior or better adjusted than the less civilized. The following list of some of the main contrasts is culled from Doob (1960), Kluckhohn (1950), Baker (1974), and Vernon (1969a).[5]

Characteristics of More Civilized Societies	Characteristics of More Primitive Societies
Complex organization.	Simple organization.
High standards of living and national wealth.	Low standards of living and national wealth.
High technological manipulation and control over environment.	Use of human and animal power.
High specialization and division of labor.	Little specialization and division of labor.
Large population, mainly urbanized.	Small communities; face-to-face contacts.
Much trading; money economy.	Each community self-sufficient; barter economy.
Forward-looking; planning for future.	Static, conservative; living for the present in the light of the past.
Encourage individual initiative and competition.	Encourage social conformity.
Scientific development; advanced health care.	Superstition; magical beliefs.
Advanced educational system; relatively high literacy.	Little or no formal education; preliterate.
High average level of Intelligence B; symbolic thinking.	Low average level of Intelligence B; primarily concrete thinking.
High development of the arts.	Sporadic artistic development (e.g., cave paintings, African and Eskimo carvings).

[5] The questions raised in this section and in the remainder of the chapter are discussed more fully in my book, *Intelligence and Cultural Environment* (1969a). I have also described there another broad dimension contrasting agricultural with hunting cultures, which links with Witkin's (1962) conception of field dependence versus independence.

While Western civilization is more complex and more advanced in many respects, it is certainly not ideal for all people. It brings with it such undesirable features as crime, neurosis, and warfare, whereas many simpler societies seem more harmonious and better integrated. It is common for developing countries, in Africa, for example, to try to acquire only some of the advantages of technological culture. They realize that if they are to become self-sufficient and improve their standard of living, they need to train professionals, teachers, and leaders in much the same kind of intellectual capacities as underlie Western civilization. Hence, they lay great stress on improved education (which largely follows Western models) as a means of supplying the needed personnel; but, at the same time, they reject many elements of Western culture and wish to retain much of thier traditional values and customs.

Although Piaget and Bruner are far from being ethnocentric, a good deal of the cross-cultural work that has grown out of their theories does appear to assume that all humanity passes through the same stages in the growth of logical thinking and that some cultures have progressed further along this continuum from sensorimotor to formal operations, or from enactic to symbolic, than others have. In contrast, there are writers such as Cole et al. (1971) who not only reject the notion that intelligence is an innate faculty differing between different groups but also strongly criticize the "social pathology" view that attributes group differences in abilities to cultural conditions inhibiting, or failing to stimulate, mental growth (see p. 127). Baratz and Baratz (1970) attack Hunt, Deutsch, Bernstein, and Hess and Shipman for regarding the American black as a "sick white man." In Cole's view, people whom we categorize as relatively primitive are not lacking in reasoning or other intellectual functions; they differ merely in the kind of situations in which they reason, or show their skills. Thus, Cole and Gay insist on first-hand study of the modes of thought and concepts in the particular group, disregarding the Euro-American type of thought in which the foreign investigators are themselves versed.

This is probably an almost impossible demand until such time as different local cultures can produce their own psychologists who can study the meaning and the criteria of the intelligence appropriate to the culture. So far, there has been very little attempt to find what kinds of behavior are regarded as most effective or crucial in intellectual development. Even in a country such as India, which does produce numerous university psychologists, scholars are trained mostly by American or English textbooks or by teachers who have learned their psychology abroad. And when they devise intelligence tests for internal use, they simply follow Western models. However, some beginning has been made in Africa (see Wober, 1971; Serpell, 1974), where it would seem that the concept of intelligence involves caution and wisdom on the one hand and social conformity on the other, rather than the rational cognitive skills emphasized by Western culture.

Intelligence Tests Across Cultures

It would indeed be naive to suppose that conventional intelligence tests can be used for assessing the comparative intellectual potentiality (Intelligence A) of different racial or ethnic groups. Insofar as our tests sample the kinds of intellectual functioning that are valued in our culture, and discriminate differences within this culture, the validity of such tests would be unsatisfactory if they did *not* yield low scores among members of different groups.

However, we should distinguish a number of factors that enter into low test scores. They can be classified under Extrinsic, Constitutional and Environmental, and Genetic factors (see Vernon, 1969a). These categories correspond to Intelligence C, B, and A (see p. 20).

Extrinsic conditions (as described by Biesheuvel, 1949) are characteristics of the test or the testing situation that are largely irrelevant to the mental abilities the psychologist wants to assess; however, they particularly handicap subjects with different cultural backgrounds who have little or no previous experience of testing and thus obtain low scores. Intrinsic factors are those which do affect the underlying abilities and that are difficult to change without long-term environmental intervention.

Extrinsic Handicaps:

1 Unfamiliarity of testees with any test situation and lack of motivation.

2 Anxiety, excitement, suspicion of tester. This is particularly likely to occur when the tester is of a different race.

3 Difficulties with particular forms of items or materials (e.g., pictures), or with such conditions as working at speed. The "odd-man-out" and any kind of multiple-choice item is an artificial way of eliciting information or problem-solving skills. Lack of test sophistication has been shown to be a considerable handicap to Western children who have had little prior experience with such tests (see Vernon, 1960), and this is probably exacerbated in more remote cultures.

4 Linguistic difficulties in understanding instructions and communicating responses. These will naturally occur if the tests are not couched in the testees' mother tongue, even if a fluent interpreter is employed.

Intrinsic Factors — Constitutional Handicaps:

5 Brain damage due to pre- or postnatal malnutrition, maternal stress, disease, birth injury, or later brain pathology and deterioration. The risk of such conditions is much greater in more primitive cultures.

Positive Environmental Factors:

6 Reasonable satisfaction of biological and social needs, including exercise and curiosity.

7 Perceptual and kinesthetic experience; varied stimulation.

8 Linguistic stimulation encouraging an "elaborated" code and clarity of concepts.

9 Demanding but democratic family climate, emphasizing internal controls, responsibility, and interest in education.

10 Conceptual stimulation by varied environments, books, television, travel, and so on.

11 Absence of magical beliefs; tolerance of nonconformity in home and community.

12 Reinforcement of items 8 and 9 by school and peer group.

13 Regular and prolonged schooling, also demanding-democratic, emphasizing discovery rather than rote learning only.

14 Appropriate methods for overcoming language problems.

15 Positive self-concepts with realistic vocational aspirations.

16 Broad and deep cultural and other leisure interests.

Genetic Factors

17 General plasticity.

18 Genes relevant to special aptitudes.

Although Western-type tests cannot tell us anything about genetic differences between remote cultural groups and Westerners, they still have some legitimate applications in other racial-ethnic groups. When suitably adapted to a particular culture, they have been proved to give valid predictions of educational and occupational success within that culture in much the same way that they do in Western societies (see Irvine, 1965; Schwarz, 1961; Vernon, 1969a). However, adaptation requires more than just eliminating culture-bound items or translating into the vernacular. Preferably, although following conventional psychometric models, the test should be constructed by local psychologists who are familiar with modes of perception and thinking within their culture, and it should be item-analyzed, validated, and renormed locally. Special precautions are needed to overcome the extrinsic difficulties mentioned above.

Under such circumstances, the test is not used for group comparisons, except those between subgroups within the particular culture. Occasionally, however, group comparisons are legitimate, even using unmodified Western tests. This is when it is necessary to assess members of a non-Western culture against Western norms. For example, applicants from abroad could hardly expect entry to advanced education if they did not reach the same standards as local Western candidates. Again, when students in a developing country are being educated for professional careers (e.g., as doctors or lawyers), it may be useful to find whether they possess intelligence comparable to that of Western students undergoing similar training. Finally, many experimental investigations of cognitive processes (e.g., Piagetian conservation) are directly concerned with the differences between members of contrasted cultural groups in particular test situations.

Even greater caution is needed in attempting to explore genetic group differences by means of tests. Many writers would deny such a possibility insofar as any groups that differ in gene pools will also have different cultural characteristics and environments that affect test scores; thus, the two kinds of factors cannot be separated. This objection will be discussed more fully in Chapter 18. While it certainly invalidates direct comparisons, there are, nonetheless, certain indirect ways of varying cultural and genetic influences independently.

Much depends on the degree of difference between the cultures concerned. Obviously, one would not expect a U.S. test to measure the genetic capacity of African bushmen, whereas it probably could be used, with the same norms, in Canada (apart from a few items such as those in WISC Information, which are geared specifically to the United States). The usual condition laid down for comparability is that the subjects should have had equal opportunities to acquire and practice the concepts and skills embodied in the test. Mercer (1972) expands this requirement by suggesting four conditions to be met before meaningful ethnic group differences can be obtained:

1   Equal likelihood on both groups of any physical disability (e.g., malnutrition).
2   Equal access to education.
3   Equal familiarity with test demands and freedom from anxieties.
4   Equal valuation by the two cultures of the skills involved.

The most contentious situations occur when there is a partial, incomplete, overlapping of cultural background, as between blacks, American Indians, Mexican Americans, and whites in the United States, or similarly contrasted groups in other countries. It would be highly disputable whether these groups meet Mercer's criteria; the same could be said of upper and lower socioeconomic classes.

In many respects, blacks and whites do share the same culture, and also a large proportion of their genes must overlap. It has been said that a black man is more like a white man than he is unlike him. This is true both genetically and culturally in the United States; hence, the difficulties in interpreting test score differences.

In the early days of testing, it was thought that the difficulties could be overcome by using nonverbal group tests or performance tests based on shapes or pictures. Few would accept this nowadays, though Cattell (1971a) still advocates his culture-fair batteries as relatively pure tests of fluid intelligence on the grounds that the test materials are not so much equally familiar as equally unfamiliar to members of different ethnic or racial groups. Ortar (1963), working in Israel with Jewish immigrants from diverse cultural backgrounds, points out that facility with nonverbal test materials needs to be learned just as much as facility with verbal problems; she makes a good case for preferring language and number material to nonverbal (see also Vernon, 1969a). Discussing the problems of individual testing, for example, of immigrant children from a non-English-speaking home, Sattler (1970) concludes that there are no culture-fair tests that overcome these children's handicaps.

An interesting commentary on attempts to provide a universally familiar type of test material is to be found in Dennis' (1960) study of the "Draw-a-Man" test. Children aged 6 to 9 in some 50 ethnic groups were tested, and the mean IQs on Goodenough norms ranged from 52 to 124. Conceivably this range could arise in part from genetic differences, but it seems far more plausible that cultural differences are responsible: (1) in the use of drawing materials; (2) in practicing two-dimensional representation of solid objects; and (3) in the encouragement given for observing the human form analytically.

In the following chapter, we will look at some of the results that have been obtained in cross-cultural comparisons and the interpretations that can legitimately be made. Inevitably, we will have to draw rather largely on black versus white studies in the United States, since these have attracted the greatest amount of research; however, much the same problems crop up in almost any investigation of group differences.

SUMMARY

1   Humanity constitutes a single species, since all its members can interbreed. However, many biological variations are recognizable, though their classification into distinct races is highly controversial and arbitrary, since the various physical attributes (height, skin color, blood group, etc.) do not coincide. To the geneticist, race implies a population possessing a common pool of genes, which differ from those of other races. Members of different races often interbreed to yield hybrids; for example, American Negroes who, on the average, possess approximately 20 percent white genes.

2   The origins of different races are obscure, though probably genetic drift and natural selection for attributes that make for survival are involved. The genetic diversity of human beings and their adaptability to a wide range of environments have been of the utmost importance in the evolution of the present worldwide racial distribution and the emergence of civilizations.

3   Ethnic groups refer to subpopulations that show particular cultural values or other characteristics, and retain these over generations, who also regard themselves as distinct. Often, though not necessarily, these groups show some genetic differentiation, and they may be geographically and/or linguistically delimited. Socioeconomic classes effectively constitute different cultures or subcultures. Though the issue is disputed by most social scientists, these classes do tend to differ genetically in intelligence as well as in their environmentally determined characteristics.

4　SES and racial-ethnic groupings often interact; but it is not legitimate to try to hold SES constant in studying racial differences, since this eliminates some of the genetic variance between the groups.

5　Although racial-ethnic differences are extremely diverse, a major dimension, ranging from the more primitive and underdeveloped to the more civilized and technologically advanced, is readily recognizable. The most advanced cultures should not be regarded as superior to, or psychologically better adjusted than, cultures lower on the scale. However, most cultural groups aim to progress on this dimension, while at the same time retaining many of their traditional values and customs.

6　Intelligence tests were devised to differentiate within advanced Western populations and are inappropriate for making comparisons between different racial-ethnic groups with different values, perceptual and conceptual structures, and languages. Thus, no test can be accepted as culture-free, even if it is based on nonverbal or pictorial materials. However, intelligence and/or achievement tests can sometimes be used, with suitable modifications, for selection purposes within a non-Western society.

7　The factors involved in high and low intelligence scores can be grouped under (1) genetic factors; (2) intrinsic factors, including constitutional (as described in Chapter 6) and cultural differences in upbringing and education that affect mental growth; and (3) extrinsic factors, such as unfamiliarity with test materials and the tester. Extrinsic factors can usually be overcome by changes in test administration and additional preliminary practice.

8　The major difficulties and controversies arise in interpreting test score differences between cultures that have much in common but also differ, such as U.S. blacks and whites.

Studies of Racial Ethnic Differe in Intellig

Many of the standard texts on individual differences, such as Anastasi (1958) or Tyler (1965), provide good surveys of work on racial-ethnic differences in intelligence, so there is no point in my trying to cover the same ground. But there are some aspects of the question that need emphasis or clarification.

Spuhler and Lindzey (1967) have outlined the historical development of cross-cultural studies, starting with the expedition by Rivers (1901) and his colleagues to the Torres Straits in Northern Australia, which found a number of differences from Caucasians in sensory and motor tests (see also Klineberg, 1935a). Probably the first measure of intelligence to be applied to numerous racial-ethnic groups was the Porteus Mazes test (though Porteus himself regarded this as a measure of planning capacity rather than all-round intellectual ability). The number of cases in most of the groups Porteus tested was quite small and not necessarily representative; hence, the reported differences often failed to accord with estimates by anthropologists of the relative abilities of these groups. The wide range of studies of American Indians, blacks, and other groups in the 1920s and 1930s, and the sophisticated awareness among psychologists of environmental and cultural problems are apt to be forgotten (see, for example, Klineberg, 1928).

BLACK–WHITE DIFFERENCES

The application in 1917–1918 of the Army Alpha and Beta tests (see p. 6) and the reported mean scores of recruits with varying racial or ethnic backgrounds led to widespread controversy. Most social scientists soon agreed that the differences were largely, if not wholly, environmental in origin. While blacks obtained the lowest average, their scores varied quite widely in different states, and it was shown that blacks who resided in four of the Northern states averaged higher than did whites in four of the Southern states (Bagley, 1924). However, this finding has been criticized by Alper and Boring (1944) on the grounds that it did not take account of recruits who took Army Beta and those who were rejected from the army. Actually, on Army Beta, the highest state average for blacks was lower than the lowest state average for whites.

Over the next 50-odd years, there were hundreds of studies of black intelligence; these were pulled together and carefully analyzed by Shuey in *The Testing of Negro Intelligence* (1958; rev. ed., 1966). Though aware of possible environmental and other effects on scores, she obviously favored a genetic explanation of the difference between blacks and whites, apparently regarding the sheer number of studies that gave generally consistent results as proof. However, reviews by Dreger and Miller (1960; 1968) helped to correct the balance and to emphasize the dangers of taking such results at their face value. More recently, Loehlin, Lindzey, and Spuhler (1975) have published their *Race Differences in Intelligence,* which is almost exclusively concerned with U.S. blacks. It is certainly the most dispassionate and scholarly discussion yet written on the question of race and intelligence, its main conclusion being that there is definite evidence on both sides but that the interpretation of such evidence is beset with so many difficulties that equally reputable scientists can justify contradictory inferences from the same facts (see also Horn, 1974).

It is now agreed by genetically and environmentally inclined psychologists alike that the mean black IQ is close to 1σ below the white, that is, about 85 when $\sigma = 15$; also, that this difference seriously impairs black educational performance. Shuey quotes means of 88.7 for black children in the Northern states and 82.6 for those in Southern states. One of the most extensive surveys of some 1800 black children in Southern states, with the Stanford-Binet, gave a mean IQ difference of 20 points. The black IQs at 5 years averaged 86; by 13 years, they had dropped to 65 (Kennedy, Van de Riet, and White, 1963).

However, this increasing retardation with age, though often accepted as typical, was due to an artifact in sampling rather than to progressive decline. Indeed, Kennedy (1969) followed up and retested 312 children after 4 years, and did not obtain any such decline. (The problem of cumulative deficit is discussed in Chapter 20.) Kennedy, Van de Riet, and White noted, as have several other writers (e.g., Last, 1976), that the Standard Deviation of black IQs is distinctly lower than that of whites, say 12 as contrasted with 15 to 16; and Jensen suggests that this could be explained partly by a lower figure for assortative mating among black parents and partly because a slower mental growth rate in blacks would reduce the IQ variance.

All writers agree, too, that there is considerable overlapping and a much wider range of differences within, than between, races. If the S.D. were 15 in both groups, we would expect some 16 percent of blacks to score above the white average of 100 and 16 percent of whites to score below the black average of 85. The actual figures obtained vary in different samples with different tests, but typically the overlap is between 10 and 20 percent; a very small proportion of blacks show IQs of 140 and over. One case has been reported with an IQ of 200 (on the old Stanford-Binet).

The deficit is much smaller at preschool level; indeed, there is either no difference or some black superiority on Gesell and other tests applied in the first 2 years. Dreger and Miller, however, consider that there is already some retardation during this period, particularly in view of the higher prematurity rate and pregnancy complications among black mothers. But Werner (1972) summarizes results of infant testing around the world and claims that Negroes, whether African or North American, show the highest scores in early psychomotor development, Caucasians the lowest. By the age of 4 or 5, when intelligence tests depend more on verbal skills and reasoning, the average IQ of black children approximates the 15-point deficit, which stays fairly constant thereafter.

One would naturally anticipate that, with improved social welfare measures, especially improved education, the mean IQ for blacks should have risen over the past 50 years. However, Loehlin, Lindzey, and Spuhler (1975) compare statistics from World Wars I and II and the Vietnam War and conclude that the deficit among black recruits was 17 IQ points in 1917–1918 and 23 points in the two later war periods. Shuey (1966) noted no differences between earlier and later studies of children. Thus, there appears to be no evidence that improvements in environment or lessening of discrimination have had any positive effect.

The Coleman report showed no tendency for the ability gap to close, although inequalities in provision of schooling (so often claimed as a major factor in black intellectual growth) have been greatly reduced, if not wiped out, in most states. The overall income gap between the racial groups has also diminished, although one-third of black families still live below the poverty line, compared to 9 percent of white families.

Possibly there has been less improvement in the occupational opportunities open to blacks, in which case the interest of black school students in education as a means to better jobs may not have altered greatly. This is especially likely with males. Black females tend to get slightly higher IQs (1 to 3 points) and to achieve considerably better at school than do males. It has been noted that the occupational distribution of black females is more similar to that of white females than are the distributions of black and white males (see Jensen, 1971b). This suggests that females are better motivated for school work and stay on longer because they have better job prospects open to them. As Thoday (1973) points out, such differences are much more likely to be cultural than genetic in origin.

However, this interpretation, together with Jensen's findings on sex differences, have been disputed by Strauch (1977). In his research, WISC-R and other ability and achievement tests were given to several samples of whites and blacks, ranging from first to eleventh grade. There were large and significant main effects of race and SES but not of sex, and the occasional significant interaction terms did not seem to be meaningful. Perhaps changes are occurring in the social structure of black culture that are affecting the IQ distribution.

A view that has received some publicity (see "The American Underclass," 1977), but little statistical verification, is that the range of differences in prosperity and achievement among blacks has widened in recent years. There are many more ambitious, middle-class black families, but also a minority—dubbed "the underclass"—who have been left behind and are stuck in conditions of abject poverty, malnutrition, underemployment, crime, and complete failure to achieve in school. If this were confirmed, it might explain the change in IQ variance noted above.

DIFFERENCES IN MENTAL FACTORS

A common stereotype is that the American blacks' main difficulty is in abstract reasoning, whereas they are more adept in practical and social situations as well as in psychomotor abilities.

However, many studies, including the Coleman report, have shown higher black scores on verbal than on nonverbal intelligence tests. Actually, the greatest difficulty is with visuospatial tasks. Higgins and Sivers (1958) gave the nonverbal Progressive Matrices to large groups of 7- to 10-year-old blacks and whites, who were matched on Stanford-Binet IQ. They found a black deficit in this test of 9.8 IQ points, and they conclude that the Matrices is not a good test of intelligence because it involves some specific ability that is lower in blacks. Conceivably, blacks could have some special perceptual difficulty; but there is ample evidence from other sources that the Matrices test is an almost pure g test among whites, apart from some unreliability and a small spatial element (see Vernon, 1969a; also p. 308 below).

Mercer and Brown (1973) noted that the lowest performance of their black sample on the WISC subtests was in Kohs Blocks; and I have obtained a similar result with blacks in Jamaica and East Africa. WISC or WAIS performance tests as a whole tend to yield lower IQs among blacks than do verbal tests (see Shuey, 1966; Loehlin, Lindzey, and Spuhler, 1975). However, Teahan and Drews (1962) found no significant differences between verbal and performance IQs among Northern U.S. blacks, but a difference of 11½ points among Southern blacks. Their means were:

	Verbal	Performance
Northern	87.4	88.4
Southern	80.3	68.8

Tuddenham (1970) obtained much the same retardation on a series of Piaget-based tasks as occurs with intelligence tests. In contrast, the Oriental students in his first- and third-grade samples averaged much the same as whites.

The type of cognitive ability in which there is least racial difference is rote memory, or Jensen's Level I. This was shown in a study by Jensen (1973d), where an extensive battery of tests was given to some 2,000 fourth- to sixth-grade children, who were representative of whites, blacks, and Mexican Americans in a rural area of California. The tests were factor analyzed to yield scores, which Jensen identified as follows:

G_f — nonverbal reasoning, for instance, Matrices.
G_c — verbal intelligence and educational achievements.
Memory — digit span.

The black children scored lower in G_f and G_c, but approximated to whites on Memory; whereas the Mexican Americans obtained their best score on G_f and were about equally handicapped on G_c and Memory.

Though there is much additional evidence that would be relevant, I would remind the reader at this point that three main types of explanation have been advanced for the lower scores of black children and adults. These correspond to C, B, and A factors discussed in Chapter 16.

1   The test materials are less familiar or comprehensible to black children, and these children are less motivated than whites to try their best.

2   The background, upbringing, and schooling of blacks has provided less stimulus to intellectual development. Poor health conditions in the prenatal and infant stages are also involved.

3   There are genetic differences between blacks and whites in Intelligence A, and possibly in some more specialized aptitudes such as spatial relations.

Clearly, the findings mentioned so far could not be fully accounted for by differences in cultural background, since blacks tend to perform less well on relatively culture-fair tests than they do on tests that are culturally or educationally loaded. It is more probable that all three factors are involved, though as yet we have no reliable evidence regarding their relative importance.

Arthur Jensen's Findings

The part played by A. R. Jensen in this controversy was outlined in Chapter 1. In 1967, he wrote an article on the special difficulties of blacks and other disadvantaged groups on intelligence tests, including the statement:

> Since we know that the Negro population for the most part has suffered socio-economic and cultural disadvantages for generations past, it seems a reasonable hypothesis that their low average IQ is due to environmental rather than genetic factors.

In his 1969 article, however, he included the now-famous words, "a not unreasonable hypothesis that genetic factors are strongly involved in the average Negro—white difference." This did not mean that all or most of the average difference is genetic, though Jensen was often so misinterpreted; it was put forward as an alternative hypothesis that should be investigated. Since then, there have appeared a number of researches, including his own, that have yielded supporting evidence, so that nowadays he does tend to regard the major part of the difference as genetic (see Jensen 1973a). His position has hardened also because he has shown that a purely environmental explanation would imply improbably large differences between the typical white and typical black environments.

On p. 208, I gave the method for calculating environmentally produced variance when heritability is known. However, this environmental variance includes within- and between-family environmental differences, probably in about equal proportions. It is only the between-family component that interests us when studying black–white differences; hence, we have to divide the figure cited earlier by $\sqrt{2}$. When h^2 is assessed at the high figure of 0.80, the between-family σ_E works out at 4.1.[1] This means that, if the whole range of environments from good to poor could be scaled, an environmental difference equivalent to 1σ on this scale would bring about an IQ difference of 4.1. Thus, if the whole 15-point difference was environmental, the black and white environments would have to differ by $^{15}/_{4.1} = 3.66\sigma$. If the average white environment falls at zero on this scale, the average black one would have to be 3.66σ lower, which is obviously impossible. However, if we take the much lower estimate of h^2 as 0.60, the σ_E increases to 6.3 points, and this implies that black environment is 2.38σ lower than that of whites; in other words, it falls within the bottom 1 percent of the scale of environments. While this is somewhat more conceivable, it still exaggerates the likely difference between black and white environments. There is no known environmental factor or combination of factors that could bring about so large a difference. Thus, in order to account for the observed difference between races, it would still seem logical to include some genetic component as well as the environmental differences.

Australian Aboriginals

Several studies of aboriginal natives have been published by Australian psychologists (see Kearney et al., 1973). Many whites tend to group them with blacks, because of their dark

---

[1] Jensen himself (1970c) used a different approach, based on environmental differences between MZA twins, to arrive at $\sigma_E = 3.35$. This is even smaller and it would imply a difference of $4.48\ \sigma$ units between black and white environments which is clearly out of the question.

skin, but, in fact, they constitute a distinct race, and their circumstances more closely resemble those of Canadian Indians and Metis. Apart from a few isolated tribes, they have been largely dispossessed of their traditional lands and mostly live in great poverty, with severe malnutrition. There has been much hybridization, but only a small minority are fully acculturated, and the majority seem to be strongly hostile to white society and education. Since the children are also handicapped by language, their progress in school is extremely poor. However, the Australian government is now putting more funds into the provision of better health measures, welfare, and schooling.

Nurcombe (1976) describes an experiment along the lines of Head Start, where 4-year-old aboriginals and low-intelligence white children were given a year's part-time preschooling before entering elementary school. Several programs were tried, and the traditional child-centered nursery school approach was the least successful. Both a drill approach, adapted from DISTAR (see Bereiter and Engelmann, 1966), and a Piaget-based cognitive approach produced positive gains, though, unfortunately, these seemed to disappear after a year or two in elementary school. However, considerable improvements in the children's confidence and in interracial parental cooperation are claimed, though these could not readily be tested.

It is widely believed (not only in Australia) that aboriginals represent one of the lowest races in intellectual potential. Nurcombe's application of the Peabody Vocabulary yielded a mean IQ of 78 for children in one area. However, McElwain and Kearney (1973) gave the Queensland performance test battery to over 1,000 aboriginals and obtained a mean about 1 Standard Deviation below whites. Other studies yielded varying results, the scores being affected both by the nature of the tests and by the amount of contact that each group had experienced with white civilization.

U.S. and Canadian Indians

Indians have been studied quite extensively in Canada and the United States. The results often differ considerably, largely because certain tribal groups, or Indians living off the reservations, have been brought up by parents speaking English as their main language; other groups, mostly living on reservations, use an Indian language at home, and the children are naturally handicapped on entering school. In addition, there are marked differences between different tribes, so that a single estimate of average IQ would be misleading.

It has frequently been found (e.g., Jamieson and Sandiford, 1928; Havighurst, Gunther, and Pratt, 1946) that Indians do better on performance and nonverbal tests than on verbal intelligence tests. In an early study, Goodenough (1926) gave her drawing test to several groups of Anglos, children of immigrants, blacks, and Indians, anticipating that the test would be fair to those with non-English language backgrounds. The medians for U.S. whites and children of Northern European descent were close to 100; Southern European somewhat lower; Indians (one tribe only) 86; Californian and Southern blacks 83 and 77, respectively. However, in later investigations (e.g., Gaddes, McKenzie, and Barnsley, 1968), Indians have shown themselves to be particularly skilled on Goodenough or Harris drawing tests, and their mean scores can exceed those of whites. Indeed, when DuBois (1939) gave a test of drawing a horse and established norms of performance for Pueblo Indian boys, white boys showed a mean IQ of only 74. Doubtless the Indians had had much more experience of horses; but they also had less experience of some of the materials used in a verbal intelligence test standardized for whites.

Some large, but probably not very representative, samples of Indians in first, sixth, ninth, and twelfth grades were tested in Coleman's survey. The younger children were greatly handicapped on the verbal and educational tests, but approximated to the white mean on nonverbal ability. The older Indian students achieved considerably higher grade equivalents than blacks or Puerto Ricans, though they did less well than Orientals. The means, in terms of percentages of white grade averages, were Orientals, 92; Indians, 78; Mexican Americans, 78; blacks, 68; Puerto Ricans, 65.

Multiple Group Comparisons

Loehlin, Lindzey, and Spuhler (1975) point out that the conventional comparison of two racial or ethnic groups constitutes poor research strategy, since, if a difference is found, there are likely to be too many underlying causal factors to be disentangled. Thus, there has been a trend in recent years to compare several groups and several contrasted types of ability, since such a design gives much more information. Jensen's and Coleman's studies fall in this category, and a few more examples will be quoted.

Between 1962 and 1967, I undertook cross-cultural comparisons of boys aged 10.1–11.11 in six very different ethnic groups: (1) English (southeastern counties); (2) Hebrideans

TABLE 17.1
Median Deviation Quotients of
Six Ethnic Groups on Four Types of Tests

Ethnic group	Inductive reasoning or g	School attainment	Rote learning	Visuo-spatial
English	100	100	100	100
Hebridean	97	104	112	93
Jamaican	75	86	92	77
Ugandan*	82	86	94	84
Canadian Indian	81	81	76	86
Eskimo	91	86	84	90

*The Ugandan sample was drawn from above-average urban schools. Much lower scores on all variables would be expected in a more representative sample. A fuller account of these investigations is given in Vernon, 1969a.

(Scotland); (3) Jamaicans; (4) Ugandans; (5) Canadian prairie Indians; and (6) Eskimos attending a large school in Inuvik, Northwest Territories, Canada. All these boys were taught in English and had sufficient experience to understand instructions given by English-speaking teachers, though the mother-tongues of all the groups except No. 1 were not standard English. Most of the testing was individual, and very full instructions and practice were given in order to reduce the effects of extrinsic (C) factors. While group No. 1 was reasonably representative of the whole range of ability in that culture at that age, and it supplied the test norms, the other groups (numbering 40 or 50) were not necessarily representative; usually, they were all the boys available within the desired age range in the local schools.

The object of the study was not to compare the basic intelligence of these groups, but to apply a variety of cognitive tests, so as to find in what ways the patterns or profiles of scores were affected by the particular cultural environment. Table 17.1 summarizes the median scores on four main sets of tests; all are expressed as Deviation Quotients from the English mean, with S.D. = 15. It will be seen that on the tests most representative of general intelligence or g, the Jamaicans scored considerably lower than the typical mean of U.S. blacks. But this is to be expected in view of the widespread poverty, poor education, and linguistic difficulties in the West Indies. Their school attainments and rote learning were somewhat higher and, as in other investigations, the visuospatial scores were particularly low.

The Canadian Indians also scored poorly on g and attainments, partly, at least, because they almost all came from non-

English-speaking homes. They did better on spatial tests, and this has been confirmed in other studies, such as that of Bowd (1974), who worked with four Indian tribes. The Eskimos were the least retarded of any group except Hebrideans. Moreover, those who lived on the land or in small communities scored distinctly higher than the town-dwellers, both on spatial and general intelligence tests. Taylor and Skanes (1976) have confirmed that Eskimo boys, when compared with sons of white fathers of similar occupational distribution, score on the average as high as white boys on WISC Arithmetic, Blocks, and Mazes, although a little inferior on Vocabulary.

Anastasi suggested as far back as 1958 that different ethnic groups might show different patterns of abilities or factors, whereas general socioeconomic or cultural advantage or disadvantage would affect the general level of performance on all aspects of intelligence. This has been confirmed in several studies, though apparently it does not apply to the rote memory factor. Not only blacks, but also whites of low SES score almost as well on this factor as white children of high SES (see Vernon and Mitchell, 1974).

The best known study is that by Lesser, Fifer, and Clark (1965), which was replicated by Stodolsky and Lesser (1967). Eighty first-grade children, representing each of four ethnic groups in New York—Jews, Chinese, Negroes, and Puerto Ricans—were tested individually (by testers of their own ethnicity) on Verbal Comprehension, Nonverbal Reasoning, Number, and Spatial Relations. Both high- and low-SES families and both boys and girls were included in each group. As may be seen from Figure 17.1, Jews were highest on Verbal and lowest on space; Chinese showed almost the opposite pattern. The best performance among Negroes was on Verbal, the other three factors all being low. Puerto Ricans did better on Space and Number and were lowest on Verbal, which obviously would be affected by their language background. Almost identical patterns, at different levels, were found in the high- and low-SES groups. However, the range of differences between SES groups was somewhat greater than that between ethnic groups.

OTHER RACIAL ETHNIC COMPARISONS

A great many other studies have been made of the intelligence and school achievements of Chinese-American and Japanese-American children and of Jews, although the samples are often doubtfully representative. Usually, the Orientals come out very close to the Anglo norms, or even above them; Jews

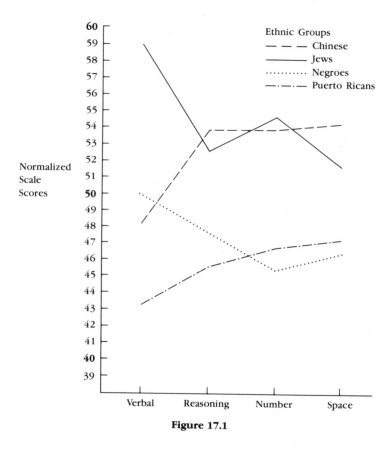

Figure 17.1

Pattern of normalized mental-ability scores for four ethnic groups. (Reprinted by permission, from G. S. Lesser, G. Fifer, and D. H. Clark. "Mental Abilities of Children from Different Social-Class and Cultural Groups," *Monographs of the Society for Research in Child Development* 30, p. 64. Copyright © 1965 by The Society for Research in Child Development, Inc.)

seem to average some 5 IQ points higher. Such results are commonly attributed to the high value placed on education and intellectual advancement by these ethnic groups; yet, at the same time, in many families, languages other than English are used, which would be expected to handicap the children, at least in elementary school.

Lynn (1977) reports on restandardization of the three Wechsler intelligence scales in Japan. Taking the Performance and Digit Span subtests (which did not require any adaptations), the mean WAIS IQ on U.S. norms was around 105; the mean WISC was 110.5 at 5 years, dropping to 101 at 14–15 years; and the mean WPPSI approximated 111.7. As Lynn points out, these figures would be difficult to explain environmentally, since the mean Japanese family income was much lower than the American. However, I would suggest that similar gains in American Wechsler means may have occurred since the scales were first standardized, corresponding to the gains found by Thorndike (1973a) in the Terman-Merrill test. Other possibilities are that (1) the Japanese standardization samples were unrepresentative, or (2) Japanese are genetically superior, particularly on performance tests.

Smilansky and Smilansky (1967) have described the situation in Israel, where about half the immigrant population is of Euro-American origin, and they have established a predominantly Western-type culture. But the other half are "orientals" (Africans, middle- and far-Easterners) who, although stated to be of similar economic status, come from more primitive backgrounds. They experience considerable difficulties of acculturation, and their children achieve poorly in school. Smilansky claims, though, that, when the community, school, and parents work together, the IQs of oriental preschoolers can be raised by some 20 points, those of adolescents by 10 points; and that, particularly in the kibbutz, such gains are maintained. (Bloom (1969) quotes similar figures.) Thus, Smilansky disagrees that the orientals are genetically inferior; they merely lack certain acquired skills fundamental to successful schooling. However, no detailed evidence for these claims is forthcoming.

Factor Analyses

Any comparative use of test scores in contrasted cultural groups must assume that the tests measure the same variables in the same way in the groups concerned. Factor analysis has been used quite widely to investigate differences in patterns or structure of abilities in contrasted groups. The results are somewhat mixed, some authors claiming to replicate most of Thurstone's primary factors on non-Caucasian groups. In my own investigation of boys in six different racial-ethnic groups (Vernon, 1969b), the same verbal-educational factor appeared in all the groups, presumably because all the samples were following much the same educational curriculum. But substantial differences in loadings of tests on the g factor and on spatial ability were noted, suggesting that these dimensions are more heterogeneous in different cultures. Irvine (1969) reports similar results on several large samples of African pupils. MacArthur (1968; 1973) has given large batteries of tests to various samples of Eskimo, Indian, and Meti subjects of various ages. When analyzed, these rather consistently yielded factors identified as Nonverbal Reasoning, Visuospatial, and Verbal-Educational. However, a different grouping was obtained with 65 Zambian children.

Flaugher and Rock (1972) obtained much the same factor structure in white, black, Mexican-American, and Oriental boys. However, Semler and Iscoe (1966) found significant differences in the loadings of WISC subtests among 5- to 9-year-old whites and blacks, and Michael (1949) reported some marked differences between the factors present in white and black Air Force recruits. Additional studies are listed by Loehlin, Lindzey, and Spuhler, some indicating pronounced differences, others not. Thus, this type of research does not seem very profitable in bringing out different ability dimensions in different ethnic groups, though it suggests that factor structures are more apt to differ between widely different cultures. And this means that it is unwise to assume that tests are measuring the same ability dimensions in such cultures. More consistent are the studies mentioned above, where the factors are much the same, but different groups achieve different patterns of factor scores.

Rural and Urban Differences

It has generally been found that children living in rural areas score significantly lower than those in urban areas, though the results vary to some extent with the tests used, and they are far from uniform in different countries. Thus, when McNemar (1942) analyzed the results obtained in standardizing the Terman-Merrill test, the mean IQ differences between urban and rural in different age groups were:

Ages	IQ Difference
2– 5½ years	5.7
6– 14	10.4
15– 18	12.2

The children classified as suburban scored a little lower than the urban. It seems probable nowadays that the more highly intelligent families tend to live in suburban areas surrounding the large cities, whereas those remaining in the inner city tend to be of low SES or to come from ethnic minority groups, and these may well score lower than rural children.

Some of the older studies, such as Gordon's (1923) in England, Sherman and Key's (1932), and Wheeler's (1942) in the

United States, suggested that the lowest scores occured in more isolated regions, where educational provisions were poor. Such samples displayed the characteristic decline of IQ with age. However, these pockets have largely disappeared (in Western societies) now that communications and education have so much improved. In the survey of all 11-year-olds by the Scottish Council for Research in Education (1939), the highest mean IQs occurred in more isolated rural areas and the lowest in the industrial belt, presumably because of the bad slum conditions and the inclusion of considerable numbers of families of Irish peasant ancestry in the latter group.

Some explanations tend to stress the lower stimulation, less need for rapidity of thought, and often poorer education, which might retard intellectual growth in rural areas. But, alternatively, differences might arise because the more progressive and intelligent families tend to migrate to urban and suburban areas, or because of genetic class differences, as farm labor is relatively unskilled.

Language differences may also confuse the issue, as illustrated by the lower scores among Welsh-speaking than among English-speaking children in Wales (see Jones, 1960). In Ireland, also, test scores tend to be lower than the English norms, especially in rural areas; and a far larger proportion of the population than in England is engaged in agriculture. Eysenck (1971) attributes the low performance to lasting genetic inferiority, consequent on the large-scale Irish emigration in the nineteenth century. However, Macnamara (1966) tested over 1,000 11-year-olds in various types of Irish schools, and found the lowest scores on English, Problem Arithmetic, and even Nonverbal Intelligence in those schools that were predominantly Irish-speaking. In Mechanical Arithmetic, there was much less difference. He accounts for these findings largely in terms of the amount of time given to instruction in the Irish language, which detracts from the acquisition of facility in English. He also stresses the extreme unfamiliarity of Irish children with any objective tests and rejects genetic explanations.

SUMMARY

1   A brief summary of the development of cross-cultural testing is given, including the U.S. group test results with Army Alpha in 1917– 1918. Groups of different racial-ethnic descent varied widely in their means, but most writers would now agree that the differences reflected differences in economic and educational conditions in the countries rather than genetic differences.

2   The mean IQ of U.S. black children and adults is approximately 1 S.D. (i.e., 15 points) below the white mean, though this is consonant with a large amount of overlapping; for example, some 16 percent of blacks score above the white average of 100. There are geographical and sex differences, girls scoring a little higher in IQ and much better in school achievement.

3   Early infant tests tend to show blacks as more advanced in many psychomotor skills. Thus, there is little difference from whites up to about 4 years, but at 5–6, the full 15-point deficit is usually established.

4   Blacks do best, relative to whites, on rote memory tests and least well on visuospatial. Their performance on verbal tests is generally better than on nonverbal, although the former tests are more culture-biased.

5   American Indian children tend to score higher than blacks, especially on nonverbal or performance tests, although their environmental handicaps are even more serious. Eskimos who live "on the land" scored considerably higher than Canadian Indians on reservations.

6   Some studies are described that included samples of several ethnic groups, and tests designed to measure different ability factors were used. The patterns of performance on such factors tend to be quite stable even when high- and low-SES children in each ethnic group are compared. Much the same factors have been found in contrasted ethnic groups, though considerable discrepancies occur in other studies, especially when the groups differ widely. In such circumstances, it is clearly not legitimate to assume that the same tests are measuring the same abilities.

7   Oriental (English-speaking) children differ little from Anglos, and Jews tend to be superior in most cognitive abilities.

8   In general, urban children tend to score higher than rural, especially if the latter live in very isolated areas. But the results are irregular and are often confounded by language differences. They could be attributed to either genetic or environmental causes, or both.

18

General Criticisms and Implications

RACISM

The study of racial differences is often wrongly confused with racism. Thus, Mercer (1972), referring to blacks and whites, defines racism as "the belief that the differences are biological." This is quite unjustified. Racism means the belief that all (or most) members of one racial group are biologically superior or inferior to members of other groups, and the belief is generally accompanied by discrimination on the basis of race. Thus, Jensen himself is certainly not open to accusations of racism, though he might be criticized on the grounds that his writings have been used by others as supporting anti-black prejudice. But clearly, he has never advocated discrimination; his point is, rather, that fuller scientific knowledge of the nature of black–white differences should make it possible to plan more effectively for diversified education to suit the needs of those with differing genetic make-up. (This viewpoint is accepted also by Bereiter (1975), in reviewing Jensen's (1973a) book.) At present, we continue to impose a single system of education on all children, and this policy inevitably produces a great deal of frustration, feelings of inferiority, and low school achievement among the majority of black and low-SES white children. It is the monolithic educational system, as much as anything, that makes conceptual learning ability or intelligence the major factor in educational success or failure.

Although Jensen believes that the gene pools of blacks and whites differ to some extent, he insists that one group is not generally inferior to the other but that they differ partly because of differences in their patterns of genetic strengths and weaknesses. He reiterates that educational treatments or employment decisions should not be based on group membership. The racist lumps together all members of a racial group and believes that all are inferior because they belong to this group; Jensen argues that every individual is unique and has different capacities and needs.

We have to recognize that, throughout history, different groups have believed so strongly in their own physical, mental, and moral superiority to other groups that such prejudices have led to innumerable crimes against humanity, culminating in Hitlerism. Unfortunately, it is also true that many who claimed to be speaking as scientists have exhibited ideological prejudices. Galton and Pearson expressed strongly anti-Semitic views and, like Spencer, they were imbued with the doctrine of Social Darwinism, which preached the superiority of Caucasians (particularly the British) to other inferior races.

Hunt and Kirk (1971) point out that American ideology, as expressed, for example, in the U.S. Constitution, has generally opposed hereditary privilege, drawing largely on Locke's empiricism; Europe, by contrast, was more wedded to Kant's nativism. However, Stanley Hall brought Galton's Darwinism to the United States, and he was the teacher of Goddard, Kuhlmann, Terman, and Gesell—the main pioneers of intelligence testing. According to Kamin (1974), Terman, Goddard, Yerkes, E. L. Thorndike, Garrett, and Brigham (until he later recanted) perverted the scientific development of intelligence testing by supporting dysgenic sterilization of the unfit and the curtailment of immigration into the United States on the grounds of low intelligence, which they linked to hereditary degeneracy and criminal tendencies.

Fine (1975) and Daniels (1976) argue that tests are currently being used to perpetuate the inferior status of ethnic-minority and low-SES families. Along with Kamin, they give the impression that the genetic view of racial differences in ability is a conspiracy thought up by fascist-minded psychologists and bolstered by Burt's "fraudulent" heritability analyses. I agree that Kamin's chapter on the distortions of psychology by political and social prejudices is a telling one, though he has probably overestimated the amount of influence that psychologists were able to exert on public opinion and political legislation. As Cronbach

(1975) suggests, economic factors had a good deal more to do with the restrictive U.S. immigration legislation in 1924 than did the adjurations of misguided psychologists.

Kamin is justified in arguing that psychological theories of human nature are always formulated in a sociopolitical context and that ideological impartiality is much more difficult to obtain than in, say, physics. At the same time, he fails to realize that his own interpretation of studies of intelligence and those of many other critics of hereditarianism are at least as likely to be biased in the opposite direction. Vernon (1957a), Cronbach (1975), and Loehlin, Lindzey, and Spuhler (1975) make the point that, while some of the early pioneers may have been misguided bigots, many, including Burt and Terman, were genuinely motivated by the belief that intelligence testing would help to break down social class barriers and enable bright children, regardless of class or race, to obtain the educational opportunities they deserved.

Another point usually ignored by social critics is that, while intelligence tests are banned in the U.S.S.R., since they are regarded as instruments for the maintenance of class discrimination and social inequality in capitalist countries, yet there is probably much more rigorous selection for higher education and the professions in the Soviet Union than in most Western countries. There is certainly not equality of educational opportunity for all.

NATURE – NURTURE CONTROVERSIES

A common theme among environmentalist writers is that Jensen and his supporters wish to maintain the status quo of white middle-class supremacy and to keep less acculturated minorities in their place (see Daniels and Houghton, 1972). Layzer (1972) suggests that people find it comforting to believe in genetic differences, since it saves them from doing anything about depressed minorities or social reform; and Lewontin (1976) accuses Jensen of putting the blame for the failure of education to teach black children on the children's defective genes, which render them incapable of ever acquiring abstract reasoning or problem-solving skills. Daniels (1976) writes that "IQ tests are really political instruments both in design and effect. They place the blame for inequalities in educational achievement squarely on the child or his home life."

It has been suggested, also, that "Jensenism" is a counter-reaction to the growing liberalism of the 1950s and 1960s. The

"Establishment" felt threatened by radical attitudes, student activism, and the rise of black power; hence, the appeal of reactionary doctrines such as hereditarianism (see Bowles and Gintis, 1974). Similarly, Rex (1972), commenting on the social strains arising from the massive influx of colored immigrants to Britain during this period, states that scientific rationalizations were revived in an attempt to stop and even to reverse the flow. The prejudices of the white population showed themselves in defamatory jokes and in the speeches of extremist politicians. Richards, Richardson, and Spears (1972) go so far as to suggest that the failure of Head Start, which largely provoked Jensen's article, was inevitable, since, if successful, it would have led to social and educational reforms that middle-class white society was unable to tolerate.

Husén (1972) writes more mildly that the Jensen fight was basically between those devoted to preserving the traditional political and educational structures on the one hand and those working to bring about radical reforms on the other hand. Possibly there does exist some association between people's sociopolitical attitudes generally and their views on the nature–nurture problem specifically. Politicians and writers who oppose social welfare or increased educational expenditure on behalf of the disadvantaged have often believed that some individuals or groups have poorer hereditary potential than others and that people with initiative and ability should not be highly taxed for the benefit of those who lack those qualities. The traditional opposition between conservative and progressive ideologies certainly tends to reflect different views of human nature in most Western countries, though this is somewhat obscured in the United States by the still pervasive rejection of hereditary privilege and the absence of any clear-cut philosophical differences between the two main political parties. Rather more marked is the tendency for opponents of genetic theory to be strongly left-wing in their general social and political attitudes. But there would certainly be many exceptions.[1] According to Eysenck (1973), Terman was decidedly liberal in his general outlook; and J. B. Watson, the arch-environmentalist, was somewhat conservative. But, in any case, ad hominem attacks, which resort

[1] An interesting alternative interpretation has been advanced by Hudson (1972), namely, that prominent test constructors tend to be "convergers" of high ability, who, therefore, make up tests that emphasize these same qualities but discriminate against the less intellectual and those given to more divergent thinking. In other words, quite apart from ideologies, the tester's own characteristics affect the kinds of tests he or she produces.

largely to probing the motives of those who hold opposing views, serve little or no purpose in stimulating the production of better research evidence (see Piel, 1974).

A common characteristic of prejudiced thinking is its tendency to be all-or-none; the extremist is incapable of allowing any truth in opposing arguments or findings. This would appear to hold true of most of the environmentalist writers referred to in the preceding paragraphs, and particularly of Kamin. On the other hand, although Jensen insists far more than most writers on the importance of genetic influences in human intelligence, he does also allow that environment makes a substantial contribution. It was natural, and right, that there should be a strong reaction against the excesses of Hitler's racism in the 1950s; but it went too far in indoctrinating social science students against any kind of genetic causation. Hence, in the period following Jensen's 1969 article, they refused to listen to any evidence contrary to their environmentalism and were unable to discuss the issues rationally and objectively.

THE SOCIAL RESPONSIBILITY OF SCIENTISTS

A frequent line of criticism is that scientists should not publish statements on matters of social concern if they are liable to be misinterpreted or misused or to do harm to the status and self-respect of some section of the community. This policy was put forward by the SPSSI (Society for the Psychological Study of Social Issues) when Jensen's article first appeared, and it was stressed that public statements are particularly undesirable when the available data and their interpretations are highly ambiguous and contentious. According to the SPSSI, scientists are accountable for the social consequences of their utterances, and Jensen was lacking in social responsibility in failing to see the furor that his article might cause. The SPSSI nevertheless claims to support free enquiry into controversial social issues, provided due caution is observed in the manner in which the conclusions are published. But it would seem to me that the critics are, in effect, saying that topics as sensitive as black–white differences should not be studied at all. In England, the editors of *Nature* (1972) insist that Jensen has the right to carry on his investigations but that people working in so controversial an area should be especially aware of the impact of their investigations and should disclaim that their results have any immediate implications for social policy. Similarly, the American National Academy of Sciences indicated that most scientists do avoid research into fields where current research methods are insufficiently advanced to produce unambiguous results. A committee was set up by the Academy to answer William Shockley's advocacy of research into the possible dysgenic effects of the high birthrate of the black population, which they saw as a particularly loaded and inflammatory question (see Shockley, 1972, for a summary of his views). Though their report (by Crow, Neel, and Stern) came out in 1967, it was remarkably farsighted and could well have been applied to the controversies that flared up in 1969 and the 1970s.

Block and Dworkin (1974) discuss these matters very fully, holding that the advancement of scientific knowledge is not the sole criterion for following a line of research and that the scientist should also take into account the likely social consequences. For example, many biologists are currently urging restrictions on certain types of genetic research; and Darwin himself seriously considered the ethics of publishing his *Origin of Species*. Jensen's reply is that any restraints on scientific enquiries, or on publication, mean that any group of people can muzzle or censor any work they happen to dislike. Scientific progress almost always involves challenging current beliefs and investigating the unconventional. I think that Block and Dworkin's view would have stifled the work of both Darwin and Galileo, which likewise shocked conventional morality and ideologies at the time they appeared. Dworkin does not admit this analogy, since Jensen's studies of race differences did not merely upset accepted psychological theories, but also were likely to do harm to, and lower the dignity of, U.S. blacks generally. Thus, his conclusions were quoted with approval (or often misquoted) by those who were essentially racist. It is possible that they led employers to discriminate more than ever against blacks, believing them to be generally inferior in ability. Despite Jensen's insistence that people should be evaluated on individual merits, not as a group, the unsophisticated reader of press reports would tend to do just that. It is unfortunate that public misunderstanding of such issues is always apt to be exacerbated by oversimplification and sensationalism in the press.

Clearly, there had been a change in the social climate by 1969 that Jensen had not anticipated. Even so, he had good grounds for believing that the accepted environmentalist position was doing greater social harm, for example, by raising false hopes of the effectiveness of compensatory education and encouraging such costly failures as Head Start. The "progressives" who ignored hereditary factors were trying to change the children instead of diversifying education in order to allow for a variety of talents. Another circumstance that was likely to be mis-understood was Jensen's apparent change of views between 1967 and 1969. When he argued that alternative hypotheses should be proposed and evaluated in the light of empirical research, it was natural that the lay reader might be put off by his treating a matter of such social importance as two straw men to be shot at.

It is doubtful whether such disputations about ethical is-sues will ever get us anywhere. Jensen may have laid himself open to some criticism for the way he presented his arguments at the particular time (see Cronbach, 1975), but that does not make him a racist. And the subsequent attacks by presumably intelligent students and many social scientists on Jensen's right to defend himself and to conduct further research on an important social issue are certainly much more blameworthy; even Hirsch (1975), who regards "Jensenism" as a moral, not a scientific, problem, deplores such attacks as "inarticulate and self-defeating hooliganism." Similarly, Horn (1974) points out that the very irra-tionality of the attacks on Jensen's right to continue his work re-bounded and led to a wide measure of support from psychol-ogists who disagree with many of his premises and conclusions.

SOME MORE SPECIFIC CRITICISMS

Test Scores Are Inadequate Measures of Phenotypic Traits

This is much the same objection as was raised in Chapter 13, but it gains added importance when statements are made about group differences that imply that Group A is superior or inferior to Group B in some socially valued trait such as intelli-gence. As Block and Dworkin (1974) argue, IQs (or other test scores) are not an exact representation of intelligence as under-stood by people generally. The layperson can hardly be expected to follow the niceties of operational constructs, and it is prevari-cation to say that there is no need to bother about the essential nature of what the tests measure (see Rex, 1972; Williams, 1970). Hirsch (1967) objects that, in view of the lack of any clear con-sensual theory of intelligence and the inconsistencies in the results yielded by different tests, we are not entitled to talk of in-telligence as a "thing" that exists in different amounts in the aver-age black and average white. The National Academy of Science, while supporting research in this area, agrees that psychologists don't really know what is being measured and should, therefore, refrain from any judgments affecting educational or social policies.

To some extent, this objection has been answered by showing that, so far as the evidence goes, intelligence tests do measure the same variable with virtually the same factorial structure and predictive validity in blacks as in whites. (This would be less true if we were comparing more dissimilar cultures.) The meaning of the term is given by whatever the tests correlate with in scientifically conducted investigations. But I would have to admit that this argument, however rational, seems coldly impersonal when some particular individual or social group may be affected by it; in other words, there are ethical implications that are sometimes not realized by psychometrists. It is unfortunate that Block and Dworkin do not tell us what "real" intelligence is; but they do have a point.

Environmental Differences Cannot Be Controlled

The most common criticism of studies of genetic group differences is that relevant environmental factors cannot be controlled or randomized. Any ethnic or racial groups that we try to compare inevitably must have been brought up in somewhat different environments and experienced different educational and economic conditions. Or, as Thoday (1973) puts it, any gene-frequency differences are to an unknown extent correlated with environmental differences. Scarr-Salapatek (1971b) makes essentially the same point with reference to U.S. blacks and whites: All blacks are disadvantaged to an unknown degree by being reared in a white-dominated environment, whereas whites do not have this handicap; hence, it is impossible to assess the between-group genetic and environmental variances. Bodmer and Cavalli-Sforza (1970), Biesheuvel (1972), Cronbach (1969), Dobzhansky (1973), and Morton (1972), all of whom recognize the importance of genetic diversity, believe that adequate evidence for genetic group differences in any psychological trait is, in the nature of the case, unobtainable; and Morton adds that, since all the relevant environmental factors are not known, they are probably underestimated. Since it is manifestly impossible to expose blacks and whites to the same environment, the problem of genetic differences is insoluble. (However, studies of the adoption of black children by white foster parents, described in Chapter 19, go some way to meet this objection.)

Several other cautious and relatively impartial commentators, such as Anastasi (1958), Tyler (1965), Dreger and Miller

(1960; 1968), and Spuhler and Lindzey (1967), conclude that, although there is a case for genetic black–white differences, it cannot be proven because of the difficulties of getting adequate and convincing evidence. It is noteworthy, however, that the authors of the most recent survey, Loehlin, Lindzey, and Spuhler (1975), find quite strongly supportive evidence in both directions. They conclude that group differences reflect both genetic and environmental factors and, usually, biases in the particular tests employed.

Within-Group Heritability Does Not Imply Between-Group Heritability

Several authors who admit that individual differences in intelligence within any one culture are quite largely genetic (e.g., 60 percent variance or over) nevertheless maintain that this does not tell us anything about the source of differences between racial-ethnic groups. Lewontin (1976) gives an example from plant breeding to show that very high within-group h^2 can coexist with zero between-group. In fact, from 1969 on, Jensen has always admitted that one cannot extrapolate from within-group findings to between-group, though his critics seldom realize this. Nevertheless, he does show that if h^2 is high, it is implausible that group differences should not also be partially genetic (1973a). The greater the value of h^2 within ethnic groups, the less the likelihood that h^2 between groups could be zero. It is interesting that Morant (1956), who is generally sympathetic to Klineberg's views on the absence of genetic race differences in mental traits, nevertheless argues that wherever there exists a wide range of genetic variance within a population, one should certainly expect to find genetic differences, even if small, between races.

DeFries (1972) has worked out the theoretical relationship of the two parameters, but, since his equation involves an unknown quantity, this method is of little help (see Jensen, 1973a). However, DeFries indicates that h^2 between groups is unlikely to be substantial when considerable cross-breeding has occured. In addition, the presence of genetic–environmental covariance makes the prediction of between-group heritability even more complex. Both of these conditions do apply in the United States.

Jensen (1975a) and Urbach (1974) further point out that, when h^2 within groups is large, between-group genetic variance could be zero only if there was a large environmental difference (see p. 267) or if some additional differentiating factor (not responsible for within-group variance) was present. In the case of blacks and whites, there would have to be some subtle disadvantage affecting all blacks that does not affect deprived whites, and it would have to be a very potent factor in order to account for the mean IQ difference. The ordinary environmental differences that affect both races would, of course, account for part of the between-group difference. But those psychologists who admit within-group and deny any between-group variance are obligated to find some special quality of black environment. Rex (1972), and Bodmer and Cavalli-Sforza (1970) state that the black environment is 200 or more years of oppression and discrimination. Obviously, this cannot be quantified, and it is, therefore, not much help to the social scientist; if the crucial factors could be isolated, psychometric researchers would gladly investigate their effects. Thoday (1973) talks of a subtle gestalt including awareness of black or slave ancestry and current discrimination; this cannot be adequately covered by a few normally distributed variables such as socioeconomic class. And Lewontin (1970) claims that psychologists simply do not know what are the major environmental differences among blacks, whites, Indians, or other groups; hence, it is impossible to assess genetic and environmental variance.

Many other suggestions come to mind, but whenever they are investigated, they fail, according to Jensen, to show any significant between-group variance over and above within-group. He therefore refers to these hypothetical differences in equality of environment as *X-factors*. If any one of these is disproved, the environmentalist can readily think up another, which means that, scientifically, the hypotheses are worthless. As Urbach (1974) remarks, "Everything in the world can be explained by factors that we know nothing about" (see also Li, 1971; Thoday, 1973).

While I accept Jensen's, Urbach's, and Li's criticisms of untestable hypotheses, I doubt whether we can, at present, go beyond a weak hypothesis, namely that U.S. blacks are affected in their intellectual and educational development by a syndrome of adverse factors — constitutional; linguistic; home upbringing, especially in the early years; and attidudinal, including reactions to white domination. I believe that, if we could more clearly define and measure the major differentiating conditions, we might be able to account for a substantial proportion of the IQ deficit blacks show. I would *not* expect them to account for the whole if it; nor do I accept that h^2 between ethnic-racial groups approximates zero, only that it is probably small relative to environmental variance. Any other conclusion would be difficult to reconcile with the large amount of evidence of environmental effects on mental growth that has been outlined in Part II of this book and further in Chapter 19.

It should be noted that this conclusion would still be criticized by writers such as Cole and Gay, Labov, and Ginsburg, who consider any notion of "social pathology" to be as insulting as attributing low test performance to genetic factors. It is difficult to see how to avoid this. Presumably, such critics would prefer our third source of racial-ethnic differences, namely unsuitability of the tests or testees' unfamiliarity with them. But it will be shown in Chapter 20 that this factor has been largely disconfirmed by recent research, at least in the case of blacks and whites.

Genetic Differences Are Relative to Current Cultural Conditions

In discussing heritability and individual differences, I admitted that obtained values of h^2 applied only to the present range of environmental differences. The same is true here; and both Dobzhansky and Hunt and Kirk make the point that, even if genetic group differences were conclusively demonstrated, say between U.S. whites and blacks, this would in no way imply that they would be interchangeable in altered circumstances. This is a tricky argument, since the authors presumably have in mind such changed circumstances as greater equalization of educational and occupational opportunity and reduced white prejudice against blacks. As in the case of individual differences, though, the outcome would be that successful reduction in environmental variance under improved conditions would actually increase the proportion of genetic variance in the remaining differences. Possibly this has some connection with the apparent lack of improvement in black IQ and achievement over the past 50 years, despite the considerable improvements in educational and other circumstances (p. 263).

SUMMARY

1   The study of racial or ethnic groups does not constitute "racism," which implies prejudice against all members of an out-group. Several early psychologists in the field of mental testing did express racist views and believed in the permanent mental and moral inferiority of low-scoring groups. But it is doubtful whether their beliefs had much influence in forging the restrictive U.S. immigration legislation.

2   Though all psychological research and writing are, to some extent, ideologically and ethnocentrically biased, mental testing originates more in the desire to break down the barriers of

wealth and privilege than to help preserve the status quo. Many of Jensen's conclusions ran counter to the prevailing environmentalism in American social science, but this is no excuse for the violence and irrationality of the attacks on his work and on any who supported his right to open discussion and further research.

3 Critics have also blamed Jensen for lack of social responsibility in expressing his views at a time when black power and student activism were increasing. Such an attitude would have stifled much original research, such as that of Galileo and Darwin. Fortunately, the period of emotive abuse has now abated, and more serious, less one-sided, discussions (such as Loehlin, Lindzey, and Spuhler's book) are being published.

4 Lack of precise definition of intelligence and the validity of intelligence tests have again been called into question. But the great volume of research on factorial content and predictive value of tests was ignored.

5 Research on the genetics of group differences is particularly complex and difficult to interpret, because racial and ethnic groups always differ also in environmental conditions, which cannot be controlled as in experimental research. Geneticists generally agree with Jensen on the importance of genetic diversity in human groups, but do not regard his analytic techniques as applicable to traits like intelligence.

6 Jensen admits that the existence of high heritability of within-group differences does not prove that group differences are genetic. But his environmentalist opponents have been unable to define the environmental conditions that would account fully for such differences, and they tend to put forward speculations rather than hypotheses that could be tested.

7 My own conclusion is that a syndrome of environmental and constitutional factors, which require more precise specification and measurement, does particularly affect the intellectual development of ethnic minority groups such as blacks and Indians. Furthermore, although it is highly probable that some genetic differences are also involved, their influence is small relative to that of cultural differences.

8 Jensen would agree, also, that group differences, such as that between white and black IQs, exist only under present circumstances, and that the situation could change with the discovery of novel types of intervention or amelioration.

19

Additional Evidence For and Against Genetic Group Differences

CHANGES IN PERFORMANCE
OF BLACK SUBJECTS
WITH CHANGED ENVIRONMENT

Two classical studies are frequently cited to show that low black IQs can be raised by improvements in the environment. Klineberg (1935b) and Lee (1951) found that black children whose families had migrated from the South to New York or Philadelphia obtained higher average IQs the longer their period of residence in the Northern cities. The authors attributed this to the somewhat better economic and educational conditions. Criticisms were raised that any differences between Northern and Southern blacks might be due to the more intelligent black parents being more likely to migrate, but this explanation was rejected by Klineberg. What we should note is that the maximum gain was some 6 to 8 points only; thus, the children did not make up the full 15 to 20 points that usually differentiate white and black means. However, it is reasonable to answer that the amount of improvement in environment was also quite limited, hence still more favorable circumstances might have had more substantial effects. Elsewhere (Vernon, 1969a), I have reported a considerably larger gain, equivalent to some 15 IQ points, between West Indian and other immigrant children who had attended schools in London for 6 to 7 years, compared with other emigrants who had attended 2 years or less. It is likely that the very low scores of the latter could be due mainly to unfamiliarity with standard English or other uncontrolled factors.

CRITICISM OF ENVIRONMENTAL THEORIES

In view of such studies as Skodak and Skeels' with foster children, or Heber's intervention experiment, and the difference of 15 points or more between four of Newman, Freeman, and Holzinger's pairs of separated twins, Jencks et al. (1972) and others have argued that the whole 15-point difference could plausibly be attributed to environmental deprivation. However, Dobzhansky rejects the argument that changes obtained in rather extreme cases can be generalized to racial population differences. And Jensen (1973a) points out that, in only 5 percent of recorded MZ twins reared apart, did the difference in IQs exceed 15 points. In Heber's work, the special intervention program would be expected to be more effective than ordinary environmental differences; indeed, his experimental group was provided with intellectual stimulation superior to that of the average white home.

Any simple explanation in terms of environmental handicap is ruled out by the finding that American Indian and Mexican-American children score higher than black children on nonverbal intelligence tests, despite even poorer economic circumstances. Coleman et al. (1966) found that these ethnic groups were more disadvantaged than blacks on several environmental indices. Jensen has since confirmed that, on relatively culture-free tests, Mexican-Americans score nearer to the white norm than do blacks, though they do less well on verbal intelligence and achievement tests, presumably because of linguistic difficulties (see p. 265). It might be possible, though difficult, to think of some environmental factor in which blacks are even worse off than other minorities, but, unless this can be operationalized and measured, it is just another "X-factor." Senna's (1973) comment on this finding is that it merely shows how invalid intelligence tests are, given that blacks have produced many more professionals and leaders of various kinds than have the other minority groups.

Though this observation is plausible at first sight, it certainly is not true of professional workers. Weyl (1966) used the

1960 U.S. census returns to analyze the proportional representation of five racial-ethnic groups in each of 12 major professions. The jobs ranged from lawyer or judge to school teacher and nurse. Weyl calculated an index that averages 100 if a certain ethnic group is represented in a profession according to its numbers in the general population. But when, for example, blacks show an index of 20 for natural scientists, this means that the number of scientists they produce are only one-fifth as many as would be expected in a representative population. Weyl's full table is reproduced in Jensen (1973a). I have taken the median index for all the professions, as follows:

Chinese	300
Japanese	155
White	110
Indian	48
Black	20

Thus, Chinese-Americans are the most productive of professionals and blacks much the lowest. However, blacks do reach over 50 in three occupations — school teacher, clergyman, and nurse. Other types of leadership, political, for instance, could not be assessed.

EFFECTS OF MULTIPLE ENVIRONMENTAL FACTORS

A common fallacy committed by writers on racial-ethnic differences is that the effects of numerous environmental handicaps is cumulative. For example, it may be shown that blacks or low-SES whites differ from middle-class whites in greater pregnancy and birth complications, poorer nutrition, unstimulating early rearing by the mother, poverty and overcrowding, linguistic differences from standard English, poorer quality schools and teachers, and so forth. It would seem only logical that, if each condition is associated with an IQ decrement, then the combination of many or most of them might readily add up to the 15-point overall black deficit. I must plead guilty myself to stating, in my comparative study of several ethnic groups (1969a), that there was a general correspondence between the *number* of adverse cultural conditions and the overall test performance.

However, Jensen (1973a) points out that this is unjustified insofar as there is always likely to be considerable correlation between the adverse conditions. The situation is quite similar to that in predicting, say, job success from a combination of different predictors by multiple correlation. Almost always, the bulk of the prediction can be effected by some three or four tests, and the inclusion of additional ones adds little or nothing to the multiple correlation with the criterion, because they are merely covering the same ground over again. In the same way, the discovery of additional factors that differentiate ethnic groups may fail to increase the variance between the groups that can be accounted for, because three or four major factors (e.g., constitutional, SES, and parental education) may cover as much ground as 10 or more additional ones.

An investigation by Fox (1972) provided some relevant data. He tested over 5,000 whites and an equal number of blacks at ninth- and twelfth-grade levels with a lengthy biographical inventory designed to elicit differences between the races in home background and life history, attitudes, goals, and so on. Item analysis was carried out on half the sample for boys, girls, and total group; the other half were retained for cross-validation. Actually, only 49 out of 1,342 possible item responses differentiated significantly between the racial groups. These were very varied in content, including size of family, parents lacking secondary education, few books in home, fear of thunder storms, negative self-concepts (girls only), and lack of experience of camping or taking trips away from home. When the control group was scored on these keyed items, the following correlations were obtained:

	Race	IQ	School Grades	Family Income
Race-difference score	0.56	0.45	0.22	0.50
Family income	— —	0.56	0.50	— —

Thus, the cross-validity of the race score was 0.56. The figures also show that race score correlates to some extent with IQ and grades, but less so than family income does. Unfortunately, the author did not attempt any multivariate regression analysis; however, it seems unlikely that scores based on the inventory would have added more than quite a small amount to the prediction of cognitive performance when family income or SES are held constant. Possibly, items that covered the various areas mentioned on p. 286 might have been more diagnostic, though the measurement of these variables would have to be based on more reliable techniques than students' recollections and perceptions.

REGRESSION EFFECTS

One of the most striking features of black and white IQ distributions, brought to notice by Shuey and Jensen, is that the children of middle-class (e.g., professional) black parents actually score slightly lower than the children of white lower-working-class parents. Surely, one would think that the former parents can and do provide a far more intellectually stimulating environment than the latter. Jensen's explanation is that this arises from the general tendency for filial regression to the mean. It is well known that the offspring of bright parents tend to obtain IQs only half as much above the mean as the IQs of the parents themselves, since the correlation between parents and children is only about 0.5. Hence, we would expect greater regression among black than white children because their population mean is lower. For example, if we take white and black parents with IQ 110, the white children are likely to average 105; whereas black children are likely to average $110 - (110 - 85) = 97\frac{1}{2}$. Similar studies have shown that the siblings of bright black children score lower than do the siblings of equally bright white children. Indeed, since there is some evidence (Scarr-Salapatek, 1971b) that the correlation between parental SES and child IQ is lower in blacks than in whites, we might expect even greater regression; that is, the mean of middle-class black children should be somewhat more than halfway toward 85.

Loehlin, Lindzey, and Spuhler (1975) point out that this phenomenon should certainly not be regarded as a kind of biological tendency among black children to relapse to a more primitive level. Regression is simply a statistical phenomenon arising from the moderately low correlation between parents and their children. These authors also mention that black parents who achieve professional jobs are more highly selected than whites of similar SES because there are fewer of them. While this is true, it hardly seems relevant to the issue. The regression toward a lower mean among blacks appears to be more readily explicable in terms of genetic differences between population means. But as Thoday (1973) points out, correlation and regression cannot tell us what the causal factors are. The same kind of regression could occur if the population mean difference was due entirely to environmental causes; though it seems difficult to explain why, for example, siblings of bright blacks should score lower than siblings of equally bright whites. Thoday also fails to mention that genetic theory can predict the amount of regression fairly accurately, whereas environmental theories can give no definite predictions.

INTERGENERATIONAL STABILITY

A strong argument for genetic racial-ethnic differences in intelligence would be provided by a demonstration that the relative levels of contrasted groups remain approximately the same from one generation to another, despite considerable environmental changes over time. The relative deficit among U.S. blacks seems to have remained pretty stable from 1918 to the present time (see p. 263), despite the obvious increased affluence and reduced discrimination against blacks over the last 60 years. Eysenck (1971) specifically suggests that the original black slaves who were captured in Africa constituted rather low-grade stock (who were not bright enough to escape), and that, during the days of slavery, those with higher intelligence were at a special disadvantage; these historical factors might account for the low present-day IQ. Likewise, he accepts the below-average IQ of Irish children as genetic and ascribes this to the more intelligent Irish stocks having emigrated during the nineteenth century (see p. 251). He admits, however, that these are speculative arguments. In the same vein might we not expect present-day Australians to be below the British average on the grounds that their ancestors consisted largely of deported criminals who were, presumably, mostly of inferior intelligence?

There is little well-documented evidence on this question, but what there is appears to be rather consistently negative. Barron and Young (1970) compared Italians living in Boston, whose great-grandfathers, of poor peasant stock, had emigrated to the United States, with Italians living in Rome, whose grandparents were more nearly of average SES. There were no significant differences on Raven Matrices or in educational level, despite the very considerable difference in ancestry. Lieblich, Ninio, and Kugelmass (1972) report the application of WISC tests to Israeli children whose parents were of quite varied origin (European, Middle Eastern, West African, and Israeli). These parents differed considerably in SES and acculturation, yet their children score not much below Western norms, and the gap between the different ethnic groups is decreasing. I have referred earlier (p. 273) to the similar studies reported by Smilansky and Smilansky (1967) and Bloom (1969). Although it is not possible to evaluate their claims until further details are published, they do fit in with other evidence suggesting that children of low-ability ethnic stock can score up to normal Western levels when reared in a Western-type environment.

It is unfortunate that higher quality research is not available. But, in my view, what there is should make us much more cautious in accepting positive evidence of genetic group differences derived from other types of investigation. One would anticipate a substantial rise among immigrant children brought up in a new land and more stimulating environment similar to that occurring among foster children. But the amount of improvement reported by Barron, Lieblich, and Smilansky seems to be larger than that obtained in most studies of fostering; if confirmed, it might even exceed what would be expected from a 30–35 percent environmental contribution to variance. Such changes would probably require several generations, since the first generation of offspring might still be greatly affected by the parental culture, the second generation less, and so on.

CROSS-RACIAL MATINGS

Loehlin, Lindzey, and Spuhler survey a number of studies in this area, concluding that the results provide no convincing support for either genetic or environmental explanations of black–white differences. For example, on genetic theory, one might expect a child of one black and one white parent to have a higher IQ than a child of two black parents, and further rises with greater proportions of white admixture. It has been claimed that this does occur (e.g., Shuey, 1966; Baker, 1974), though Anastasi (1958) specifically denies it. Moreover, Baker's statement that the outstanding black intellectual leaders have an unusually high proportion of white ancestry does not seem to have been substantiated. According to Shockley (1972), there is an average increase of 1 IQ points among blacks for each 1 percent of white ancestry. But the available evidence is often contradictory, and possible environmental explanations have not been ruled out. For example, families with greater white admixture might well provide environments more similar to those of pure whites. And lighter colored individuals of mixed birth would tend to be more acceptable socially and occupationally than the very dark skinned.

In view of the difficulties of getting accurate information on ancestry, many more studies have simply taken lightness of skin, or the presence of other genetic markers, as measures of the proportion of white ancestry. These tend to give positive correlations with IQ, but the coefficients are quite low and inconsistent, so that they probably contradict as much as they confirm genetic determination.

The poor reliability of any findings might also be attributed to the chancy nature of the social situation in which children of mixed ancestry are reared. Some would be rejected, others (particularly those with light skin) accepted by the white community; and some might be treated as outcasts by both groups; that is, their environment would be even more abnormal than that of full-bloods. In any case, the data seem to contradict the common superstition that children of a mixed marriage tend to be degenerate, or lower in ability than their parents, as well as the opposite view that cross-racial breeding produces hybrid vigor, or heterosis, resulting in IQ gain.

Several studies of full-blood American Indians, mixed-bloods, and whites have also suggested that IQs tend to rise with greater admixture of white genes (e.g., Jamieson and Sandiford, 1928). However, it is at least as difficult as with blacks to determine ancestry. Moreover, those identified as full-bloods are more apt to isolate themselves from white U.S. or Canadian cultural influences, and they are more likely to make little use of the English language.

Jensen cites one study apparently favoring genetic determination, that of De Lemos (1969) on conservation abilities of Australian aboriginal children. Thirty-eight of the children studied were full-blooded, 34 had some admixture of white ancestry. The two groups, it is claimed, lived under the same environmental and educational conditions. The full-bloods were significantly inferior to the mixed group on 6 Piaget-type tasks. Thoday (1973) has criticized this study on the grounds that the two groups were not matched for age, and more full-bloods fell in the 8–11 year range, which was naturally less successful than the 12–15 year range, whereas more of the mixed group fell in the older range. However, he is not justified in dismissing the results as attributable merely to age; they persist at much the same level when age is held constant. What is more serious is that Dasen (1972) attempted to replicate the research under somewhat different, but well-controlled, conditions and obtained no confirmation. Thus, the case is not proven either way.

In most of the studies of blacks and whites, race has been determined by social classification of the children of their parents, that is, by skin color. But there are also numerous genetically determined blood-group characteristics that differentiate to some extent between blacks and whites. Loehlin, Vandenberg, and Osborne (1973) calculated the presence or absence in black children of 16 blood-group genes more common among whites and correlated these with IQ. The correlations were zero or negative; in other words, there was no tendency for blacks with white-type genes to show higher intelligence. A more extensive study was carried out by Scarr et al. (1977) with 144 pairs of black twins, who took 5 ability tests. When they were ranked for white-type blood-group genes, the correlations were not significant. It is true that these measurable genes constitute only a very small proportion of the total possible racially different loci and thus may be no more reliable than skin color alone, but the absence of any positive association with ability is certainly inconsistent with the theory of genetic racial differences in ability.

Returning to black hybridization, a striking finding is that the mating of black fathers with white mothers seems to produce children of higher intelligence than those of white fathers with black mothers. In one study of 4-year-olds by Willerman, Broman, and Fiedler (1970), the mean IQ of the former was 9 points higher than that of the latter. While a genetic explanation is plausible, there is also the possibility that white mothers tend to provide a better prenatal and early childhood environment for their offspring.

Some valuable data are provided by the white parents' adoption of children of presumably low-scoring minority group parentage. Loehlin, Lindzey, and Spuhler mention two such follow-up reports, one dealing with American Indian adoptees, the other with West Indians in England. Both claim that the children were growing up to be of apparently the same general intelligence level as normal white children. However, there was no control over the extent of selective placement and the true parents could well hvae been of above-average intelligence. In an early investigation by Garth (1935), eight adopted Indian children obtained mean Stanford-Binet IQs of 102, compared with 87 among Indian orphans in an institution.

DeLacey, and Seagrim (1973) have published a similar study of 22 Australian aboriginal children adopted or fostered in white families. Their Peabody Picture Vocabulary test scores were comparable to white norms, and there was little difference on several Piaget tests. However, on conservation tasks, they fell between the white and aboriginal standards.

Much fuller evidence came from recent research by Scarr and Weinberg (1976). Ninety-nine black or part-black children were adopted into superior white homes, mostly during their first year of life. They were tested with Stanford-Binet or WISC between the ages of 4 and 16. The educational levels of the natural mothers and of a small number of fathers were known and, apparently, they corresponded closely to the typical distribution for blacks in the area. Thus, the authors claim that the likely mean IQ, had the children been raised in their own homes, would be about 90. The 29 children known to have two black parents had a mean of 97; 68 others with one black parent averaged 109. For 25 white adoptees in similar homes, the mean was 111.5; for 21 American Indian or Asian-American children, it was 100. Many of the foster parents had children of their own, and these averaged 118; the foster parents themselves averaged 121 IQ on WAIS.

The authors conclude that black children show much the same gain in IQ when reared in superior homes as do white adoptees, though they do not catch up with natural children of the same foster parents. However, the results were complicated by the finding that early-adopted children tended to score higher than late adoptees.[1] The figures quoted above suggest that children with two black parents and those of Asian or Indian stock gain only some 7 to 10 points, though those with one black parent do much better. This type of investigation, which casts doubt on genetic theories of race differences, should be replicated with larger numbers. Another promising source of information that has not yet been explored would be tests of half-sibs; for example, children of the same mother but of white and black fathers.

An interesting study by Eyferth (1961) was based on illegitimate children of American soldiers stationed in Germany. The mothers were German, the fathers were either whites or blacks. Overall, there appeared to be no differences in WISC IQ distributions, but the results varied considerably with the sex and age of the children (5 – 13 years), and with the different WISC subtests. Further, the black soldiers would have been a rather superior sample, because of the Army policy of selecting recruits, particularly those sent to Europe. Thus, no definite conclusions can be drawn.

FURTHER STUDIES

Some of the attackers of Jensen's 1969 article in the *Harvard Educational Review* tried to show that there were alternatives to his Analysis of Variance model, which yield very different estimates of heritability. Thus, Light and Smith (1969) proposed what they call a social allocation model, relating black IQ and SES distribution and involving an interaction term between heredity and environment; they claimed this would account completely for the mean deficit without any genetic racial differences. However, as Shockley (1971) has shown, although the

---

[1] Thus, the mean for 13 early-adopted children with 2 black parents was as high as 104.

model is ingenious, it is untenable; it leads to absurd IQ distributions and far too large an IQ variance in blacks, among other inconsistencies (see also Jensen, 1973a).

Two investigations by Mercer (1972) and Mercer and Brown (1973) were designed to show that intelligence tests measure cultural or ethnic handicap rather than racial differences in ability. In the first, Mercer devised a scale of "behavior skills" along the same lines as the Vineland Scale of Social Maturity. She found that a great many children and adults who had been classified as mentally retarded—largely on the basis of low IQ—were able to function adequately in daily life situations. This was particularly true of blacks and Chicanos, who were far more frequently labeled mentally retarded than were whites.

In the main study, 180 each of white, black, and Chicano children were given the full WISC, Raven's Matrices, and Peabody Vocabulary. In addition, their homes were visited and nine major cultural indices were assessed by the interviewer, including Anglo values, English-speaking experience, and SES. The multiple correlations of these background variables with child's full-scale IQ were 0.42 in the white group, 0.43 in the black group, and 0.51 for the Chicanos. Scoring white as 2, black as 1, and Chicano as 0, there was a correlation of 0.47 with IQ. Mercer and Brown showed that those black or Chicano children whose families scored positively on all five of the main indices obtained IQs as high as the average white, implying that, if the environments of the minority groups could be raised to white level, there would be no ethnic group differences in intelligence left. To verify this, the environmental indices were held constant by partial correlation, and almost all the test differences between the groups disappeared. (However, for the Peabody and Block Design tests, 7 percent of additional variance was attributable to ethnic group differences, presumably because the Chicanos were particularly handicapped on Vocabulary, the blacks on Block Designs).

Mercer and Brown are aware of the obvious criticism that their environmental assessments may have involved some genetic components, but they dismiss this as a more complex hypothesis than their own claim that ethnic group differences are entirely environmental. Jensen, however, regards the research as a flagrant example of the "sociologist's fallacy" (see p. 251), that is, failure to recognize that partialling out the environment also partials out much, or the whole, of the genetic differences. For example, one of the cultural variables was "living in a white majority neighborhood versus segregated minority neighborhood." If this is held constant, it is hardly surprising that between-group differences in ability tend to disappear. This study has been quoted at some length because it illustrates in sophisticated form the weakness of much environmental argument and research.

CUMULATIVE DEFICIT

Several writers, Klineberg and Deutsch, for example, have claimed that the scholastic retardation of disadvantaged children is cumulative. Because they are backward when they first come to school, they do badly from the start; progressively, they become more frustrated and disheartened and therefore fall more and more behind in later grades. This situation is sometimes referred to as the Progressive Achievement Gap (PAG), or Progressive Decrement. It is important because, if confirmed, it would plainly support environmental explanations of intellectual retardation. It would imply that the longer the exposure to a deprived or nonstimulating environment, the more IQ and achievement might be expected to drop below the white average. With genetic theory, on the other hand, we might expect low-IQ children to show a certain deficit as soon as their school work depends on conceptual learning, say by second or third grade, and that this would persist with little alteration (other than individual fluctuations) till the end of their school careers.

There is no doubt that the deficit in ability and achievement does become more pronounced with age when tests are scored in grade or age units. For example, the Coleman report showed that black children in sixth grade scored 1¼ grades lower in verbal ability than whites, those in ninth grade averaged 2¼ grades lower, and those in twlefth grade were 3¼ grades lower. But much the same increase in spread of scores with age occurs with Mental Ages on intelligence tests or, for that matter, with heights measured in inches. Clearly, we should concern ourselves not with absolute decrements, but with decrement relative to age level. This occurs when classical IQs are calculated or when the scores are expressed in terms of sigma units. When this is done, it has been found in several studies in different parts of the United States, that black scholastic achievement falls approximately 1 sigma below that of whites, just as their mean IQ does, regardless of age. Their rate of growth in achievement is below average, but no more so than what would be expected from their rate of intellectual maturation.

However, the Coleman report did find some evidence of *relative* deficit increasing with age among blacks in the Southern states. In verbal ability, the mean scores at fifth, ninth, and twelfth grades were, respectively, 1.5, 1.7, and 1.9 sigma units below those of whites. This does suggest some genuine cumulative deficit during the adolescent years, but there are a lot of difficulties in any cross-sectional comparative studies. We do not possess any strictly equal-interval or absolute scales for measuring growth in achievement. Furthermore, we cannot guarantee the representativeness of the available samples of students at different ages. For example, it is possible, though somewhat unlikely, that the more able students in the South drop out, leaving a piling up of duller students in the later grades.

There have been some attempts to carry out longitudinal investigations in order to show whether the same students, tested at successive ages, fall further behind, but the results seem contradictory. Jensen (1974c) used a different approach with some 8,000 California students in fifth to twelfth grades, of whom 40 percent were black. He compared siblings who, of course, differed in age, but who would be expected to show the same average ability. Twenty tests were given, and it was found that the results were not affected by birth order or by family size. Only on one test, the Lorge-Thorndike Verbal, was there a greater cumulative deficit among black boys than among whites, or among girls of either race.

But in a more recent study (Jensen, 1975b), some 1,300 students in rural Georgia, aged 6 to 16 years, were given the California Test of Mental Maturity, which yields verbal and nonverbal IQs. Almost half the group was black, and these students did show a significant decrement with age, particularly on verbal quotients, which did not occur among the whites. It should be noted that the overall mean IQs were 71 for blacks and 102 for whites. The blacks came from very low-SES agricultural families. Jensen admits that, at this unusually low-grade level, a cumulative deficit does occur, which was not present among the rather less disadvantaged California blacks; and he finds an environmental explanation the most plausible. Educational achievement, as such, was not studied, but almost certainly a similar or greater decrement would have been found.

These investigations do, therefore, tend to support environmentalist theories of IQ deficit, though only when the disadvantaged blacks are living in extremely poor circumstances. In other words, the findings are similar to those noted by Jensen when he proposed his threshold hypothesis (see p. 139). Over the more normal range of environments and IQs, cumulative deficit phenomena do not occur.

SUMMARY

1   There is some tendency for black children's IQs to rise the longer they live in an environment where there are relatively good economic and educational conditions. But the amount of increase is quite limited.

2   The fact that a 15-point black–white IQ difference is no larger than that found among occasional MZ twins reared apart, or than the increases brought about in intervention studies, does not prove that the difference is purely environmental. The weakness of environmental explanations is illustrated by the higher nonverbal IQs of American Indians and Mexican Americans than those of blacks, despite their considerably poorer environmental backgrounds.

3   It is pointed out that, when a group undergoes multiple handicaps in home and school upbringing, all of which are associated with lowered IQ, the combination of all these handicaps does not necessarily account for a larger proportion of IQ variance than a few of the major variables.

4   There is clear evidence for regression to a lower mean IQ among relatives of high-ability blacks than among relatives of equally able whites. This phenomenon is more readily explicable genetically than environmentally.

5   There is little evidence that the offspring of low-IQ parents who emigrate to a Western country continue to show low ability. Several studies suggest that they catch up with local norms in one or two generations.

6   When cross-racial mating occurs, genetic theory would predict a regular rise in mean IQ the greater the proportion of white ancestry. Evidence for such a tendency based on parentage or on skin color is unconvincing, and such differences as do occur appear to be more readily explicable by environmental factors. When blood-group markers are used to classify blacks according to amount of white ancestry, there is no significant correlation with ability.

7   Blacks, Indian, or Australian aboriginal children who are adopted by white foster parents show considerable gains over the IQs expected from their ancestry, though they do not catch up with the natural children of the foster parents.

8   Two studies by Mercer of black, Chicano, and white children are outlined. Larger proportions of nonwhites get classified as mentally retarded, though their functioning in everyday life is adequate. The second investigation showed that, when environmental differences between whites and nonwhites were held constant, there was little or no group difference in mean IQs.

However, this conclusion is invalidated, since the assessments of environment would also tend to hold genetic differences constant.

9 The commonly observed Progressive Achievement Gap, or Cumulative Deficit, among black children usually disappears when the achievement or intelligence scores are expressed as sigma scores (or deviation quotients). Jensen showed that investigations in this area could be improved by using older and/or younger sibs of the experimental group as controls. Among California blacks, there was slight evidence of cumulative deficit in boys on verbal intelligence. But in a lower-grade sample from rural Georgia, the cumulative deficit phenomenon was much more marked.

20

Cultural Bias in Intelligence Tests

We turn at last to the most common criticism of testing deprived or minority group children—namely, that the tests were originally constructed for white children by white middle-class psychologists; hence, they are obviously unfair to children who have not had the same cultural background and linguistic experience. It is on these grounds that intelligence testing is being banned in parts of the United States, and numerous broadcasters or writers in the popular press reiterate the unfairness of the tests in such a way that the general public is beginning to believe it. This point was discussed rather fully in Chapter 2, and the criticism that intelligence tests merely measure acquired information was rejected. The fact that verbal intelligence tests usually correlate quite highly with scores on achievement test batteries is sometimes taken to mean that they measure the same thing. However, I pointed out (p. 175) that the heritability percentages are much lower for achievement tests than for intelligence tests, which is as it should be.

In this chapter, I will reivew a number of researches that support or, more often, contradict the criticism that tests are specially biased against low-SES or ethnic-minority children. It is true, of course, that such children tend to get low scores on conventional tests, whether of intelligence or achievement. But I hope to show that there are no difficulties in particular tests or kinds of test items that specifically affect minority-group or disadvantaged children. In fact, it is found that these children do just about as poorly on the tests least open to the accusation of cultural bias as they do on tests that appear to be strongly biased in content, language, and so on.

COMPLEXITY VERSUS CULTURAL BIAS

Jensen (1974d) points out that there are two aspects of test difficulty that are often confused, although they can vary quite independently. One is rarity, unfamiliarity, or unusualness of the concepts appearing in the test items. As admitted in Chapter 2, many of the difficult items in vocabulary and information subtests do draw on recondite information. But the other aspect is the level of complexity versus simplicity; that is, the extent to which the problems require mental manipulation, transformation, or information processing. For example, one very useful nonverbal g test depends on copying a series of geometrical figures, starting with simple circle, square, and diamond, and ranging up to a cube seen obliquely. The materials—paper, pencil, and line drawings—can hardly be said to be unknown to disadvantaged children in the United States. Several tests depend on seeing relationships, classifying, or finding analogies between quite well-known words, numbers, or figures. It is the operation, not the materials or content, that causes the difficulty.

It would certainly be possible to devise a test that depends largely on culture-biased knowledge. Shimberg (1929) constructed an information test containing numerous agricultural or rural terms and knowledge; she found, as might be expected, that urban children no longer scored higher as they do on most tests. R. L. Williams, a black psychologist, has published what he calls the BITCH test (1970), which draws on materials far more likely to be familiar to black slum children than to white middle-class ones; again, the scores of the former are higher. However, no evidence has been provided to show that this test is valid for any practical purpose. Nowadays, most test constructors tend to avoid items involving specialized information, although, in fact, vocabulary and information subtests generally work quite well, because testees who are capable of more complex mental processes are also more likely to have picked up advanced words and miscellaneous unusual information.

There is further evidence that it is complexity, rather than lack of learned information, that makes a test difficult for retarded children. Jensen points out that simple reaction-time tests, which involve a minimum of mental processing, show low correlations with intelligence, and no difference in performance between blacks and whites. But in choice-reaction times, the correlation with intelligence, and the racial differences, increase the greater number of choices provided, that is, the more complex the task. Similarly, in digit span tests, digits forward, which involves the very simple task of attending and memorizing for a few seconds, show little race difference; whereas digits backwards, which requires more concentration and manipulation, shows a greater difference and correlates more highly with other intelligence subtests (Jensen and Figueroa, 1975).

Another complaint raised by psychologists who regard tests as culture-biased is that middle-class white children receive much more extensive training in English word usage in their everyday environments. But this, too, seems to be contradicted by some awkward facts. As we saw earlier (p. 136), up till the age of about 2 years, language acquisition seems to consist of a maturating and acquired skill, which has remarkably little connection with intelligence. Though it must, of course, depend on the child's hearing plenty of varied speech from parents and older siblings, it may be that even the poorest families supply sufficient stimulation at this early stage of linguistic development. It is not until about 5 years, when language is becoming a tool for conceptual thinking rather than a means of communicating, that white children tend to draw ahead of blacks.

Surely, though, it will be said, black children who mainly hear a dialect different from standard English and use it at home and with their peers will be handicapped compared with white children who are tested in the same language as they normally use. But this was contradicted in a research by Quay (1971), who had the Stanford-Binet test translated into black dialect. This version and the original standard English version were given to 100 black 4-year-olds, and the mean IQs were practically identical. It would be useful to carry out a similar study at later ages, say 7–14 years, since it might turn out that older black children are better able to carry out verbal reasoning tasks in their habitual language. However, Hall and Turner (1974) found only slight differences between blacks and whites (of the same SES) in repeating sentences and in verbal comprehension. They conclude that even lower-class blacks experience so much standard English on television, at school, or elsewhere, that they can automatically translate what they hear into black English for processing purposes and vice versa.

A further point made by Haggard (1954) and later critics is that low-SES children are handicapped in taking written tests because of their reading difficulties, and they perform better on tests given orally. One suspects that the same would be true of blacks. But Shuey's survey of test results of black elementary school children indicated no difference between mean group test and individual test IQs. In fact, the Standard Deviations of group test distributions in either race often differ from those of individual tests, but there seems to be no convincing evidence of lower mean IQs.

The possible effects on black children of such factors as poor rapport and motivation or anxiety when tests are given by white testers are considered later.

TEST NORMS

Some writers raise the objection that most intelligence tests are standardized on white populations and that blacks are then evaluated against white norms. This shows a lamentable ignorance of the nature of test norms. If tests were standardized on mixed populations, containing the same proportion of blacks as in the total population (and recent restandardizations of Terman-Merrill and WISC-R *were* normed in this way), the relative standing of the two racial groups would not be in the slightest degree affected. The actual numerical values might change; for instance, whites might average 105 and blacks 90, instead of 100 and 85, respectively. But the same percentage of blacks—around 16 percent—would still score higher than the white mean and the same proportion of whites lower than the black mean.

Recently, some interesting comparative data have become available through the restandardization of WISC-R. J. R. Mercer organized the testing of highly representative samples of 600 white and 600 black children in California. Her material was subjected to an analysis of variance by Jensen (1975b), with the results shown in Table 20.1. The variance contributions of SES, race, and family differences are shown, together with the approximate average differences between members of different social classes, races, and so on.

The WISC is often regarded as a strongly culturally biased test—biased against blacks or against low-SES children. But if this were so, how is it that differences between racial means are no larger than the differences between siblings (either white or black) brought up in the same family, under presumably identical cultural and linguistic conditions; or that the differences between siblings are much larger than those between the different

TABLE 20.1
Effects of SES, Race,
and Family on WISC-R IQs

Source of variance	Percentage variance	Average IQ differences
Between social classes (within races)	8	6
Between races (within social classes)	14	12
Between families (within races and SES)	29	9
Within families (between sibs)	44	12
Measurement error	5	4
	100	

social class groups? Likewise, there is a larger difference between families (within any social class) than between the different classes. This analysis does not, as it stands, demonstrate any genetic factors in WISC IQs, but it does raise questions that would be very difficult to answer satisfactorily with a purely environmentalist theory. Such a theory might well have predicted exactly the opposite rank order of variance contributions; for instance, that differences in cultural stimulation of members of the same family would have the smallest influence, then differences between racial groups, and differences in the environments of upper and lower socioeconomic groups the largest influence.

AN INVESTIGATION OF CULTURE BIAS IN TWO TESTS

Perhaps the most striking contradictions of culture bias in intelligence tests are provided by Jensen's (1974d) analyses of the Peabody Picture Vocabulary Test and Raven's Progressive Matrices among some 600 white and 400 black pupils in California schools. The first test is obviously very likely to be culturally biased, since high scores depend on recognizing pictures of rare words; the second is generally admitted to approximate as closely as any test in common use to being relatively culture-fair. High scores depend on the complexity of the patterns that testees can grasp and interrelate. Yet, with few exceptions, virtually no significant differences could be discovered in the statistical properties of the contrasted tests in the two racial groups.

The order of item difficulties on either test was almost the same in the two groups, the correlations being over 0.98, though one would surely expect some items to be relatively easier or more difficult for whites than for blacks. The correlations are as high as those between the sexes in either group. In contrast, Irvine and Sanders (1972) found correlations of item-difficulty order in a reading comprehension test of 0.98 between two groups of white students, and 0.96 for two groups of African students, but an average of only 0.60 between whites and blacks. Thus, this index undoubtedly reveals differences between two very different cultures. Jensen noted a greater discrepancy in PPVT item difficulty between London and California students than between Californian whites and blacks.

The internal consistency reliability coefficients were the same for blacks and whites, although they might be expected to drop among the blacks if their responses were more haphazard or more affected by biasing conditions. Moreover, those items that discriminated best within either group were also the items that showed the largest between-group differences. When the items were subjected to factor analysis, the same ones came out with the highest first-factor loadings. In other researches, summarized by Jensen, factorization was applied to batteries of very varied cognitive tests and to a certain range of items in the Stanford-Binet test. Here, too, there was no evidence that some tests or items were relatively easier or more difficult, or better measures of the general intelligence factor in one race than the other (see p. 274).

Another technique of analysis was to select from the white pupils' results a set of PPVT items exactly matched in difficulty to each Matrices item. When the blacks were scored for these vocabulary items, their mean was the same as for the Matrices, just as in the white group. The wrong choices given to PPVT items were also tabulated, and here there were certain differences between the groups. But it was found that the wrong choices of blacks more closely resembled the wrong choices of whites who were 2 years younger. In other words, sixth-grade blacks were more like fourth-grade whites in their responses than they were like fifth-grade blacks.

In sum, the blacks, as expected, obtained lower scores than the whites on both tests, but there was no respect in which the test responses of the blacks could be distinguished statistically from those of whites about 2 years younger. Both tests could be called "culturally loaded" in the sense that the racial group means differed, whether from genetic or environmental causes or both. But neither showed any signs of "culture bias," that is, of presenting unusual difficulties, or different patterns of response, in the two groups. Indeed, Jensen found more sex bias than race bias.

Finally, it has been found that psychologists cannot even predict in advance what items will specially favor or disfavor contrasted racial groups. McGurk (1953) constructed two tests, one of apparently culture-biased, the other of nonbiased, items. He found that his black subjects scored better on the former.

CULTURE FAIRNESS OF TESTS

The layperson is apt to assume that a culture-fair test should yield the same means and distributions for members of any cultural or racial group to which it is applied. But a little consideration shows that this could not work. Tests merely record samples of the abilities that people show under present conditions. Members of the different SES groups, for example, clearly differ in their job potentialities and in their educational achievements; hence, a test on which children of unskilled laborers score lower on the average than children of doctors and lawyers is not unfair. As Linn (1973) points out, the scores do not tell us anything about causes, nor can they show what scores the laborers' children might obtain if they were brought up under different conditions. The same applies to differences in the means of racial-ethnic groups; the 15-point deficit of blacks does accord with the ability they show in schools and universities or in jobs that depend largely on intellectual skills. Actually, no test that shows equal means for different SES or racial-ethnic groups possesses any useful validity. Eells' Games test (see Eells, Davis, and Havighurst, 1951) was constructed to eliminate social class differences; however, it still continued to show some SES differences, and it was too lacking in validity to have had any practical use.

What *would* be unfair would be a test that yielded low scores among people who turned out to be average or above-average on any criterion that the test is supposed to predict. Thus, an intelligence or scholastic aptitude test used for admission to a university should not show that a smaller proportion of blacks than whites reach the cut-off required for admission unless it is true that a similarly low proportion of blacks are capable of getting satisfactory university grades. This situation can be analyzed by drawing the regression lines of grades on scholastic aptitude tests separately for black and white students (see Messick and Anderson, 1974; Hunter and Schmidt, 1976). A great many studies using educational achievement or success in various military or civilian jobs as criteria, have shown that the correlation coefficient is much the same for blacks as whites; in other words, the test is equally predictive for the two races. Moreover, the regression lines do usually coincide closely, meaning that blacks who obtain scores as high as the average white eventually achieve the same school grades or job competence as the average white. In fact, insofar as there is any bias, it seems to be slightly in favor of blacks, in that those who reach a certain standard on the criterion do not have to obtain quite as high scores on the selection tests as do whites who achieve the same standard. Hunter and Schmidt further point out that any selection tests or tests that are low in reliability tend to favor blacks as against whites.

However, we are not entitled to assume that any test constructed for, or validated on, one cultural group would give equally good predictions in another group. In fact, one study in the U.S. Army Air Force during World War II (Michael, 1949) did yield a different regression equation for black than for white recruits. Thus, it is reasonable that civil rights legislation in the United States should demand that tests must not be used for the selection of nonwhite individuals for jobs unless the relevance or the validity of these tests has been proved.

Recently, this regression line technique, which was formulated by Cleary (1968), has been shown by R. L. Thorndike (1971) to be inadequate in certain respects. Thorndike found that a test that maximizes the accuracy of prediction of an individual's performance on the criterion task is yet likely to underestimate the proportion of members of a low-scoring group who should be selected. This situation occurs because of the imperfect validity of any test or test battery. Thus, although the standard method of selection for college on the basis of achievement and/or aptitude scores gives the best prediction for each individual case, regardless of race, it does result in many fewer blacks being selected than might have managed the college courses. The opposite approach is the so-called quota system, whereby the same proportion of blacks and whites as exist in the general population are admitted. This means setting a considerably lower cut-off on the predictors for blacks than for whites, and legal cases have been fought by white students who were denied admission although they scored more highly on the entrance tests than some of the admitted blacks. This policy has other disadvantages, since a considerable proportion of admitted blacks find the course work too difficult and their motivation and morale suffer or they drop out (see Stanley, 1971). Alternatively, easier courses may be arranged, and this means that the overall educational standards of the college are lowered. Current systems of selection seem to be based on an uneasy compromise between the demands for greater representation of blacks and the desire to employ the most valid predictors possible.

In fact, as Hunter and Schmidt (1976) point out, there is no perfect psychometric solution to the problem of selecting fairly from among disparate populations. The best decision depends, for example, on the relative importance attached to "false positives" (i.e., individuals passed by the test who fail to reach the desired criterion) and "false negatives" (those failed by the test who would have reached the criterion). In selection for university entry, it is preferable to be lenient about false positives to avoid keeping out students who might have done well. On the other hand, in selecting aircraft pilots, false positives should be stringently avoided, since they might have accidents involving loss of life and damage to property.

MOTIVATIONS AND ATTITUDES OF TESTEES

Apart from the possible culture-bias in the test content, the factors most often cited as reducing the scores of low-SES or ethnic-minority children are motivation and cooperation. I have already surveyed relevant research on the effects of motivational differences (Chapter 2) and concluded that such effects are difficult to substantiate. However, it did appear that the test performance of maladjusted children is likely to be upset by their anxiety, distractibility, and so on. Jensen himself mentions in his 1969 article that, when giving individual tests to disturbed children in a psychological clinic, he found it advisable to let them become familiar with the clinic playroom and to accept him as a friendly adult. This seemed to produce a marked gain of about 8 to 10 points in the children's IQs. However, he believes that, with careful instruction and ample pretest practice, low-SES and black children can be quite adequately motivated to do their best on group tests.

In Chapter 16, it was pointed out that particular attention must be paid to extrinsic factors in testing individuals or groups who are members of a remote culture and unfamiliar with Western tests and testers. Biesheuvel (1972) mentions that blacks in South Africa are often either overanxious and unduly cautious about committing themselves to any test response or else over-keen and not stopping to think; either of these attitudes may lower their scores. The difficulties of motivation are discussed, also, by Brislin, Lonner, and Thorndike (1973).

Here we are concerned with cultures that overlap Western society and with the suggestion that American blacks, Indians, and Mexican Amercans are particularly likely to feel anxious or resentful and uncooperative when given tests devised for whites, especially when the tester is a white. Erikson (1950) observes that the testing situation is a kind of microcosm of the total social contest, so that children's reactions to tests will reflect the everyday social relations or attitudes of the ethnic, SES, or age groups involved.

Katz and Greenbaum (1963), who have done extensive work on the motivation of black college students, particularly stress the expectation of failure when blacks feel themselves to be in competition with whites, and their humiliation because they regard testing merely as another occasion for showing how stupid they are. Older students, who have acquired strong feelings of group solidarity and black power, may cooperate unwillingly, or not at all, especially if the tester seems unsympathetic and domineering.

However, although Katz is often cited as having proved the disturbing effects of motivational conditions on black test performance, he actually carried out his investigation with tests such as speeded arithmetic or coding (digit-symbol), which are likely to be much more susceptible to the influence of conditions of administration and emotional arousal than are intelligence tests. Moreover, as these tests were given to black college students (without any white control group), they have little relevance to the performance of black school children. Katz did obtain significant differences in scores under conditions where fear of failure, threat of punishment, or competition with white norms were involved. The race of the tester did not in itself produce any consistent effects, though more authoritarian testers tended to induce lower performance. As Sattler (1970) points out in reviewing these studies, the results were quite variable, and Katz frequently resorted to ad hoc hypotheses to patch up his findings (see also Urbach, 1974).

In England, Watson (1973) also regards the motivational and personality characteristics of West Indian (i.e., black) children, along with the low socioeconomic level of black families, as the main sources of poor test performance. He carried out experiments similar to those of Katz and obtained comparable results on the effects of testing conditions, though these were more marked with 7 to 8-year-olds than with 14 to 15-year-olds. Watson draws attention also to the well-known effects of stress and anxiety on performance at complex tasks and their lesser effect on simpler tasks. He accounts in this way for the better results of blacks on rote learning tasks, preferring it to Jensen's explanation of the differences among blacks and low-SES children on Level I and Level II tests. However, Jensen and Figueroa (1975) report an experiment on forward and backward digit span that clearly contradicted the anxiety hypothesis.

RACE OF THE TESTER

Shuey was able to trace 19 studies of Southern black children where intelligence tests were given by black testers. The mean IQ was almost identical with that found in other studies where the tester was white. Similar results were obtained with secondary school students. In an extensive review, Sattler (1970) also concludes that there is no consistent evidence of any effect. Jensen (1974a) carried out a comparative study in which whites and blacks from kindergarten to sixth grade were given several tests by white or black student testers who had been equally thoroughly trained. The only test on which any significant differences occurred was the Making Xs test of speed and persistence, where both black and white pupils did better with white testers. This test involves first writing Xs in a series of boxes for 90 seconds and then, after a rest, doing the same thing with the instructions to write as quickly as possible. Jensen regards this as a test that does not involve intelligence, but where the increase in scores at the second round provides a measure of motivation and concentrated attention.

A recent study by Samuel et al. (1976a) was carefully designed to compare black and white junior high students of each sex who were tested on four of the WISC subtests by a black or a white tester. They were further subdivided according to the test "atmosphere," half the students being tested in a very formal manner, half in a more relaxed atmosphere; in addition, half were given the expectation of doing well, half of doing badly. Thus, there was a fivefold classification, yielding a total of 32 sets of conditions; 13 students were tested under each of these conditions. Samuel found variations in the mean IQs of the 32 subgroups from 89.3 to 105.6, and concluded that these conditions, including race of students and of tester, had important effects on performance. Though there were some significant interactions, most of the variations could be attributed to chance in view of the small numbers in the different subgroups; the most significant factors were race of students and testers. Whites averaged 111.1 under all conditions and blacks 96.7; white testers elicited higher IQs in both races, namely, a difference of 6.9 points with white testees and 3.6 with black testees. Thus, the blacks did not do better with black testers, and the varying instructions or procedures had little consistent effects. However, negative correlations were found between performance and scores on an anxiety scale, and Samuel suggests that, in either race, the acceptance by the subjects of a challenge to do well raised the IQ. A follow-up study with boys who were subclassified for high versus low SES likewise showed that certain combinations of testing atmosphere and student expectations yielded some significant interactions. In yet another study (Samuel, 1976), this time with girls, male or female testers of each race were compared. Here, students showed significantly higher IQs with female testers than with males, though, again, there were several complex interactions.

NEGATIVE SELF-CONCEPTS

In regard to feelings of inferiority or negative self-concepts, which are often supposed to lower the scores of minority or disadvantaged groups, the evidence is again generally contradictory. The Coleman report on the abilities and achievements of different ethnic groups in the United States included an attitude scale. Most of the items relating to positive or negative self-concepts showed little differences between groups and insignificant relations to abilities. However, the item "Good luck is more important than hard work for success" was more frequently endorsed by blacks and was negatively related to test scores. Some writers have generalized this to imply that blacks feel at the mercy of their environment, that they have little control over what happens to them. Similar results were obtained with two more statements suggesting lack of personal control. However, it has not been shown that these sentences represent a generalized trait or attitude, though further investigation might be worthwhile. Jensen points out some difficulties of interpretation; we do not know whether the attitude affects test performance or whether the less intelligent children are more likely to stress "luck."

Another characteristic of blacks that has often been suggested as responsible for low intelligence and achievement (particularly among boys) is the frequent absence of the father from the home. Lacking any model for identification, and living in a home dominated by the mother, they are more likely to rebel against the female teachers who take most of the elementary school grades (see Glazer and Moynihan, 1963). In Broman,

Nichols and Kennedy's (1975) sample, the fathers were absent in 38 percent of black families and 18 percent of white families; and the IQs of the father-present children were slightly higher than those of father-absent children. But this factor was also included in Coleman's investigation, and no differences in ability and achievement scores were found there between the father-present and father-absent children (see also Jensen, 1969).

Several other investigators have applied personality inventories to black and white children and either found no difference in positive versus negative self-concepts or else that blacks show a higher positive score. Zirkel and Moses (1971) used the Coopersmith Self-Esteem inventory with fifth- and sixth-grade children and found no difference, though a third group of Puerto Ricans did score lower than either blacks or whites. However, the authors draw attention to the many weaknesses in such self-assessments, which Wylie (1961) had previously exposed. Much depends on the particular instrument, and those that focus on self-esteem in everyday life may measure something different from those covering confidence in academic achievement. It seems quite likely that compensatory mechanisms are involved such that those who feel inferior are more likely to reject suggestions of failure. Nevertheless, the fact remains that psychologists who attribute low ability or achievement among blacks to negative attitudes have not been able to define these attitudes in such a way that their effects can be measured. That is, we have another "X-factor."

Jensen (1973a) carried out a large-scale study with 1,588 whites and 1,242 blacks in fourth to sixth grades, using several tests designed to distinguish between motivational conditions and intellectual ability. One was the Making Xs test, described above, where willingness to cooperate and motivation to do well are obviously important, but intellectual ability is minimized. In each grade, the blacks improved more when urged to work at speed. Digit memory span tests do have some g saturation, but blacks tend to do them better than tests involving conceptual skills; yet here, too, children who are inadequately motivated to attend carefully would be expected to do badly. Another test of listening attention, involving following simple directions, likewise showed no black–white differences. Particularly interesting was a simple recall test in which a series of 20 familiar objects was shown, one at a time, and subjects wrote down as many as they could remember after each of several trials. One set of objects was quite miscellaneous; in a second set, the objects could be categorized into four groups — furniture, animals, clothing, and foods. The possibility of clustering was not pointed out, but the more intelligent children realized it for themselves and tended to write out, say, all the furniture items, then the clothing, and so on. The black or low-SES children scored quite close to the whites on the unclassified set, but they did relatively less well at the second set. Here, then, we have two situations where the instructions and motivational conditions are identical. The only difference is that the second set permits clustering, so that the scores depend on organizing and seeing relations between the objects. It is at this point that the racial differences in ability become evident, not at a point where motivational differences might have intervened.

In conclusion, the general trend of this chapter has been entirely negative. Obviously, no investigation is likely to be perfect; there may have been inadequate sampling or lack of controls in those I have cited, or alternative explanations might be plausible. Furthermore, there still may be differences between racial-ethnic groups such as blacks and whites that have not attracted attention but do play an important part in success at cognitive tests. Clearly, though, it is no use just thinking up other possibilities or X-factors; they must be sufficiently defined to be testable.

SUMMARY

1   Intelligence testing of nonwhite racial or ethnic groups such as blacks is criticized by many psychologists on the grounds that blacks have less familiarity with the test materials or poorer motivation than whites. Though such factors are admittedly important in comparing remote cultural groups, black difficulties with tests depend far more on complexity of mental processing than on unfamiliar content or conditions of administration.

2   Even lesser familiarity with standard English than with black dialect has not been found to affect black children's performance. The inclusion or omission of blacks in standardizing intelligence or achievement tests makes no difference to their scores relative to those of white children.

3   A standardization study of the WISC-R showed, unexpectedly, that individual differences between sibs in the same family and differences between families contributed more to IQ variance than differences between races or SES groups.

4   A further study by Jensen of two tests, one apparently culture-biased (the Peabody Picture Vocabulary), the other relatively culture-fair (Raven's Matrices), demonstrated that no statistical property of the scores or the item responses confirmed the operation of culture bias. The black children's responses more closely resembled those of whites who were 2 years younger than they did those of blacks who were 1 year younger.

5   A test cannot be regarded as culturally unfair merely because it yields different mean scores for two or more contrasted racial-ethnic groups. What is important is that low scores in either group should be equally predictive of low performance on some external criterion, college grades, for instance. However, the problem of selecting fairly from disparate populations is a complex one, which inevitably involves value judgments regarding the proportion of each population that should be selected.

6   The motivation and attitudes of testees have a significant influence on test performance of maladjusted white children or on members of some non-Western cultures. But it has not been possible to prove the effects of any such condition on the scores of more closely overlapping cultures, such as U.S. blacks and whites.

7   Katz's studies showed some effects of type of administration and instructions on certain tests performances by black college students, though not on intelligence test scores of black children. Numerous studies of the race of the tester, including some well-designed experiments by Samuel, failed to show any adverse effects of white testers on black children's test performance.

8   Contrary to expectations, black children do not show more negative self-concepts than white, which might affect their scores. In addition, absence of the father, relatively common in black families, has no consistent effects on children's abilities. Another study designed by Jensen to elicit motivational effects on cognitive test performance of blacks and whites showed that the only racial difference was the lower ability of the former to do complex tasks.

21

Conclusions Regarding Racial-Ethnic Differences

Having surveyed most of the empirical evidence, I have tried to pull it together in Table 21.1, which lists 30 main points, each classified as:

G   Definitely points to genetic influence.
G? Probably genetic, but might also be explained environmentally.
E? Probably environmental, but might also be explained genetically.
E   Definitely points to environmental determination.

There are also some points that seem to fit Either or Neither E or G. Points that apply to individual differences rather than group differences are omitted. Most of the evidence summarized here is derived from studies of U.S. blacks and whites, but some of it has been partially replicated elsewhere with similar findings.

Naturally, I would not expect all psychologists to agree with my classification, though I have certainly aimed at impartiality. It may be seen that, although the total number of items favoring genetic influences (G and G?) is roughly balanced by the number of environmental points (E and E?), more of the highly convincing items are G than E. Although there is a great deal of evidence pointing to the importance of environmental influ-

TABLE 21.1

Evidence Favoring Genetic or Environmental Explanations of Racial-Ethnic Group Differences in Intelligence

Evidence	Genetic/Environmental
1. Races show certain physical differences that are clearly inherited. Genetic diversity has played an important part in the historical evolution of humanity. This would suggest genetic differences in mental abilities and traits also (see p. 231f.).	G?
2. Socioeconomic classes differ, to some extent, genetically as well as environmentally (for example, see Lawrence's orphaned children). This would be expected in any society where assortative mating and considerable social mobility coexist (see p. 250f.).	G
3. The high correlation between mean Army Alpha scores of recruits from different ethnic backgrounds and the economic and educational level of such groups is more suggestive of environmental than genetic difference (see p. 262).	E?
4. Klineberg and Lee found that improved conditions in Northern cities tended to raise black IQs by some 6 to 8 points, but not more than this. Also, selective migration cannot be ruled out entirely (see p. 289).	E?
5. American Indians and Mexican Americans are much more economically handicapped than blacks, but they score higher on nonverbal reasoning tests, although they are linguistically backward on some verbal tests. Orientals are also liable to be discriminated against, yet they approximate white standards on intelligence and achievement tests (see p. 265).	G
6. A recent study of large and representative samples of white and blacks in California showed that the variance in scores between families and within families (regardless of race or SES) accounts for far more variance than SES or race (see p. 307f.).	G?
7. Different racial-ethnic groups show rather consistent differences in patterns of scores on ability factors. Thus, blacks do better on more culturally loaded verbal tests than on nonverbal or spatial tests (see p. 270f.).	Either

8. There are considerable similarities in factor structure when the same battery of tests is given to racial-ethnic groups that overlap in their cultures. This suggests that Western-type tests are measuring much the same abilities in these groups. However, there are also differences, especially between more widely different racial-ethnic groups (see p. 273f.).	Either
9. Rural children tend to score lower than urban children in most (though not all) countries. Improvements in education and communication have reduced these differences (see p. 274f.).	E?
10. The earlier psychomotor precocity of black infants and their later retardation on tests involving more reasoning are suggestive of different gene patterns (see p. 263).	G?
11. Though there have been considerable improvements in the economic and educational circumstances of blacks over the past 30 years or so, there is no sign of any rise in mean IQ or achievement. Likewise, schemes of compensatory education, such as Head Start, have generally failed (see pp. 263–264).	G
12. Some of the writings of pioneers in mental testing displayed obvious racial prejudice and antiprogressive views. Current supporters of genetic explanations always admit some effects of environment, whereas environmentalist writers often reject any genetic differences (see p. 278f.).	Neither
13. Intelligence is more ambiguous and difficult to define than physical attributes, hence the techniques of genetic analysis devised for the former may be inapplicable to the latter. On the other hand, there is a considerable amount of factorial and follow-up evidence to show that intelligence is a major dimension of mind, which can be operationalized (see p. 283f.).	Neither
14. Even if heritability is high within groups, this does not prove its existence between groups. However, the rejection of any between-group genetic variance would imply much larger environmental differences than normally occur in Western countries (see pp. 285–286).	G?

TABLE 21.1 *(continued)*

Evidence	Genetic/Environmental
15. Children of high-SES black families tend to regress to the black population mean, not to the general average. Siblings of bright black children do the same. Conceivably, some environmental explanation is possible (see p. 293).	G?
16. The descendants of immigrants who were probably of below-average intelligence appear to approximate to the intelligence distribution of the new country within a few generations. However, the evidence is not strong enough to disprove any intergenerational stability (see pp. 294–295).	E?
17. In cross-racial matings of blacks and whites, there is very little reliable evidence of increases in the children's IQs the greater the proportion of white ancestry, nor of any substantial correlation with lightness of skin color or with blood-group genetic indices. Even if these were proved, environmental explanations would still be quite plausible (see pp. 295–296).	E
18. Children of black fathers and white mothers score significantly better than those of white fathers and black mothers (see p. 297).	Either
19. Black children adopted into white homes obtain IQs considerably higher than would be expected from their parentage. However, the evidence is inconclusive, since insufficient information is available on the abilities of the true parents or on the possibility of selective placement (see pp. 297–298).	E?
20. With more intensive and well-planned intervention programs, or with fostering into good homes, children of poor black origin obtain IQs of 20 points above expectation (as in Heber's research). In other words, they surpass the white mean; so far, this improvement appears to be permanent (see pp. 133–135).	E
21. Disadvantaged children appear to drop further below average in intelligence and achievement with increasing age. But when scores are converted to σ units	E?

(e.g., Deviation IQs), this cumulative deficit, or progressive achievement gap, generally disappears. However, in an exceptionally low-grade sample of Southern blacks (mean IQ, 71), Jensen did find some cumulative deficit that was absent in more nearly average populations (see pp. 300–301).

22. Tests devised in one cultural group are usually unsuitable in other ethnic groups because Intelligence B is essentially culture-bound (see p. 255f.).   E?

23. In tests of children or adults in non-Western cultures, the unfamiliarity of the test materials and instructions and of a foreign tester have a considerable influence on scores. There is no clear evidence that the same holds for ethnic minority groups in Western countries (see p. 312f.).   E?

24. There is no substantial evidence that the cultural bias of many intelligence test items particularly affects the scores of ethnic minority children. It is the complexity of the mental operations required by a test, rather than the unusualness of content, that lowers performance (see p. 305f.).   G

25. Jensen's analysis of the Peabody Vocabulary and Raven Matrices for white and black children showed that their responses to both tests were indistinguishable, except that the black scores and item-difficulty distributions more closely resembled those of whites 2 years younger than themselves than they did those of blacks 1 year younger. In reliability, factor content, etc., no significant racial differences occurred (see pp. 308–309).   G

26. When intelligence tests are used for selection to schools, universities, or jobs, they do *not* generally underestimate the later success of minority group testees. However, the issue of "test-fairness" is complex and controversial (see p. 310f.).   G?

27. The fact that most blacks make little use of standard English in daily life has not been found to lower their performance on verbal intelligence tests (see p. 306).   G?

Conclusions Regarding Racial–Ethnic Differences   323

TABLE 21.1 (continued)

Evidence	Genetic/Environmental
28. If the tester is of a different race from the testees, this, in itself, does not reduce their scores. However, there may be some effects of anxiety or suspicion among the testees or of the tester's manner, though no reliable trends have been isolated (see pp. 314–315).	E?
29. Black children and students do not usually score lower on positive self-concept scales than whites; hence, performance on ability tests is not necessarily affected by feelings of inferiority. Direct experiments by Jensen on motivation in group test situations showed no significant differences from whites (see pp. 312–317).	G?
30. Western-type tests can be validly used in Africa, India, and other countries—for instance, for educational or occupational selection—though a good deal more instruction and practice should be given to unsophisticated testees. The results should not, of course, be compared with the norms for whites. It would be preferable for similar tests to be constructed, item-analyzed, standardized, and validated by psychologists belonging to the same culture as the testee (see pp. 255–258).	Either

ences, it is seldom as conclusive as the genetic evidence. This might well be due to the difficulties of defining, controlling, and measuring the crucial environmental variables, which were mentioned earlier (p. 286). Thus, I agree with Jensen's criticism of the weak logic of most environmentalistic arguments and accept the greater cogency of much of his work on genetic differences, but nevertheless I feel that the case is not proven. Owing to the confounding of race or ethnicity with environmental differences, it does not seem possible to separate their effects. Even in analyzing the heritability of individual differences, I stressed the inadequacy of current attempts to assess GE–covariance; this is still more true in discussing group differences. Much the same conclusion is reached by J. L. Horn in his 1974 review of Jensen's book *Educability and Group Differences* (1973a).

Clearly, no definitive conclusion is justified in either direction. Much as with individual differences, both heredity and environment are involved and interact with one another. Even if some quantitative estimate of between-group heritability could be calculated, this would, of course, apply only to the particular populations studied, and environmental variance would certainly be higher between groups that differed more widely in habitat, cultural conditions, and child rearing than do blacks and whites.

WHAT DIFFERENCE DOES IT MAKE?

Several writers who have also studied the evidence and found it to be mixed have asked, So what? Does it really make any practical difference whether heritability between groups is high or low? The American National Academy of Sciences (Crow, Neel, and Stern, 1967) pointed out that there is no doubt as to the gross inequalities in the environments of ethnic or racial groups around the world. Hence, social action is urgently needed without having to wait for convincing proof of the strength of h^2. "Even a strong hereditary component ... does not imply that the conditions cannot be cured or ameliorated." At the same time, this does not mean that further research in the area should be discouraged.

Others have suggested that the controversy is mainly carried on by academics who favor different ideologies; it is not directed for or against the blacks, and it makes no practical difference to the need for social and educational reform. According to Chomsky (1974), the existence of any correlation between race and intelligence makes no difference, except to people who hold racist views and wish to obtain scientific justification for discrimination against a group or groups of lower intelligence. Morton (1972) states that the problem is methodologically insoluble and has no practical consequences; hence, the controversy is entirely emotionally based. Even if genotypical differences in intelligence were demonstrated, they would provide no better guide for action than can be obtained from our current knowledge of the phenotypic differences. Block and Dworkin (1974) similarly deny that social policy would be affected and add that, although we know only the phenotype, psychologists such as Terman, Burt, Jensen, Herrnstein, and Shockley do put forward recommendations on education, fertility, and the like as though we knew the genotype. To all these critics, I would reply that fuller knowledge of heritability and of environmental variance or covariance are of the greatest theoretical importance for developmental psychology and for our understanding of human nature, quite apart from any practical consequences.

Jensen himself believes that the acceptance of substantial genetic variance would have important social and educational consequences, though he specifically disagrees that such acceptance would in any way detract from our efforts to achieve greater humanity and justice in race relations. Further, the more we understand the origins of certain conditions, the better we are able to deal with them and plan effective remedial measures, as in the case of diabetes or of PKU deficiency; hence, the justification for more intensive research. Jensen also contradicts Gage (1972), who believes that the demonstration of high between-group heritability would lead to a reduction in expenditures or efforts on behalf of minority and deprived groups on the grounds that any attempts to overcome inborn defects would be useless. Nevertheless, I am concerned lest the undue emphasis on genetic differences might affect the self-images of such groups and might be quoted in support of racial prejudices. Public attention might be distracted from needed changes in school organization if psychologists and administrators believed that most of the differences are due to the characteristics of individual children, their parents, and their racial-ethnic background, rather than to the shortcomings of the educational system.

A rather clear example of the consequences of genetic bias is provided by Burt's influence on educational developments in Britain from the 1920s to the 1940s. His advice to the Ministry of Education was almost certainly one factor in the reorganization of secondary schooling and the eleven-plus selection procedure. Although this system did have considerable merits (see Vernon, 1957a), it was also unjust to a minority of working-class children whose superior ability was not recognized until the age of 12 or later. The consequent reaction against it in the 1950s and 1960s, which led to its virtual abolition and to the substitution of a system of comprehensive schools, seems to have resulted in a serious decline in the efficiency of British education.

Both Dobzhansky (1973) and Spuhler and Lindzey (1967) insist that the admission of genetic diversity has no bearings on the socioethical problems of equality and justice. It is merely loose thinking to identify social equality with biological identity, though this is what radical environmentalists seem to believe. People are certainly not born all alike and cannot be thought of as "created equal." But regardless of our views on genetic determination, we should aim to provide equal educational, economic, and political rights and opportunities for all, irrespective of race. However, there are bigots—for instance, in South Africa and Rhodesia and, to a lesser extent, in North America and Europe—who resist this ideal, and others who do disservice to society by denying any differences in inborn potential.

It is curious that the prejudice against biological differences seems to be confined so largely to the kind of conceptual and symbolic reasoning that we call intelligence. Very few, if any, would object to people with outstanding physique and athletic promise (who often happen to be black in the United States) being given more training and opportunities than average; few would hold that any individual, regardless of basic potentiality, could equally well be trained to be a concert violinist. As Eysenck (1973) puts it, "if meritocracy and élitism are encouraged in athletics, why should mediocrity be preferred in education?" Those with athletic and musical talent are likely to be rewarded by prestige and monetary success, certainly to a greater extent than people with very high IQs can count on worldly rewards. Maybe this difference is, in part, the psychologist's fault for overstressing the value of abstract thinking; more likely, it is the high valuation that contemporary Western society places on education and academic success for which, admittedly, a high IQ is a useful qualification, though not the only requisite.

Jencks et al. (1972) suggest that the issue of racial-ethnic differences has been exaggerated out of all proportion, considering the very wide range of ability within all the racial-ethnic groups found in the United States. Jensen (see p. 278) insists that each individual should be treated on his or her own merits, not as a member of a particular ethnic, socioeconomic, or other group. Thoday (1973) suggests, too, that if we recognized the importance of individual differences in our educational or social planning, there would be much less need to bother about group differences. He considers Jensen's stress on the genetic components in racial-ethnic differences an unwise move, since, because it is an unpopular view, the public may not realize the much stronger case for genetic influence in individual differences.

Diversification in Education

I have already touched on the differences in educational policy that might be expected if the heritability of intelligence were proved to be either quite large or quite small. If it were known that group or individual differences were purely cultural, educationists would probably continue to try to improve on schemes like Head Start, designed to acculturate children from disadvantaged backgrounds to white middle-class norms. On the other hand, if we knew that the genetic component was considerable, the educational reformer might more profitably explore new types of intervention and give major priority to diversification of curricula and methods of instruction. The latter view is, of course, Jensen's, and he is backed up by Bereiter (1975). Jencks believes that parents and their offspring should have greater freedom of choice among a variety of types of schooling, especially at secondary level; this would be much preferable to using homogeneous grouping or other forms of acceleration and retardation, or segregation, in trying to allow for individual differences.

I would suggest, however, that the goal of diversification within or between schools is beset with many difficulties, partly because most administrators and a good many teachers are opposed to it; but chiefly because it might raise as many and as serious social problems as has the desegregation by busing in the United States. Parents would tend to base their choices on the reputation of the school and the socioeconomic level of its students rather than on the type of education provided. Consider, for example, Jensen's scheme to differentiate pupils higher in Level I (associative) than Level II (conceptual) learning, and cater to them by different approaches to instruction (p. 66). It is surely inevitable that Level I– type schools would be regarded as supplying an inferior education. Most parents would opt for Level II, and it would be very difficult to choose those children better suited to Level I (especially at the age of about 6 years) other than perhaps by skin color or socioeconomic class. Moreover, those who started in Level I might later develop unsuspected Level II ability, and it would be difficult to transfer them. Since making the original proposal, Jensen has not attempted to describe more fully how it could be put into practice. I would see it myself as most applicable to mathematics teaching, where, in the past, a lot of pupils made fairly good progress largely by rote memory and drill but are now as retarded in this subject, as in English, because modern mathematics involves far more verbal and conceptual understanding.

Another example of the difficulties in specialized instruction is provided by the schools or special classes for the physically handicapped, severely retarded, and maladjusted, which have done excellent work both in Britain and the United States. Currently, they are under attack, probably largely because parents are anxious to avoid having their children labelled as abnormal, and it is being argued that "normalization" or "mainstreaming" is preferable. The result must surely be that the handicapped do less well because they cannot get as much individual help as in smaller classes, and the rest of the class suffers because the teacher has less time to spend on their needs. Further problems are raised by the introduction of the "quota" system into all schools, whether for the gifted, the average, or the retarded. This is a retrograde step that is being enforced in many American education districts for political reasons. Obviously, it is not possible to provide special remedial classes for all children who need it if such classes are not allowed to contain a larger proportion of blacks than of whites.

Nevertheless, some attempts to provide diversification are giving promising results. In many cities, groups of parents have set up private schools that come nearer to meeting their aspirations for their children than the public system. Often these alternative schools do not last, or they become conventionalized or absorbed into the regular system. But they do some good, especially, for example, for gifted children with special talents that might otherwise have gone to waste.

Another development is the spread of individualized instruction based on behavioral objectives, which was briefly outlined in Chapter 2. Both this approach and mastery learning are worthwhile if they reduce the correlation between general intelligence and achievement, since this implies that the methods and content of instruction are better adapted to a wide range of abilities. They have escaped, to some extent, from the single-track system where success depends almost wholly on conceptual learning ability and convergent thinking (see p. 277).

The Uses of Intelligence Tests

In the previous paragraph, I appear to be attacking the educational uses of the IQ; and earlier in the chapter, I said that I do not regard IQ differences between racial-ethnic groups as having much importance. But this certainly does not mean that I consider individual testing as having outlived its usefulness. True, I concluded (in Chapter 2) that mass group testing is generally undesirable, at least in the elementary school, though it can help in grading of students into classes at secondary level or provide valuable information to the educational and vocational counselor. I agreed, also, that the standard Terman-Merrill or Wechsler tests could usefully be supplemented by more flexible, process-based instruments. Where alternate types or levels of education are available, there is no doubt that the trained psychologist, with the aid of standardized tests, could usually make more accurate rec-ommendations for the placement of any child than the parents or the child's present teachers.

Eysenck (1973) points out that the judgments and decisions that are taken on matters of social or educational policy are based largely on the public's or the politician's preconceived ideas about human nature. Factual information, which is either already available or could fairly easily be gathered from tests and social surveys, tends to be ignored. Unfortunately, at the present time, such problems are usually considered purely in terms of manipulating the environment. No one stops to ask whether the majority of children, or adults, who will be affected have suffi-cient literacy or reasoning capacity for the desired goal to be practicable. When Eysenck, and I myself, claim that more use should be made of empirical psychological data in educational planning, and when we stress that individual differences in abil-ity are partly, or largely, genetic, this does *not* mean that we are merely trying to preserve privilege and the status quo. Modern psychology and psychometry can and should be instruments for progress. To take a concrete example: It is absurd to legislate that all students should receive the same number of years of educa-tion. Not only does this mean watering down of curricula and lowering of academic standards, but it is also probably responsi-ble for the amount of violence and vandalism so common in schools today. Yet some writers are even claiming that university education should be available to everyone.

FINALE

I intend to end on a contentious note. Throughout history, youth has tried to rebel against the traditional values of their elders and to attack "the Establishment." Since the end of World War II, this clash has been more bitter and widespread than ever before, since the growing generation has much more evidence of the failure of their parents to provide a secure and stable envi-ronment for them to live in. Probably the main reason the world seems to be in such a mess is simply that we are living in a technological civilization that is vastly more complex and dif-ficult to control than ever before. But, naturally, this does not satisfy the youthful idealists and reformers. Nor does it placate them to be told that, when they grow up and become self-sufficient, with a family and home to work for, they will think more as we do.

Simultaneously, the parental generation, being less sure of themselves and more open to progressive ideas and reforms, have brought up their children much more permissively than in the past, with the result that children and adolescents have little respect for the authority of school teachers or anyone else. Psychologists and other social scientists have encouraged this trend, and they generally belittle the idea that firm control during childhood produces adults who can control themselves and are capable of living well-adjusted lives in a civilization that rewards ability, hard work, responsibility, and reasonable conformity to social norms. Child-centered, or progressive, education seems to assume that children must be sheltered from any frustrations, any competition against other members of their age group, or any failure when their work is not good enough. It is forgotten that, as they grow up, they will have to face frustration, competition, and sometimes failure. Surely it is better for them to learn gradually to cope with life's trials and tribulations before and during the adolescent years, at a time when they are most resilient and adaptable, rather than to be protected from the real world as long as possible. I find it difficult to conceive of any society that does not constantly evaluate its members and differentiate people with desired qualities and abilities from those who lack them. Everyday life consists of a whole series of tests that are often far more arbitrary and less valid than the tests constructed by psychologists. Parents, peers, and other people make children aware of successes and failures long before they even come to school.

Another sign of the times is the derogation of intellect and the rejection of the values that society previously attached to different jobs and different kinds of behavior. The young can hardly be expected to work hard at school when they see the janitors and city street cleaners getting paid more than many school teachers or university instructors and when they hear so many stories of students with good degrees, even higher degrees, failing to gain employment in the areas for which they have been trained. I would link the current attacks on intelligence tests, or on any kind of educational evaluation or achievement examinations, with this downgrading of intellect and responsibility. Unless there is another swing of the pendulum and the social climate regains some of its earlier assurance and stability, I fear that we may experience a gradual breakdown of Western mores and standards.

Doubtless, many readers will regard this diatribe as just another example of the old trying to hang on to their privileges and complaining that the world has gone to the dogs. But I believe that the contemporary social climate is temporary, and that psychology and education have much to contribute in building up a more stable and just society. One aspect of this change for the better should be the recognition and wider use of psychologists, with their cognitive tests and experimental techniques, for diagnosing the strengths and weaknesses of any child, and in devising educational procedures to suit the more, and the less, able.

SUMMARY

1 Thirty items of evidence regarding the relative influence of genetic and of environmental factors on intellectual differences between racial-ethnic groups are summarized in Table 21.1. Classification according to G or E shows almost as many environmentally favorable as genetically favorable items, though the environmental tend to be less convincing than the genetic because of difficulties in identifying and measuring the crucial environmental variables.

2 Like many other recent writers, I conclude that there is no clear verdict in either direction. Genetic and environmental factors are always both involved, and their relative variance cannot, as yet, be quantified. It is doubtful, though, whether the proof or disproof of a strong hereditary component would make much practical difference to social, political, and educational policies. Such proof should not imply any discrimination against members of lower scoring racial-ethnic groups.

3 Insofar as heritability is substantial, psychologists should search for novel methods of intervention. Greater diversification of educational curricula and methods would be of value to children born with different gene patterns. Though Jensen's plan for different schools for children with high associative (as distinct from conceptual) learning ability has not been followed up, various kinds of "alternative" schools, and of individualized instruction, are working well.

4 Despite current attacks on tests in general (as well as on genetic explanations), they have much to contribute to the diagnosis of the type of education best suited to a child's needs and potentialities. The present malaise is probably linked with the current rejection of traditional values and the down-grading of intellect, which, it is hoped, will be a passing phase.

Glossary

Affective   See *Cognitive*.

Alleles   Two alternative forms of a gene occupying a particular locus on a chromosome.

Anova   Analysis of Variance. See *Variance*.

Assortative mating   The tendency for spouses to choose one another for the possession of similar traits (e.g., age, religion, education).

Attenuation   The reduction in correlation between variables arising from imperfect reliability or errors of measurement. The expected true correlation can be corrected for attenuation by dividing the obtained correlation by the square root of the respective reliability coefficients.

Centroid factors   Factors that are calculated by Thurstone's method. Though easier to apply, this method is less mathematically accurate than *Principal components*.

Chromosome   See *Gene*.

Cognitive   Mental processes concerned with perception, recognition, comprehension, recollection of or reasoning with our experiences. Distinguished from emotional, feeling, motivational, or affective processes.

Correlation coefficient   The degree of correspondence between two sets of measurements of the same individuals (e.g., IQ and achievement), expressed as a coefficient ranging from 0.0

(no correspondence) to +1.0 (perfect correspondence) or to −1.0 (complete inverse relationship). The symbol r refers to this coefficient.

Correlation, nonlinear   See *Nonlinear regression.*

Criterion-referenced tests   Tests designed to show what stage individuals have reached in learning a particular subject, or their ability defined in terms of the tasks they can actually accomplish. Distinguished from norm-referenced tests, where an individual's proficiency is assessed from high or low score relative to the distribution of scores in the population of which he or she is a member (e.g., the *Deviation Quotient*).

Developmental Quotient   A score comparable to an intelligence quotient, obtained from developmental tests or scales applied to young children (e.g., 1 week to 3 years old). Such tests are based on sensorimotor and other functions that develop in early life rather than on intellectual problems.

Deviation Quotients   IQs or educational quotients, which are "standard scores," that is, scores that run from 3 *Standard Deviation* units above the mean to 3 units below. In the case of IQs the Standard Deviation is usually taken as 15; hence a Deviation Quotient of 130 represents 2σ above the mean and cuts off the top 2¼ percent of the distribution in a representative population.

Dizygotic twins   Nonidentical or fraternal twins, developed from two separately fertilized ova. Their genetic resemblance to each other is the same as that of a pair of siblings.

Dominance   Interaction between two *alleles* at the same locus on a chromosome, one of which is dominant, the other recessive. A certain trait results if either or both of a person's alleles are dominant; the recessive trait appears only if both alleles are recessive.

Ethnic group   A society or group of people who share the same customs, culture, traditions, language, religion, and the like. Usually they are resident in a single nation or tribe. They tend to interbreed and thus to share a common gene pool, but this is not a necessary condition as it is with *race.*

Factors   The main dimensions present in a set of tests that appear to measure the same psychological ability or trait. Factor analysis determines these dimensions by analyzing a matrix of correlations within a battery of tests. When the factor loadings are multiplied together they should closely reproduce the original correlation matrix.

Fraternal twins   See *Dizygotic twins.*

g   The general ability factor believed by Spearman to be present, to a greater or lesser extent, in all cognitive abilities.

Subsequent factor analysts found that *g* alone could not account for all the correlations in a set of diverse tests; hence *group factors* were recognized, or Thurstone's and Guilford's *multiple primary factors* were preferred.

Gene   The unit of heredity. A part of the DNA molecule that transmits a particular hereditary attribute. It is responsible for the production of a specific protein required for the development of the organism. Long chains of genes constitute the chromosomes that are present in the nucleus of the living cell.

Genotype   The overall pattern of genes that make up the hereditary constitution of the individual. Contrasted with *Phenotype.*

Group factor   A factor running through a set of similar tests (e.g., verbal or spatial) but not common to all tests. It accounts for the residual correlations within this set of tests, over and above their *g* content.

***h²* (heritability)**   The proportion of *variance* in intelligence, or other, tests that is attributable to the combined effects of the genes.

Hawthorne effect   The tendency for the output or achievement of a group of adults or children to rise when members become aware that they are of particular interest to an investigator. Such special attention is apt to increase their motivation to succeed.

Intelligence A   D. O. Hebb's term for the basic genetic potentiality of each individual for intellectual growth.

Intelligence B   Hebb's term for the observed all-round cognitive ability, which results from interaction between Intelligence A and the stimulating nature of the environment in which the individual is reared.

Intelligence C   Vernon's term for the IQ or other score from a particular intelligence test, which provides a limited sample of the skills involved in Intelligence B.

Intraclass correlation   Instead of a comparison between scores on two variables obtained by each of a set of persons, a comparison can be made of the scores of paired individuals (such as siblings or twins) on a single variable. The method may also be used in calculating test reliabilities by analysis of variance.

Locus   The position of a particular *gene* (or its *allele*) on a chromosome.

LTM   The long-term storage of memories, associations, concepts, and the like in the brain.

Matrices test   An intelligence or reasoning test constructed by J. C. Raven, based on recognition of the patterning or sequence in 3 × 3 figures or designs. The main version, with 60 items, was published in 1938; other versions are available for young children or for superior adults.

Mean   The average score of a group, obtained by summing the scores of all members and dividing by their number.

Median   The middle score in a distribution of scores, which divides the top half from the bottom half. Usually close to the mean, unless the distribution is skewed or asymmetrical.

Mental Age   The score or level reached by children of average ability on a scale of mental tests. Thus a dull 6-year-old might reach the same level as an average 5- or 4-year-old.

Mid-parent   The IQ of a child can be correlated with that of either parent or with the average of both parents. This is called the mid-parent; similarly, foster mid-parent.

Monozygotic twins   Identical twins, derived from the splitting of a single fertilized ovum, and therefore having the same genotype.

Multiple correlation   The correlation of a combination of several predictor variables with a criterion variable, each predictor being optimally weighted. Denoted by the symbol R.

Multiple factors   The analysis of a battery of tests into a number of distinct factors rather than into g plus additional group factors.

Multiple regression   The equation for calculating each individual's predicted score on a criterion from the weighted scores on several predictor variables.

Nonlinear regression   In an ordinary correlation there is a straight line relationship between scores on variable X and variable Y, known as the regression line. In a nonlinear correlation the regression line is curved; thus a certain change in X is associated with a larger or smaller change in Y at different points on the scale. The overall correlation is measured by the correlation ratio (eta) instead of the correlation coefficient (r).

Norm-referenced tests   See *Criterion-referenced tests.*

Oblique factors   Factors are usually assumed to be orthogonal; that is, their axes are at right angles. Sometimes a more meaningful factor structure, giving a better fit to the data, is obtained by factors that are oblique to one another and are therefore intercorrelated.

Path analysis   A method of analysis of the correlations between a set of variables based on assuming a plausible chain of causal connections between these variables.

Performance test   A test of intelligence (or of some other ability or aptitude) based on certain concrete materials, such as blocks, pictures, etc., rather than on verbal problems. The instructions regarding the required performance may be given orally.

Phenotype   The actually observed traits or characteristics of the individual, developed through the interaction between genetic potentiality and environment. Contrasted with *Genotype* (see *Intelligence B* and *Intelligence A*).

Primary factors   A set of multiple factors obtained from analyzing a battery of tests, which meets Thurstone's criterion of "simple structure," namely, that each test should, as far as possible, be loaded on a single factor. When the same factors recur in several investigations (as do Thurstone's) they tend to be regarded as basic mental faculties or traits.

Principal components   A factorial technique that extracts the dimensions underlying as much as possible of the variance in a number of tests. That is, the components include the specific factors in each test as well as the common factors that account for the test intercorrelations.

Race   A population of people who are of common ancestry, and who share a common pool of genes that differ from those of other races. The distinctive genes often produce characteristic physical attributes, such as skin color, height, or blood-group frequencies. But many of the observed differences between races are not so much genetic as cultural.

Regression effect, or **regression to the mean**   When the scores on two variables, X and Y, are correlated, and a subgroup is selected of high X-scorers above the mean (or low X-scorers below the mean), the Y scores for these subgroups will be closer to the mean. The smaller the correlation, the greater the regression effect.

s factors   That part of any test score that is not attributable to *g* or to other common (e.g., group or multiple) factors. There is no correlation between the specific components of any two or more tests.

Second-order factors   When factors intercorrelate (see *Oblique factors*), these correlations can themselves be factor-analyzed to give one or more second-order, or more generalized, factors.

SES   Socioeconomic status, or social class. Generally assessed by level of father's occupation. For other methods of assessment, see p. 117.

Standard Deviation   Often abbreviated to S.D. or σ. The generally accepted measure of the range or dispersion of a distribution of test scores. It is calculated from the square root of the average squared deviations of all scores from the mean. In a normal distribution, almost all the scores fall within a range of +3 to −3 S.D.'s from the mean.

Standard scores A test score expressed in terms of number of *Standard Deviation* units above or below the mean, or some fraction or multiple of the S.D. (see *Deviation Quotients*).

Statistical significance The probability that an obtained statistic (e.g., a mean, a difference between means, a Standard Deviation, or a correlation) could have arisen from chance biases in the selection of cases observed or tested. Degrees of significance are usually expressed as $<.001$ (highly improbable), $<.01$ (improbable), $<.05$ or 1 in 20 (moderately improbable), or $>.05$ (could have arisen from chance characteristics of the sample).

Variance A measure of the total individual differences between scores of a group of subjects; calculated from the squares of deviations of each score from the mean. When divided by the number of cases (minus 1), we get the mean square variance, which is the same as the Standard Deviation squared. By Fisher's Analysis of Variance, it is possible to partition the total variance into proportions attributable to differences between subgroups, different conditions of testing, and so on.

WAIS Wechsler Adult Intelligence Scale. Contains 6 verbal and 6 performance subtests, individually administered. It is normed from 16 to 64+ years.

WISC Wechsler's Intelligence Scale for Children. Parallel to WAIS, but normed from 5.0 to 15.0 years.

References

Aikin, W. M. *The story of the eight-year study.* New York: Harper, 1942.

A.I.R. (American Institutes for Research) *Report on educational research.* Washington, D.C.: A.I.R., 1971.

Airasian, P. W., and Madaus, G. F. Criterion-referenced testing in the classroom. In R. W. Tyler and R. M. Wolf (eds.), *Crucial issues in testing.* National Society for the Study of Education. Berkeley, Ca.: McCutchan, 1974, pp. 73–88.

Alper, T. G., and Boring, E. G. Intelligence-test scores of northern and southern white and Negro recruits in 1918. *Journal of Abnormal and Social Psychology,* 1944, **39**: 471–474.

Altus, W. D. Birth order and its sequelae. *Science,* 1966, **151**: 44–49.

Amante, D., Margules, P. H. et al. The epidemiological distribution of CNS dysfunction. *Journal of Social Issues,* 1970, **26**(4): 105–136.

The American underclass. *Time,* August 29, 1977, pp. 14–27.

Amrine, M., Brayfield, A. H. et al. The 1965 Congressional inquiry into testing. *American Psychologist,* 1965, **20**: 857–992.

Anastasi, A. Further studies on the memory factor. *Archives of Psychology,* 1932, No. 142.

Anastasi, A. *Differential psychology.* New York: Macmillan, 1958.

Anastasi, A. *Psychological testing* (3rd ed.) New York: Macmillan, 1968.

Anderson, J. E. The prediction of terminal intelligence from infant and preschool tests. *Yearbook of National Society for the Study of Education,* 1940, **39**(1): 385– 403.

Ashline, N. F., Pezzullo, T. R., and Norris, C. I. *Education, inequality, and national policy.* Lexington, Mass.: D. C. Heath, 1976.

Astin, A. W., and Ross, S. Glutamic acid and human intelligence. *Psychological Bulletin,* 1960, **57**: 429– 434.

Bagley, W. C. The Army tests and the pro-Nordic propaganda. *Educational Review,* 1924, **67**: 179– 187.

Bajema, C. J. Estimation of the direction and intensity of natural selection in relation to human intelligence by means of the intrinsic rate of natural increase. *Eugenics Quarterly,* 1963, **10**: 175– 187.

Baker, J. R. *Race.* New York and London: Oxford University Press, 1974.

Baldwin, A. L., Kalhorn, J., and Breese, F. H. Patterns of parent behavior. *Psychological Monographs,* 1945, **58**, No. 268.

Baller, W. R. A study of the present social status of a group of adults who, when they were in elementary schools, were classified as mentally deficient. *Genetic Psychology Monographs,* 1936, **18**: 165– 244.

Baltes, P. B., and Schaie, K. W. On the plasticity of intelligence in adulthood and old age: Where Horn and Donaldson fail. *American Psychologist,* 1976, **31**: 720– 725.

Baratz, S. B., and Baratz, J. C. Early childhood intervention: The social science base of institutional racism. *Harvard Educational Review,* 1970, **40**: 29– 50.

Barker, D. J. P. Low intelligence and obstetric complications. *British Journal of Preventive and Social Medicine,* 1966, **20**: 15– 21.

Barron, F., and Young, H. B. Rome and Boston: A tale of two cities and their differing impact on the creativity and personal philosophy of Southern Italian immigrants. *Journal of Cross-Cultural Psychology,* 1970, **1**: 91– 114.

Bartlett, F. C. *Remembering.* Cambridge, England: Cambridge University Press, 1932.

Baumrind, D. Current patterns of parental authority. *Developmental Psychology Monographs,* 1971, **4**, 1 (Pt. 2).

Bayley, N. Consistency and variability in the growth of intelligence from birth to eighteen years. *Journal of Genetic Psychology,* 1949, **75**: 165– 196.

Bayley, N. On the growth of intelligence. *American*

Psychologist, 1955, **10**: 805– 818.

Bee, H. L. The effects of poverty. In H. L. Bee (ed.), *Social issues in developmental psychology.* New York: Harper & Row, 1974, pp. 219– 239.

Bell, A. E., Zipursky, M. A., and Switzer, F. Informal or open-area education in relation to achievement and personality. *British Journal of Educational Psychology,* 1976, **46**: 235– 243.

Bennett, S. N., Jordan, J. et al. *Teaching styles and pupil progress.* London: Open Books, 1976.

Bereiter, C. Review of A. R. Jensen's *Educational differences. Contemporary Psychology,* 1975, **20**: 455– 457.

Bereiter, C., and Engelmann, S. *Teaching disadvantaged children in the preschool.* Englewood Cliffs, N.J.: Prentice-Hall, 1966.

Bernstein, B. B. Social class and linguistic development: A theory of social learning. In A. H. Halsey (ed.), *Education, economy and society.* Glencoe, N.Y.: Free Press, 1961, pp. 288– 314.

Bernstein, B. B. *Class, codes, and control.* London: Routledge and Kegan Paul, 1971.

Bernstein, B. B., and Young, D. Some aspects of the relationship between communication and performance in tests. In J. A. Meade and A. S. Parkes (eds.), *Genetic and environmental factors in human ability.* Edinburgh: Oliver and Boyd, 1966, pp. 15– 23.

Biesheuvel, S. Psychological tests and their application to non-European peoples. *Yearbook of Education.* London: Evans Bros., 1949, pp. 87– 126.

Biesheuvel, S. An examination of Jensen's theory concerning educability, heritability, and population differences. *Psychologia Africana,* 1972, **14**: 87– 94.

Bijou, S. W. Environment and intelligence: A behavioral analysis. In R. Cancro (ed.), *Intelligence: Genetic and environmental influences.* New York: Grune and Stratton, 1971, pp. 221– 239.

Binet, A., and Simon T. Application des méthodes nouvelles au diagnostic du niveau intellectual chez des enfants normal et anormaux d'hospice et d'école primaire. *L'Année Psychologique,* 1905, **11**: 245– 336.

Bing, E. Effect of childrearing practices on development of differential cognitive abilities. *Child Development,* 1963, **34**: 631– 648.

Birch, H. and Gussow, J. *Disadvantaged children: Health, nutrition, and school failure.* New York: Grune and Stratton, 1970.

Blewett, D. B. An experimental study of the inheritance of

intelligence. *Journal of Mental Science,* 1954, **100**: 922–933.

Block, J. H., ed. *Schools, society, and mastery learning.* New York: Holt, Rinehart and Winston, 1974.

Block, N. J., and Dworkin, G. IQ: Heritability and inequality. *Philosophy and Public Affairs,* 1974, **3**: 331–407; **4**: 40–99.

Bloom, B. S. *Stability and change in human characteristics.* New York: Wiley, 1964.

Bloom, B. S. Letter to the Editor. *Harvard Educational Review,* 1969, **39**: 419–421.

Bloom, B. S. *Human characteristics and school learning.* New York: McGraw-Hill, 1976.

Bock, R. D., and Kolakowski, D. Further evidence of sex-linked major-gene influence on human spatial visualizing ability. *American Journal of Human Genetics,* 1973, **25**: 1–14.

Bodmer, W. F. Race and IQ: The genetic background. In K. Richardson and D. Spears (eds.), *Race, culture and intelligence.* Harmondsworth: Penguin, 1972, pp. 83–113.

Bodmer, W. F., and Cavalli-Sforza, L. L. Intelligence and race. *Scientific American,* 1970, **223**: 19–29.

Bowd, A. Practical abilities of Indians and Eskimos. *Canadian Psychologist,* 1974, **15**: 281–290.

Bower, T. G. R. *Development in infancy.* San Francisco: Freeman, 1974.

Bowlby, J., Ainsworth, M., Boston, M., and Rosenbloch, D. The effects of mother–child separation: A follow-up study. *British Journal of Medical Psychology,* 1956, **29**: 211–247.

Bowles, S., and Gintis, H. IQ in the United States class structure. In A. Gartner, C. Greer, and F. Riessman (eds.), *The new assault on equality.* New York: Harper & Row, 1974, pp. 7–84.

Bowman, M. J. Through education to earnings? *Proceedings of the National Academy of Education,* 1976, **3**: 221–292.

Bracht, G. H. Experimental factors related to aptitude-treatment interactions. *Review of Educational Research,* 1970, **40**: 627–645.

Bradley, R. H., and Caldwell, B. M. The relation of infants' home environments to mental test performance at fifty-four months: A follow-up study. *Child Development,* 1976, **47**: 1172–1174.

Breland, H. M. Birth order, family configuration, and verbal achievement. *Child Development,* 1974, **45**: 1011–1019.

Brislin, R. W., Lonner, W. J., and Thorndike, R. M. *Cross-cultural research methods.* New York: Wiley, 1973.

Broman, S. H., Nichols, P. L., and Kennedy, W. A. *Preschool IQ: Prenatal and early developmental correlates.* Hillsdale, N.J.: Lawrence Erlbaum, 1975.

Bronfenbrenner, U. The changing American child: A speculative analysis. *Journal of Social Issues,* 1961, **17**: 6– 18.

Bronfenbrenner, U. Is early intervention effective? *Teachers College Record,* 1974, **76**: 279– 303.

Bruner, J. S. The beginnings of intellectual skill. *New Behavior,* 1975, 20– 24, 58– 61.

Bruner, J. S. et al. *Studies in cognitive growth.* New York: Wiley, 1966.

Burks, B. S. The relative influences of nature and nurture upon mental development. *Twenty-seventh Yearbook of the National Society for the Study of Education,* Part I, 1928, pp. 219– 316.

Burt, C. L. *The backward child.* London: University of London Press, 1937.

Burt, C. L. The relations of educational abilities. *British Journal of Educational Psychology,* 1939, **9**: 45– 71.

Burt, C. L. Ability and income. *British Journal of Educational Psychology,* 1943, **13**: 83– 98.

Burt, C. L. *Intelligence and fertility.* London: Eugenics Society, 1946.

Burt, C. L. The structure of the mind: A review of the results of factor analysis. *British Journal of Educational Psychology,* 1949, **19**: 100– 111, 176– 199.

Burt, C. L. The evidence for the concept of intelligence. *British Journal of Educational Psychology,* 1955, **25**: 158– 177.

Burt, C. L. The inheritance of mental ability. *American Psychologist,* 1958, **13**: 1– 15.

Burt, C. L. The genetic determination of differences in intelligence: A study of monozygotic twins reared together and apart. *British Journal of Psychology,* 1966, **57**: 137– 153.

Burt, C. L. *The gifted child.* London: Hodder and Stoughton, 1975.

Burt, C. L., and Conway, J. Class differences in intelligence. *British Journal of Statistical Psychology,* 1959, **12**: 5– 33.

Burt, C. L., and Howard, M. The multifactorial theory of inheritance and its application to intelligence. *British Journal of Statistical Psychology,* 1956, **9**: 95– 131.

Burt, C. L., Jones, E., Miller, E., and Moodie, W. *How the mind works.* London: Allen and Unwin, 1933.

Burt, C. L., and Williams, E. L. The influence of motivation on the results of intelligence tests. *British Journal of Statistical Psychology,* 1962, **15**: 129– 136.

Butler, N. R., and Alberman, E. A. (eds.), *Perinatal problems.* Edinburgh: Livingstone, 1969.

Caldwell, E., and Richmond, J. The children's center in

Syracuse, New York. In C. Chandler, R. Lourie, and A. Peters (eds.), *Early child care: New perspectives.* New York: Atherton, 1968, pp. 326–358.

Campbell, S. B., and Douglas, V. I. Cognitive styles and responses to the threat of frustration. *Canadian Journal of Behavioral Science,* 1972, **4**: 30–42.

Cancro, R. Genetic contributions to individual differences in intelligence: An introduction. In R. Cancro (ed.), *Intelligence: Genetic and environmental influences.* New York: Grune and Stratton, 1971, pp. 59–64.

Cancro, R., ed. *Intelligence: Genetic and environmental influences.* New York: Grune and Stratton, 1971.

Carlsmith, L. Effect of early father-absence on scholastic aptitude. *Harvard Educational Review,* 1964, **34**: 3–21.

Carroll, J. B. A factor analysis of verbal abilities. *Psychometrika,* 1941, **6**: 279–307.

Carroll, J. B. A model of school learning. *Teachers College Record,* 1963, **64**: 723–733.

Carroll, J. B. Psychometric tests as cognitive tasks: A new "Structure of Intellect." Princeton, N.J.: Educational Testing Service, *Technical Report* No. 4, 1974.

Cattell, R. B. The fate of national intelligence: Test of a thirteen-year prediction. *Eugenics Review,* 1950, **42**: 136–148.

Cattell, R. B. The multiple abstract variance analysis equations and solutions: For nature–nurture research on continuous variables. *Psychological Review,* 1960, **67**: 353–372.

Cattell, R. B. Theory of fluid and crystallized intelligence: A critical experiment. *Journal of Educational Psychology,* 1963a, **54**: 1–22.

Cattell, R. B. The interaction of hereditary and environmental influences. *British Journal of Statistical Psychology,* 1963b, **16**: 191–210.

Cattell, R. B. *Abilities: Their structure, growth and action.* Boston: Houghton Mifflin, 1971a.

Cattell, R. B. The structure of intelligence in relation to the nature–nurture controversy. In R. Cancro (ed.), *Intelligence: Genetic and environmental influences.* New York: Grune and Stratton, 1971b, pp. 3–30.

Cattell, R. B., Stice, G. F., and Kristy, N. F. A first approximation to nature–nurture ratios for eleven primary personality factors in objective tests. *Journal of Abnormal and Social Psychology,* 1957, **54**: 143–159.

Cavalli-Sforza, L. L., and Bodmer, W. F. *The genetics of human populations.* San Francisco: Freeman, 1971.

Charles, D. C. Ability and accomplishment of persons earlier judged mentally deficient. *Genetic Psychology Monographs,* 1953, **47**: 3–71.

Chomsky, N. The fallacy of Richard Herrnstein's IQ. In A. Gartner, C. Greer, and F. Riessman (eds.), *The new assault on equality.* New York: Harper & Row, 1974, pp. 85–101.

Clarke, A. M., and Clarke, A. D. B. *Mental deficiency: The changing outlook* (3rd ed.). London: Methuen, 1974.

Clarke, A. M., and Clarke, A. D. B. *Early experience: Myth and evidence.* London: Open Books, 1976.

Cleary, T. A. Test bias: Prediction of grades of Negro and white students in integrated colleges. *Journal of Educational Measurement,* 1968, **5**: 115–124.

Coan, R. W. Facts, factors and artifacts: The quest for psychological meaning. *Psychological Review,* 1964, **71**: 123–140.

Cohen, E. Examiner differences with individual intelligence tests. *Perceptual and Motor Skills,* 1965, **20**: 1324.

Cole, M., and Bruner, J. S. Cultural differences and inferences about psychological processes. *American Psychologist,* 1971, **26**: 867–876.

Cole, M., Gay, J., Glick, J. A., and Sharp, D. W. *The cultural context of learning and thinking: An exploration in experimental anthropology.* London: Methuen, 1971.

Coleman, J. S. et al. *Equality of educational opportunity.* Washington, D.C.: U.S. Office of Education, 1966.

Conrad, H. S., and Jones, H. E. A second study of familial resemblance in intelligence. *Thirty-ninth Yearbook of the National Society for the Study of Education,* Pt. II, 1940, pp. 97–141.

Conway, J. The inheritance of intelligence and its social implications. *British Journal of Statistical Psychology,* 1958, **11**: 171–190.

Coon, C. S. *The origin of races.* New York: Knopf, 1971.

Coopersmith, S. *The antecedents of self-esteem.* San Francisco: Freeman, 1967.

Cowley, J. J., and Griesel, R. D. The effect on growth and behaviour of rehabilitating first and second generation low protein rats. *Animal Behavior,* 1966, **14**: 506–517.

Crandall, V. J., Preston, A., and Rabson, A. Maternal reactions and the development of independence and achievement behavior in young children. *Child Development,* 1960, **31**: 243–251.

Cravioto, J., Birch, H. G. et al. The ecology of infant weight gain in a pre-industrial society. *Acta Paediatrika Scandinavica,* 1967, **56**: 71–84.

Cronbach, L.J. Heredity, environment, and educational policy. *Harvard Educational Review,* 1969, **39**: 338– 347.

Cronbach, L. J. *Essentials of psychological testing* (3rd ed.). New York: Harper & Row, 1970.

Cronbach, L. J. Five decades of public controversy over mental testing. *American Psychologist,* 1975, **30**: 1– 14.

Crow, J. F., Neel, J. V., and Stern, C. Racial studies: Academy states position on call for new research. *Science,* 1967, **158** (3803): 892– 893.

Daly, M. Early stimulation of rodents: A critical review of present interpretations. *British Journal of Psychology,* 1973, **64**: 435– 460.

Daniels, N. IQ, intelligence and educability. *Philosophical Forum,* 1976, **6**: 56– 69.

Daniels, N., and Houghton, V. Jensen, Eysenck, and the eclipse of the Galton paradigm. In K. Richardson and D. Spears (eds.), *Race, culture and intelligence.* Harmondsworth: Penguin, 1972, pp. 68– 80.

Darlington, C. D. *The evolution of man and society.* London: Allen and Unwin, 1969.

Darlington, C. D. Genetics of intelligence: Bearing on education. Letter to *The Times* (London), November 23, 1976.

Dasen, P. R. The development of conservation in aboriginal children: A replication study. *International Journal of Psychology,* 1972, **7**: 75– 85.

Dasen, P. R., De Lacey, P. R., and Seagrim, G. N. Reasoning ability in adopted and fostered aboriginal children. In G. E. Kearney, P. R. De Lacey, and G. R. Davidson (eds.), *The psychology of aboriginal Australians.* New York: Wiley, 1973, pp. 97– 104.

Davids, A., and DeVault, S. Maternal anxiety during pregnancy and childbirth abnormalities. *Psychosomatic Medicine,* 1962, **24**: 464– 470.

Davie, R., Butler, N., and Goldstein, H. *From birth to seven.* London: Longman, 1972.

Davis, K. Final note on a case of extreme isolation. *American Journal of Sociology,* 1947, **52**: 432– 457.

Dearborn, W. F., and Rothney, J. W. M. *Predicting the child's development.* Cambridge, Mass.: SciArt, 1941.

DeFries, J. C. Quantitative aspects of genetics and environment in the determination of behavior. In L. Ehrman, G. S. Omenn, and E. Caspari (eds.), *Genetics, environment and behavior.* New York: Academic Press, 1972, pp. 5– 16.

De Groot, A. D. War and the intelligence of youth. *Journal of Abnormal and Social Psychology,* 1951, **46**: 596– 597.

De Lemos, M. M. The development of conservation in aboriginal children. *International Journal of Psychology,* 1969, **4**: 255– 269.

Dennis, W. The human figure drawings of Bedouins, *Journal of Social Psychology,* 1960, **52**: 209–219.

Dennis, W., and Narjarian, P. Infant development under environmental handicap. *Psychological Monographs,* 1957, **71**, No. 436.

Deutsch, C. P. Environment and perception. In M. Deutsch, I. Katz, and A. R. Jensen (eds.), *Social class, race and psychological development.* New York: Holt, Rinehart and Winston, 1968, pp. 58–85.

Deutsch, M. The role of social class in language development and cognition. *American Journal of Orthopsychiatry,* 1965, **35**: 78–88.

Dobbing, J. Effects of experimental undernutrition on development of the nervous system. In N. S. Scrimshaw and J. E. Gordon (eds.), *Malnutrition, learning and behavior.* Cambridge, Mass.: M.I.T. Press, 1968, pp. 181–202.

Dobzhansky, T. *Genetic diversity and human equality.* New York: Basic Books, 1973.

Doob, L. W. *Becoming more civilized.* New Haven: Yale University Press, 1960.

Douglas, J. W. B. "Premature" children at primary schools. *British Medical Journal,* 1960, **1**: 1008–1013.

Douglas, J. W. B. *The home and the school.* London: McGibbon and Kee, 1964.

Douglas, J. W. B., Ross, J. M., and Simpson, H. R. *All our future.* London: Peter Davies, 1968.

Dreger, R. M., and Miller, K. S. Comparative psychological studies of Negroes and whites in the United States. *Psychological Bulletin,* 1960, **57**: 361–402.

Dreger, R. M., and Miller, K. S. Comparative psychological studies of Negroes and whites in the United States: 1959–1965. *Psychological Bulletin Supplement,* 1968, **70**, No. 3, Pt. 2.

DuBois, P. H. A test standardized on Pueblo Indian children. *Psychological Bulletin,* 1939, **36**: 523.

Duncan, O. D. Ability and achievement. *Eugenics Quarterly,* 1968, **15**: 1–11.

Dunn, J. *Distress and comfort.* Cambridge, Mass.: Harvard University Press, 1977.

Dye, N. W., and Very, P. S. Growth changes in factorial structure by age and sex. *Genetic Psychology Monographs,* 1968, **78**: 55–88.

Eaves, L. J., and Jinks, J. L. Insignificance of evidence for differnces in heritability of IQ between races and social classes. *Nature,* 1972, **240**: 84–88.

Ebel, R. L. The social consequences of educational testing. In A. Anastasi (ed.), *Testing problems in perspective.* Washington,

D.C.: American Council on Education, 1966, pp. 18–28.

Eckland, B. K. Genetics and sociology: A reconsideration. *American Sociological Review,* 1967, **32**: 173–194.

Eells, K., Davis, A., and Havighurst, R.J. *Intelligence and cultural differences.* Chicago: University of Chicago Press, 1951.

Ekstrom, R. B. *Experimental studies of homogeneous grouping: A review of the literature.* Princeton, N. J.: Educational Testing Service, 1959.

Elashoff, J. D., and Snow, R. E. *"Pygmalion" reconsidered.* Worthington, Ohio: Charles A. Jones, 1971.

Elkind, D. Piagetian and psychometric conceptions of intelligence. *Harvard Educational Review,* 1969, **39**: 319–337.

Erikson, E. H. *Childhood and society.* London: Imago, 1950.

Erlenmeyer-Kimling, L., and Jarvik, L. F. Genetics and intelligence: A review. *Science,* 1963, **142**: 1477–1478.

Ertl, J. P. Evoked potentials and intelligence. *Revue de l'Université d'Ottawa,* 1966, **36**: 599–607.

Esposito, D. Homogeneous and heterogeneous ability grouping: Principal findings and implications for evaluating and designing more effective educational environments. *Review of Educational Research,* 1973, **43**: 163–179.

Estes, W. K. Learning theory and intelligence. *American Psychologist,* 1974, **29**: 740–749.

Exner, J. E. Variations in WISC performances as influenced by differences in pretest rapport. *Journal of General Psychology,* 1966, **74**: 299–306.

Eyferth, K. Leistungen verschiedener gruppen von besatzungskindern in Hamburg-Wechsler intelligenztest für kinder (HAWIK). *Archiv für die Gesamte Psychologie,* 1961, **113**: 222–241.

Eysenck, H. J. Intelligence assessment: A theoretical and experimental approach. *British Journal of Educational Psychology,* 1967, **37**: 81–98.

Eysenck, H. J. *Race, intelligence and education.* London: Temple Smith, 1971.

Eysenck, H. J. *The inequality of man.* London: Temple Smith, 1973.

Fehr, F. S. Critique of hereditarian accounts of "intelligence" and contrary findings. *Harvard Educational Review,* 1969, **39**: 571–580.

Feldman, S. E., and Sullivan, D. S. Factors mediating the effects of enhanced rapport on children's performance. *Journal of Consulting and Clinical Psychology,* 1971, **36**: 302.

Ferguson, G. A. On learning and human ability. *Canadian Journal of Psychology,* 1954, **8**: 95–112.

Fine, B. *The stranglehold of the IQ.* New York: Doubleday, 1975.

Fisher, R. A. Contribution to UNESCO. In *The race concept: Results of an enquiry.* Paris: UNESCO, 1952.

Flaugher, R. L., and Rock, D. Patterns of ability factors among four ethnic groups. *American Psychologist,* 1972, **27**: 1126.

Fleishman, E. A. On the relation between abilities, learning and human performance. *American Psychologist,* 1972, **27**: 1017–1032.

Foulds, G. A., and Raven, J. C. Normal changes in the mental abilities of adults as age advances. *Journal of Mental Science,* 1948, **94**: 133–142.

Fowler, W. Cognitive learning in infancy and early childhood. *Psychological Bulletin,* 1962, **59**: 116–152.

Fox, D. G. *An investigation of the biographical correlates of race.* Unpublished M.Sc. thesis, University of Utah, 1972.

Francis, H. Social background, speech and learning to read. *British Journal of Educational Psychology,* 1974, **44**: 290–299.

Fraser, E. *Home environment and the school.* London: University of London Press, 1959.

Freeberg, N. E., and Payne, D. T. Parental influence on cognitive development in early childhood: A review. *Child Development,* 1967, **38**: 65–87.

Freeman, F. N., Holzinger, K. J., and Mitchell, B. C. The influence of environment on the intelligence, school achievement, and conduct of foster children. *Twenty-seventh Yearbook of the National Society for the Study of Education,* 1928, Pt. 1, pp. 103–217.

French, J. W., Ekstrom, R. B., and Price, L. A. *Manual for kit of reference tests for cognitive factors.* Princeton, N.J.: Educational Testing Service, 1963.

Fried, M. H. The need to end the pseudoscientific investigation of races. In M. Mead, T. Dobzhansky et al. (eds.), *Science and the concept of race.* New York: Columbia University Press, 1968.

Fujikura, T., and Froehlich, L. A. Mental and motor development in monozygotic co-twins with dissimilar birth weights. *Pediatrics,* 1974, **53**: 884–889.

Fulker, D. W. Review of "The Science and Politics of IQ" by L. J. Kamin. *American Journal of Psychology,* 1975, **88**: 505–519.

Furth, H. G. Linguistic deficiency and thinking: Research with deaf subjects, 1964–1969. *Psychological Bulletin,* 1971, **76**: 58–72.

Gaddes, W. H., McKenzie, A., and Barnsley, R. Psychometric

intelligence and spatial imagery in two northwest Indian and two white groups of children. *Journal of Social Psychology,* 1968, **75**: 35– 42.

Gage, N. L. IQ heritability, race differences, and educational research. *Phi Delta Kappan, Special Supplement,* 1972, pp. 308– 312.

Garber, H., and Heber, R. The Milwaukee project. In P. Mittler (ed.), *Research to practice in mental retardation.* Baltimore: University Park Press, 1977, pp. 119– 127.

Garn, S. M. *Human races* (3rd ed.). Springfield, Ill.: Thomas, 1971.

Garrett, H. E. A developmental theory of intelligence. American Psychologist, 1946, **1**: 372– 378.

Garron, D. C. Intelligence among persons with Turner's syndrome. *Behavior Genetics,* 1977, **7**: 105– 127.

Garth, T. R. A study of the foster Indian child in the white home. *Psychological Bulletin,* 1935, **32**: 708– 709.

Getzels, J. W., and Jackson, P. W. *Creativity and intelligence.* New York: Wiley, 1962.

Gibson, D. Chromosomal psychology and Down's syndrome (mongolism). *Canadian Journal of Behavioral Science,* 1975, **7**: 167– 191.

Gillie, O. *Who do you think you are? Man or Superman: The genetic controversy.* London: Hart Davis, MacGibbon, 1976.

Ginsburg, H. *The myth of the deprived child.* Englewood Cliffs, N.J.: Prentice-Hall, 1972.

Glaser, R. *Adaptive education: Individual diversity and learning.* New York: Holt, Rinehart and Winston, 1977.

Glazer, N., and Moynihan, D. P. *Beyond the melting pot.* Cambridge, Mass.: M.I.T. Press, 1963.

Golden, M., and Birns, B. Social class and infant intelligence. In M. Lewis (ed.), *Origins of intelligence.* New York: Plenum Press, 1976, pp. 299– 351.

Goldfarb, W. Variations in adolescent adjustment of institutionally-reared children. *American Journal of Orthopsychiatry,* 1947, **17**: 449– 457.

Goldstein, K., and Scheerer, M. Abstract and concrete behavior. *Psychological Monographs,* 1941, **53**, No. 555.

Goodenough, F. L. Racial differences in the intelligence of school children. *Journal of Experimental Psychology,* 1926, **9**: 388– 397.

Goodenough, F. L. Some special problems of nature– nurture research. *Thirty-ninth Yearbook of the National Society for the Study of Education,* 1940, Pt 1, pp. 367– 384.

Goodenough, F. L. *Mental testing*. New York: Rinehart, 1949.

Gordon, H. Mental and scholastic tests among retarded children. *Board of Education Pamphlet*, 1923, No. 44. London: HMSO.

Gordon I. J. *The infant experience*. Columbus, Ohio: Merrill, 1975.

Goslin, D. A. *The search for ability: Standardized testing in perspective*. New York: Wiley, 1963.

Gottesman, I. I. Biogenetics of race and class. In M. Deutsch, I. Katz, and A. R. Jensen (eds.), *Social class, race, and psychological development*. New York: Holt, Rinehart and Winston, 1968, pp. 11–51.

Gottfried, A. W. Intellectual consequences of perinatal anoxia. *Psychological Bulletin*, 1973, **80**: 231–242.

Gray, J., and Satterly, D. A chapter of errors: Teaching styles and pupil progress in retrospect. *Educational Research*, 1976, **19**: 45–56.

Gross, M. L. *The brain washers*. New York: Random House, 1962.

Guilford, J. P. Creativity. *American Psychologist*, 1950, **5**: 444–454.

Guilford, J. P. *The nature of human intelligence*. New York: McGraw-Hill, 1967.

Guilford, J. P., and Hoepfner, R. *The analysis of intelligence*. New York: McGraw-Hill, 1971.

Guinagh, B. J., and Gordon, I. J. *School performance as a function of early stimulation*. Gainesville: University of Florida, College of Education, 1976.

Haggard, E. A. Social-status and intelligence: An experimental study of certain cultural determinants of measured intelligence. *Genetic Psychology Monographs*, 1954, **49**: 141–186.

Hall, V. C., and Turner, R. R. The validity of the "different languages explanation" for poor scholastic performance by black students. *Review of Educational Research*, 1974, **44**: 69–81.

Halsey, A. H. Genetics, social structure and intelligence. *British Journal of Sociology*, 1958, **9**: 15–28.

Hambley, J. Diversity: A developmental perspective. In K. Richardson and D. Spears (eds.), *Race, culture and intelligence*. Harmondsworth: Penguin, 1972, pp. 114–127.

Hamilton, V. Motivation and personality in cognitive development. In V. Hamilton and M. D. Vernon (eds.), *The development of cognitive processes*. London: Academic Press, 1976, pp. 451–506.

Hamilton, V., and Vernon, M. D., (eds.) *The development of cognitive processes* London: Academic Press, 1976.

Hargreaves, H. L. The "faculty" of imagination. *British Journal of Psychology, Monograph Supplements,* 1927, No. 10.

Harlow, H. F. The formation of learning sets. *Psychological Review,* 1949, **56**: 51–65.

Harrell, R. F., Woodyard, E., and Gates, A. I. *The effects of mothers' diet on the intelligence of the offspring.* New York: Teachers College, Columbia University, Bureau of Publications, 1955.

Havighurst, R.J., Gunther, M.K., and Pratt, I.E. Environment and the Draw-a-Man test: The performance of Indian children. *Journal of Abnormal and Social Psychology,* 1946, **41**: 50–63.

Hebb, D.O. *The organization of behavior.* New York: Wiley, 1949.

Heber, R., and Garber, H. Report No. 2: An experiment in the prevention of cultural–familial retardation. In D. A. A. Primrose (ed.), *Proceedings of Third Conference of the International Association for the Scientific Study of Mental Deficiency.* Warsaw: Polish Medical Publishers, 1975, pp. 34–43.

Heinis, H. A personal constant. *Journal of Educational Psychology,* 1926, **17**: 163–186.

Herrnstein, R. J. *IQ in the Meritocracy.* Boston: Little, Brown, 1973.

Hess, R. D., and Shipman, V. C. Early experience and the socialization of cognitive modes in children. *Child Development,* 1965, **36**: 869–886.

Higgins, C., and Sivers, C. H. A comparison of Stanford-Binet and Colored Raven Progressive Matrices IQs for children with low socioeconomic status. *Journal of Consulting Psychology,* 1958, **22**: 465–468.

Hirsch, J. Introduction and Epilog. In J. Hirsch (ed.), *Behavior-genetic analysis.* New York: McGraw-Hill, 1967.

Hirsch, J. Behavior-genetic analysis and its biosocial consequences. In R. Cancro (ed.), *Intelligence: Genetic and environmental influences.* New York: Grune and Stratton, 1971, pp. 88–106.

Hirsch, J. Jensenism: The bankruptcy of "Science" without scholarship. *Educational Theory,* 1975, **25**: 3–28.

Hirsch, N. D. M. An experimental study of the East Kentucky mountaineers: A study in heredity and environment. *Genetic Psychology Monographs,* 1928, **3**: 183–244.

Hirsch, N. D. M. *Twins: Heredity and environment.* Cambridge, Mass.: Harvard University Press, 1930.

Hoffman, B. *The tyranny of testing.* New York: Crowell-Collier, 1962.

Hoffman, L. W., and Lippitt, H. The measurement of family life variables. In P.H. Mussen (ed.), *Handbook of research methods in child development.* New York: Wiley, 1960, pp. 945–1013.

Hofstaetter, P.R. The changing composition of "intelligence": A study in T-technique. *Journal of Genetic Psychology,* 1954, **85**: 159–164.

Honzik, M.P. Developmental studies of parent–child resemblance in intelligence. *Child Development,* 1957, **28**: 215–228.

Honzik, M. P., MacFarlane, J. W., and Allen, L. The stability of mental test performance between two and eighteen years. *Journal of Experimental Education,* 1948, **17**: 309–324.

Hopkins, K. D., and Bracht, G. H. Ten-year stability of verbal and nonverbal IQ scores. *American Educational Research Journal,* 1975, **12**: 469–477.

Horn, J. L. Review of "Educability and group differences," by A. R. Jensen. *American Journal of Psychology,* 1974, **87**: 546–551.

Horn, J. L. Human abilities: A review of research and theory in the early 1970s. *Annual Review of Psychology,* 1976, **27**: 437–485.

Horn, J. L., and Donaldson, G. On the myth of intellectual decline in adulthood. *American Psychologist,* 1976, **31**: 701–719.

Horn, J.L., and Knapp, J.R. On the subjective character of the empirical base of Guilford's structure-of-intellect model. *Psychological Bulletin,* 1973, **80**: 33–43.

Hudson, L. *The cult of the fact.* London: Jonathan Cape, 1972.

Humphreys, L. G. Theory of intelligence. In R. Cancro (ed.), *Intelligence: Genetic and environmental influences.* New York: Grune and Stratton, 1971, pp. 31–42.

Humphreys, L. G. A factor model for research on intelligence and problem solving. In L. B. Resnick (ed.), *The nature of intelligence.* New York: Wiley, 1976, pp. 329–339.

Humphreys, L. G., and Dachler, H. P. Jensen's theory of intelligence. *Journal of Educational Psychology,* 1969, **60**: 419–433.

Hunt, J. McV. *Intelligence and experience.* New York: Ronald Press, 1961.

Hunt, J. McV., and Kirk, G. E. Social aspects of intelligence:

Evidence and issues. In R. Cancro (ed.), *Intelligence: Genetic and environmental influences.* New York: Grune and Stratton, 1971, pp. 262–306.

Hunt, J. V. Environmental risk in fetal and neonatal life and measured infant intelligence. In M. Lewis (ed.), *Origins of intelligence: Infancy and early childhood.* New York: Plenum Press, 1976, pp. 223–258.

Hunter, J. E., and Schmidt, F. L. Critical analysis of the statistical and ethical implications of various definitions of test bias. *Psychological Bulletin,* 1976, **83**: 1053–1071.

Husén, T. The influence of schooling upon IQ. *Theoria,* 1951, **17**: 61–88.

Husén, T. *Psychological twin research.* Stockholm: Almquist and Wiksell, 1959.

Husén, T. *International study of achievement in mathematics.* Stockholm: Almquist and Wiksell, 1967.

Husén, T. *Social background and educational career.* Paris: OECD, Center for Educational Research and Innovation, 1972.

Hutt, M. L. A clinical study of "consecutive" and "adaptive" testing with the revised Stanford-Binet. *Journal of Consulting Psychology,* 1947, **11**: 93–103.

Hutt, S. J. Cognitive development and cerebral dysfunction. In V. Hamilton and M. D. Vernon (eds.), *The development of cognitive processes.* London: Academic Press, 1976, pp. 591–643.

Inhelder, B., Sinclair, H., and Bovet, M. *Learning and the development of cognition.* Cambridge, Mass.: Harvard University Press, 1974.

Irvine, S. H. *Selection for secondary education in Southern Rhodesia.* Salisbury: University College of Rhodesia and Nyasaland, 1965.

Irvine, S. H. Factor analysis of African abilities and attainments: Constructs across cultures. *Psychological Bulletin,* 1969, **71**: 20–32.

Irvine, S. H., and Sanders, J. T. Logic, language and method in construct identification across cultures. In L. J. Cronbach and P. J. D. Drenth (eds.), *Mental tests and cultural adaptation.* The Hague: Mouton, 1972.

Jamieson, E., and Sandiford, P. The mental capacity of southern Ontario Indians. *Journal of Educational Psychology,* 1928, **19**: 313–328.

Jarvik, L. F., and Erlenmeyer-Kimling, L. Survey of familial correlations in measured intellectual functions. In J. Zubin and G. A. Jervis (eds.), *Psychopathology of mental development.* New York: Grune and Stratton, 1967, pp. 447–459.

Jastak, J. F. Intelligence is more than measurement. *Harvard Educational Review,* 1969, **39**: 608–611.

Jencks, C. et al. *Inequality: A reassessment of the effect of family and schooling in America.* New York: Basic Books, 1972.

Jensen, A. R. The culturally disadvantaged: Psychological and educational aspects. *Educational Research,* 1967, **10**: 4–20.

Jensen, A. R. How much can we boost IQ and scholastic achievement? *Harvard Educational Review,* 1969, **39**: 1–123.

Jensen, A. R. IQs of identical twins reared apart. *Behavior Genetics,* 1970a, **1**: 133–148.

Jensen, A. R. Hierarchical theories of mental ability. In W. B. Dockrell (ed.), *On intelligence.* Toronto: Ontario Institute for Studies in Education, 1970b, pp. 119–190.

Jensen, A. R. Note on why genetic correlations are not squared. *Psychological Bulletin,* 1971a, **75**: 223–224.

Jensen, A. R. The race × sex × ability interaction. In R. Cancro (ed.), *Intelligence: Genetic and environmental influences.* New York: Grune and Stratton, 1971b, pp. 107–161.

Jensen, A. R. *Genetics and education.* New York: Harper & Row, 1972.

Jensen, A. R. *Educability and group differences.* New York: Harper & Row, 1973a.

Jensen, A. R. The IQ controversy: A reply to Layzer. *International Journal of Cognitive Psychology,* 1973b, **1**(4): 427–452.

Jensen, A. R. Let's understand Skodak and Skeels, finally. *Educational Psychologist,* 1973c, **10**: 30–35.

Jensen, A. R. Level I and Level II abilities in three ethnic groups. *American Educational Research Journal,* 1973d, **10**: 263–276.

Jensen, A. R. The effect of race of examiner on the mental test scores of white and black pupils. *Journal of Educational Measurement,* 1974a, **11**: 1–14.

Jensen, A. R. Kinship correlations reported by Sir Cyril Burt. *Behavior Genetics,* 1974b, **4**: 1–28.

Jensen, A. R. Cumulative deficit: A testable hypothesis? *Developmental Psychology,* 1974c, **10**: 996–1019.

Jensen, A. R. How biased are culture-loaded tests? *Genetic Psychology Monographs,* 1974d, **90**: 185–244.

Jensen, A. R. The meaning of heritability in the behavioral sciences. *Educational Psychologist,* 1975a, **11**: 171–183.

Jensen, A. R. Test bias and construct validity. *Proceedings of American Psychological Association,* 83rd Annual Convention, 1975b.

Jensen, A. R. Genetic and behavioral effects of nonrandom

mating. In C. E. Noble, R. T. Osborne, and N. Weyl (eds.), *Human variation: Biogenetics of age, race and sex.* New York: Academic Press, 1977a.

Jensen, A. R. Cumulative deficit in IQ of blacks in the rural south. *Developmental Psychology,* 1977b, **13**: 184– 191.

Jensen, A. R. Did Sir Cyril Burt fake his research on heritability of intelligence? *Phi Delta Kappan,* 1977c, **6**: 471, 492.

Jensen, A. R. The problem of genotype-environment correlation in the estimation of heritability from monozygotic and dizygotic twins. *Acta Geneticae, Medicae et Gemellologiae,* 1977d.

Jensen, A. R., and Figueroa, R. A. Forward and backward digit span interaction with race and IQ: Predictions from Jensen's theory. *Journal of Educational Psychology,* 1975, **67**: 882– 893.

Jinks, J. L. and Eaves, L. J. IQ and inequality: Review of Herrnstein (1973) and Jencks (1972). *Nature,* 1974, **248**: 287– 289.

Jinks, J. L., and Fulker, D. W. Comparison of the biometrical-genetical, MAVA, and classical approaches to the analysis of human behavior. *Psychological Bulletin,* 1970, **73**: 311– 349.

Joffe, J. M. *Prenatal determinants of behaviour.* Oxford: Pergamon, 1969.

Johnson, R. C. Similarity in IQ of separated identical twins as related to length of time spent in the same environment. *Child Development,* 1963, **34**: 745– 749.

Jones, M. C., Bayley, N., MacFarlane, J. W., and Honzik, M. P. *The course of human development.* Waltham, Mass.: Xerox Publishing, 1971.

Jones, W. R. A critical study of bilingualism and nonverbal intelligence. *British Journal of Educational Psychology,* 1960, **30**: 71– 77.

Juel-Nielsen, N. Individual and environment: A psychiatric-psychological investigation of monozygotic twins reared apart. *Acta Psychiatrica et Neurologica Scandinavica (Monograph Supplement),* 1965, **183**.

Kagan, J. Biological aspects of inhibition systems. *American Journal of Diseases of Children,* 1967, **114**: 507– 512.

Kagan, J. What is intelligence? In A Gartner, C. Greer, and F. Riesmann (eds.), *The new assault on equality.* New York: Harper & Row, 1974, pp. 114– 130.

Kagan, J. Resilience and continuity in psychological development. In A. M. Clarke and A. D. B. Clarke (eds.), *Early experience; myth and evidence.* London: Open Books, 1976, pp. 97– 121.

Kagan, J., Kearsley, B., and Zelazo, P. R. Day care is as good as home care. *Psychology Today,* May 1976, pp. 36–37.

Kagan, J., and Klein, R. L. Cross-cultural perspectives on early development. *American Psychologist,* 1973, **28**: 947–961.

Kamin, L. J. *The science and politics of IQ.* Potomac, Md.: Lawrence Erlbaum, 1974.

Kamin, L. J. Comment on Munsinger's review of adoption studies. *Psychological Bulletin,* 1977a (in press).

Kamin, L. J. Comment on Munsinger's adoption study. *Behavior Genetics,* 1977b, **7**: 403–406.

Kamin, L. J. Transfusion syndrome and the heritability of IQ: A case study. Princeton, N.J.: Princeton University, unpublished paper, 1977c.

Kaplan, B. J. Malnutrition and mental deficiency. *Psychological Bulletin,* 1972, **78**: 321–334.

Karnes, M. B., Teska, J. A., Hodgins, A. S., and Badger, E. D. Educational intervention at home by mothers of disadvantaged infants. *Child Development,* 1970, **41**: 925–935.

Katz, I., and Greenbaum, C. Effects of anxiety, threat, and racial environment on task performance of Negro college students. *Journal of Abnormal and Social Psychology,* 1963, **66**: 562–567.

Kearney, G. E., De Lacey, P. R., and Davidson, G. R. (eds.), *The psychology of aboriginal Australians.* New York: Wiley, 1973.

Kellmer Pringle, M. *The needs of children.* London: Hutchinson, 1975.

Kennedy, W. A. A follow-up normative study of Negro intelligence and development. *Monographs of the Society for Research in Child Development,* 1969, **34**, No. 126.

Kennedy, W. A., Van de Riet, V., and White, J. C. A normative sample of intelligence and achievement of Negro elementary school children in the southeastern United States. *Monographs of the Society for Research in Child Development,* 1963, **28**, No. 90.

Kent, N., and Davis, D. R. Discipline in the home and intellectual development. *British Journal of Medical Psychology,* 1957, **30**: 27–33.

Kirk, S. A. *Early education of the mentally retarded.* Urbana, Ill.: University of Illinois Press, 1958.

Kirkland, M. C. The effects of tests on students and schools. *Review of Educational Research,* 1971, **41**: 303–350.

Klineberg, O. An experimental study of speed and other factors in "racial" differences. *Archives of Psychology,* 1928, No. 93.

Klineberg, O. *Race differences.* New York: Harper, 1935a.

Klineberg, O. *Negro intelligence and selective migration.* New York: Columbia University Press, 1935b.

Kluckhohn, F. R. Dominant and substitute profiles of cultural orientations: Their significance for the analysis of social stratification. *Social Forces,* 1950, **28**: 376–393.

Knehr, C. A., and Sobol, A. Mental ability of prematurely born children at early school age. *Journal of Psychology,* 1949, **27**: 355–361.

Knobloch, H. Pasamanick, B., and Lilienfeld, A. M. The effect of prematurity on health and growth. *American Journal of Public Health,* 1959, **49**: 1164–1173.

Koluchova, J. Severe deprivation in twins: A case study. *Journal of Child Psychology and Psychiatry,* 1972, **13**: 107–114.

Krech, D., Rosenzweig, M. R., and Bennett, E. L. Relations between brain chemistry and problem-solving among rats reared in enriched and impoverished environments. *Journal of Comparative and Physiological Psychology,* 1962, **55**: 801–807.

Kuper, L. *Race, science and society.* Paris: UNESCO, 1975.

Labov, W. The logic of non-standard English. In F. Williams (ed.), *Language and poverty.* Chicago: Markham, 1970, pp. 153–189.

Last, K. *Genetical aspects of human behaviour.* Unpublished M.Sc. thesis, University of Birmingham (England), 1976.

Lawrence, E. M. An investigation into the relation between intelligence and inheritance. *British Journal of Psychology, Monograph Supplements,* 1931, No. 16.

Layzer, D. Science or superstition: A physical scientist looks at the IQ controversy. *International Journal of Cognitive Psychology,* 1972, **1**: 265–299.

Layzer, D. Heritability analyses of IQ scores: Science or numerology? *Science,* 1974, **183** (4131): 1259–1266.

Leahy, A. M. Nature–nurture and intelligence. *Genetic Psychology Monographs,* 1935, **17**: 235–308.

Lee, E. S. Negro intelligence and selective migration: A Philadelphia test of the Klineberg hypothesis. *American Sociological Review,* 1951, **16**: 227–233.

Lerner, I. M., and Libby, W. J. *Heredity, evolution, and society.* San Francisco: Freeman, 1976.

Lesser, G. S., Fifer, G., and Clark, D. H. Mental abilities of children from different social class and cultural groups. *Monographs of the Society for Research in Child Development,* 1965, **30**, No. 102.

Levenstein, P. Cognitive growth in preschoolers through verbal interaction with mothers. *American Journal of Ortho-*

psychiatry, 1970, **40**: 426– 432.

Levine, S. Stimulation in infancy. *Scientific American,* 1960, **202**(5), 80– 86.

Lévi-Strauss, C. Race and history. In *The race question in modern science.* Paris: UNESCO, 1956, pp. 123– 163.

Lewin, R. "Head Start" pays off. *New Scientist,* 1977, **73** (1041): 508– 509.

Lewis, M. *Origins of intelligence.* New York: Plenum Press, 1976.

Lewis, M. M. *Language, thought and personality.* London: Harrap, 1963.

Lewontin, R. Race and Intelligence. *Bulletin of the Atomic Scientists,* 1970, **26**(3): 2– 8.

Lewontin, R. The fallacy of biological determinism. *The Sciences,* 1976, **16**(2): 6– 10.

Li, C. C. A tale of two thermos bottles: Properties of a genetic model for human intelligence. In R. Cancro (ed.), *Intelligence: Genetic and environmental influences.* New York: Grune and Stratton, 1971, pp. 162– 181.

Lieblich, A., Ninio, A., and Kugelmass, S. Effects of ethnic origin and parental SES on WPPSI performance of pre-school children in Israel. *Journal of Cross-Cultural Psychology,* 1972, **3**: 159– 168.

Light, R. J., and Smith, P. V. Social allocation models of intelligence: A methodological enquiry. *Harvard Educational Review,* 1969, **39**: 484– 510.

Lilienfeld, A. M., and Pasamanick, B. The association of prenatal and paranatal factors with the development of cerebral palsy and epilepsy. *American Journal of Obstetrics and Gynecology,* 1955, **70**: 93– 101.

Linn, R. L. Fair test use in selection. *Review of Educational Research,* 1973, **43**: 139– 161.

Loehlin, J. C., Lindzey, G., and Spuhler, J. N. *Race differences in intelligence.* San Francisco: Freeman, 1975.

Loehlin, J. C., Vandenberg, S. G., and Osborne, R. T. Blood groups genes and Negro-white ability differences. *Behavior Genetics,* 1973, **3**: 263– 270.

Lorge, I. Schooling makes a difference. *Teachers College Record,* 1945, **46**: 483– 492.

Lynn, D. B., and Sawrey, W. L. The effects of father-absence on Norwegian boys and girls. *Journal of Abnormal and Social Psychology,* 1959, **59**: 258– 262.

Lynn, R. The intelligence of the Japanese. *Bulletin of the British Psychological Society,* 1977, **30**: 69– 72.

Lytton, H. Comparative yield of three data sources in the

study of parent-child interaction. *Merrill-Palmer Quarterly,* 1974, **20**: 53– 64.

Lytton, H. Do parents create, or respond to, differences in twins? *Developmental Psychology,* 1977, **13**: 456– 459.

Lytton, H., Conway, D., and Sauvé, R. The impact of twinship on parent– child interaction. *Journal of Personality and Social Psychology,* 1977, **35**: 97– 107.

MacArthur, R. S. Some differential abilities of northern Canadian native youth. *International Journal of Psychology,* 1968, **3**: 43– 50.

MacArthur, R. S. Some ability patterns: Central Eskimos and Nsenga Africans. *International Journal of Psychology,* 1973, **8**: 239– 247.

McAskie, M., and Clarke, A. M. Parent-offspring resemblance in intelligence: Theories and evidence. *British Journal of Psychology,* 1976, **67**: 243– 273.

McCall, R. B. Toward an epigenetic conception of mental development in the first three years of life. In M. Lewis (ed.), *Origins of intelligence.* New York: Plenum Press, 1976, pp. 97– 122.

McCall, R. B., Hogarty, P. S., and Hurlburt, N. Transitions in infant sensorimotor development and the prediction of childhood IQ. *American Psychologist,* 1972, **27**: 728– 748.

McClelland, D. C. Testing for competence rather than "intelligence." *American Psychologist,* 1973, **28**: 1– 14.

McElwain, D. W., and Kearney, G. F. Intellectual development. In G. E. Kearney, P. R. DeLacey, and G. R. Davidson, (eds.), *The psychology of aboriginal Australians.* New York: Wiley, 1973, pp. 43– 50.

McGurk, F. C. On white and Negro test performance and socioeconomic factors. *Journal of Abnormal and Social Psychology,* 1953, **48**: 448– 450.

MacKay, G. W. S., and Vernon, P. E. The measurement of learning ability. *British Journal of Educational Psychology,* 1963, **33**: 177– 186.

McKeown, T., and Record, R. G. Early environmental influences on the development of intelligence. *British Medical Bulletin,* 1971, **27**: 48– 52.

Macnamara, J. *Bilingualism and primary education.* Edinburgh: Edinburgh University Press, 1966.

McNemar, Q. A critical examination of the University of Iowa studies of environmental influences upon the IQ. *Psychological Bulletin,* 1940, **37**: 63– 92.

McNemar, Q. *The revision of the Stanford-Binet scale.* Boston: Houghton Mifflin, 1942.

McNemar, Q. Lost: Our intelligence? Why? *American Psychologist,* 1964, **19**: 871– 882.

Madden, J., Levenstein, P., and Levenstein, S. Longitudinal IQ outcomes of the mother– child home program. *Child Development,* 1976, **47**: 1015– 1025.

Marjoribanks, K., Walberg, H. J., and Barger, M. Mental abilities: Sibling constellation and social class correlates. *British Journal of Social and Clinical Psychology,* 1975, **14**: 109– 116.

Martin, N. G., and Martin, P. G. The inheritance of scholastic abilities in a sample of twins. *Annals of Human Genetics,* 1975, **39**: 213– 229.

Medawar, P. B. Are IQs nonsense? *New York Review,* 1977, **24**(1): 13– 18.

Meichenbaum, D. H., Turk, L., and Rogers, J. M. Implications of research on disadvantaged children and cognitive training programs for educational television: Ways of improving "Sesame Street." *Journal of Special Education,* 1972, **6**: 27– 50.

Mercer, J. R. IQ the lethal label. *Psychology Today,* 1972, **6**(4): 44– 47, 95– 97.

Mercer, J. R., and Brown, W. C. Racial differences in IQ: Fact or artifact. In C. Senna (ed.), *The fallacy of IQ.* New York: The Third Press– Josph Okapu, 1973, pp. 56– 113.

Messer, S. B. Reflection-impulsivity: A review. *Psychological Bulletin,* 1976, **83**: 1026– 1052.

Messick, S., and Anderson, S. Educational testing, individual development and social responsibility. In R. W. Tyler and R. M. Wolf (eds.), *Crucial issues in testing.* Berkeley, Ca.: National Society for the Study of Education: McCutchan, 1974, pp. 21– 34.

Michael, W. B. Factor analysis of tests and criteria: A comparative study of two AAF pilot populations. *Psychological Monographs,* 1949, **63**, No. 298.

Miller, G. A., Galanter, E., and Pribram, K. H. *Plans and the structure of behavior.* New York: Holt, Rinehart and Winston, 1960.

Miller, G. W. Factors in school achievement and social class. *Journal of Educational Psychology,* 1970, **61**: 260– 269.

Miller, L. B., and Dyer, J. L. Four preschool programs: Their dimensions and effects. *Monographs of the Society for Research in Child Development,* 1975, **40**, No. 162.

Millman, J., Bishop, C., and Ebel, R. An analysis of test-wiseness. *Educational and Psychological Measurement,* 1965, **25**: 707– 726.

Money, J. Two cytogenetic syndromes: Psychologic comparisons. *Journal of Psychiatric Research,* 1964, **2**: 223– 231.

Morant, G. M. The significance of racial differences. In *The* race question in modern science. Paris: UNESCO, 1956, pp. 285–325.

Morrow, W. R., and Wilson, R. C. Family relations of bright high-achieving and under-achieving high school boys. *Child Development*, 1961, **32**: 501–510.

Morton, N. E. Human behavioral genetics. In L. Ehrman, G. S. Omenn, and E. Caspari (eds.), *Genetics, environment and behavior*. New York: Academic Press, 1972, pp. 247–265.

Moss, H. A., and Kagan, J. Stability of achievement and recognition seeking behaviors from early childhood through adulthood. *Journal of Abnormal and Social Psychology*, 1961, **62**: 504–513.

Mosteller, F., and Moynihan, D. P. *On equality of educational opportunity*. New York: Random House, 1972.

Munsinger, H. The adopted child's IQ: A critical review. *Psychological Bulletin*, 1975a, **82**: 623–659.

Munsinger, H. Children's resemblance to their biological and adopting parents in two ethnic groups. *Behavior Genetics*, 1975b, **5**: 239–254.

Munsinger, H. The identical-twin transfusion syndrome: A source of error in estimating IQ resemblance and heritability. *Annals of Human Genetics*, 1977a, **40**: 307–321.

Munsinger, H. A reply to Kamin. *Behavior Genetics*, 1977b, **7**: 407–409.

Mussen, P. H., ed. *Handbook of research methods in child development*. New York: Wiley, 1960.

Nature, Editors of. How much of IQ is inherited? *Nature*, 1972, **240**(5376): 69.

Nebes, R. D. Hemispheric specialization in commissurotomized man. *Psychological Bulletin*, 1974, **81**: 1–14.

Neff, W. S. Socioeconomic status and intelligence: A critical survey. *Psychological Bulletin*, 1938, **35**: 727–757.

Newman, H. H., Freeman, F. N., and Holzinger, K. J. *Twins: A study of heredity and environment*. Chicago: University of Chicago Press, 1937.

Newson, J., and Newson, E. Intersubjectivity and the transmission of culture: On the social origins of symbolic functioning. *Bulletin of the British Psychological Society*, 1975, **28**: 437–446.

Nichols, R. C. The inheritance of general and specific ability. *National Merit Scholarship Research Reports*, 1965, No. 1.

Nichols, R. C. Heredity and environment: Major findings from twin studies of ability, personality, and interests. *Conference of the American Psychological Association*, invited address, 1976.

Nurcombe, B. *Children of the dispossessed*. Honolulu: University of Hawaii Press, 1976.

Office of Economic Opportunity. *Experiment in education*

performance contracting. Columbus Laboratories, Battelle Memorial Institute, 1972.

Oléron, P. *Récherches sur le développement mental des sourds-muet*. Paris: Centre National de la Récherche Scientifique, 1957.

Ortar, C. R. Is a verbal test cross-cultural? *Scripta Hierosolymitana* (Publications of the Hebrew University, Jerusalem), 1963, **13**: 219– 235.

Page, E. B. Miracle in Milwaukee: Raising the IQ. *Educational Researcher,* 1972, **1**(10): 8– 16.

Pasamanick, B., and Knobloch, H. Retrospective studies on the epidemiology of reproductive casualty: Old and new. *Merrill-Palmer Quarterly,* 1966, **12**: 7– 26.

Pasamanick, B., Knobloch, H., and Lilienfeld, A. M. Socioeconomic status and some precursors of neuropsychiatric disorder. *American Journal of Orthopsychiatry,* 1956, **26**: 594– 601.

Pedersen, F. A., and Wender, P. H. Early social correlates of cognitive functioning in six-year-old boys. *Child Development,* 1968, **39**: 185– 193.

Penfield, W. Some mechanisms of consciousness discovered during the electrical stimulation of the brain. *Proceedings of the National Academy of Science,* 1958, **44**: 51– 66.

Penfield, W. *Speech and brain mechanisms*. Princeton, N.J.: Princeton University Press, 1959.

Penrose, L. S. A clinical and genetic study of 1280 cases of mental defect (Colchester Survey). *Report Series of the Medical Research Council,* 1938, No. 229.

Piaget, J. *The psychology of intelligence*. London: Routledge, 1950.

Piel, G. Ye may be mistaken. Address given at the Conference of the American Psychological Association, 174.

Pinneau, S.R. *Changes in intelligence quotient*. Boston: Houghton Mifflin, 1961.

Plomin, R., DeFries, J. C., and Loehlin, J. C. Genotype-environment interaction and correlation in the analysis of human behavior. *Psychological Bulletin,* 1977, **84**: 309– 322.

Poli, M. D. Heredity and environment. Address at the Proceedings of the 21st Congress of the International Psychological Association, Paris, 1976.

Price, B. Primary biases in twin studies. *American Journal of Human Genetics,* 1950, **2**: 293– 352.

Quay, L. C. Language dialect, reinforcement, and the intelligence-test performance of Negro children. *Child Development,* 1971, **42**: 5– 15.

Rasch, G. *Probabilistic models for some intelligence and*

attainment tests. Copenhagen: Danish Institute for Educational Research, 1960.

Ravich, D. The revisionists revised: Studies in the historiography of American education. *Proceedings of the National Academy of Education.* 1977, **4**: 1–84.

Record, R. G., McKeown, T., and Edwards, J. H. An investigation of the difference in measured intelligence between twins and single births. *Annals of Human Genetics,* 1970, **34**: 11–20.

Reed, T. E. Caucasian genes in American Negroes. *Science,* 1969, **165**: 762–768.

Reitan, R. M. Impairment of abstraction ability in brain damage. *Journal of Psychology,* 1959, **48**: 97–102.

Reitan, R. M. Diagnostic inferences of brain lesions based on psychological test results. *Canadian Psychologist,* 1966, **7**: 368–383.

Reitan, R. M., and Davison, L. A., eds. *Clinical neuropsychology: Current status and applications.* Washington, D.C.: V. H. Winston, 1974.

Resnick, L. B., ed. *The nature of intelligence.* New York: Wiley, 1976.

Rex, J. Nature versus nurture. The significance of the revived debate. In K. Richardson and D. Spears (eds.), *Race, culture and intelligence.* Harmondsworth: Penguin, 1972, pp. 167–178.

Richards, M., Richardson, K., and Spears, D. Conclusion: Intelligence and society. In K. Richardson and D. Spears (eds.), *Race, culture and intelligence.* Harmondsworth: Penguin, 1972, pp. 179–196.

Richards, M. P. M. The development of psychological communication in the first year of life. In K. J. Connolly and J. S. Bruner (eds.), *The growth of competence.* New York: Academic Press, 1974, pp. 119–132.

Riessman, F. *The culturally deprived child.* New York: Harper & Row, 1962.

Rist, R. C. Student social class and teacher expectations: The self-fulfilling prophecy in ghetto education. *Harvard Educational Review,* 1970, **40**: 411–451.

Rivers, W. H. R. Vision. In A. C. Haddon (ed.), *Reports of the Cambridge anthropological expedition to the Torres Straits.* Cambridge, England: Cambridge University Press, 1901.

Roberts, J. A. F. The genetics of mental deficiency. *Eugenics Review,* 1952, **44**: 71–83.

Robinson, H. B., and Robinson, N. M. Longitudinal development of very young children in a comprehensive day care program: The first two years. *Child Development,* 1971, **42**: 1673–1683.

Rose, S. Environmental effects on brain and behavior. In K. Richardson and D. Spears (eds.), *Race, culture and intelligence.* Harmondsworth: Penguin, 1972, pp. 128–144.

Rosenthal, R. Experimenter effects in behavioral research. New York: Appleton-Century-Crofts, 1966.

Rosenthal, R., and Jacobson, L. *Pygmalion in the classroom.* New York: Holt, Rinehart and Winston, 1968.

Rourke, B. P. Issues in the neurological assessment of children with learning disabilities. *Canadian Psychological Review,* 1976, **17**: 89–102.

Royce, J. B. The development of factor analysis. *Journal of General Psychology,* 1958, **58**: 139–164.

Rutter, M. *Maternal deprivation reassessed.* Harmondsworth: Penguin, 1972.

Ryle, G. *The concept of mind.* London: Hutchinson, 1949.

Samuel, W. L. *Test environment and race, sex, and social class of the testee as determinants of observed IQ.* Sacramento: California State University, unpublished paper, 1976.

Samuel, W. L., Soto, D., Parks, M., Ngissah, P., and Jones, B. Motivation, race, social class and IQ. *Journal of Educational Psychology,* 1976, **68**: 273–285.

Sarason, S. B., Davidson, K. S., Lighthall, F. F., Waite, R. R., and Ruebush, B. K. *Anxiety in elementary school children: A report of research.* New York: Wiley, 1960.

Sattler, J. M. Racial "experimenter effects" in experimentation, testing, interviewing, and psychotherapy. *Psychological Bulletin,* 1970, **73**: 137–160.

Sattler, J. M. *Assessment of children's intelligence.* Philadelphia: Saunders, 1974.

Savage, I. R. Review of Loehlin, Lindzey and Spuhler. *Proceedings of the National Academy of Education,* 1975, **2**: 1–37.

Scarr, S., Pakstis, A. J., Katz, S. H., and Barker, W. B. The absence of a relationship between degree of white ancestry and intellectual skills within a black population. *Human Genetics,* 1977, **37**: 1–18.

Scarr, S., and Weinberg, R. A. IQ test performance of black children adopted by white families. *American Psychologist,* 1976, **31**: 726–739.

Scarr-Salapatek, S. Unknowns in the IQ equation. *Science,* 1971a, **174**(4015): 1223–1228.

Scarr-Salapatek, S. Race, social class and IQ. *Science,* 1971b, **174**(4016): 1285–1295.

Scarr-Salapatek, S. Review of Kamin's "The Psychology and Politics of IQ." *Contemporary Psychology,* 1976, **21**: 98–99.

Schaefer, E. S., and Bayley, N. Maternal behavior, child behavior, and their intercorrelations from infancy through adolescence. *Monographs of the Society for Research in Child Development,* 1963, **28**, No. 87.

Schaffer, H. R. *The growth of sociability.* Harmondsworth: Penguin, 1971.

Schaffer, H. R. Early social behaviour and the study of reciprocity. *Bulletin of the British Psychological Society,* 1974, **27**: 209–216.

Schaffer, H. R., and Emerson, P. E. The development of social attachments in infancy. *Monographs of the Society for Research in Child Development,* 1964, **29**, No. 94.

Schaffer, R. *Mothering.* Cambridge, Mass.: Harvard Univeristy Press, 1977.

Schaie, K. W., and Strother, C. R. A cross-sequential study of age changes in cognitive behavior. *Psychological Bulletin,* 1968, **70**: 671–680.

Schooler, C. Birth order effects: Not here, not now! *Psychological Bulletin,* 1972, **78**: 161–175.

Schull, W. J., and Neel, J. V. The effects of inbreeding on Japanese children. New York: Harper & Row, 1965.

Schull, W. J., and Neel, J. V. The effects of parental consanguinity and inbreeding in Hirado, Japan. V. Summary and interpretation. *American Journal of Human Genetics,* 1972, **24**: 425–453.

Schwartz, M., and Schwartz, J. Evidence against a genetical component to performance on IQ tests. *Nature,* 1974, **248**: 84–85.

Schwarz, P. A. *Aptitude tests for use in developing nations.* Pittsburgh, Pa.: American Institutes for Research, 1961.

Scottish Council for Research in Education. *The intelligence of Scottish children.* London: University of London Press, 1933.

Scottish Council for Research in Education. *The intelligence of a representative group of Scottish children.* London: University of London Press, 1939.

Scottish Council for Research in Education. *The trend of Scottish intelligence.* London: University of London Press, 1949.

Scottish Council for Research in Education. *Social implications of the 1947 Scottish mental survey.* London: University of London Press, 1953.

Scrimshaw, N. S., and Gordon, J. E., eds. *Malnutrition, learning and behavior.* Cambridge, Mass.: M.I.T. Press, 1968.

Seemanova, E. A study of children of incestuous matings. *Human Heredity,* 1971, **21**: 108–128.

Segall, M. H., Campbell, D. I., and Herskovits, M. J. Cultural differences in the perception of geometric illusions. *Science,* 1963, **139**: 769–771.

Semler, I. J., and Iscoe, L. Structure of intelligence in Negro and white children. *Journal of Educational Psychology*, 1966, **57**: 326–336.

Senna, C. *The fallacy of IQ*. New York: The Third Press–Joseph Okapu, 1973.

Serpell, R. Estimates of intelligence in a rural community of eastern Zambia. *H.D.R.U. Reports*, 1974, No. 25.

Sherman, M., and Key, C. B. The intelligence of isolated mountain children. *Child Development*, 1932, **3**: 279–290.

Shields, J. *Monozygotic twins*. London: Oxford University Press, 1962.

Shimberg, M. E. An investigation into the validity of norms with special reference to urban and rural groups. *Archives of Psychology*, 1929, No. 104.

Shockley, W. Negro IQ deficit: Failure of a "Malicious Coincidence" model warrants new research proposals. *Review of Educational Research*, 1971, **41**: 227–248.

Shockley, W. Dysgenics, geneticity, raceology. *Phi Delta Kappan, Special Supplement*, 1972, pp. 297–307.

Shucard, D. W., and Horn, J. L. Evoked cortical potentials and measurement of human abilities. *Journal of Comparative and Physiological Psychology*, 1972, **78**: 59–68.

Shuey, A. M. *The testing of Negro intelligence*. New York: Social Science Press, 1958; rev. ed. (expanded) 1966.

Sigel, I. E. How intelligence tests limit understanding of intelligence. *Merrill-Palmer Quarterly*, 1963, **9**: 39–56.

Sims, V. M. The influence of blood relationship and common environment on measured intelligence. *Journal of Educational Psychology*, 1931, **22**: 56–65.

Skeels, H. M. Adult status of children with contrasting early life experiences: A follow-up study. *Monographs of the Society for Research in Child Development*, 1966, **31**, No. 105.

Skeels, H. M., and Dye, H. B. A study of the effects of differential stimulation on mentally retarded children. *Proceedings of the American Association for Mental Deficiency*, 1939, **44**: 114–136.

Skodak, M. and Skeels, H.M. A follow-up study of children in adoptive homes. *Journal of Genetic Psychology*, 1945, **66**: 21–58.

Skodak, M., and Skeels, H. M. A final follow-up study of one hundred adopted children. *Journal of Genetic Psychology*, 1949, **75**: 85–125.

Smilansky, M., and Smilansky, S. Intellectual advancement of culturally disadvantaged children: An Israeli approach for research and action. *International Review of Education*, 1967, **13**: 410–431.

Smith, R. T. A comparison of socioenvironmental factors in monozygotic and dizygotic twins. In S. G. Vandenberg (ed.), *Methods and goals in human behavior genetics*. New York: Academic Press, 1965, pp. 45–61.

Snygg, D. The relation between the intelligence of mothers and of their children living in foster homes. *Journal of Genetic Psychology*, 1938, **52**: 401–406.

Sontag, L. W. Implications of fetal behavior and environment for adult personalities. *Annals of New York Academy of Science*, 1966, **134**(2): 782–786.

Sontag, L. W., Baker, C. T., and Nelson, V. L. Mental growth and personality development: A longitudinal study. *Monographs of the Society for Research in Child Development*, 1958, **23**, No. 68.

Spearman, C. "General intelligence," objectively determined and measured. *American Journal of Psychology*, 1904, **15**: 201–293.

Spearman, C. *The nature of "Intelligence" and the principles of cognition*. London: Macmillan, 1923.

Spearman, C. *The abilities of man*. London: Macmillan, 1927.

Spitz, R. A. Anaclitic depression: An enquiry into the genesis of psychiatric conditions in early childhood. In A. Freud (ed.), *The psychoanalytic study of the child*. New York: International Universities Press, 1946.

Spuhler, J. N., and Lindzey, G. Racial differences in behavior. In J. Hirsch (ed.), *Behavior-genetic analysis*. New York: McGraw-Hill, 1967, pp. 366–414.

Stanley, J. C. Predicting college success of the educationally disadvantaged. *Science*, 1971, **171**: 640–647.

Stein, Z., Susser, M., Saenger, G., and Marolla, F. Nutrition and mental performance. *Science*, 1972, **178**: 708–713.

Stenhouse, D. *The evolution of intelligence*. London: Allen and Unwin, 1974.

Stoch, M. B. The effect of undernutrition during infancy on subsequent brain growth and intellectual development. *South African Medical Journal*, 1967, pp. 1027–1030.

Stoddard, G. D., and Wellman, B. L. Environment and IQ. *Thirty-ninth Yearbook of the National Society for the Study of Education*, 1940, Pt. I, pp. 405–442.

Stodolsky, S. S., and Lesser, G. Learning patterns in the disadvantaged. *Harvard Educational Review*, 1967, **37**: 546–593.

Stone, L. J. A critique of studies of infant isolation. *Child Development*, 1954, **25**: 9–20.

Stott, D. H. Physical and mental handicaps following a disturbed pregnancy. *The Lancet,* 1957, **171**: 1006– 1012.

Stott, D. H. Behavioral aspects of learning disabilities: Assessment and remediation. *Experimental Publications System,* April 1971, **11**, No. 400– 36.

Strauch, A. B. More on the sex × race interaction on cognitive measures. *Journal of Educational Psychology,* 1977, **69**: 152– 157.

Suedfeld, P. The clinical relevance of reduced sensory stimulation. *Canadian Psychological Review,* 1975, **16**: 88– 103.

Swift, D. What is the environment? In K. Richardson and D. Spears (eds.), *Race, culture and intelligence.* Harmondsworth: Penguin, 1972, pp. 147– 166.

Taylor, L. J., and Skanes, G. R. Cognitive abilities in Inuit and white children from similar environments. *Canadian Journal of Behavioral Science,* 1976, **8**: 1– 8.

Teahan, J. E., and Drews, E. M. A comparison of northern and southern Negro children on the WISC. *Journal of Consulting Psychology,* 1962, **26**: 292.

Terman, L. M. et al. *Genetic studies of genius.* Vol. I: *Mental and physical traits of a thousand gifted children.* Stanford, Ca.: Stanford University Press, 1925.

Terman, L. M., Burks, B. S., and Jensen, D. W. *Genetic studies of genius.* Vol. III: The promise of youth. Stanford, Ca.: Stanford University Press, 1930.

Terman, L. M., and Merrill, M. A. *Measuring intelligence.* Boston: Houghton Mifflin, 1937.

Terman, L. M., and Oden, M. H. *Genetic studies of genius.* Vol. IV: *The gifted child grows up.* Stanford, Ca.: Stanford University Press, 1947.

Terman, L. M., and Oden, M. H. *Genetic studies of genius.* Vol. V: *The gifted group at mid-life.* Stanford, Ca.: Stanford University Press, 1959.

Thoday, J. M. Review of Jensen's "Educability and Group Differences." *Nature,* 1973, **245**(5426): 418– 420.

Thompson, W. R. The inheritance and development of intelligence. *Proceedings of the Association for Research in Nervous and Mental Diseases,* 1954, **33**: 209– 231.

Thompson, W. R., and Grusec, J. E. Studies of early experiences. In P. H. Mussen (ed.), *Carmichael's manual of child psychology* (3rd ed.). New York: Wiley, 1970, pp. 565– 654.

Thomson, G. H. *The factorial analysis of human ability.* London: University of London Press, 1939.

Thorndike, E. L. et al. Intelligence and its measurement. *Journal of Educational Psychology,* 1921, **12**: 123f.

Thorndike, E. L., Bregman, E. O., and Cobb, M. V. *The mea-*

surement of intelligence. New York: Teachers College, Columbia University, 1927.

Thorndike, R. L. The effect of the interval between test and retest on the constancy of the IQ. *Journal of Educational Psychology,* 1933, **24**: 543–549.

Thorndike, R. L. Concepts of culture-fairness. *Journal of Educational Measurement,* 1971, **8**: 63–70.

Thorndike, R. L. *Stanford-Binet intelligence scale: 1972 norms table.* Boston: Houghton Mifflin, 1973a.

Thorndike, R. L. Reading comprehension education in fifteen countries. *International Studies in Evaluation.* No. III. New York: Wiley, 1973b.

Thorndike, R. L., and Hagen, E. *Ten thousand careers.* New York: Wiley, 1959.

Thurstone, L. L. The absolute zero in intelligence measurement. Psychological Review, 1928, **35**: 175–197.

Thurstone, L. L. Primary mental abilities. *Psychometric Monographs,* No. I. Chicago: University of Chicago Press, 1938.

Thurstone, L. L. *The differential growth of mental abilities.* Chapel Hill, N.C.: University of North Carolina, Psychometric Laboratory, 1955.

Thurstone, L. L., and Thurstone, T. G. Factorial studies of intelligence. *Psychometric Monographs,* No. 2, 1941.

Tizard, B. *Preschool education in Britain: A research review.* London: Social Science Research Council, 1974.

Tizard, B., and Rees, J. A comparison of the effects of adoption, restoration to the natural mother, and continued institutionalization, on the cognitive development of four-year-old children. *Child Development,* 1974, **45**: 92–99.

Tizard, J. *Community services for the mentally handicapped.* London: Oxford University Press, 1964.

Torrance, E. P. *Rewarding creative behavior.* Englewood Cliffs, N.J.: Prentice-Hall, 1965.

Trevarthen, C. Conversations with a two-month-old. *New Scientist,* 1974, **62**(896): 230–235.

Tuddenham, R. D. Soldier intelligence in World Wars I and II. *American Psychologist,* 1948, **3**: 54–56.

Tuddenham, R. D. A "Piagetian" test of cognitive development. In W. B. Dockrell (ed.), *On intelligence.* Toronto: Ontario Institute for Studies in Education, 1970, pp. 49–70.

Tyler, L. E. *The psychology of human differences* (3rd ed.). New York: Appleton-Century-Crofts, 1965.

Tyler, R. W., and Wolf, R. M., eds. *Crucial issues in testing.* National Society for the Study of Education. Berkeley: McCutchan, 1974.

UNESCO. *The race concept: Results of an enquiry.* Paris: UNESCO, 1952.

Urbach, P. Progress and degeneration in the IQ debate. *British Journal of the Philosophy of Science,* 1974, **25**: 99– 135, 235– 259.

Uzgiris, I. C., and Hunt, J. McV. *Assessment in infancy.* Urbana, Ill.: University of Illinois Press, 1975.

Van Alstyne, D. The environment of three-year-old children: Factors related to intelligence and vocabulary tests. *Teachers College Contributions to Education,* 1929, No. 366.

Vandenberg, S. G. The hereditary abilities study: Hereditary components in a psychological test battery. *American Journal of Human Genetics,* 1962, **14**: 220– 237.

Vandenberg, S. G. What do we know today about the inheritance of intelligence and how do we know it? In R. Cancro (ed.), *Intelligence: Genetic and environmental influences.* New York: Grune and Stratton, 1971, pp. 182– 218.

Vernon, P. E. Recent investigations of intelligence and its measurment. *Eugenics Review,* 1951, **43**, 125– 137.

Vernon, P. E. The assessment of children. *University of London Institute of Education Studies in Education,* No. 7. London: Evans Bros., 1955, pp. 189– 215.

Vernon, P. E., ed. *Secondary school selection.* London: Methuen, 1957a.

Vernon, P. E. Intelligence and intellectual stimulation during adolescence. *Indian Psychological Bulletin,* 1957b, **2**: 1– 6.

Vernon, P. E. *Intelligence and attainment tests.* London: University of London Press, 1960.

Vernon, P. E. *The structure of human abilities* (2nd ed.). London: Methuen, 1961.

Vernon, P. E. The pool of ability. *Sociological Review Monographs,* 1963, No. 7, pp. 45– 57.

Vernon, P. E. Ability factors and environmental influences. *American Psychologist,* 1965, **20**: 723– 733.

Vernon, P. E. *Intelligence and cultural environment.* London: Methuen, 1969a.

Vernon, P. E. Cross-cultural applications of factor analysis. *Proceedings of the 16th International Congress of Applied Psychology.* Amsterdam: Swets and Zeitlinger, 1969b, pp. 762– 768.

Vernon, P. E. The distinctiveness of field independence. *Journal of Personality,* 1972, **40**: 366– 391.

Vernon, P. E., Adamson, G., and Vernon, D. F. *The psychology and education of gifted children.* London: Methuen, 1977.

Vernon, P. E., and Mitchell, M. C. Social class differences in associative learning. *Journal of Special Education,* 1974, **8**: 297– 311.

Vernon, P. E., and Parry, J. B. *Personnel selection in the British Forces.* London: University of London Press, 1949.

Very, P. S. Differential factor structures in mathematical abilities. *Genetic Psychology Monographs,* 1967, **75**: 169– 207.

Vincent, D. F. The linear relationship between age and score of adults in intelligence tests. *Occupational Psychology,* 1952, **26**: 243– 249.

Wachs, T. D., Uzgiris, I. C., and Hunt, J. McV. Cognitive development in infants of different age levels and from different environmental backgrounds: An explanatory investigation. *Merrill-Palmer Quarterly,* 1971, **17**: 283– 317.

Wallace, G., and McLoughlin, J. A. *Learning disabilities: Concepts and characteristics.* Columbus, Ohio: Charles Merrill, 1975.

Wallach, M. A., and Kogan, N. *Modes of thinking in young children: A study of the creativity-intelligence distinction.* New York: Holt, Rinehart and Winston, 1965.

Waller, J. H. Achievement and social mobility: Relationships among IQ score, education, and occupation in two generations. *Social Biology,* 1971, **18**: 252– 259.

Warburton, F. The British intelligence scale. In W. B. Dockrell (ed.), *On intelligence.* Toronto: Ontario Institute for Studies in Education, 1970, pp. 71– 98.

Warren, N. Malnutrition and mental development. *Psychological Bulletin,* 1973, **80**: 324– 328.

Watson, P. Race and intelligence through the looking glass. In P. Watson (ed.), *Psychology and race.* Harmondsworth: Penguin, 1973, pp. 360– 376.

Wechsler, D. *The measurement and appraisal of adult intelligence.* Baltimore: Williams and Wilkins, 1958.

Weil, P. G. Influence du milieu sur le développement mental. *Enfance,* 1958, No. 2: 151– 160.

Werner, E. E. Infants around the world: Cross-cultural studies of psychomotor development from birth to two years. *Journal of Crosscultural Psychology,* 1972, **3**: 111– 134.

Werner, H. *Comparative psychology of mental development.* New York: Follett, 1940.

Westinghouse Learning Corporation/Ohio University. *The impact of Head Start.* Springfield, Va.: U.S. Office of Economic Opportunity, 1969.

Weyl, N. Some comparative performance indexes of American ethnic minorities. *Mankind Quarterly,* 1969, **9**: 106– 119.

Wheeler, L. R. A comparative study of the intelligence of East Tennessee mountain children. *Journal of Educational Psychology,* 1942, **33**: 321– 334.

WHO (World Health Organization). Malnutrition and mental development. *WHO Chronicle,* 1974, **28**: 95– 102.

Willerman, L., Broman, S. H., and Fiedler, M. Infant development, preschool IQ, and social class. *Child Development,* 1970, **41**: 69– 77.

Willerman, L., Naylor, A. F., and Myrianthopoulos, N. C. Intellectual development of children from interracial matings. *Science,* 1970, **170**: 1329– 1331.

Williams, R. L. Black pride, academic relevance, and individual achievement. *The Counseling Psychologist,* 1970, **2**: 18– 22. Also published in R. W. Tyler and R. M. Wolf (eds.), *Crucial issues in testing.* Berkeley: National Society for the Study of Education. McCutchan, 1974.

Williams, T. Competence dimensions of family environment. Address at meeting of American Educational Research Association, Chicago, 1974.

Wiseman, S. *Education and environment.* Manchester, England: Manchester University Press, 1964.

Witkin, H. A., Dyk, R. B., Faterson, H. F., Goodenough, D. R., and Karp, S. A. *Psychological differentiation: Studies of development.* New York: Wiley, 1962.

Wober, M. Culture and the concept of intelligence: A case in Uganda. *Journal of Cross-cultural Psychology,* 1972, **3**: 327– 328.

Wolf, R. The measurement of environment. In A. Anastasi (ed.), *Testing problems in perspective.* Washington, D.C.: American Council on Education, 1966, pp. 491– 503.

Woodworth, R. S. *Heredity and environment.* New York: Social Science Research Council, 1941.

Wulbert, M., Inglis, S., Kriegsmann, E., and Mills, B. Language delay and associated mother– child interactions. *Developmental Psychology,* 1975, **11**: 61– 70.

Wylie, R. C. *The self concept.* Lincoln, Neb.: University of Nebraska Press, 1961.

Yarrow, L. J. Maternal deprivation: Toward an empirical and conceptual re-evaluation. *Psychological Bulletin,* 1961, **58**: 459– 490.

Yarrow, L. J. Research in dimensions of early maternal care. *Merrill-Palmer Quarterly,* 1963, **9**: 101– 114.

Yarrow, L. J., and Pedersen, F. A. Attachment: Its origins and course. *Young Children,* 1972, **27**: 302– 312.

Yarrow, L. J., and Pedersen, F. A. The interplay between cognition and motivation in infancy. In M. Lewis (ed.), *Origins of intelligence*. New York: Plenum Press, 1976, pp. 379–399.

Yarrow, M. R., Campbell, J. D., and Burton, R. V. *Child rearing: An inquiry into research and methods*. San Francisco: Jossey-Bass, 1968.

Yerushalmy, J. Statistical considerations and evaluation of epidemiological evidence. In G. James and T. Rosenthal (eds.), *Tobacco and health*. Springfield, Ill.: Thomas, 1962, pp. 208–230.

Yoakum, C. S., and Yerkes, R. M. *Army mental tests*. New York: Holt, 1920.

Yudkin, S., and Holme, A. *Working mothers and their children*. London: Michael Joseph, 1963.

Zajonc, R. B., and Markus, G. B. Birth order and intellectual development. *Psychological Review,* 1975, **82**: 74–88.

Zigler, E., and Butterfield, E. C. Motivational aspects of changes in IQ test performance of culturally deprived nursery school children. *Child Development,* 1968, **39**: 1–14.

Zingg, R. M. Feral man and extreme cases of isolation. *American Journal of Psychology,* 1940, **53**: 487–517.

Zirkel, P. A., and Moses, E. G. Self-concept and ethnic group membership among public school students. *American Educational Research Journal,* 1971, **8**: 253–265.

Name Index

Adamson, G., 31, 32, 65
Aikin, W. M., 151
A. I. R. (American Institutes of Research), 11, 92
Airasian, P. W., 36
Alberman, E. A., 97
Allen, L. 70 n, 74
Alper, T. G., 262
Altus, W. D., 98
Amante, D., 86, 90
The American Underclass, 264
Amrine, M., 16
Anastasi, A., 33, 66, 261, 271, 284–285, 295
Anderson, J. E., 76, 82
Anderson, S., 310
Ashline, N. F., 159 n
Astin, A. W., 96

Bagley, W. C., 8, 262
Bajema, C. J., 100
Baker, J. R., 112, 246, 247, 253, 295
Baldwin, A. L., 112
Baller, W. R., 123
Baltes, P. B., 81
Baratz, S. B., 127, 254
Baratz, J. C., 127, 254
Barger, M., 99
Barker, D. J. P., 87

Barnsley, R., 269
Barron, F., 294, 295
Bartlett, F. C., 44, 52
Baumrind, D., 110
Bayley, N., 28, 70 n, 71–72, 76, 78, 82, 107, 109
Bee, H. L., 136, 142
Bell, A. E., 151, 341
Bennett, S. N., 152
Bereiter, C., 12, 35, 126, 147, 268, 277, 328
Bernstein, B. B., 117, 124–125, 126–127, 128, 137, 157, 158, 212, 254
Biesheuvel, S., 210, 255, 284, 312
Bijou, S. W., 202, 212
Binet, A., 3–4, 7, 17, 19, 40, 62, 64
Bing, E., 111
Birch, H., 85, 86, 93, 95, 97, 100
Birns, B., 136, 139
Bishop, C., 25
Blewett, D. B., 186
Block, J. H., 36, 154, 156, 161
Block, N. J., 20, 54, 55, 61–62, 201, 209, 211, 214, 282, 283, 284, 325
Bloom, B. S., 36, 76–77, 78, 82, 118, 119, 154–156, 159, 161, 273, 294
Bock, R. D., 64, 111
Bodmer, W. F., 245, 251, 284, 286

375

Ekstrom, R. B., 32, 49
Elashoff, J. D., 26
Elkind, D., 206, 212
Emerson, P. E., 104
Engelmann, S., 12, 35, 126, 268
Erikson, E. H., 104, 313
Erlenmeyer-Kimling, L., 166–167, 169, 170, 180, 210
Ertl, J. P., 43
Esposito, D., 32
Estes, W. K., 50
Exner, J. E., 27–28
Eyferth, K., 298
Eysenck, H. J., 13, 43, 59, 60, 131, 140, 148, 182, 237, 275, 280, 294, 327, 330

Faterson, H. F., 373
Fechner, G., 3
Fehr, F. S., 179
Feldman, S. E., 28
Ferguson, G. A., 47, 52, 60
Fiedler, M., 116, 297
Fifer, G., 271–272
Figueroa, R. A., 306, 314
Fine, B., 19, 21, 31, 75, 278
Fisher, R. A., 165, 181, 203, 249, 338
Flaugher, R. L., 274
Fleishman, E. A., 58
Foulds, G. A., 79–80
Fowler, W., 73
Fox, D. G., 292
Francis, H., 127
Fraser, E., 118
Freeberg, N. E., 12, 118
Freeman, F. N., 9, 133, 170, 172, 173, 174, 175, 179, 180, 194, 218–219, 220, 223, 228, 230, 290
French, J. W., 49
Fried, M. H., 249
Froehlich, L. A., 88, 177
Fujikura, T., 88, 177
Fulker, D. W., 169 n, 170, 172, 174–175, 176, 183, 184, 190–191, 199, 223
Furth, H. G., 142

Gaddes, W. H., 269
Gage, N. L., 326
Galanter, E., 44, 49, 52
Galileo, G., 282, 288
Galton, Francis, 2–3, 17, 98, 237, 278
Garber, H., 133–135
Garn, S. M., 245
Garrett, H. E., 57, 278
Garron, D. C., 235
Garth, T. R., 297
Gates, A. I., 93
Gay, J., 254, 287

Gesell, A., 73–74, 103, 278
Getzels, J. W., 65
Gibson, D., 164, 234
Gillie, O., 171–172
Ginsburg, H., 33, 156, 157, 287
Gintis, H., 121, 123, 156, 159 n, 280
Glaser, R., 35–36, 38, 154
Glazer, N., 315
Goddard, H. H., 5, 7, 278
Golden, M., 136, 139
Goldfarb, W., 140
Goldstein, H., 97, 99, 111, 150
Goldstein, K., 90
Goodenough, F. L., 24, 136, 269
Gordon, H., 8, 145, 274
Gordon, I. J., 104, 136, 137–138
Gordon, J. E., 93
Goslin, D. A., 7, 15, 24, 32, 40
Gottesman, I. I., 201, 245, 248
Gottfried, A. W., 89
Gray, J., 152
Greenbaum, C., 313
Griesel, R. D., 93
Gross, M. L., 15, 18
Grusec, J. E., 140
Guilford, J. P., 21, 49, 51, 58–60, 61, 62–63, 64–65, 67, 89, 90–91, 335
Guinagh, B. J., 137–138
Gunther, M. K., 269
Gussow, J., 85, 86, 93, 95, 97, 100

Hagen E., 123
Haggard, E. A., 306–307
Hall, Stanley, 278
Hall, V. C., 306
Halsey, A. H., 250
Halstead, W. C., 90, 91
Hambley, J., 202, 250
Hamilton, V., 102 n, 110
Hargreaves, H. L., 64
Harlow, H. F., 35, 47, 105, 131
Harrell, R. F., 93, 94
Harris, D. B., 269
Hauser, R. M., 146 n
Havighurst, R. J., 269, 310
Head, H., 44
Hebb, D. O., 10–11, 17, 20, 42, 45–46, 48, 52, 80, 139, 143, 335
Heber, R., 133–135, 136, 138, 143, 208, 210, 290, 322
Heinis, H., 78
Helmholtz, H. von, 3
Herrnstein, R. J., 13, 123, 193, 204, 209, 325
Herskovits, M. J., 252
Hess, R. D., 125, 129, 254
Higgins, C., 265
Hirsch, J., 201, 203, 204, 205, 208, 210, 245, 283

Levenstein, S., 137
Levine, S., 130–131
Lévi-Strauss, C., 252
Levy-Bruhl, L., 252
Lewin, R., 12 n
Lewis, M., 71, 73, 116–117, 125
Lewis, M. M., 142
Lewontin, R., 61, 201, 202, 204, 205, 233, 279, 285, 286
Li, C. C., 239, 286
Libby, W. J., 164, 202, 234
Lieblich, A., 294, 295
Light, R. J., 183 n, 298
Lilienfeld, A. M., 86, 89, 94
Lindzey, G., 20, 94, 165, 172, 191–192, 195, 196, 198, 199, 200, 226, 235, 236, 245, 251, 261, 262, 263, 265, 269, 274, 279, 285, 288, 293, 295, 326
Linn, R. L., 310
Lippitt, H., 117
Locke, John, 278
Loehlin, J. C., 20, 94, 165, 172, 181–182, 183, 191–192, 195, 196, 198, 199, 200, 226, 227–228, 229, 235, 236, 237, 245, 251, 262, 263, 265, 269, 274, 279, 285, 288, 293, 295, 296, 297
Lonner, W. J., 312
Lorenz, K., 41
Lorge, I., 145
Lynn, D. B., 112
Lynn, R., 272–273
Lytton, H., 88, 108, 177, 359–360

MacArthur, R. S., 273–274
McAskie, M., 166 n
McCall, R. B., 71, 73, 82, 106
McClelland, D. C., 120 n
McElwain, D. W., 268
MacFarlane, 70 n, 74
McGurk, F. C., 310
MacKay, G. W. S., 21 n
McKenzie, A., 269, 349–350
McKeown, T., 87, 88, 177–178
McLoughlin, J. A., 92
Macnamara, J., 275
McNemar, Q., 6, 21, 60, 62, 274
Madaus, G. F., 36
Madden, J., 137
Marcus, G. B., 100
Marjoribanks, K., 99
Martin, N. G., 175
Martin, P. G., 175
Medawar, P. B., 201, 202, 205, 208, 211, 234, 249, 250
Meichenbaum, D. H., 125–126, 127
Mercer, J. R., 258, 265, 277, 299, 302, 307
Merrill, M. A., 115
Messer, S. B., 34

Messick, S., 310
Michael, W. B., 274, 311
Miller, G. A., 44, 49, 52
Miller, G. W., 109, 120, 212
Miller, K. S., 14, 246, 262, 263, 284–285
Miller, L. B., 12 n, 147
Miller, S. M., 159 n
Millman, J., 25
Mincer, J., 146 n
Mitchell, B. C., 133, 179, 218–219, 220, 228, 230
Mitchell, M. C., 66, 196, 271
Money, J., 235
Morant, G. M., 285, 361–362
Morrow, W. R., 120, 362
Morton, N. E., 169, 191–193, 199, 200, 201, 203, 284, 325
Moses, E. G., 316
Moss, H. A., 112
Mosteller, F., 147
Moynihan, D. P., 147, 315
Munsinger, H., 88–89, 133, 177, 183, 216 ff, 226–227, 228, 229, 230
Mussen, P. H., 107

Narjarian, P., 132
National Academy of Science, 281, 283–284
Nature, editors of, 198, 281
Nebes, R. D., 42
Neel, J. V., 232, 236, 250, 282, 325
Neff, W. S., 115
Nelson, V. L., 112
Newman, H. H., 170, 172, 174–175, 179, 180, 290
Newson, E., 103
Newson, J., 103
Nichols, P. L., 85, 87, 88, 97, 316
Nichols, R. C., 169, 186
Ninio, A., 294
Norris, C. I., 159 n
Nurcombe, B., 268

Oden, M. H., 78, 121
Office of Economic Opportunity, 148
Oléron, P., 142
Ortar, C. R., 258
Osborne, R. T., 296
Otis, A. S., 6

Page, E. B., 135
Parry, J. B., 29, 80
Pasamanick, B., 86, 87, 89, 94, 100
Paterson, D. G., 6
Payne, D. T., 12, 118
Pearson, K., 278
Pedersen, F. A., 73, 104, 126
Penfield, W., 42, 90
Penrose, L. S., 234
Pezzullo, T. R., 159 n

Piaget, J., 11, 17, 21, 33, 42, 44,
    45– 47, 52, 59, 73, 78, 102, 153,
    157, 254
Piel, G., 281
Pinneau, S. R., 76
Pintner, R., 6
Plomin, R., 181– 182, 183
Poli, M. D., 203
Porteus, S. D., 40, 261
Pratt, I. E., 269
Preston, A., 111
Pribram, K. H., 44, 49, 52
Price, B., 88, 177, 178
Price, L. A., 49

Quay, L. C., 306
Quetelet, L. A. J., 2

Ramphal, C., 144
Rasch, G., 78
Raven, J. C., 79– 80, 335
Ravich, D., 159 n
Record, R. G., 87, 88, 177– 178
Reed, T. E., 246
Rees, J., 141
Reitan, R. M., 81, 90, 91, 92
Resnick, L. B., 48– 50
Rex, J., 280, 283, 286
Richards, M., 280
Richards, M. P. M., 103
Richardson, K., 280
Richmond, J., 105
Riessman, F., 33
Rist, R. C., 26
Rivers, W. H. R., 261
Roberts, J. A. F., 234
Robinson, H. B., 136
Robinson, N. M., 136
Rock, D., 274
Rogers, J. M., 125– 126, 127
Rose, S., 95, 202, 210
Rosenthal, R., 24, 25– 26
Rosenzweig, M. R., 130
Ross, J. M., 78
Ross, S., 96
Rothney, J. W. M., 74
Rourke, B. P., 92
Royce, J. B., 62
Rutter, M., 141 n
Ryle, G., 39

Samuel, W. L., 314– 315, 318
Sanders, J. T., 309
Sandiford, P., 269, 296
Sarason, S. B., 28– 29
Satterly, D., 152
Sattler, J. M., 24, 28, 29, 33, 313, 314
Sauvé, R., 88, 177
Savage, I. R., 202

Sawrey, W. L., 112
Scarr, S., 296– 297
Scarr-Salapatek, S., 170, 174,
    196– 198, 200, 209, 249, 284,
    293
Schaefer, E. S., 107, 109– 110
Schaffer, H. R., 102, 103, 104, 105, 142
Schaie, K. W., 80– 81
Scheerer, M., 90
Schmidt, F. L., 310, 312
Schooler, C., 98
Schull, W. J., 236
Schwartz, J., 173, 198
Schwartz, M., 173, 198
Schwarz, P. A., 257
Scottish Council for Research in
    Education, 99, 119, 275
Scrimshaw, N. S., 93
Seagrim, G. N., 297
Seemanova, E., 236
Segall, M. H., 252
Semler, I. J., 274
Senna, C., 290
Serpell, R., 255
Sewell, W. H., 146 n
Sherman, M., 274– 275
Shields, J., 170, 172, 174, 180, 190,
    194
Shimberg, M. E., 305
Shipman, V. C., 125, 129, 254
Shockley, W., 13, 232, 282, 295,
    298– 299, 325
Shucard, D. W., 43
Shuey, A. M., 14, 246, 251, 262, 263,
    265, 293, 295, 307, 314
Siegel, I. E., 33
Simon, T., 3, 40
Simpson, H. R., 78
Sims, V. M., 179
Sinclair, H., 47
Sivers, C. H., 265
Skanes, G. R., 271
Skeels, H. M., 9, 133, 135, 138, 143,
    183, 208, 210, 224– 226, 228,
    229, 230, 290
Skodak, M., 9, 135, 183, 210,
    224– 226, 228, 230, 290
Smilansky, M., 273, 294, 295
Smilansky, S., 273, 294, 295
Smith, P. V., 183 n, 298
Smith, R. T., 176
Snow, R. E., 26
Snygg, D., 223– 224, 229, 230
Sobol, A., 88
Sontag, L. W., 88, 112
Spearman, C., 4– 5, 17, 18– 19, 37,
    40, 43– 44, 47, 49, 52, 55– 56,
    57, 61, 62– 63, 65– 66, 67, 185,
    210– 211, 334

Young, H. B., 294
Yudkin, S., 105

Zajonc, R. B., 100
Zelazo, P. R., 136

Subject Index

Abilities
  acquired, 9, 10, 21–23, 37
  construct of, 40
  parent–child resemblance in, 2,
    238 (*see also* Foster children)
  and special talents, 56, 60, 63–64,
    67, 114 n, 211
Achievements, educational, 50–51,
  53, 120, 123, 134, 148, 149,
  151 ff, 205, 304, 310–311
  assessments of, 5, 20 n, 25, 30, 32,
    34, 36, 64, 151, 270, 301
  expectations, of, 26, 119–120
  formative and summative,
    154–155
  need for, 98, 112
  quotient, 50–51
Adopted children. *See* Foster
  children
African natives, abilities of, 64, 95,
  140, 246, 248, 254, 255, 257,
  263, 270–271, 273, 294, 312
Age
  and changes in intelligence, 5–6,
    8, 74, 77–81, 82, 145
  increasing isolation with, 142
  in factor structure, 57–58, 67
Alleles, 165, 333
Animal studies of deprivation and
  stimulation, 45, 85, 93, 100,
  130–131, 139, 143

Anoxia, 89–90, 100
Antisemitic views, 278
Aptitude-treatment interactions (ATI),
  149, 183, 208
Aptitudes, 50–51
Army Alpha and Beta tests, 6–7, 8,
  17, 21, 113, 186, 262, 275
  General Classification test, 115
Artistic abilities, 60
Aspirations, effects of on mental
  growth, 118, 119, 120, 150
Association of Black Psychologists, 15
Assortative mating, 166, 184–185,
  186, 188, 192–193, 196, 199,
  225, 250, 333
Attenuation, 77, 333
Australian aboriginals, 261, 267–268,
  296, 302
Authoritarian homes, 110, 112

Bayley scales, 28, 71, 72, 73, 116
Behavioral objectives, 35, 38
Behavior modification, 34–35
Berkeley growth studies, 109, 114 n
Binet-Simon test, 4, 5, 8, 17, 21, 56,
  73, 75, 175, 176
Biometrical-genetical analysis, 190,
  199–200
Birth order, effects of, 98, 101
Blacks. *See* Negroes, American

383

Brain
changes in with age, 81, 83
localization of function, 42, 52, 90
relation of to abilities, 42–43, 44, 45, 52, 90–92
Brain damage, 48, 73, 84, 87, 90–92, 95, 96, 101, 246
Halstead and Reitan test, 90–91
minimal, 91, 101, 126
Brazil, unschooled peasants in, 145
British Intelligence Test, 21 n, 78
Burt's adjusted IQs, 171, 172
Burt's work on heritability, criticisms of, 170–173, 180

California growth studies, 70–71, 72, 74, 113–114, 226
Cattell culture-fair tests, 48, 52, 189
Cattell infant scale, 81, 116, 132
Celts, 247
Chicanos. See Mexican-American children
Child-rearing practices, 74, 102, 105–106, 107, 114, 117–119, 125, 131–134, 157, 182, 208, 240, 330–331
methods of study of, 107–109
Chromosomes, 164–165, 234–235, 335
Civilization, Western, 157, 238, 252–254, 260
Cognitive growth, 3–4, 33, 44, 49, 52, 102–103, 109–114, 124–125, 132, 139–140, 183, 207, 333
Cognitive styles, 33–34, 38, 39, 65, 126, 129, 252
Coleman Report, 147, 160, 264, 265, 269, 300–301, 315, 316
Collaborative Prenatal Project, 85
Competency versus performance, 127–128, 156–157
Complexity of tests versus culture bias, 22, 305, 308–309, 317
Concept development, 44, 50–51, 102, 140, 153
Concept formation tests, 15, 33–34, 142
Consanguinity, 236
Conservation, cognitive, 34, 46–47, 257
Constitutional determinants of abilities, 48, 52, 84–101, 238, 240, 265, 286, 288
Constructs, operationalizing of, 40, 51, 54–55, 63, 67, 202, 209–211, 214, 283
Continuum of reproductive casualty, 86, 100
Conversations, prelinguistic, 103–104, 114

Correlation, 3, 4, 333–334
Cousin marriages, effects of on intelligence, 236, 241
Creativity, 30, 32, 62, 64–65, 67, 114 n. See also Divergent thinking tests
Criterion-referenced tests, 36, 37, 38, 154–155, 334
Critical periods, 45, 139, 143
Cross-cultural testing, 255, 256–258, 261, 310–311
Cross-racial breeding. See Race, hybrids
Crystallized ability, 46–47, 52, 60–61, 67, 79, 81, 82, 116, 189–190
Cultural group differences, 8, 10, 17, 32–33, 64, 86, 127, 130, 157, 196, 244, 247 ff, 257, 259–60, 261 ff, 284–285, 288, 319 ff, 334
Cumulative deficit, 263, 300–301, 303
in rural Georgia, 301
Cypriot immigrants to the United Kingdom, 124

D scale (Bayley), 78
Day-care centers and nursery schools, 105, 136, 138
Deafness, 142, 143
Democratic home climate, 110, 112
Demographic differences in abilities, 119–120
Deprivation
environmental, 12, 22, 23, 32–33, 45, 115–116, 123–124, 130–141, 143, 149–150, 161, 196, 207, 290, 305
maternal, 103, 105, 141–142
sensory and perceptual, 45, 92, 131, 139–140, 143
syndromes of, 85–86, 135
Developmental or infant tests. See Intelligence, preschool tests
Deviation quotients, 6, 17, 76, 334
Differential Aptitude Tests, 62
Digit Memory test, 49, 66, 306, 314, 316
Disadvantaged children. See Deprivation
Dispositional properties, 39–40
Divergent thinking tests, 59, 60, 64–65, 67, 280 n
Dominance, 165, 166, 183–185, 186, 188–189, 192–193, 199, 202, 233, 334
Down's syndrome, 87, 164, 234, 241
Draw-a-man test, 259, 269
Dyslexia, 91–92, 101

Education
 adaptive (individualized), 35–36,
  151, 153, 282
 compensatory, 11, 17, 35,
  146–147, 157, 158, 159, 160
 diversification of, 66, 158, 208, 277,
  327–329, 332
 effects of, 80, 144–156
 influence of on vocational success,
  146
Educational Testing Service, 24, 37,
 49, 113
Eight-Year Study, 151
EKJ kinship correlations, 166–168,
 170, 176, 180, 191, 192,
 193–194, 199, 200, 210
Electroencephalographic indices, 43,
 52, 91
Eleven-plus examination, 7, 16, 122,
 326
Environmental factors in
 intelligence, 3, 8–9, 10, 12, 14,
  17, 45, 50–51, 62, 70, 75, 77, 80,
  85, 94, 95, 98, 99, 115–129,
  130–135, 139, 168, 172, 179,
  181 ff, 187–188, 195–196,
  200 ff, 211–212, 214, 220, 230,
  232, 237–238, 240, 247 ff, 256,
  265, 267, 284, 285–286, 289,
  294–295, 299, 300, 319 ff, 332.
  See also Deprivation
Environmental factors, multiple,
 291–292, 302
Environmentalism, 13–14, 17, 23,
 46–47, 168, 195, 203, 206, 212,
 279, 281, 282, 286, 288, 300, 308
Environments, modification of by
 children, 153, 181
Equality, social and educational, 146,
 156–160, 193–195, 200, 204,
 209, 287, 326–327
Equilibration, 46
Error (unreliability) in heritability
 analyses, 185, 186, 212
Eskimos, abilities of, 140, 249,
 270–271, 274, 276
Ethnic groups. See Cultural group
 differences
Eugenic beliefs, 278, 282
Europe, testing in, 7, 8, 16
Extrinsic factors. See Tests, extrinsic
 and intrinsic influences on

Factor analysis, 4, 48, 50, 55–67, 72,
 73, 210–211, 214, 334
 cross-cultural comparisons,
  273–274, 276
 of test items, 309
 score patterns, 270–271, 276
 two-factor theory, 4–5, 17

Factors
 centroid, 56, 67, 333
 changes with practice, 58, 59, 67
 group, 44, 55–57, 61, 67, 335
 heritability of, 186–187, 189
 multiple, 56–61, 67, 336
 oblique versus orthogonal, 48,
  56–57, 59, 61, 67, 336
 primary, 44, 56–57, 59, 62, 67, 337
 reality of, 63
 s (specific), 5, 18, 43, 337
 second order, 56–57, 60, 337
 speed versus power, 60
Faculty theory, 4, 56, 66
Families, between and within
 heritability, 185, 188, 189–190,
 191, 194, 267, 307–308
Family size, 99–100, 101, 119
Father's role in child development,
 112–113, 114, 136
Fels Institute, 109, 114
Feral children, 131
Field dependence-independence, 64,
 111–113, 126, 253 n
Fluency factor, 60–61, 62, 64, 65 n,
 79
Fluid ability, 43, 46–47, 52, 60–61,
 67, 79, 80, 81, 82, 116, 189, 190
Foster children, 9, 132, 133, 140, 141,
 143, 166, 168, 179, 182, 183, 185,
 192, 212, 215–230, 239, 240
 effects of age of adoption, 217, 218
 effects of home quality, 118, 218,
  220
 gains in intelligence, 218, 220, 222,
  225, 226, 228, 230, 297–298
 methodological difficulties,
  216–218, 229
 regression effects, 218, 219, 223,
  225
 relation to biological parent ability,
  221–222, 223–224, 226, 227,
  228, 229, 230
 relation to foster-parent ability,
  219, 220, 222–223, 226, 227,
  228–229, 230
 selective placement of, 173, 180,
  217, 219, 220, 222, 224, 226,
  227, 228–229
 unrepresentative sampling, 216
Foster parents, atypicality of, 217,
 221, 223, 226

g (general ability factor), 4, 17, 18,
 19, 37, 43, 44, 47, 50, 55–57, 58,
 61, 62, 65–66, 67, 72, 82, 99, 111,
 185, 207, 210, 232, 240, 265, 270,
 273, 305, 316, 334–335
Gene pools, 207, 213, 245, 246, 248,
 257, 259, 278

National Survey of Health and
Development (U.K.), 78
Natural selection. *See* Selective
mating and breeding
Negro English, 127–128, 306, 317
Negroes, American, 8, 12–13,
29–30, 66, 94, 97, 100, 122, 124,
127, 128, 133, 145, 184,
193–194, 196, 197–198, 200,
245 ff, 251 ff, 258, 259, 260,
261 ff, 271, 274, 276, 277, 284,
285, 286, 287, 289–303, 305 ff,
317–318
effects of father absence, 315–316
effects of race mixing, 295–296
selection for college, 310–312
stereotype of, 246 n
Negro test results
differences between sexes, 264
at different ages, 263
on different factors, 264–265, 269
in different parts of the United
States, 262, 265–266
at different periods, 263–264
motivational differences, 313–315
Normalization of school
organization, 328–329
Number and mathematical abilities,
53, 64, 111, 113
Number factor, 58, 61, 63, 79, 271
Nursery and preschooling, effects of,
11, 27, 105, 126, 135–137, 143,
146

Object permanence, 104
Observational techniques, 106, 108,
109, 125
Open plan schools, 151–153. *See
also* Schooling, structured
versus permissive
Oriental Americans, 95, 127–128,
246, 269, 271, 274, 276, 291
Overlap hypothesis, 76–77, 82

Pakistani immigrants in the United
Kingdom, 124
Parental attitudes, dimensions of,
107–108, 109, 110, 117, 120
Parent-offspring IQ correlations, 166,
168, 222, 223, 227, 229,
237–238
Path analysis, 120, 191, 195, 200, 336
Perceptual abilities. *See* Spatial
abilities and tests
Perceptual deficit, 34, 92
Perceptual development, 44–47,
131. *See also* Cognitive growth
Perceptual speed factor, 58, 79
Performance contracting, 148, 160

Personal constant (Heinis), 78
Personality factors in mental growth,
63, 74, 193. *See also*
Self-concept, effects of tests on
Phenylketonuria, 164, 326
Piagetian stages of development, 21,
33, 34, 45–46, 73, 78, 140,
157–158, 254, 268
Piagetian tests, 15, 33–34, 37, 142,
144, 297
Polygenetic inheritance, 165,
179–180, 205, 233–234, 241
Porteus Mazes test, 261
Pregnancy, complications of, 10,
84–90, 100
Premature births, 86, 88, 89, 97, 100,
263
Prenatal and perinatal conditions, 10,
84, 85–92, 96, 100–101, 117,
238, 263
unreliability of evidence on,
84–85, 89, 100
Preschooling. *See* Nursery and
preschooling, effects of
Primary Mental Abilities test
(Thurstone), 79
Principal components, 56, 67, 333
Privacy, invasions of, 16, 30
Progressive Matrices test, 48, 80, 94,
142, 144, 145, 186, 265, 299,
308–309, 317, 335
Project Talent, 148
Protein deficiency, 93, 95
Puerto Rican children, 271–272

Race
definition of, 244 ff, 259, 337
differences in abilities, 13–14,
244, 251, 261–276, 277–288,
290, 306, 307–308, 324–325
differences in health, 86, 94–95
differences, multiple, 269–271
discrimination, 14, 246, 247, 249,
252, 264, 277, 282, 326, 332
hybrids, 245–246, 259, 295–298,
302
Races, evolution of, 237–248, 259
Racial-ethnic groups, dimensions of,
252–254
Racism, 158, 244, 277, 278, 282, 287,
325
Range of reaction, 202, 213
Raven Matrices. *See* Progressive
Matrices test
Reaction time, simple and choice,
305–306
Regression to the mean, 238–239,
336–337